A DICTIONARY OF

MEDIEVAL TERMS AND PHRASES

in memoriam

V.E.N.

S.C.S.

A DICTIONARY OF

MEDIEVAL TERMS AND PHRASES

Christopher Corèdon

with Ann Williams

D. S. BREWER

First published 2004
D. S. Brewer, Cambridge

ISBN 1 84384 023 5

D. S. Brewer is an imprint of Boydell & Brewer Ltd
POBox 9, Woodbridge, Suffolk IP12 3DF, UK
and of Boydell & Brewer Inc.
668 Mt Hope Avenue, Rochester, NY 14620, USA
website: www.boydellandbrewer.com

A CiP catalogue record for this book is available
from the British Library

Library of Congress Cataloging-in-Publication Data

Corèdon, Christopher, 1945–
    A dictionary of medieval terms and phrases / Christopher Corèdon with Ann Williams.
      p.   cm.
    Includes index.
    ISBN 1-84384-023-5 (hardback : alk. paper)
    1. Great Britain – History – Medieval period, 1066–1485 – Dictionaries. 2. Great
Britain – History – Anglo-Saxon period, 449–1066 – Dictionaries. 3. Latin language,
Medieval and modern – Great Britain – Dictionaries. 4. English language – Middle
English, 1100–1500 – Dictionaries. 5. English language – Old English, ca. 450–1100 –
Dictionaries. 6. Historiography – Great Britain – Dictionaries. 7. Middle Ages –
Historiography – Dictionaries. 8. Civilization, Medieval – Dictionaries. I. Williams,
Ann, 1937– II. Title.
    DA129.C67 2004
    909.07′01′4 – dc22   2004003845

Typeset in Palatino by Word and Page, Chester

Printed in Great Britain by
Antony Rowe Ltd, Chippenham, Wiltshire

CONTENTS

PREFACE

In recent years, history has become the focus of increasing popular interest, both in book form and on television. This dictionary is intended not for historiographers (who will not need it) but rather for the readers of history who are neither specialists nor academically trained.

There is an astonishing amount of material that is readily available today. *Domesday Book* can be bought in a modern translation, in one paperback volume, for less than the cost of a ticket to a football match – all two million words. There are paperback editions of texts of the period, in which the voice of the time can still be heard, while *Bracton* is easily accessible on the Internet. And there is, of course, the literature. From Geoffrey of Monmouth to Chaucer, to Thomas Malory – it is all available, sometimes in modern English, and there the imagination of the past can be seen and heard at work. The people are recognisable. Chaucer is subject to adaptations which attempt to make him 'relevant': but modernisation strips his characters of just what it is that makes them recognisably flesh-and-blood human beings: their voice and milieu. Malory's *Morte D'Arthur* was being printed by Caxton in the same year as the Battle of Bosworth, 1485: a decisive exposition of the Arthurian legend which had persisted throughout this period appeared simultaneously with the battle which was the last of the era we call medieval.

The period can be made to look very good, even glamorous, with well-chosen pictures. Iconic knights in armour on gorgeously arrayed horses, the castles and tournaments, the brightly coloured clothing of the men and women of the nobility, so rich in comparison with ours, so unlike that of the little-seen peasantry – all provide evocative images. But all that they thought and believed was utterly different, even alien, to our ways of thought and belief. The Church and its place in the lives of those people, its power over actions and its intimate place in daily life and thought is just one such profound difference among many.

The medieval period is separated from us by language as much as time. This was a time of languages: English, French and Latin. English, and its several dialects, was spoken by the majority; French/Anglo-Norman was the language of power, while Latin was used by scholars here and throughout Europe and in the writing of history and the making of records, e.g. the rolls which record government business. Therefore this dictionary includes words and terms in those languages, because to write about the past, the modern historian must use the terms and language used in that past. Inevitably, the non-specialist reader encounters words which are either unfamiliar or, more often, words being used which are 'sort of' understood, are familiar, but which, when checked, turn out to have unexpected meanings.

In an attempt to aid a better understanding of these terms, an etymology has been given to many of them: the unfamiliar becomes clearer if one can see something of its origin. However, no claim to originality is being made by including etymologies. All have been checked against those offered in *The Oxford English Dictionary* and Onions's *The Oxford Dictionary of English Etymology*. They have been placed at the end of each definition, so as not to obtrude.

So far as possible, persons have been kept out of definitions. Bede (*c*.673–735), Geoffrey of Monmouth (*c*.1100–54) and the great chronicler and court historian, Jean Froissart (*c*.1333–1400/01), are mentioned, as is John Wyclif (*c*.1330–84). Fortunately, historical terms do not rely upon individuals. However, the time of their use is important and therefore monarchs are named without hesitation. (For those who are a little uncertain about the regnal dates of the Henrys and Edwards, and others, a list has been appended.) To include less familiar names without an entry and details of their life would be unhelpful; information on those few which are included should be readily available.

ACKNOWLEDGEMENTS

Thanks are due to David Ferris, Curator of Rare Books and Manuscripts at Harvard Law Library, for permission to quote from their on-line edition of Bracton's *De Legibus et Consuetudinibus Angliæ*. This site gives both the Latin text and an English translation. The URL of the home page is: http://hlsl5.law.harvard.edu/bracton/index.htm, where there can be found details about both text and translation.

I wish to express my great debt of gratitude to Dr Ann Williams, who kindly read this dictionary in its final stages, at a time of ill-health and when she was occupied with valuable work of her own. The lightness with which she wore her scholarship only enhanced her suggestions and made her corrections a pleasure – which learning always should be. This dictionary is much improved as a result of her scrutiny. Further thanks are owed to Clive Tolley for his editorial rigour and his *kotkansilmä*. Obviously, errors that remain are mine. Thanks are also due to PHG for encouragement and an easy hand when pouring drinks.

ABBREVIATIONS

abbr.	abbreviation, abbreviated
AL	Anglo-Latin
AN	Anglo-Norman
approx.	approximately
Ar.	Arabic
AS	Anglo-Saxon
ASC	*Anglo-Saxon Chronicle*
c	century
c.	*circa*
d	penny/pence, e.g. 30d = 30 pennies/pence
d.	died
DB	*Domesday Book*
dim.	diminutive
Du.	Dutch
Fr.	French
Gr.	Greek
Her.	heraldry
Ir.	Irish
Ital.	Italian
L	Latin
LHP	*Leges Henrici Primi*
lit.	literally (of a translated word or phrase)
ME	Middle English, between *c.*1066 and *c.*1500
MS	manuscript
OE	Old English, between *c.*500 and *c.*1066
OFr.	Old French
ON	Old Norse
orig.	original, originally
s	shilling, e.g. 2s = two shillings
W	Welsh
[ ]	brackets enclose alternative forms of headwords, and etymologies
<	is derived from
*	cross-reference to a **Headword**

A

À outrance. The term used to describe jousting in a hostile manner, when injury or death were expected and even wished for. Jousting could also be *à plaisir*, for pleasure. [< OFr. *outrance* = beyond bounds, extreme; Fr. *à outrance* = to the bitter end] – *Cf.* À PLAISIR; JOUST OF PEACE; JOUST OF WAR

À plaisir. Term used to describe jousting for pleasure, as a test of skill, rather than mortal combat. In such an event points were variously scored. – *Cf. previous;* JOUST OF PEACE; JOUST OF WAR

Abacus. Orig. a flat surface or board covered with sand and used as a drawing board by mathematicians; architecturally the top, flat part of a capital (supporting the architrave); latterly the computing device made of rows of beads.

Abaddon [Apollyon]. Angel of the Bottomless Pit; also, hell itself. Hell seemed powerfully real at this time. The terror of spending eternity in hell added greatly to the universal fear of death. The fires were not considered to be metaphorical but to be real: it was the Inferno, the place of punishment.

Abatement [rebatement]. *Her.* A *charge or mark of disgrace. It was either sanguine or *tenné in colour. An older version of the names of the colours was 'staynande colours'. Such marks were rarely, if ever, used: no one willingly displayed signs of disgrace. [ME *abate* = to bring down, curtail] – *Cf.* GUSSET

Abba. Christ used this Aramaic word when speaking of God; from this came the title *abbot. St Benedict determined on the use of abbot in his *Rule*. A similar title, *abuna*, was used by Syrian Christians and Ethiopians of a priest. The Arabic *abuna* = father.

Abbacy. Office of either an *abbot or *abbess; the Latin form is *abbatia*.

Abbess. The head of a community of nuns; after the Dissolution of the monasteries, the madam of a brothel, a usage which suggests vigorous Protestantism. The Latin form was *abbatissa*. – *Cf.* ABBOT

Abbey. A community of monks or nuns, governed by an *abbot or *abbess; thus the building of such a community – each was part of one of the monastic orders; after the Dissolution, a church once belonging to such a community. [< OFr. *abbeie* < L *abbatia* = abbey, monastery]

1

Abbey lubber. A lubber = an idle person, a sponger. Abbey lubber was one who existed on *doles and alms given out by abbeys and religious houses. They were considered professional beggars. – *Cf.* BEGGING; CUSTOM HOUSE

Abbot. The head of a community of monks; also spelt 'abbat' till the 17c. [< L *abbas* < Aramaic *abba* = father] – *Cf.* ABBA; ABBESS; FILIATIO

Abbreviatio. An abbreviation of the *DB* was made during the early part of the 13c by the monks of Westminster Abbey for presentation to King Henry III by way of thanks for the work he had done in rebuilding the abbey.

Abecedarius. A name given to a school pupil just beginning to read.

Abel. Second son of Adam and Eve; considered a kind of Christ-figure because of his good life and particularly his violent death. – *Cf.* CAIN

Abjure. To renounce something under oath usually on the Bible: in a time of faith, a solemn act. – *Cf. next*

Abjure the realm. Permanent exile. The sentence to leave the kingdom was applied to many who had sought *sanctuary. Once the 40 days' sanctuary was over, a criminal was given the chance to abjure the realm. The guilty person was assigned a port to leave the kingdom from and a specific route to follow; the time permitted might be as little as seven days or as much as 40 days. He was dressed in a long white garment, of the kind usually worn by someone under sentence of death. He also carried a cross to show he was under protection to discourage the aggrieved from punishing the man themselves – which happened often enough. – *Cf. previous*; NORTHAMPTON, AS-SIZE OF

Abraham, bosom of. Phrase used of the place of bliss found by the righteous dead. It was an image much used by medieval artists, expressed by showing figures sitting on the lap of Abraham the patriarch.

Abutment. That point where a support and what is supported meet, e.g. a supporting wall, pillar, buttress and an arch.

Abyss. *Her.* The centre of an *escutcheon. – *Cf.* FESS POINT

Acceptor. Latin term for a hawk. The word was qualified by many adjectives. For example, *acceptor de pertica* = a hawk off the perch; *acceptor mutatus* = a mewed hawk; *acceptoricius canis* = a spaniel accompanying hunts with hawks. – *Cf.* MEW

Accident. A medieval philosophic concept indicating the material body of an object, as distinct from its essence (referred to as 'substance'). Thus in eucharistic transubstantiation the accident of the bread, i.e. its material quality as bread, was believed to remain, while the words of consecration had changed its substance or essence into the body of Christ.

Accidentia. Accidental or non-predictable items of royal income. While a rent and *farm might be fixed, a *fine or *tallage could be increased in number and value.

Accidie. What today we might call depression: a torpid state, lacking interest in anything and suggesting sloth. It was a condition which afflicted monks, as despair was considered one of the seven deadly sins. [< L *acedia* = weariness of body or soul] – Cf. SINS, SEVEN DEADLY

Acclamation. Word used for the loudly voiced acceptance of a new monarch at his coronation. It was a part of the procedure of electing monarchs before the Conquest. At William I's coronation on Christmas Day, 1066, in Westminster Abbey, the cry of acclamation was so loud that William's soldiers, on guard outside, thought he was being attacked and went on a rampage, killing many people and burning down a great many buildings. [< L *acclamo* = to acclaim]

Accolade. Ceremonial embrace or salute at the bestowal of a knighthood after the familiar tap, *adoubement*, on the shoulder with a sword. Orig. the important moment was the girding on of the knight's sword and spurs. [OFr. *acoler* = embrace about the neck] – Cf. CINGULUM MILITARE; DUB

Accompanied. *Her.* Used of a *charge which is found between two others. – Cf. ACCOSTED

Accorné. *Her.* Having horns of a different *tincture from the body's. [< OFr. *corne* = horn]

Accosted. *Her.* Term for two charges placed either side of a third. [< L *accosto* = to be beside] – Cf. ACCOMPANIED

Accroupi. *Her.* Resting, of a lion. [< OFr. *croup* = an animal's rear]

Accrued. *Her.* Describes a *charge in the form of a full-grown tree. [< L *accresco* = to grow]

Achievement. *Her.* A word synonymous with the more common 'hatchments'. It was used esp. of coats of *arms displayed at a funeral, or on the front of the house of one who had died, or before a *tournament, which indicated a particularly distinguished feat of arms. When a monarch died his or her arms were blazoned on a *sable field.

Acolyte. A priest's assistant who carried out lesser tasks, such as carrying candles. He would have been a member of one of the four *minor orders. [< L *acolitus* < Gr. *akolouthos* = follower]

Acre. Orig. a piece of arable, tillable land; a unit of measure = 4,840 sq yards. – *Cf.* FURLONG; ROOD 1

Acrostic. Poems in which the first or last letters of successive lines formed a word or phrase were popular in this period. The hiddenness of the acrostic gave it a didactic quality which accorded with an impulse which found more evident expression in the *mendicant preachers. – *Cf.* CAYME'S CASTLES

Acton [aketon]. A padded, stuffed vest or undergarment worn beneath *mail. [< Ar. *al-qutun* = cotton]

Acts of mercy. *See* CORPORAL ACTS OF MERCY

AD. *See* ANNO DOMINI

Ad aratrum. Lit. 'at the plough'. – *Cf.* IN PECUNIA

Ad limina. Lit. 'to the threshold'. Phrase used of an archbishop's visits to the threshold of the apostles, i.e. Rome. Having received the *pallium it was expected that he should go to Rome every three years, if possible.

Ad malam. Lit. 'at rent'. The term used in records and accounts for land rented out. The OE word, *mal*, was simply latinised. [< OE *mal* = rent] – *Cf.* AD OPUS; MALMAN

Ad opus. Lit. 'at work'. Land worked by villeins was known as *ad opus*, i.e. being worked. – *Cf.* AD MALAM; MALMAN

Ad pondum. Lit. 'by weight'. Method of payment in which coins were weighed, rather than counted. Latin *pondus* = pound, from which our monetary pound. – *Cf.* TALE

Ad quod damnum. Lit. 'at what damage?' The phrase was used of inquisitions undertaken to discover what damage or loss of revenue the king might incur in a district or town if he granted a market licence.

Ad succurrendum. Lit. 'towards salvation'. The medieval Latin term used of the benefactor of a monastery who, late in life, joined that house as a full member. [< L *succurro* = run to the aid of, to help]

Adder. *Her.* When used heraldically, adder referred to any kind of snake, for which 'serpent' was a synonym; asps were also named in this context. Visually there was no difference except for the *tincture.

Addice. *See* ADZE

Addorsed [endorsed]. *Her.* Term used of two animals shown back to back; it could be used of any object in a *blazon. – *Cf.* AFFRONTANT

Adelingus. Latin form of *ætheling*.

Adjure. To put a person on oath. [< L *adjuro* = to swear]

Admiral. Although ships had always been used in war, the first time an English admiral was appointed with that title to be in charge of a fleet was 1303, when Gervaise Alard was so appointed by Edward II as captain and admiral of the *Cinque Ports' fleet. However, a commission had been issued in 1295 naming Barrau de Sescas as admiral. Later that year two further appointments were made by royal writ. One of those named, Sir William Leyburn, was described as *amiraux de nostre navie Dengleterre*. The title captain and admiral of the fleet was used until 1344. An admiral of all the fleets was commissioned in 1360, there being North, West and Other fleets at the time. Clerks of the king's ships provided administration between times of war from the 13c until a navy board was created in 1546. [< Ar. *amirail* = a *Saracen ruler or commander; *amir-al-bahr* = commander of the sea; thus admiral; cf. *emir*] – Cf. next

Admiralty, Black Book of the. MS containing documents connected with the admiralty of Sir Thomas Beaufort, 9 Hen. VI; ordinances of war made in 1385 and 1419. Volumes II–IV contain the Domesday of Ipswich, the laws of *Oléron, the Spanish *Consolat de la Mar*, the maritime laws of Gotland, Visby, Flanders, etc. The book is a collection of laws, in French and Latin, relating to the navy, the original MS of which is preserved in the admiralty archives at Whitehall.

Adoubement. The ceremonial tap on the shoulder at the knighting ceremony. – Cf. ACCOLADE; DUB

Adscriptus glebae. The term describing the status of a *serf as 'belonging to the land'; one who could be transferred with it were the land to change lord. [< L *adscriptus* = stated in writing (and belonging) + *glebae* = to the land] – Cf. ATTORN

Adulterine castle. Modern term for castles built without the king's permission. In *LHP building a castle without licence (*castellatio sine licentia*) placed the builder *in misericordia regis* = in the king's mercy. During the *anarchy of King Stephen's reign many hundreds of such castles were built. However, these were not the stone-built castles which still stand. Rather they were all hastily thrown up, wooden stockades on earth mounds. One such construct, given the name of castle, was nothing more than a wooden square atop a church tower.

Adumbration. *Her.* A figure shown in outline or in shadow.

Adventus Saxonum. Lit. 'the advent or arrival of the *Saxons (in England)'. Just when they began to settle here is far from clear. Between the departure of the Romans in 410 and the late 6c there is not much that can with certainty be given a year date. Bede has the Saxons settling 450–5; the *ASC* gives 449 as their first entry into England.

Advocatus ecclesiae. Lit. 'advocate of the church'. Latin term for a lord who undertook to protect a monastery or church from secular enemies and to act as patron. There was a ceremony at which he took an oath and his sword was blessed. This ceremony evolved from the *Truce of God which had emerged in the 10c. It was, however, a position with the potential for abuse: the advocate could too easily ask for money by way of confirmation. In other words, protection money could be demanded. The *advocatus* was also known sometimes in the Latin records as *actor ecclesiae* = acting (in the sense of doing something) for the church.

Advowson. The right to present a clergyman for appointment to the bishop of the diocese by one who had the patronage or was guardian of a *benefice or an ecclesiastical house. Advowson was an incorporeal inheritance. The Latin used in 13c records was *advocatia*. [< L *advoco* = to summon (a priest to serve)]

Adze [addice]. *Her.* An axe.

Æhtemann. A serf or bondsman. [< OE *æht* = possessions, a serf]

Ærendraca. A king's agent or messenger, though perhaps not officially so as was the *nuncius regis* of later times; rather a *legatus regis*, or ambassador perhaps, charged with specific tasks. The rank is now unclear but was akin to that of *staller and *pedesecus*. [< OE *ærende* = message + *raca* = someone who moves forward]

Æthel. First element of numerous aristocratic AS names = noble. [< OE *æðel* = noble, of good birth] – *Cf. next*

Ætheling. Prince or lord. A member of a royal AS family; a prince of the blood royal and heir to the throne; a person considered worthy of the throne. When used in the *ASC* it was nearly always applied to members of the West Saxon royal family. [< OE *æðeling* = prince] – *Cf. previous*

Affer. *See* AVER

Affinity 1. *Canon law was strict in forbidding marriage between couples too closely related by marriage or by being a godparent. Such marriages could be rendered null by the Church. Thus, though a later instance, Henry VIII's marriage to Catherine of Aragon was deemed null because she had allegedly been married to Henry's brother, Arthur. When, in the 11c and 12c, the Latin *affinitas* was used it was this sense that was intended, not the second political sense found in the following entry. [< L *affinitas* = relationship] – *Cf. next*

Affinity 2. Affinity is used today to describe the network of relations within a magnate's own country. This comprised knights and esquires who supported him in local affairs. During Edward III's reign, and the emergence of *bastard feudalism, magnates began to take on permanent retainers; they were also extending their power and were able to influence local courts through which they intimidated those they wished to constrain. While the *justice-in-eyre system might bring central authority to justice, local politics remained comfortably within the magnate's hands. – *Cf. previous;* BUZONE; FAUTOR

Afforestation. The conversion into a designated forest with the legal trappings attaching thereto which circumscribed or forbade hunting by any but the lord. The Normans were particularly avid hunters and greatly extended forest law. Perhaps a third of England was subject to such law under the Norman kings and early Plantagenets. The New Forest, as it is still known a millennium later, was created by William I in 1079. – *Cf.* DISAFFORESTATION; FOREST ASSIZES; FOREST, CHARTER OF THE

Affrontant. *Her.* Describes two animals facing each other. Synonyms are 'confronting' and 'respecting'. – *Cf. next;* ADDORSED

Affronty. *Her.* The term for a *charge shown facing outwards at the viewer, particularly when that charge is a lion. This is known as 'full aspect' when used of birds. – *Cf. previous*

-age. Suffix which gives a quality to a word it is attached to, e.g. *courage. [< Fr. *age* < L *-aticus*] – *Cf.* -AGIUM

Agist. To admit livestock into a forest but more usually to pasture for a set time, and/or at a specified cost. The term is still used in Cumbria when sheep farmers move their flocks to lower pasture in winter. [< AN *gister* = to lodge] – *Cf. next*

Agistment tithe. The *tithe imposed upon the owner of land used for agisting; later, the right to the use of forest land, its *herbage. – *Cf. previous;* GISEMENT

Agistor. Officer in charge of *agistment; an officer who watched over the king's forests. – *Cf.* AGIST; FOREST ASSIZES

-agium. Second element of Latin words such as *ancoragium, *barragium, *berbiagium, *hibernagium,* functioning as the equivalent English element *-age* which gives a quality, and here a sense of right or privilege, e.g. *faldage. – *Cf.* -AGE

Agnate. Term indicating common descent within a kindred group from one particular male ancestor, usually on the male side. – *Cf.* LLWYTH

Agnung. Ownership, possession; also proof of ownership of land. [< OE *agnung* = ownership] – *Cf.* TALU

Agnus Dei. Lit. 'lamb of God'. The phrase used by John the Baptist of Christ, taken from the book of Isaiah 53:7. Later the two words became the opening a part of the mass. The lamb became a familiar icon or symbol of Christ, e.g. in Æthelred the Unready's coinage of *c.*1009 and later in both medieval and Byzantine painting.

Ague. Feverish sickness with high fever, perhaps the *sweating sickness or malaria. Severe cases were probably genuine influenza; others, the bad head-cold we persist in calling 'flu. [< L *acuta* = acute]

AH. The Latin abbreviation of *Anno Hejira*, the year of Mohammed's flight to Medina, which in the Christian calendar was 622. This year is considered the beginning of the Islamic era and thus of the Islamic calendar. It is analogous to *AD.

Aide de la venerie. Lit. 'helper of the hunt'. AN title for an assistant hunts-man, used of young men with some years experience of hunting, with horses of their own. This was a route into the knighthood for ambitious young men not nobly born. As an *aide* the young man, perhaps 20 years old, would have a *varlet of his own. The horses used on these occasions were not esp. bred; the *courser and *palfrey were ridden to hounds. Such riding skills acquired as an aide were considered vital to one who might become a knight. – *Cf.* LYMER; VARLET DES CHIENS

Aids. One of the obligations or *feudal incidents of a tenant requiring him to make payments of money to his lord. Requests were prompted by many occasions; however, *Magna Carta imposed limits. *Bracton distinguished between services or concomitant services and 'reasonable aids', i.e. the giving of money. The occasions permitted for the request of an aid were: the knighting of an eldest son, and the first marriage of an eldest daughter. Others were for the need or indigence of the lord, e.g. the giving of money for a ransom to release the lord. – *Cf.* TALLAGE

Aiguise. *Her.* Pointed, esp. sharply so. [< Fr. *aiguiser* = sharpen]

Aislé. *Her.* Used of a creature depicted with wings which it does not have naturally. [< Fr. *aile* = a wing]

Ait. *See* EYOT; WICK

Ajouré. *Her.* The term used of a *chief which can be seen through or is *crenellé.

Aketon. *See* ACTON

al-. The Arabic definite article. It is still to be found in English words such as *algebra and *alchemy, the consequence of Europe benefiting from Arabic learning.

Alant. *Her.* A *charge showing a short-eared mastiff.

Alb. The white vestment, usually floor length, worn by all *clergy, from *acolyte to bishop. [< L *albus* = white]

Alba firma. Lit. 'white *farm, white payment'. The annual rent payable to a lord, esp. the king, in 'white money', i.e. assayed silver. – *Cf.* BLANCH FARM; INBLANCH; WETHERSILVER

Alberia. *Her.* Used of a shield devoid of charges, being wholly white or *argent. [< L *albus* = white]

Alce. *Her.* Another term for a *griffin.

Alchemy. The science and chemistry of the Middle Ages, popularly known for the search for a means of turning base metal into gold, and also for an elixir of life. It was a resource of great knowledge of metals, allied with a belief that a perfectly pure substance could purify what was base by contact. Dante placed alchemists in the eighth circle of the *Inferno* with all other falsifiers. [< Ar. *al-kimiya* = art of transmuting metals]

Alcoran. The *Koran.

Alderman. The senior member or warden of a *guild; latterly, a borough magistrate or officer equivalent to mayor. [< OE *ealdorman* = a prince or chief, ruler of a district]

Ale. A pale brew made without hops. Without tea or coffee, and the water not reliable, those unable to get wine drank ale, small beer or cider. [< OE *ealu* = ale, beer]

Ale-conner. An inspector of ale; every village or place with an *ale-house would have had one. [*conner* = an inspector or examiner < OE *cunnan* = to know] – *Cf.* ASSIZE

Alegar. Malt vinegar, a vinegar made from ale; for the poor who brewed ale but did not drink wine. [14c ale + *egar* = acidic, pungent < OFr. *aigre* = keen, sharp < L *acer* = sharp, bitter]

Ale-house. It is not clear that every village had an ale-house, but one without an ale-house or brewster would be unlikely. Often they would be found at or near cross-roads. The Latin term used was *domus potationis* = a drinking house. This ale or beer was not very strong. [OE = *ealahus*]

Aleppo boil [oriental sore]. Conditions in the Eastern Mediterranean were unfamiliar and hostile to ill-equipped European crusaders. The boil was the outward sign of a disease known to modern medicine as leishmaniasis. It was the consequence of a parasitic infection, with unpleasant symptoms of boils, ulcers and liver damage; it was frequently fatal (disease was a more effective killer of crusaders than the Saracens). Aleppo was in today's north Syria. Then it was an important garrison town of the Muslim forces.

Alerion. *Her.* Eagle depicted without beak or feet but with wings spread wide. [< L *alario* = of the wings of an army] – *Cf.* MARTLET 2

Ale-stake. Taverns used to sport a pole like a flag-pole, on which a bush was hung. An ivy bush was the sign used, ivy being sacred to Bacchus.

Ale-wife. *See* BREWSTER

Algebra. This word is derived from the title of an Arabic text, *Kitab al-jabr wa al-muqabalah* (The Book of Integration and Equation) written by al-Khwarizmi (d. 850). The word *al-jabr* of the title is of two parts: *al* = the + *jabr* = reunion of parts. – *Cf. next;* AL-

Algorism. System of Arabic numeration, arithmetic. European acquaintance with and adoption of Arabic numerals came from translations of Arab mathematicians, esp. in Moorish Spain. [< Ar. *al-Khwarizmi* = a 9c Arab mathematician; thus also, algorithm] – *Cf. previous;* THETA

Alidad. Device for measuring angles with e.g. an *astrolabe. [< Ar. *al-idada*]

Alien priory. A monastery or convent established in England yet subject to a mother-house in another country, usually France. These were small establishments, sometimes with only two or three monks in residence. Their function was administrative, looking after the lands belonging to the mother-house. In 1294 many such properties were confiscated, at a time of war with France. In 1378 all the monks in alien priories were expelled, their lands being acquired by the crown. – *Cf.* CLUNY; DENIZEN

Alienation. This term is used of property given by its owner to another, e.g. from a lord to a monastery, and particularly of lands given by the king to supporters, or those he wished to become supporters. – *Cf.* DE DONIS; ENFEOFFMENT TO USE

Alkanet. A red dye taken from plants of the borage family, *Alkanna lehmannii.* The colour is known today as henna. [< Ar. *al-hanna*]

Alkaron. The *Koran. An instance of an Arabic word entering the English language, if temporarily, and retaining the definite article *al-* prefix, *cf.* *algebra and *algorism.

Allegiance. Loyalty due to one's lord. At Salisbury, in 1086, William I had all landowners in England swear allegiance to him. It was a sign, if one were needed, of the new king's power: all land in the kingdom was his. – *Cf.* Do-MAIN

Alliteration. A distinctive feature of OE poetry, alliteration employed similar or identical sounds from the beginning of stressed syllables. It continued in use until the late 14c, alongside French-influenced forms of rhyme and metre. Of the great English poets, William Langland was the last to use alliteration. In OE verse the poetic line was divided in two: generally, each half-line had two stressed syllables, of which either or both from the first half-line alliterated with the first from the second half-line.

Allodium [allod]. An *allodium* was inherited, family land held absolutely, rather than of a lord or monarch. – *Cf.* ALLEGIANCE; FIEF

Almagest. Ptolemy's great treatise on astronomy; translated by Arab scholars in the 9c; this Arabic text was translated into *Latin in the 12c, making it accessible to European scholars. The works of Aristotle followed this path back into Europe via Moorish Spain.

Almesfeoh. Lit. 'alms' fee'. The cash render to the pope from the kingdom of England, first given by Alfred the Great. This was also known as *Peter's pence or *Rome-scot.

Almoign. An ecclesiastical possession. [< AN *almoin* < L *eleemosyna* = alms] – *Cf. next;* FRANKALMOIGN

Almoner. An official who dispensed *alms for some other person or institution, e.g. the king and queen each had an almoner, as would a religious house; an alms-giver. Robert Mannyng (*c.*1330) uses *aumenere* in *Handlyng Synne*: 'Seynt John, the aumenere'. [< AN *aulmoner* = an almoner < L *eleemosyna* = alms] – *Cf. next;* AUMENER

Almonry. The place from which *alms were dispensed. [< OFr. *aulmosnerie* < L *eleemosyna* = alms] – *Cf. previous*

Alms. Charity for the destitute and poor. Such giving was deemed one of the duties of a monastery and the wealthy. Alms were doled out on a monastery's patron saint's day, for example, or on the anniversary of its founder's death, and on Good Friday; also on Good Friday one penny was given to all who came. Endowments were left for alms-giving. [< OE *ælmysse, ælmesse* = alms] – *Cf.* ALMONER; DOLE

Almuce. A large cloth cape, often with attached hood turned down over the shoulders and lined with fur. Doctors of Divinity and canons wore one lined with grey fur.

Alnage. *See* AULNAGE

Altarage. The revenue of a church or *cathedral received through oblations to an altar. The Latin form was *altaragium*. – *Cf.* -AGIUM

Alure. A passage or gallery to walk in; particularly a parapet or gallery behind battlements or a church roof; also a *cloister. [< AN *aleür* = a passage < L *alura*] – *Cf.* AMBULATORY

Alveary. A bee-hive. [< L *alvearium* = a group of beehives, *alvarus* = a beehive] – *Cf.* BEOCEORL; MELLITARIUS

Amber. A dry measure of four *bushels; a liquid measure of 48 *sesters. [< L *amphora*]

Ambidexter. The Latin term for a juror who took money from both sides; generally, a swindler. [< L *ambidexter* = both sides] – *Cf.* ANTITHETARIUS

Ambler. As its name suggests, a slow-moving horse; one not bred as, nor suited to be, a *destrier* or a *courser.

Ambo [ambon]. Latin word for the desk from which the Epistle and *Gospel were read in early Christian churches. It was replaced by the now familiar pulpit during the 14c.

Ambry [aumbry]. A small cupboard let into the wall of a church for storing the vessels of the mass; a place where books were kept. [< L *armarium* = chest, closet]

Ambulant. *Her.* Walking.

Ambulatory. A place for walking, e.g. the *cloister of a monastery or convent; also, the aisle around the *sanctuary of a church or *cathedral; the space behind the high altar of a church. – *Cf.* ALURE

Amen. Lit. 'so be it'. The Hebrew word which ends a prayer.

Amerce. To impose a fine, of the kind imposed by a lord of the *manor. [< AN *amercier, à merci* = at (the) mercy (of another)] – *Cf. next*

Amercement. The imposition by a lord of a discretionary penalty; later the penalty itself. The greatest imposer of amercements was the king; they were a royal fine. *Magna Carta deals with such royal penalties. Thus, ch. 20 states of freemen: 'A free man shall be fined only in proportion to the degree of his offence, and for a serious offence correspondingly, but not so heavily as to deprive him of his livelihood.' Magnates were to be treated similarly in ch. 21: 'Earls and barons shall be fined only by their equals, and in proportion to the gravity of their offence.' [< AN *amercier, à merci* = at (the) mercy (of another)] – *Cf. previous*

Amice. A white scarf worn on the shoulders by celebrant priests; sometimes expensively decorated, perhaps like *orphrey. [< L *amicio* = to clothe, cover]

Amiens, Mise de. An attempted reconciliation or settlement (*mise*) between the king, Henry III, and Simon de Montfort, arbitrated by Louis IX of France in January 1264. De Montfort declined to accept and the Barons' War was the result.

Amour courtois. A term coined by Gaston Paris in the late 19c to describe the kind of adoration found, for example, in Chrétien de Troyes's romances and the *Roman de la Rose. – Cf.* COURTLY LOVE

Ampula [ampulla]. A small container or phial of water. These were sold as souvenirs for pilgrims to take home; at Canterbury *ampulae* of 'Becket water' were considered to have medicinal or miraculous powers. The word was also used of the containers of the sacramental oils.

Anarchy. A large part of King Stephen's reign from approximately 1135 to 1154 is so called, although a better term might well be civil war. The term is no longer favoured, as it suggests a more general state of disorder than actually existed at the time.

Anathema. *Excommunication and condemnation, usually of a heretic. The word can also be used to indicate someone damned, e.g. 'he was anathema'. – *Cf.* EXCOMMUNICATION

Anchor. *Her.* When used in *heraldry the anchor is a sign of hope, from its being something which gives security.

Anchor-hold. The cell of an anchorite or anchoress. [< anchor + ME *hold* = confinement, constraint] – *Cf. next;* ANCORSETL; *Ancrene Riwle*

Anchorite. Anchoress is the female form. A recluse; a person persuaded by faith to reject the world and live in isolation. Sometimes such persons were immured, wholly confined and even literally walled in. Before one could be 'bricked in' permission was required from a bishop. One of his duties would be to officiate, for which ceremonies in *pontificals survive. Indeed, an anchoress received the last rites, and had the office of the dead said over her. She then entered her cell and was bricked in, accompanied at each stage by various prayers. Strange as it may seem today, such women felt they were entering a community. The *Ancrene Riwle* makes plain, as it praises the feeling of communality, that the anchoresses communicated with one another through servants, described as 'maidens', who carried spoken messages to and fro between the cells. These cells typically had three windows, a private altar, and a bed and crucifix. One of the windows gave a view of the altar of the church to which the cell was attached; a second window opened into servants' quarters through which food and, presumably, a chamber-pot were passed; the third and smallest, known as the 'parlour' window, faced out-wards and was used to speak to visitors. This was the smallest so as to mini-mise the temptation implicit in seeing the outside world. This last was simi-lar to the *fenestra parvula* of Gilbertine monasteries. The *Ancrene Riwle* offers the following as definition of an anchorite: 'an anker is called an anker . . . [for being] anchored under the church like an anchor under the ship [to hold it] so that waves and storms don't overturn it'. [< Gr. *anakhoro* = to withdraw]

Ancilla. Latin for 'female slave'. Nuns would sometimes refer to themselves as *ancillae* (i.e. handmaids of the Lord). – *Cf.* SERVUS

Ancoragium. The Latin term for the fee or duty paid by a ship for anchorage in a port or haven.

Ancorsetl. The cell of an *anchorite; an *anchor-hold. [< OE *ancor* = anchorite, hermit + *setl* = place, residence] – *Cf.* CHIRCHETHURL

Ancrene Riwle. *A Rule for Anchoresses.* This is sometimes also known as *Ancrene Wisse.* This text gives rules for the behaviour of female recluses who were not within one of the established orders. The *Riwle* was written in English anony-mously for three sisters of gentle birth. Both Latin and French versions were available until the 16c. Its use of alliteration is highly ornamental, while its tone has the fervour of sermon and the intensity of poetry. The *Riwle* is one of the earliest surviving examples of sustained ME prose. – *Cf.* ANCHORITE

Ancrene Wisse. See previous

Andred. The Weald, the great forest in Kent and Sussex. – *Cf.* WOLD

Angel 1. Angels were beings believed to be incorporeal but which when mani-festing themselves to human beings assumed a body of air, the least corpo-real of the *elements. They existed in God's presence in heaven, having sev-eral classes or degrees. These were: *seraphim, *cherubim, thrones, domin-ions, virtues, powers, principalities, *archangels and angels. Angels are the closest order of spiritual beings to men.

Angel 2. An English gold coin, known as the 'angel *noble', worth one third of a pound, 6s 8d, first issued in 1464. Its name derived from the image of St Michael spearing a dragon on the obverse; the reverse displayed a ship at sea with rays of the sun from its masthead. The angel replaced the noble. It was also known as an *angelot*, and *ange d'or* (gold angel).

Angelcynn [Ongelcyn]. The English people. *Angelcynneslond* = land of the English.

Angelica. An aromatic plant, *Angelica sylvestris*, used as a plague remedy throughout this period, in England and elsewhere. It is to be found in medi-eval art used as the flower of the Trinity.

Angelot. *See* ANGEL 2

Angevin. The adjectival form of *Anjou and name of a dynasty which came to rule in England from the reign of Henry II, beginning in 1154. They were later known as the *Plantagenets. [< L *Andegavensis* = region of *Civitas Andegavensis*, today Anjou]

Angild. A single payment or the rate of compensation for damage. [< OE *an* = one + *gild* = money, payment]

Angles. Bede mentioned the Angles as one of the groups of Germanic people who migrated to Britain in the 5c; their home territory was in today's Holstein. They were known to the Roman historian Tacitus (d. *c*.117), who wrote about them in his *Germania*. They overwhelmed local populations in eastern England. – *Cf.* SAXONS

Anglo-Norman. A French dialect which became after 1066 the vernacular of the court, law, the Church and parliament. It was also a literary language, from the 12c taking second place only to Latin. It was the language of the aristocracy in England; its use became necessary for merchants and traders. However, in the 14c, and during the *Hundred Years' War, feeling turned against France and the language began to fall out of favour, English reclaiming lost ground. Anglo-Norman persisted in the law for some time after English came to be deemed acceptable for use in parliament in 1362.

Anglo-Saxon. AS is used to refer to the Germanic peoples, i.e. Angles and Saxons and others, who settled in what today we call England in the 400 years after the 5c when the Romans left and before the *Viking incursions of the 9c and later. When speaking of the language, 'Old English' is preferred to 'Anglo-Saxon'. [< OE *Angulseaxe*] – *Cf.* ANGLES

Anglo-Saxon Chronicles [Old English Chronicles]. An extraordinary and fascinating document begun during the reign of Alfred the Great. The *ASC* is one of the few continuous Western histories in a native language, here OE. It begins with Alfred's genealogy. The annals themselves begin in 410, with the last being for 1154, and record the many events of English history over these years (the earlier entries in particular being less factually reliable).

Animé. *Her.* The term is used of the eyes of an animal which are of a different *tincture from that of its body; also when the animal is posed as if ready to fight. – *Cf.* BEQUE; CRINED; MEMBERED; RAMÉ; UNGULED

Annal. A year by year record of events set out in a *codex often with a single sentence for each year: it was a laconic, epigrammatic record of the past, chronicling the little news there was, when for most, the village or monastery was all they knew. [< L *annalis* = of a year] – *Cf. Anglo-Saxon Chronicles*

Annales Cambriae. The Annals of Wales. A collection of annals recording Welsh history from the 5c to the mid-10c. The surviving text, contained in MS Harley 3859, is 11c. [L *Cambria* = Wales] – *Cf. previous*

Annates. *See* FIRST FRUITS

Anno Domini. Lit. 'in the year of the Lord'. The decision to use the present dating system in the West – using the birth of Christ as the base year – evolved from work by Dionysius Exiguus (d. 550). However, it is now accepted that Christ was born some years earlier, between 7 and 4 BC.

Annodated. *Her.* Lightly curved in the shape of an 'S'.

Annona. Orig. a year's crop of wheat; then used of a levy on that wheat to supply the soldiery.

Annulet. *Her.* A *charge in the shape of a ring. [< L *annulus* = a ring] – *Cf.* CADENCY, MARK OF

Ansetla. A *hermit.

Antecessor. A term used in *DB*, synonymous with 'predecessor'. It usually indicated a person who held land before the Conquest, i.e. those in possession *TRE, whose land had been granted to a Norman by William I. The process of grants of land to new landlords was methodical and slow; dispossession did not take place overnight.

Ante portas. *See* CAPELLA EXTRA PORTAS

Anthony, Order of Hospitallers of St. Founded *c.*1100, the house at Grenoble became a site of pilgrimage for those suffering from *Saint Anthony's fire. They were black-robed itinerants, ringing small bells for alms. They owned many pigs which were permitted to run freely in town streets and were required to wear bells as a sign of their ownership. (St Anthony was the patron saint of swineherds.) All other citizens had to keep their pigs in their house.

Anthropophagi. Man-eaters believed to live in distant regions of the world; part of the exotica which filled the medieval imagination for want of real knowledge. [< Gr. *anthropophagos* = *anthropos* = man + *phagos* = eating] – *Cf.* BABEWYN

Antiphon. Orig. something sung by two choirs in turn. Texts from the Bible sung during a service, at the beginning and end of psalms. – *Cf. next*

Antiphonary [antiphoner]. A liturgical book containing the *antiphons sung during service. Antiphonaries were large books for use by the choir, often decorated and *historiated. – *Cf.* CANTICLE

Antithetarius. The Latin term used in court documents for the accused who in response accuses his accuser of the same crime. [L *antithetarius* = antithesis] – *Cf.* AMBIDEXTER

Ap. Lit. 'son of'. Welsh word similar to the Ir. *mac* = son. When some names are anglicised, the *ap* is fused with the patronymic, e.g. ap Rhys becomes Price.

Apanagium. The Latin word for arrangements made for the support of children of a royal person; later, the term applied to any child with a portion of an estate. The English form is 'apanage'. [< OFr. *apaner* = dower, the estate left a widow for life. [< L *panis* = bread]

Apaumy. *Her.* A hand held up, palm facing the viewer, e.g. the three red hands of Ulster.

Apostate. Someone who abandoned or rejected their faith or moral allegiance, esp. after taking an oath; someone who was unfaithful. Apostasy was also applied to infidels, i.e. non-Christians, regardless of oath. This apostasy eliminated any scruple about waging war on the Saracens, for example.

Apparitor [apparator]. The servant or officer of a court, ecclesiastical or civil, with the duty of summoning attendance; later an usher or *herald. The Latin word was taken and used in English without change. [< L *apparitor* = a civil, public, servant] – *Cf.* BEADLE

Appellants. The name derives from the 'appeal' of treason against the friends of Richard II in parliament in 1387 made by the group of magnates who opposed the king. They were the earls of Arundel, Derby (later Henry IV) and Warwick, and Thomas of Woodstock. Those accused were defeated when they fought to defend themselves at the Battle of Radcot Bridge. For a while the Appellants ruled the country through parliament. Those accused who had not fled to Europe were tried and executed. It was some 10 years before Richard was able to turn the tables and accuse the Appellants themselves. – *Cf.* MERCILESS PARLIAMENT

Apprentice. A boy legally bound to an employer for a set number of years during which time he learnt a trade. It was a means by which *guilds controlled the numbers within a particular trade or handicraft. [< OFr. *apprendre* = to learn]

Appurtenances. The lesser rights and agreements attaching to land, e.g. pasture rights on particular strips of land, with specified quantities of wood and rights of way. Appurtenances were heritable. They were not necessarily all found within one *manor or vill but could be within neighbouring land. *Bracton, using the Latin word *pertinentia*, was clear that in land claims appurtenances must be specified: 'the demandant must at the outset describe the thing he claims, . . . that it may be known whether he claims land or a rent or a *tenement with the appurtenances . . . or without.' [< OFr. *apartenance* < L *pertineo* = to concern, pertain to]

Aquabagelus [aquebachelus]. Lit. 'carrier of holy water'. Students, ever short of funds, supported themselves by alms given for carrying holy water to the houses of parishioners. The practice was approved by Church authorities; indeed, the archbishop of Canterbury, Simon Sudbury, called it a 'laudable custom' in 1393.

Arable. Land for use with crops; land which could be ploughed and cultivated. [< L *arabilis* = ploughable]

Aramaic. Ancient Syriac; language of the Persian Empire from the 6c BC. Aramaic was the language of Christ and Jews in the Near East.

Aratura. The amount of land ploughable in one year by one plough. [< L *aratro* = to plough] – *Cf.* CARUCATE; TERRAE CARUCAE

Arbalester [arblast]. Soldier who used a crossbow, i.e. an arbalest. An English form is 'balister'. [< L *arcuballista* < *arcus* = shape of a bow + *ballista* = a missile thrower] – *Cf.* CROSSBOW; LOOPHOLE

Arber. *See* ERBER

Arcarius. Latin for a treasurer, not to be confused with the homonym meaning 'archer', the etymology being quite different. [< L *arca* = chest, strong box]

Archangel. An angelic order, the best known members of which were Gabriel, Michael and Raphael. It was Raphael who, in Milton's *Paradise Lost*, was sent by God to put man on guard against Satan. This forewarning rendered all excuse for disobedience null. Michael was the archangel who fought against Satan and those angels who sided with him during his three-day rebellion in heaven. Gabriel (the name means Man of God) was charged with protecting Adam and Eve and he expelled Satan from the garden of Eden; he was also the angel of the Annunciation.

Archbishop. The principal bishop of a province of the Church. [< Gr. *arkhos* = chief + bishop] – *Cf. next*

Archdiocese. The term for the province over which an archbishop holds jurisdiction, comprised of several *dioceses. – *Cf. previous*

Archery. Under law in the 14c all able-bodied men were required to practise archery at least once a week, and also on Sundays and holidays; to use a *longbow required both strength and long practice. Bow staves had to be imported by merchants: four staves for every ton of goods imported, 10 for butts of Malmsey. However, although large numbers of bowmen were on foot, there were also many mounted archers, which gave them considerable flexibility, allowing quick movements on the battlefield. The use of mounted archers emerged in the 1330s, allowing them to fight on foot or horseback, as needed. The foot archer was worth 2d or 3d a day; during the *Hundred Years' War, fighting on horseback, an archer was worth 6d a day. The Latin form was *arcarius*. [< L *arcus* = bow] – *Cf.* CROSSBOW; LONGBOW

Arches, Court of. *See* CURIA DE ARCUBUS

Arcuation. A curve shaped like an arch or bow; 'arcuated' is the adjectival form.

Ard-ri. High king of Ireland. High kings ruled in Ireland but rarely without some opposition, as they were not always acknowledged by provincial kings.

Argent. *Her.* A white or silver *tincture.

Argenteus. A silver shilling. [L *argenteus* = silver (adjective)]

Arglwydd. The Welsh word for a lord, or one of the lesser rulers within Wales. When translated into Latin, *dominus* was used. *Arglwydd* replaced the Welsh word *brenin* in the late 12c and the early 13c when the overlordship of the English king was acknowledged. – *Cf.* BRENIN

Arles. Colloquial term for money given as an earnest of good intent; also, money given when a servant was hired. There was no connection with the town named Arles; rather the word is *arra* with a dim. sense contributed by *-le*.

Armarium [armadium]. The Latin term for a chest in which vessels for use in the mass were kept. The English version was *'ambry'. It was also the place where books were kept. [L *armarium* = a chest, closet] – *Cf. next*

Armarius. The monk who was responsible for what was read by his fellow monks, either privately or publicly, e.g. at meal time in the *frater. – *Cf. previous*; SCRIPTORIUM

Armed. *Her.* Term used when the teeth or claws of an animal are shown in a *tincture different from the animal's body.

Armes courtoises. The general term for the arms employed in tournaments which had had their 'killing edge' removed: swords were blunted and the points of lances changed to minimise the danger of fatal injuries. It echoes the phrase *amour courtois*, i.e. *courtly love, the convention prescribing how ladies and their knights conducted themselves. – *Cf.* À PLAISIR; ARMS, STATUTE OF; CORONAL; CURTANA

Armet. A round metal helmet, with pieces covering the cheek bones, i.e. with visor, *beaver and *gorget and secured with chin straps. It became the arche-typal helmet, used throughout Europe. – *Cf.* BASINET

Armiger. An esquire; orig. a young man who attended a knight by carrying his shield. The Latin form was *armigerus*. The word was used as the title esquire, as knight was used, e.g. when John Leland mentioned in his *Itinerary* two members of a 14c family, 'Thomas Golaffre, armiger, . . . and Syr Morice Brun, knight'. It was the Latin form for what we know as a country squire, a man with land, well-born but not knighted. [< L *armiger* = bearing arms, armed] – *Cf. next*

Armigerous. Term used now for someone entitled to bear heraldic arms. – *Cf. previous*

Armil. A bracelet, part of the royal *regalia; also, later, a stole used at coronations, made of cloth of gold, which indicated the sacerdotal aspect of a king conferred by anointing.

Arms, Assize of. 1181. This *assize extended the obligations of military equipment and service to those not previously affected. Under *fyrd* law, only free landholders had been liable. This assize summoned all burgesses, all freeholders, regardless of wealth; also included were artisans and traders with income of 10 marks or more a year. Men worth 16 marks were to be equipped as knights. The rich were required to have sword, lance, helmet and mail shirt; the less well-off leather jerkin, lance and skull cap. – *Cf.* ARRAIATOR

Arms, coat of. *Her.* The heraldic insignia or *bearings of a king, or *knight, or of a family granted such hereditary devices. To bear arms it was necessary to inherit or receive a grant from the king or a *herald, or proof was required of an ancestor's use of the arms from 'time immemorial', which in common law began in 1189, but in the law of arms in 1066. – *Cf.* ARMS, COLLEGE OF; ARMS, KING OF

Arms, College of. *Her.* A royal corporation founded by King Richard III in 1484. It comprises the Earl Marshal, three Kings of *Arms – Garter, Clarenceux and Norroy – and the following Heralds: Chester, Lancashire, York, Somerset, Richmond and Windsor. There are also four pursuivants – Rouge Croix, Blue Mantle, Rouge Dragon and Portcullis. – *Cf.* ARMS, COAT OF

Arms, King of. *Her.* The title of the three chief heralds of the College of Arms, i.e. Garter, Norroy and Ulster, Clarenceux. – *Cf.* ARMS, COAT OF; ARMS, COLLEGE OF; HERALDS, COLLEGE OF

Arms, Statute of. Statutum armorum, 1292. This was intended to regulate tournaments and limit the dangers inherent in the sport. Weapons were to be blunted or *rebated: swords were not to be pointed and lances were to have a *coronal. There were also to be arbitrators to settle disputes. – *Cf.* ARMES COURTOISES

Armures de fer. Lit. 'armour of/armed with iron'. The collective term for knights and squires because they wore iron *mail.

Arpent. A measure of land equal to approx. one acre. It was used by the Normans when measuring or describing the size of vineyards.

Arra [arrhe]. Term for money paid in advance by merchants to monasteries for their wool; this was often paid two or three years in advance. These were effectively loans and the merchants made their interest by discounting. As much as one fifth of the sum might have been paid early in this way. It happened when merchants were cash-rich and monasteries the opposite. The *Cistercian order, so prominent in the wool trade, took such money, although the chapter-general frequently forbade such transactions. It led inevitably to debt when flocks were ruined by outbreaks of *murrain. [< L *arrha* = a deposit, a pledge of money] – *Cf.* ARLES

Arraiator. The Latin term for the officer charged with ensuring that mustered troops were properly clothed and equipped. An English equivalent would perhaps be 'arrayer'. – *Cf.* ARMS, ASSIZE OF; ARRAY, COMMISSION OF

Arras. The town in Flanders, near Lille, after which a rich kind of tapestry was named, depicting figures and scenes, esp. mythological. Its reputation for quality was Europe-wide, giving rise to the Italian word for tapestry, *arrazzo*, and the Spanish *drap de raz*. Curtains of this material were often hung on the walls around a room; screens also were made of arras. Polonius famously hides behind one in *Hamlet*.

Array, Commission of. Raising a large fighting force presented problems during the 13c and 14c. The procedure adopted was the Commission of Array. Commissioners were sent out by the crown to assess all men between 16 and 60 years of age in every township and *hundred in every shire. The best were selected and would be paid by the king; equipment had to be paid for by the recruit's home hundred. Commissioners were usually experienced soldiers themselves, and well able to select suitable men. Simultaneously, there were proclamations asking men to join up. For some there were pardons for criminal offences. However, the pay was assured; and if the troops were to serve abroad, they were paid from the day they left their home county. France was particularly popular, as it offered plenty of opportunity for plunder and looting, esp. during the *chevauchées*. – *Cf.* ARRAIATOR; CONTRACT CAPTAIN

Arrivagium. The Latin term for the toll payable by a ship for mooring at a dock or wharf. [L *arrivo* = to arrive] – *Cf.* -AGIUM

Arrow loop. A narrow, vertical opening in a wall or *merlon for arrows to be shot through. *Crossbows required horizontal openings, some of which with vertical openings also looked like crosses and were called 'crosslets' or 'arbalestinas'. An arrow loop could also be called a 'porthole'.

Arrowsmith. A smith who specialised in the making of metal arrow-heads.

Ars dictaminis. Lit. 'the art of letter-writing; letter composition'. University students were, then as now, short of funds. As part of the course in *dictamen*, the teacher would distribute specimen letters as guides to the writing of begging letters. – *Cf.* MULIERCULAE

Ars scribendi artificialiter. Lit. 'the art of writing artificially'. The Latin phrase used by printers for their new craft of printing books.

Arthurian romance. Much medieval literature centres on a British king, Arthur. Although mentioned in a 9c chronicle, Arthur's role was perhaps founded in literature in the *Historia Regum Britanniae* (*History of the Kings of Britain*) by Geoffrey of Monmouth. A French translation by the Jersey poet, Wace (*c.*1100–75), added the story of the Round Table, after which the court of Arthur became the focus of chivalric tales of courtly romance in England and the continent. One of the last medieval contributions to the literature was Malory's *Morte d'Arthur*, which was being prepared for printing by Caxton at the time of the Battle of Bosworth Field in 1485.

Articles of the Barons. *See* BARONS, ARTICLES OF THE

Artillator. *See* ATTILLATOR

Artiller. A maker of weapons; from this we have 'artillery'. [< OFr. *artiller* = arms] – *Cf.* ATTILLATOR

Artist. In the 13c 'artist' (Latin records used *artista*) was applied to those who studied the **trivium*: the liberal arts – grammar, **rhetoric, and logic – which were all language-based. The word was used of a knowledgeable person. [< L *ars* = skill, craft] – *Cf.* QUADRIVIUM

Arx. A small fortified position or small building. [< L *arx* = a stronghold or defensive position]

Ascendant. *Her.* Describes flames or smoke rising upwards.

Aseity. A theological term for a being (i.e. God) which depended upon no other cause than itself. [< L *a* = from + *se* = itself]

Ashlar. Large blocks of masonry smoothed and/or squared for use in horizontal courses. [< OFr. *aisselier* < L *axilla* = plank board]

Asinarium festum. *See* FEAST OF FOOLS

Aspect. *See* AFFRONTY

Assart. The grubbing up of trees and scrub, thus the turning of waste and woodland into cropland or pasture. Such land was also known as *terra nova* = new land. It was a serious offence to assart lands within a forest without a licence, forests being largely reserved for royal hunting. [< OFr. *assarter* = to grub up trees] – *Cf.* AFFORESTATION; SARTIS

Assisa panis et cervisiae. Lit. *'assize of bread and beer'. It was first issued during the reign of Henry II. The purpose was to set prices for the sale of bread in accordance with the cost of grain. Similarly, the price of beer was dependent on the cost of its ingredients. Punishments were set out: a culprit would be subject to *amercement; but persistent breaking of the assize could result in the *pillory. The Latin term for a brewer was *cervisarius*.

Assize. The meeting of the king and his council; the decrees issued by the king after such meetings; also, an ordinance such as that regulating prices of bread and ale, and weights and measures; such decrees became statutory. Later, the Grand Assize meant the Last Judgement. [< L *assideo* = to sit in council, to assess] – *Cf. previous*; ARMS, ASSIZE OF; MONEYERS, ASSIZE OF; PILLORY

Astroid. *Her.* Another term for a *mullet.

Astrolabe. A device for use in making astronomical measurements, in particular for measuring the altitude of stars. – *Cf.* ALIDAD

Astrology. Intense interest in astrology emerged in 14c England, prompted by that century's calamities of plague and famine; it was vigorously condemned by the Church, but this did not diminish its popularity or persistence. It came into England from the world of the Arabic scholars.

Astronomy. Astronomy was one of the subjects of the medieval *quadrivium*. Astronomy then was based upon Ptolemy of Alexandria's *Almagest*, written in the second quarter of the 2c. (The Arabic *al-magest* = the greatest.) The text was translated from the Greek into Arabic in the early 9c, and from Arabic into Latin in the 12c. The Ptolemaic description of the universe was geocentric; it was argued that since all objects fall to the centre of the universe, objects that were dropped on earth would fall elsewhere than to earth if it were not the centre of the universe. Not until Copernicus (d. 1543) was it shown that the earth moved. Astronomical observation served the needs of astrology, and of navigation. – *Cf.* PRIMUM MOBILE

Asylum. Usually a specific place of refuge, e.g. a church altar: a person seeking asylum could not be removed by force. [< Gk *asulon* = refuge] – *Cf.* ABJURE THE REALM; SANCTUARY

Atheling. *See* ÆTHELING

Atilt. The position in which a lance was held by a rider on horseback, tucked under the arm.

Atonement. The state of being 'at one'; unity and reconciliation between a person and God. This idea received its fullest treatment in St Anselm's *Cur Deus Homo?* (*Why Did God Become Man?*). Anselm himself used the term 'redemption'; the word 'atonement' emerged during the 16c.

Atour. The French name, used in England, for a specific style of women's headwear. The English word was *tire. These were tall, slender cones, using silver wire as a structure around which light materials would be hung. As a foundation they used the bonnet or *wimple. These were expensive items for fashionable women of the court: silk might be decorated, e.g. with pearls; costly transparent materials were also used. The *atour* was both a fragile and ephemeral creation, made for one occasion and one wearer. These diaphanous confections remain one of the most distinctive items of medieval clothing.

Attachias. A *chancery writ issued to ensure a person's attendance at its court by making him find pledges to appear or by arresting him.

Attainder, Act of. A convenient parliamentary device by which political opponents could be convicted of *treason without the inconvenience of a trial. Simply by being named in the act meant being attainted, i.e. guilty. As a result all property was forfeit, civil liberties were rendered null, and the guilty party's 'blood' was deemed corrupted. Consequently, descendants lost whatever inheritance there might have been. But just as many magnates banished by the king were forgiven and allowed to return, so also many of those attainted had the sentence reversed in parliament at a later date. [< ME *attain* = convict, bring to justice] – *Cf. next*

Attaint 1. The word was used of a nobleman convicted of an act seriously dishonourable, such as *treason. The punishment was usually death and the forfeiture of all lands and estates, leaving descendants without inheritance. – *Cf. previous*

Attaint 2 [atteint]. A hit, blow or strike. The term was used in jousting to signify a hit scored by one knight on another. When jousting in a friendly spirit, points were scored in various ways, e.g. by an attaint, by breaking a lance. – *Cf.* JOUST OF PEACE; JOUST OF WAR; TOURNAMENTS

Attillator. The craftsman working in the royal armouries, specialising in making the ammunition for *longbows, *crossbows, their winches and *quarrels; also the metal heads for the arrows and bolts. – *Cf.* ARTILLER; FLETCHER

Attire 1. A soldier's complete set of clothing and equipment necessary for going to war. Attire was also used as a verb = to equip a soldier for war. Later it came to indicate clothing in general. [< OFr. *atirer* = to equip] – *Cf.* TIRE

Attire 2. *Her.* Antlers used as a *charge. 'Attire' was used in the singular; when both antlers were meant, 'attires' was used.

Attorn. The process of transferring allegiance and homage from one lord to another. It was also used when land changed lords and the tenants who went with the land agreed to transfer all services and dues. The Latin form was *attornamentum.* [< OFr. *atorner* = assign < *torner* = turn] – *Cf.* ADSCRIPTUS GLEBAE

Aubade [aube]. The 16c term for a medieval Provençal love poem welcoming or lamenting the arrival of dawn. Such laments became a conventional trope in much European literature within and beyond the medieval period. They came to England with the Angevin kings. – *Cf.* PASTOURELLE; REVERDIE

Augustinian. Monastic order named after St Augustine (of Hippo), one of the Fathers of the Church; the order followed the Rule of St Augustine and had two branches, *Augustinian canons and *Augustinian friars. They established themselves in England first near Colchester, at St Botolph's, *c.*1106. At their peak they had more than 200 houses. – *Cf. next*; PATRISTIC

Augustinian canons [Austin canons]. Their full name was Canons Regular of St Augustine. They were sometimes known as Black Canons because of their black cassock. Their rule was based on care of the sick, on self-discipline, on love of God and of neighbour. They lived in the world, leading a common life. By 1200 they were a frequent sight in towns, where they established hospitals and almshouses. Canons took the same vow as monks but they served also in parish churches. Part of the impulse behind the establishment of new orders in the 13c was the reluctance of monastics to serve in the world, outside their walls, as parish priests, a need met by the canons. – *Cf. previous and next*

Augustinian friars (or hermits). Full name: Order of the Hermit Friars of Saint Augustine, OSA. The *hermits or friars were separate from the canons until unified by the pope in 1256, after which the friars worked in the world and were active in the universities. – *Cf.* AUGUSTINIAN

Aula regis. Lit. 'king's hall'. An 18c coinage referring to the Norman kings of England's court, which met in a great hall, such as that at Westminster built by William Rufus. – *Cf.* CURIA REGIS

Aulnage. Orig. the process of measuring by the *ell; this came to refer both to the measuring and inspection of cloth, and also the fee paid for that service. Aulnage accounts were made up for all home-produced cloth from the 13c to the 14c. These were made by the crown for taxation purposes: the wool industry, being so large, was at the centre of the English economy and crucial to royal revenues. These accounts provide a broad, if not precise, picture of the fortunes and fluctuations of the English sheep industry: before the mid-14c healthy and expanding; after the *Black Death in decline and stagnating. The Latin term was *alnagium*. [< OFr. *alner* = to measure by the *ell.]

Aumbry. *See* AMBRY

Aumener [aumonière]. A pouch or purse attached to a belt and worn both by men and women. It was used to carry coins and other small objects. A woman of high status would have carried an aumener as a purse; a woman of lower status would have carried a bourse. [< OFr. *aumoner* = an almoner] – *Cf.* AL-MONER

Aurifabria. The goldsmiths' quarter of London, near West Cheap. [< L *aurum* = gold + *faber* = a craftsman]

Austin. Contraction of 'Augustine'.

Auxilium. Lit. 'assistance, resource'. A feudal aid; the service, including military service, owed by *vassal to lord. – *Cf.* AIDS

Avagium. Latin word for payment made for the right to pannage in the lord's woods. – *Cf.* PANNAGE

Avalagium. Toll paid for going down the River Thames.

Avalon. The island of the blessed in Celtic mythology. It was also the place in legend where King Arthur sought refuge to recover from his wounds. Since the 12c Avalon has been linked in popular imagination with Glastonbury.

Avant-garde. The vanguard of an army, the leaders of the attack. [< Fr. *avant* = before, forward + *garde* = guard]

Avawmbrace. *See* VAMBRACE 1

Avellon. *Her.* A cross composed of four *filberts touching each other. Filberts were sometimes referred to as avellons, after Avella, in the Italian Campania, where they grew copiously.

Avenagium. The Latin word for a rent paid to a lord in oats. [< L *avena* = oats, straw] – *Cf. next*

Avenary. The largest department of the king's household, with a staff of between 100 and 200 grooms and valets. Under the charge of the *avener, they tended, groomed and fed the horses of the entire household, king, officials, attendants etc., and also those of visitors. [< L *avena* = oats, straw] – *Cf. next*

Avener. The chief officer of the king's stables; the officer in charge of provisioning the king's horses. The Latin term was *avenarius*. [< L *avena* = oats, straw] – *Cf. previous*; AVENAGIUM

Aventail. The mouthpiece of the helmet of a suit of armour which was movable to allow easier breathing; later this movable unit incorporated the *visor. [< AN *aventaille* < L *ventus* = wind, air]

Aver [affer]. An old horse or nag; a draught horse used on the farm. [< OE *eaffor* = a draught horse] – *Cf. next*

Avera. Service owed to his *sheriff by a *sokeman to carry messages, or anything else, while the king was in the *county; e.g. in Hertfordshire, the sheriff was supplied with 9d or 2¼ *averae*, i.e. each carrying service was valued at 4d. The word was also used of the work done by a ploughman and horse in one day. 'Avera' is the English form of the Latin *averagium*. [< OE *aferian* = to carry] – *Cf.* EQUITATIO; *previous*

Averagium. *See previous*

Averia de pondere. Spices and other fine goods weighed in units of one pound when (import) duty was paid, using the official scale or balance. From Latin *averia de pondere* is derived French *avoirdupois* = to have by weight. [< L *averia* = goods, merchandise + *pondere* = to weigh] – *Cf.* GARBLER

Aylet. *Her.* A Cornish *chough.

Ayne [eigne]. AN legal term for the first-born and heir. The spelling 'eigne' is also found, forming legal terms such as 'eigne title' = prior title (to something claimed or in dispute). [< OFr. *ainz né* = prior born, born before, i.e. eldest]

B

Baber-lipped. Thick-lipped. – *Cf. next*; BABEWYN

Babery. Grotesque images used as decoration in architecture, also in illuminated MSS. Today, we call them 'gargoyles'. [< ME *babywynrie*] – *Cf. next*

Babewyn. Any of the ugly or demonic creatures which populate medieval artwork; many are to be found cut in *cathedral stone, tucked away from first gaze. [< OFr. *babuin* = grimace, baboon; ME *babywynrie* = something monstrous] – *Cf. previous*; BAGWYN; BESTIARY; BLEMMYA; CYNOCEPHALUS; GRYLLUS

Babylon. Geography in medieval Europe was rudimentary. In this period Cairo was known in the West as Babylon. China was thought to be at the source of the Nile, as its silk was shipped down that river to Babylon/Cairo.

The Western name derives from classical usage: the Roman fortress, next to which al-Kahirah was founded, was called Babylon-on-the-Nile. – *Cf.* T/O MAP

Baccalarius. The Latin term for a graduate of a university who had not achieved his doctorate; he was a bachelor. The word was used also of lowly clerics and young novices in arms.

Bacchants. A nickname given to students who frequently changed their school or university. Then as now, students had a reputation for parties. [< L *bacchantes* = followers of Bacchus, god of wine] – *Cf.* GOLIARD

Bacele. A fighting group of several knights and their attendants; a group of lances. [?< L *baculo* = to batter, cudgel] – *Cf.* LANCE 2

Bachelor. A young man who wished to be a *knight; later, a young knight in the service of another senior; a novice in arms and warfare, thus by extension, a craftsman or *journeyman not yet of master status; also a student whose degree is below that of a master; a junior member of a *guild. The Latin word is *baccalarius*. [< OFr. *bacheler*] – *Cf.* KNIGHT BACHELOR

Bacinettum. *See* BASINET

Badge. *Her.* Orig. known as a *'cognisance'. An emblematic figure prominently displayed or an image composed of something easily recognisable, and associated with a particular person or family, e.g. the broom sprigs of the *Plantagenets, the ostrich feathers of Edward, the Black Prince, or the sun in splendour of Richard II, with the sun behind a cloud when used on his effigy.

Badling. An effeminate man or sodomite. [< OE *bædling* = a womanish man]

Baggage train. A number of wagons travelling together, e.g. the baggage trains of the king with all the household goods and administrative paperwork required during his *itinerary. If oxen were used to pull wagons, some 10 miles a day might be covered; a similar train drawn by horses would be expected to cover 25 miles a day. – *Cf.* CABALLUS; GARDEIN; PREEQUITATOR

Bagwyn. *Her.* An imaginary creature resembling an antelope but with the tail of a horse and horns grown over the ears. – *Cf.* BABEWYN

Bail [bayle]. Release from prisoner of a person on security; custody, jurisdiction; also the walls of a courtyard (*bailey) within a castle; a castle's outer defences, e.g. some kind of palisades. – *Cf.* CURTAIN WALL

Bailey. The courtyard within the walls of a castle. The London court known as the Old Bailey once stood in the city's ancient bailey. The word is a form of *bail. [< OFr. *bail, baille* = an enclosure] – *Cf.* MOTTE AND BAILEY

Bailiff. The chief officer of a *hundred or other district, representing the monarch; a justice officer under the *sheriff; the steward of the lord of the manor who would collect rents. [< OFr. *bailiff* < L *bajulus* = manager, administrator] – *Cf. next;* WICKNER

Bailiwick. The district within the jurisdiction of a *bailiff. [< *bailiff* + OE *wic*= office, function] – *Cf. previous;* -WICK

Baillonné. *Her.* Carrying a *baton in the mouth (of an animal).

Bajulus aquilae. A *steward officer in the Order of St John of Jerusalem. In English he was known as the Baillie of the Eagle. [L *bajulus* = steward; *aquilae* = of the eagle]

Bakers, Worshipful Company of. The bakers of London are first found in the *Pipe Rolls of 1155, when they made an annual payment to the *exchequer. The bakers were given authority by London's aldermen to enforce the assize of bread within two miles of the city, excluding the city of Westminster. Although short weight was an obvious failing, this might be evaded by adding sand to flour – something bakers themselves might easily discover, as would the buyer's mouth. Those who infringed were dragged through the city's streets, the offending loaf hanging from the neck. In time, a white, refined bread became popular; this caused a split in the 14c between white- and brown-bread makers. All loaves were required to carry the baker's mark, known as a *'dock', as smiths were required to mark their wares. – *Cf.* ASSISA PANIS ET CERVISIAE; BOLINGARIUS

Balcanifer. The *standard-bearer of the *Knights Templar. The standard itself was known as *balcanum*.

Baldachin [baldacchino, baldaquin, baudekin]. Material richly woven with silk and gold thread (known as *olosericum*) of the 14c and the 15c; a freestanding cover or canopy over the altar; also the canopy used at the most solemn moment during the coronation of an English monarch, as a protection against the mystical instant of the anointing with holy oil being witnessed by ordinary mortals, and used as such in 1953 during the coronation of Elizabeth II to exclude the television cameras; also, an elaborate cover of stone and wrought metal fixed to the roof or supported by the columns of tomb or niche; it reached a pinnacle of elaborate ornamentation during the Baroque, 17–18c. [?< Baldacco = Italian form of Baghdad] – *Cf.* ARMIL

Baldric [baldrick, bawdryk]. A belt worn crossways from the shoulder to carry a sword, usually richly decorated; a belt worn over one shoulder and under the opposite arm, supporting a horn; the strap from which the clapper of a bell was hung.

Bale. *Her.* *Charge used by the companies of dyers and silkmen; obviously descriptive of their trade. The cord or rope which bound the bale was of a *tincture different from the bale itself.

Baleen. A whale; whale-bone used in weapon-making. [< L *balena* = whale] – *Cf. next*; BATON 1

Balinger. A small vessel used close to shore, possibly without a forecastle. [< L *balingaria* = whaling boat < L *balena* = whale, whale-bone] – *Cf. previous*

Balistarius. Latin term for a soldier who operated a *mangonel or *trebuchet.

Balister. *See* ARBALESTER

Balistraria. The hole in the wall of a castle or other fortified building for a *crossbow or arbalest; they were also known as an *arbalestina*. – *Cf.* LOOP-HOLE

Ban. In its original Germanic use this word meant a king's or a lord's area of power or authority. Later, it signified a king's power to command and pro-hibit under pain of punishment or death, mainly used because of a breach of the *king's peace. Also, a royal proclamation, either of a call to arms, or a decree of outlawry; in clerical terms, *excommunication on condemnation by the Church.

Banality. The fees a feudal lord imposed for various usages, such as his mill, oven, etc. It might have included part of a fish catch or a proportion of the catch from a rabbit warren. – *Cf.* FORNAGIUM; FOUR BANAL

Banifer. A standard bearer; also known as a *baneur*. [< L *banera, banarium* = a banner] – *Cf. next*

Banner. *Her.* A banner was intended to indicate some distinctly valorous ac-tion of its user. The primary distinction between banners and standards and *pennons was that banners were square, having had the elongated fork-tail of the others cut off. Banners were meant to be of a size proportional to the owner's status, e.g. an emperor's was two or three times that of a *baron. A *badge would be shown on a banner for easy identification. The city of Lon-don's banner bore the image of St Paul in gold, with face, hands, feet in sil-ver. It was borne out of St Paul's Cathedral's west door on occasions of battle, when Londoners were led by the lord of Baynard's Castle. – *Cf. previous*; BAT-TLE; SAINT PAUL'S CROSS

Banneret. The title of a *knight permitted to take his *vassals into battle be-neath his *banner; this usually meant five or six knights with *squires and *sergeants; also, a person on whom a knighthood was bestowed on the field of battle; a rank of knighthood. The term banneret was used to differentiate between knights of higher rank and ordinary knights bachelor. The banneret was entitled to display his arms on a square banner; the ordinary knight bachelor had to use a triangular *pennon. He would have had a larger retinue than the knight, perhaps as many as 20 men. On campaign with the king, he received 4s a day, the knight 2s. He was responsible for commanding retinues in the field and garrisoning castles. Thus, Edward Montagu as a banneret at Crécy (1346) fought at the head of 9 knights, 15 esquires and 20 archers. In the 14c the title banneret began to be applied to those promoted to the baronage but possessing no land. They thus fell below a full *baron but above a knight. When summoned to parliament, the barons insisted upon their distinction. However, by the first quarter of the 15c this had been blurred by succeeding bannerets going to parliament and it fell out of use.

Banquet. A light collation or dessert. – Cf. FEAST 2

Bar 1. *Her.* An *ordinary in the form of a stripe no broader than one quarter of the *field. – Cf. BARRULET

Bar 2. A bar across the room or hall that separated judges from defendant, his spokesman and those watching. From this arose the practice of English *barristers being 'called to the bar'.

Barbarian. A Greek, then Roman word. Orig. someone who was neither Greek nor Roman, whose speech was unintelligible. Connotations of 'uncouth, barbaric' are to be observed from its earliest uses, and these came to predominate. – Cf. GOTHIC; HERETIC; SEELY

Barbe. The tall pleated linen collar worn by nuns and widows.

Barbers of London, Company of. The Company of Barbers (i.e. surgeons) was established in 1461 by Edward IV, in an attempt to deal with the problem of unqualified surgeons. By the time of Henry VIII, an examination was required to practise in London, overseen by the bishop of London and four qualified doctors. Also in London, four corpses (of criminals) were allowed each year for anatomy, i.e. dissection.

Barbican. An external defence for *castle or city; extra defence for a city gate or bridge. [< Ar. *barbahanne* = shelter]

Barbute. Soldier's helmet which possessed a projection covering the wearer's beard. [< L *barba* = beard] – Cf. BEAVER

Bard 1. Armour for a knight's horse, covering both breast and flanks; sometimes mail was used; also the decorative material, often velvet, covering the same parts of the animal's body. (By the 18c the term had been reduced to meaning a strip of bacon used to cover a chicken in the oven.) [< Ar. *bard'a* = saddle cloth, a saddle with stuffing] – Cf. CHAMFRON; COOPERTUS; DESTRIER

Bard 2 [bardings]. *Her.* A horse's trappings, sometimes with the owner's arms. [< Ar. *bard'a* = a saddle cloth] – Cf. *previous*

Bard 3. Irish or Welsh poet.

Bardi. Family of Florentine bankers and merchants in the 13c and 14c. In the last half of the 13c they provided regular funding to the crown. Edward III borrowed up to £20,000 a year from the Bardi. However, loans to Edward III during the *Hundred Years' War overstretched their resources and they were bankrupted in 1345. The Peruzzi family also made large loans to Edward, sometimes in concert with the Bardi, and was similarly bankrupted.

Barehide. A leather chest or trunk. The Latin equivalent was *bahudum*, a version of which survives in the medieval and modern French *bahut*.

Barker. Bark stripped from a tree was used to make an infusion in which the leather was steeped, as part of the tanning process. The barker would make that infusion. Hence the phrase, to bark one's knee = to strip skin from.

Barley. *Her.* A charge found in the insignia of brewers. The term for a sheaf of barley, as for one of wheat, is 'garb'; ears of wheat were also used as a *charge. Barley was an important crop, being the raw material for malt and hence ale.

Barmkyn. The *rampart or outer fortification of a castle's *barbican. 'Barmkyn' may be a corrupt form of 'barbican'.

Baron. Before the 13c, the rank held by all tenants-in-chief, i.e. those who held land directly of the king. In the 14c baronies were created for which land was not the basis. *Magna Carta distinguished two kinds of barony: those summoned by personal writ to parliament and those summoned by a general writ or summons. Also the lowest rank of the peerage. Officers of the *exchequer, assessors, were referred to by Henry I as his barons of the exchequer. – *Cf.* BARONET; WRIT OF SUMMONS

Baronage. The *vassals of a feudal chief; later an assembly of barons; all the barons as a class.

Baronet. A lesser *baron, though summoned to parliament, without tenure of the king.

Barons, articles of the. An initial agreement, arrived at on 15 June 1215, which immediately preceded the signing of *Magna Carta. What was agreed were basic heads or matters to be detailed in the final document.

Barons' War. This was civil war by another name. Between 1264 and 1268, Henry III struggled with the barons led by Simon de Montfort. The barons sought to circumscribe the king's powers in the ways described by the provisions of *Oxford of 1258 and the following year's provisions of *Westminster. In 1264 the king was captured by de Montfort at the Battle of Lewes, but in 1265 de Montfort was killed at the Battle of Evesham. – *Cf.* AMIENS, MISE DE; MARLBOROUGH, STATUTE OF

Barrace. A barrier or palisade in front of a fortress; also the barriers around the lists where knights jousted; hence the place of such contests. [< OFr. *barre* = a bar]

Barragium. Latin term for a toll paid for crossing a bridge or passing a barrier. – *Cf.* PONTAGE

Barrator. One who sold and bought ecclesiastical preferment and offices; also a politician who took bribes. Later the word came to be applied to troublemakers in general. [< OFr. *barateor* = cheat, trickster]

Barrister. Title of an English lawyer who has been called to the bar and can plead in the higher courts. The first element of barrister comes from the word 'bar'; the *-ister* element is perhaps cognate with the French *-ist* suffix which forms agent nouns. – *Cf.* BAR 2

Barrulet. *Her.* A narrow horizontal stripe, no broader than one twentieth of the *field, or one quarter of a bar. [< AN *barre* = a stripe + dim.] – *Cf.* BAR 1

Bartizan. A corner turret, usually embattled; more elaborately and, when used pacifically, an overhanging gallery.

Barton 1. The threshing floor in a barn. [< OE *bere* = barley + *ton* = an enclosure] – *Cf. next*

Barton 2. A *demesne farm, i.e. one reserved for the lord's own use. Barton is still found in many placenames. [< OE *bere* = barley + *ton* = an enclosure] – *Cf. previous;* CAPUT HONORIS

Baselard. A *dagger worn from a waist-band or girdle; frequently forbidden (in the 13–14c) to beneficed *clergy by Church councils.

Basilisk. A reptile of fable, whose breath was fatal; it was hatched by a serpent from a cock's egg. [< Gr. *basiliskos* = a serpent] – *Cf.* COCKATRICE

Basinet [bascinet, basnet]. A metal helmet, often with visor or *aventail. [< OFr. *bacin* = basin + *et* as a dim.] – *Cf.* ARMET; VISOR 1

Bastard. This term was applied to many, e.g. William I, known as William the Bastard. However, the word did not carry a negative freight of abuse; rather, it simply stated the bearer was born out of wedlock. In *canon law illegitimacy could be remedied by the parents' marrying; English common law said illegitimacy was irremediable, with marriage having no retrospective powers. [< OFr. *bastart* < L *bastum* = baggage, pack-saddle; i.e. a bastard = one conceived on such an *ad hoc* bed; or unwanted baggage] – *Cf.* FITZ

Bastard feudalism. A modern term for the changes in the forms of lordship in the 14c. Whereas 'classical' feudalism relied upon oaths and service owed through *fief and obligation, 'bastard feudalism' is distinctive because cash payments were at its heart. Contracts with cash rewards were drawn up; annuities were offered and accepted; *liveries also were offered. Much of the old world had gone by the middle of Edward III's reign. Villeins were demanding cash for work, reflecting a society caught in the cash cycle. – *Cf.* FEUDALISM

Bastide. The term sometimes used of the fortified or castle boroughs established by Edward I. Bastides were first established in Gascony by Kings John and Henry III. Being of military as well as economic value they were somewhat like the English *burhs, although such fortifications were more widespread and stronger in France, where there are walled towns still. The word *bastide* is Provençal. A slightly later Latin form, *bastila*, formed the basis of the name of the well-known Parisian prison, the Bastille. [< L *bastida*]

Bastion. A fortified structure built outside but attached to the main structure of a castle or the walls of a town; e.g. corner bastions which, projecting out, allowed a wider range of fire. Such structures were added to many forts in the late 4c to the early 5c and throughout the medieval period. [< Provençal *bastir* = to build]

Baston. A stick or club; also used of a staff of office. [< Spanish *baston* = stick, baton < L *bastum* = a stick] – *Cf.* TRAILBASTON

Bat. A pack-saddle; from the combination 'bat-horse' (*cheval de bât*), which carried an officer's baggage, we have 'batman' = an officer's servant. [< OFr. *bat* = pack-saddle]

Bath, Order of the. The full modern name is The Most Honourable Order of the Bath; but in the Middle Ages it was not a formal order of knighthood. The name represents a relic of the rituals attendant on the conferring of a knighthood. After a night of vigil in a church, the candidate took a purifying bath before he heard mass. Dubbing knights at a state occasion was common in Henry V's reign. The order fell out of fashion until the early 18c, when it was revived by the then *Garter King of Arms.

Batillagium. The fee for hiring a boat. [< ME *batelle* = a boat or barge] – *Cf.* -AGIUM

Baton 1. A stick used as a weapon; also, a sword made from whale-bone, used as a practice weapon in a *tournament when wounding was frowned upon. – *Cf.* BALEEN; BÉHOURD; JOUST OF PEACE

Baton 2. *Her.* An *ordinary like a *truncheon used to indicate bastardy, known as 'baton *sinister' or *'bar sinister'.

Battle. Term used for a squadron of 10 banners fighting at the front. Each such *'banner' was assembled about a particular knight's banner. However,

Edward I forced all horsemen to fight on foot, after disastrous defeats at the hands of the Scots.

Battle, trial by. The resolution of conflict between two people could be achieved by a legal fight, a trial or ordeal, however small the dispute – even over a chicken. Peasants fought with staves, the nobility with a sword. Members of the Church sought exemption from such conflicts. When charges were serious, the punishment, short of death, was equally serious and very unpleasant.

Bauble. A jester's rod of office, a *baton carved with an elaborate head with the ears of an ass. [< OFr. *bauble* = a child's toy]

Baudekin [baudkin, baudkyn]. A cloth also known as *'baldachin'; not related to *bodkin.

Bauderye [baudré]. The piece of cloth, predominantly brown in colour and usually well embroidered, hung over a saddle; often it would almost reach the ground. – *Cf.* BARD 2; TRAPPINGS

Baulk. A ridge left after ploughing, used as a dividing mark between strips of land worked by different people. [< OE *balc, balca* = a bank, ridge] – *Cf.* BUTT 2; LYNCHET

Bawdstrot. Combination of 'bawd' = lively, shameless, immoral + 'trot' = an old woman; abbr. as 'bawd' in common usage. Originally used of elderly women, the madams of the time, the term became gender-free and was applied to anyone who acted as a pimp and provided women.

Baxter. A baker; the female form was 'baxtere'. [< OE *bæcere; bæcestere* is the female form] – *Cf.* BEGGESTERE

Bayard. A bay-coloured horse; also 'blynde bayarde' = a foolish, self-confident person. The name of the magical horse given by Charlemagne to Renaud de Montaubon, which became famous for blind recklessness. The story is told in the *chanson de geste* known as *Les Quatre Fils Aymon (The Four Sons of Aymon)*.

Bayeux Tapestry. This remarkable work depicts events in England following a journey to France by Earl Harold with instructions by King Edward. In a sequence of scenes we see Harold in Normandy, and the infamous oath-swearing, the death of Edward, Harold's becoming king, and then the Battle of Hastings itself. The work, measuring *c.*70m by *c.*0.5m, is actually an embroidery, not woven tapestry. It was worked with coloured wools on a linen ground. The stitching is laid and couched work in the solid shapes, with details in stem stitch. It was made between 1066 and 1082 – perhaps at Canterbury in the late 1070s – and was probably commissioned by Bishop Odo of Bayeux. It should be borne in mind that the tapestry tells the victor's story, showing the downfall of King Harold II from the moment he took an oath before William, duke of Normandy, to his death at Hastings. – *Cf.* ARRAS

BC. Abbr. of 'Before Christ'. – *Cf.* ANNO DOMINI

Bead. Orig. prayer with a rosary, whence by transference small, decorative, pieces of glass or metal. [< OE *gebed* = prayer]

Beadle. In **DB* there are references to (the Latin) *bedellus*, following *reeve, which suggest he might have acted as an assistant. As a junior law-officer it is likely his activities were restricted to the *manorial court. Later, he acted as messenger and town crier. [< OE *bydel* = an *apparitor, a herald]

Beam. A tree, as in 'hornbeam' and *'whitebeam'. 'Beam' was used as a synonym for the Cross. – *Cf.* TREE

Bearing. What is displayed on a coat of *arms; when 'bearing' is used in the singular, one charge is referred to.

Bearward. The owner or keeper of a bear used for performing tricks or taking part in shows of bear-baiting. The bearward was itinerant, as were most entertainers, setting up at fairs and other occasions when people gathered with some money to spend. The Latin term was *ursinarius*. [< OE *bera* = a bear; L *ursus* = bear]

Beaver. The movable lower part of a helmet. [< OFr. *baviere* < *baver* = slaver, i.e. where spittle runs from the mouth] – *Cf.* ARMET; BARBUTE

Bedel. A messenger or *herald. [< OE *bydel* = an *apparitor, a herald] – *Cf.* BEADLE

Bede-roll. This was a roll, i.e. list, of all persons of a parish for whom prayers were to be said on the anniversary of their death. Such lists were of great local importance and would refer back a considerable time. They were an integral part of any parish's religious life. – *Cf.* BEAD; OBIT [< OE *gebed* = prayer]

Bedhus. A house of prayer. – *Cf.* BEAD

Bedlam. A hospital of last resort, which took in those who had nowhere else to go. Its name was the Hospital of St Mary of Bethlehem, which usage garbled to Bedlam. It was founded in 1247 in Bishopsgate Street (where Liverpool Street railway station in London can be found today). In 1330 it was granted a licence to collect alms in England. As it was nominally an *alien priory it was taken by the crown in the latter half of the 14c. In the 14c it was being used as a place for the insane, whence our use of 'bedlam' = a place of chaos.

Bedrepium. *Cf. next;* BOON WORK

Bedrip. Work on the harvest performed by tenants as part of the customary dues to their lord. This was usually for a specified amount of time, one or two days. The Latin form was *bedrepium*. [< OE *beodan* = command + *ripa* = harvest]

Beggestere. A female beggar. – *Cf.* -ESTERE

Begging. The request for money or food to be given in a charitable spirit; an important part of a culture in which charity was deemed an essential quality. It was far from demeaning; indeed the *Franciscan friars had literally to beg for a living.

Beghard. A lay brother who lived a life of devotion modelled on that of the *Beguine.

Beguine. A woman who led a life of religious devotion without taking vows. They were known as *mulieres sanctae* = holy women and lived in communities. The movement began in Liége in the late 12c but during the 13c, while it grew, it also attracted some condemnation through being seen as potentially heretical or even actually so. In 1311, the Council of Vienne did condemn some of the teaching as heretical. As with the more conventional organised religious communities, there were many aristocratic and middle-class beguines. Their lay brothers were known as the *Beghard. – *Cf.* MULIERCULAE

Behemoth. A word used of an unusually large animal, without being specific. It is found in the Bible: 'Behold now behemoth, . . . he eateth grass as an ox' (Job 40:15). The reference is probably to a hippopotamus.

Béhourd. A *tournament held on friendly, non-destructive, terms in which participants wore padded garments of *bumbace, using lightweight weapons made of *baleen. It was intended as an exercise in skill, judged by scoring points. Tournaments were only allowed under licence; one such held in 1226 occasioned a writ, in which the Latin form of *béhourd* was used: *buhurdicio*. – *Cf.* À PLAISIR; ATTAINT 2

Bellatores. Latin word used for the order of fighting men. The singular *bellator* meant a warrior or fighting man; a description of King Stephen calls him *bellator robustissimus* = a most doughty warrior. – *Cf.* THREE ORDERS

Belled. *Her.* The term for a hawk shown with a bell attached to a leg.

Belvedere. A raised tower or pavilion, even a summerhouse. [Ital. equivalent of Belvoir, i.e. *bel* = beautiful + *vedere*/*voir* = to see; thus a place with a beautiful view]

Bely-ioye. Belly joy, i.e. appetite.

Bend. *Her.* An *honourable ordinary, one of nine, being a broad line or strap drawn from the shield's *dexter *chief to the *sinister base, i.e. top right to bottom left. A bend usually occupies one third of the field. – Cf. next; BENDY; ORDINARY 2

Bend sinister. Her. An *honourable *ordinary drawn as mirror opposite to a *bend, i.e. from the shield's *sinister chief to *dexter base. It was a mark of bastardy. – Cf. BATON 2

Bendlet. Her. A *charge, half the width of a *bend.

Bendy. Her. Used of a shield covered by *bends of alternate tinctures. In this case, each bend is one fifth of the width of the shield.

Benedictines [black monks]. The monks and nuns belonging to the Order of St Benedict (OSB). The rule dominated Europe from the 9c. They were required to remain in their community, always obeying the abbot. In England the order possessed great areas of land, becoming very rich and powerful. At the time of the Conquest their monasteries were the only sources of education and art in England: the Benedictine rule specified that a set number of hours each day should be set aside for work in the *scriptorium. – Cf. CLUNY; POOR

Benedictional [benedictionary]. These were service books containing the blessings given during mass and arranged according to use through the liturgical year They were known as *Liber Benedictionum* or *Liber Benedictionalis*. The 10c *Benedictional of St Æthelwold* is an esp. fine example. [< L *benedictionalis* = concerned with blessing, praising]

Benefice. An office held by a priest, *vicar or rector, the duties for which were recompensed with land and its attendant revenues; known colloquially as a 'living'; land granted in tenure, a *fief. [< L *beneficus* = a kindness, a benefit]

Benefit of clergy. One of the issues at the centre of the dispute between Henry II and the archbishop of Canterbury, Thomas Becket. The benefit released *clergy, 'criminous clerks', from the power of secular courts regarding various charges of felony and other offences, esp. when there was the possibility of the death penalty. This release could be claimed by the literate, proof of which was the ability to read the Scriptures. In time, though, men simply learned a text to recite by rote as proof. After Becket's death, benefit of clergy was conceded by the Church, apart from offences against forest law.

Bent entrance. The entrance to a fortified place with a right-angled left turn which would expose an invader's unshielded right side to attack.

Beoceorl. Lit. 'bee *ceorl'. The person who tended an estate's beehives. If the hives were *gafol*-hives, i.e. those on which rent was to be paid, he would be required in the 11c to pay five *sesters of honey.

Beodemon. A beadsman; one who prays for another (for money); one who has been granted a pension in order to pray for a patron. [OE < *gebed* = prayer] – *Cf.* BEAD; OBIT

Beque. *Her.* The beak of a bird with a *tincture different from that of its body. – *Cf.* ANIMÉ; CRINED; MEMBERED; RAMÉ

Berbiagium. The term for rent paid in sheep; the word was also used of tax paid on sheep.

Bere. Barley. – *Cf.* BEREWICK

Berebretus. The Latin term for the official in charge of a *berewick.

Berefredum. An unusually large siege tower, as used at Courcy in the 1090s. By the 14c, they had become movable on wheels. Many were tall enough to allow bowmen to fire on the place besieged at eye-level. They were also referred to in OFr. as a *berfrois*, being used as a watch tower. The tower was perhaps named after a belfry, which in the Latin of the time was called a *berefredus*. 'Belfry' was used equally of a military tower and the bell tower of a church, attached or separate. The word's second element, *-fredum* or *-fredus*, may well be derived from *frith* and carried a sense of protection. – *Cf.* SOW

Berewick. A place belonging to a *manor but situated elsewhere, growing crops for the home place; also *grange and outlier; remembered in the placename 'Berwick'. In *DB*, it is clear that berewick land belonged to the lord of the home estate, the *caput honoris*. Such places were in the charge of a *berebretus*. [< OE *bere* = barley + *wick* = village, i.e. a place where barley was stored.] – *Cf.* BERE; INLAND

Berfrois. A grandstand constructed to allow spectators a view of the *tournament from above ground-level. The word was also used to refer to a watch tower and is the AN form of *berefredum*. – *Cf.* RECET

Berm. That area between a plain or *curtain wall of a castle and its ditch or moat.

Bernardines. A name given sometimes to the Cistercian order in recognition of St Bernard of Clairvaux, their most distinguished member. The name Bernadine Sisters was used of an order of *Franciscan sisters in Poland in the mid-15c.

Beryl. Bluish-green, aquamarine, precious stones, much used in decoration of *reliquaries.

Besant. *See* BEZANT 1

Bestiary. The illustrated bestiary, depicting real and imagined creatures, is a distinctive medieval construct. Bestiaries first appeared in England in the 12c and were derived ultimately from a Greek text, the *Physiologus*, from 4c Alexandria. They display a strange imagination alongside what we would consider a complete disregard for empirical or scientific assessment and judgement. There are fine versions, for example, in the Bodleian Library (MS 764), which is based on a version of 30 or so years earlier and dates to *c*.1230; and in the library at Aberdeen University (MS 24), which dates to *c*.1200. The bestiary, in displaying the 'wonders' of the world to its readers, was showing the wonders of God's way, in which could be found moral significance. For those who knew so little of the world beyond the immediate horizon, these images satisfied a deep hunger for the strange and wonderful. [< L *bestia* = farm animal; beast for hunting] – *Cf.* BABEWYN; BLEMMYA; CYNOCEPHALUS; GRYLLUS

Betagh. One of the customary tenants of Ireland who rendered a food rent. The Irish form was *biatach*, the Latin *betagius* (with variant spellings such as *petagius*), while *betagium* referred to the *betagh*'s tenure. However, *nativus* was also used as a synonym. – *Cf.* -AGIUM

Bezant 1 [byzant]. Gold or silver coin minted at Byzantium (named Constantinople in 330; Istanbul since 1926) of which 'bezant' is a corruption. Through much of the early Middle Ages, the only gold coins in circulation were Byzantine; the quality, and therefore their value, was always reliable. In the West only silver coins were minted, while the bezant was universally accepted. – *Cf.* ANGEL 2; BISANTIUS ALBUS

Bezant 2. *Her.* A gold *roundel.

Bible 1. The sacred scriptures of Christianity and (without the Christian New Testament) of Judaism. Until the Reformation the text generally used in the West was that of the *Vulgate. At a time when all texts were handwritten, Bibles were usually to be found in two or three or more large folio volumes. Monasteries would have one as a treasured possession. The earliest complete Bible, i.e. both Old and New Testaments, surviving in the West is the 7c Codex Amiatinus. – *Cf.* BIBLIA PAUPERUM; BIBLIOTHECA

Bible 2. This word, with a lower-case initial 'b', was given to the long moralising works common in 14c literature. This usage, orig. French, was familiar in England, where French literature exerted much influence.

Biblia pauperum. Lit. *'Bibles of the poor'. These Bibles were in fact versions replete with illustrations but with little text. As with paintings on the walls of churches, they were intended to teach the illiterate. Such books are also known as 'block books', that is they were made from wood blocks onto which the picture and minimal text were engraved for printing. (This was before Gutenberg and the use of movable type.) These Bibles first appeared during the 13c.

Bibliotheca. A library.

Bight. A bend; used geographically, a bend in a river. It has a rare use at Lincoln, in a street named East Bight: an eastward street with a sharp bend.

Bisantius albus. A silver or white *bezant. – *Cf.* ALBA FIRMA; INBLANCH

Bishop's Lynn. King's Lynn was known thus until the reign of Henry VIII.

Bivallate. A defensive structure comprising two encircling walls. [< L *bi* = two + *vallatus* = walled] – *Cf.* VALLATE

Black canons. *Augustinian monks, so called after the colour of their *habit. – *Cf.* BLACK MONKS

Black Death. *Yersinia pestis*, 1348. In the words of a contemporary chronicler, the year 1348 was the year of 'the great mortality', though there were other outbreaks in the 14c (1362, 1369, 1375). Some 25 million are thought to have died across Europe in the outbreak. It was spread by the fleas carried by rats. There were bubonic and pneumonic versions; a third, the septicaemic form, killed before the other two even had a chance to develop. The bubonic version showed as buboes, the swelling of lymph nodes; the pneumonic attacked the lungs; septicaemic poisoned the blood invisibly and fatally. Echoes of it survive in the children's rhyme 'Ring a ring of roses' and in the saying of 'Bless you' when someone sneezes. It reached England, probably Dorset, in June 1348; by January 1349 it had reached London. It is readily treatable today with antibiotics such as tetracycline, but not penicillin. In 1348 there was also a 'great *murrain' which killed large numbers of sheep. The price of everything fell: for example, a 40s horse sold for half a *mark, i.e. 6s 8d. By 1400, the population had approximately halved from around 5 million in 1300. – *Cf.* MORTALITÉ DES ENFANTS; SWEATING SICKNESS

Black friars. Colloquial term for the *Dominicans.

Black letter. Typographer's phrase for the Gothic fonts used from the beginning of printing, which persisted particularly in Germany.

Black monks. Term used to describe Benedictine monks, after the colour of their *habit. – *Cf.* BLACK CANONS

Black Rod. The office of Chief Gentleman Usher to the Lord Chamberlain; he is usher to the House of Lords. The post was founded in 1350. His most visible rôle in parliament today is as attendant to the monarch at state openings of parliament. It is Black Rod who summons the House of Commons to attend the monarch in the upper house: he knocks on the door thrice and issues the call. The rod is the symbol of his office.

Black Rood of Scotland. A relic described as being a casket made in the form of a cross and said to contain a piece of the 'true Cross' set in a piece of ebony, also cruciform – hence the name. It is first heard of as belonging to the Wessex princess, Margaret, sister of Edgar *Ætheling, who married Malcolm, king of Scotland, *c.*1070. She left it in her will to her children, after which it remained in Scotland. In 1346, David II, king of Scots, invaded England, taking the rood with him in the hope of its bringing success. Instead, at the Battle of Neville's Cross, David himself was captured and the rood fell into English hands. It was taken to Durham Cathedral and placed in St Cuthbert's shrine. At some time during the Dissolution it disappeared. – *Cf.* ROOD 2

Black Rood of Waltham. The chief relic of Waltham Abbey, a life-size crucifix. A new church was consecrated in 1060, its chief patron being Harold Godwineson, later King Harold II. It was said that when Harold visited Waltham on his way from the Battle of Stamford Bridge to Hastings in 1066, the figure of Christ bowed its head in sorrow, having foresight of the king's death. One fable also had it that Harold was secretly buried at the abbey.

Bladesmith. A smith who specialised in every kind of blade.

Blanc. Silver coin minted in France by Henry V, worth 5d. It was also known as a *blancum.* The term 'blanc' or 'blanch' indicated the coins had been assayed. – *Cf.* BLANCH FARM; INBLANCH

Blanch. *Her.* A synonym for 'white' and *'argent'. – *Cf. previous*

Blanch farm. A rent which was required to be paid in coin, whose silver content had been determined by chemical assay. – *Cf.* ALBA FIRMA; BLANC; FARM; INBLANCH

Blasted. *Her.* Used of a tree without leaves.

Blaze. *Her.* The white spot on a horse's face. The word is incorrectly used to mean to cover or adorn with heraldic devices; the correct verb is 'to emblazon'. – *Cf. next*; EMBLAZON

Blazon. *Her.* The description of a coat of *arms. 'Blazonry' is sometimes used as a noun. 'Blaze' is also used sometimes but this is incorrect. – *Cf. previous*

Blemmya. One of the many kinds of monster found in the margins of illuminated MSS or in cathedrals. Blemmyae were creatures somewhat like human beings, except they lacked heads: their eyes and mouths were on the chest. The name is taken from a people of Nubia, known to the Romans in the 3c and later. Fable and ignorance transformed them into acephalous creatures. – *Cf.* BABEWYN; CYNOCEPHALUS; GARGOYLE

Blesevin [Blésois]. Adjectival form of Blois.

Blind document. Modern term for a document that has become separated from others it was originally associated with. Often enough such documents can be placed in the appropriate department by the style of writing which had been used, clerks being taught the house style.

Blockhouse. A building (often timbered) separate from the main defences but fortified; a building designed to block access.

Blood-letting. The practice of blood-letting or bleeding (phlebotomy) was general throughout the medieval period. It was considered a panacea for a variety of ills. In monasteries, monks were treated at set times of the year, which were known as *tempora minutionis* = time of lessening. They would spend three days in the infirmary, the time the loss of blood – the *minutio* – was thought to affect the patient. The person in charge of the operation was known as the *minutor*. During this time, those in the infirmary would not be required to attend matins. In this rather special period outside the monastery's regular routine, it was common for the monks to chatter and gossip in a way that would have been inappropriate elsewhere, although by the 15c much of the inner discipline of the monasteries had dissolved. – *Cf.* LÆCECRÆFT; SANGUINATI

Bloodwite [blodwite]. A penalty imposed for the shedding of blood in the *AS period. – *Cf.* WERGELD; WITE

Blue Mantle. One of the four *pursuivants of the (English) College of Arms; he wears a blue robe. The others are: *Rouge Croix, *Rouge Dragon and *Portcullis. – *Cf.* ARMS, COLLEGE OF

BMV. Abbr. of the Latin *Beata Maria Virgo* = Blessed Virgin Mary.

Boclæden. Book-Latin, i.e. the language of learning and scholarship.

Bocland. Bookland, land given by a king by the book, i.e. the gift was recorded in a *charter or *land-boc*. Two placenames record this as Buckland: one in Lincolnshire, another, Buckland Monachorum (= belonging to the monks) in Devon. A royal grant by the book created a *ius perpetuum* = perpetual right. Such land could be bequeathed and inherited. For this reason, charters were extremely valuable, being the only evidence of such a grant. (The charter recorded the grant; it was not the grant itself.) Many monasteries resorted to forgery in the *scriptorium at times of crisis when their charters could not be found. In *LHP*, anyone proclaimed an *outlaw would forfeit such land, which reverted to the king.

Bocstæf. A letter of the alphabet; that letter which is alliterative in a line of OE poetry; modernised as 'bookstave'.

Bodkin. A small, pointed implement for piercing materials e.g. cloth, leather etc.; a pin used to fasten hair; most familiarly, and later, a *dagger or a stiletto. Bodkin and pin (the seamstress's and hairpin) were used synonymously until the 16c and later; up to six inches or more in length, they were potentially lethal.

Bog ore. Iron ore, used by blacksmiths, was often found in deposits near the surface of bogs.

Boist [boiste]. The bag used by the king's and other messengers to carry the post entrusted to them. – *Cf.* Nuncius regis

Bolingarius. Latin word for a baker; from which the French still have *boulanger*. – *Cf.* Bakers, Worshipful Company of

Boll. A unit of dry measure for goods such as grain, which varied but was sometimes two *bushels.

Bolt. A short heavy arrow fired from a *crossbow, from which we have the phrases 'he has shot his bolt' and 'a bolt from the blue'. The bolt was also known as a *'quarrel'. – *Cf. next*

Bolted arrow. A *crossbow arrow used for shooting birds, e.g. rooks and duck. – *Cf. previous*

Bombard. An early, primitive cannon, which fired stone balls; first used at the Battle of Crécy, in August 1346. Through use it gave its name to a new kind of warfare, featuring bombardment and the bombardier.

Bonda. Orig. a freeman, a householder. The ME *bonde* and *bonde-man* was a serf, a peasant, even a slave.

Bondsman. Broad term for a man bound to a lord through the various degrees of villeinage, owing a variety of services for his tenure of land. *Bracton defines him as 'either born or made such. They are born of a *villein and a *naif'. Bracton also says a bondsman 'is procreated of an unmarried naif though of a free father, for he follows the condition of his mother' married or unmarried, whether they are under the **potestas* of a lord or outside it. – *Cf. next*; Bonda

Bondus. This word began to appear in Latin documents in the late 11c as a synonym for *villanus*, i.e. a *villein. Its use suggests a wish to abandon the old word with its negative connotations of a person unfree. The Latin term for this person's status was *bondagium*, replacing *villanagium*. *Bondacra* was the acre of land held by a *bondus*. – *Cf. previous*

Bonfire. Writing in the 1540s, John Leland commented that Lincolnshire people were known to light large fires of bones in the streets; this suggests the word and its etymology as being from 'bone fire' were not particularly familiar. Vikings were said to make the burning of the winter's pile of waste bones a special occasion. That they appear to have accumulated bones is implicit in the circumstances of the death of St Ælfheah (St Alphege), who the *ASC states was taken to a *husting and there pelted with bones and cattle heads. This suggests a large quantity of such things was not out of the ordinary: boned, not stoned, to death.

Bons hommes. *See* PROBI HOMINES

Book. Books were both scarce and expensive items before Gutenberg invented printing with movable type in the late 15c. The number of copies of any text was always necessarily small. Before Gutenberg everything had to be written, the only means of reproducing being hands and pens. Men went to great lengths to acquire books: Benedict Biscop (d. *c*.690) travelled to Rome, much of the journey on foot, at least four times, returning on each occasion with books and relics. By the end of the 12c, the Benedictine monastery at Canterbury had a famous collection of 600 volumes. The *codex form required the skins of many animals, usually sheep, to use as folios, i.e. the pages. This was a principal item of cost. By the 14c there were professional copyists and illuminators, e.g. *Luttrell Psalter*. [< OE *boc* = something written, a charter, record] – *Cf.* LAPIS LAZULI; VELLUM

Book language. *See* LATIN

Book of Fees. *Liber Feodorum.* A book kept as a reference in the *exchequer containing details of tenures, particularly *serjeanties, and associated services: an index of persons and places which when printed in the 1920s filled almost 700 double-column pages. – *Cf.* FIEF

Book of Hours. These MS books were also called *horae* (L = hours). They were variations of the *breviary and used mostly for private devotions. The central text, the Little Office of the Blessed Virgin, was a shorter version of the devotions performed in the eight *canonical hours. The text, known from the 10c, entered into lay use by the end of the 12c, often attached to the psalter. Owned mostly by the nobility of the 14c, these books were often illuminated in a highly elaborate and expensive fashion. The best-known such work is perhaps the *Très Riches Heures du Duc de Berry*, produced in Flanders by the Limbourg brothers *c*.1416 (but finished later).

Bookland. *See* BOCLAND

Bookstave. *See* BOCSTÆF

Boon work. Extra work done by villeins for the *lord of the *manor e.g. at harvest and haymaking. The Latin word was *precarium. The days on which such work was done were known as 'boon days'; the lord would provide food, of a type fixed by custom. Meat, broth or cheese might be offered, and bread with ale (*precaria madida*, 'wet') or without (*precaria sicca*, 'dry'). – *Cf.* BEDRIP; CENSARIUS

Booth. A temporary shelter, of the kind used at summer pastureland; later, the covered structure used for selling at a market, from which we have the contemporary use of 'booth'. [< Danish *bod* = a shop or stall] – *Cf.* HAFOD

Bordage. The tenure of a *bordar; services owed by one. The Latin term was *bordagium*. [< OFr. *borde* = small farm, cottage] – *Cf.* -AGIUM

Bordalisander. *See* OAK BOOK

Bordar. One who holds land of his *lord in return for menial work; a low-ranking *villein; generously, a smallholder. He might have had five acres but would not have been able to supply even one ox to a plough-team. In *DB the bordar was referred to by the Latin form, *bordarius*. [< AL *bordarius*, OFr. *borde* = small farm, cottage] – *Cf.* BORDAGE

Bordarius. *See previous*

Bordure [birder]. *Her.* A *bearing in the form of a stripe which ran round the edge of a shield, being one fifth of the shield in breadth.

Borhbryce. The breaking of a pledge or surety given. [< OE *borh* = pledge + *bryce* = break] – *Cf. next*

Borhfæstan. To bind by a pledge or surety. [< OE *borh* = pledge + *fæstnian* = fasten, bind] – *Cf. previous*

Borough. The English boroughs emerged from modest beginnings as local centres of trade within a protective wall. Many were created from new by King Alfred, who established such places as centres of strength and defence against the Vikings. By the 12–13c new towns were being created by lords of the *manor for the holding of markets and fairs as a way to make extra money. [< OE *burh, burg*] – *Cf.* BURH; FIVE BOROUGHS

Borough-English. The term given to ultimogeniture, i.e. inheritance by the youngest son or daughter, which was customary among unfree AS peasants; it continued in English boroughs after the Conquest. The term arose after a case in the early 14c at Nottingham which drew attention to the operation of two systems of inheritance in one town, primogeniture operating among free peasants within Norman law. The AN term was *tenure en Burgh Engloys*.

Borrow. A pledge or guarantee. [< OE *borh* = a pledge]

Bosky [boske]. Bushy, woody or full of thickets; the *bocage*. This landscape of lanes, small woods and high hedges was characteristic of Normandy. [< ME *bosk* = a version of bush, thus 20c *bosky*; *cf.* also Fr. *boscage* = woody]

Bot 1. Compensation paid to someone for injury caused. – *Cf. next;* BOTLEAS; WITE

Bot 2 [bote]. An advantage, e.g. a tenant's right to take supplies such as timber for the necessary repair of property. – *Cf.* BURHBOT; HAYBOT

Botleas. Without recompense. A crime for which monetary compensation was inadequate. In *LHP* among such offences were *husbreche* and arson; also, treachery towards one's lord and endangering the king through killing. – *Cf.* BOT 1

Botony. *Her.* A cross with its four ends split, as if budded. [< OFr. *boutonné* = covered with buds]

Bottle glass. *See* CROWN GLASS

Bouche en court. Meal/mouthful in court. The AN term for the right to eat at the king's table, or that of a prince. It was granted as part of a salary or pension to someone like the king's physic and many others who had variously served the king. – *Cf.* CONSTITUTIO DOMUS REGIS

Bouget. *Her.* An old kind of water container made of leather; sometimes a yoke with a vessel on either end was shown.

Bourdy. A farce or ludicrous play. [< OFr. *bourde* = lie, cheat] – *Cf.* MIRACLE PLAY

Bovarius. Latin term for a tenant who looked after the plough and oxen belonging to a *manor. [< L *bos* = ox]

Bovata. The amount of land (between 10 and 20 acres) which notionally supplied one ox to a team of eight. *Bovata* is to found throughout *DB. The English form is 'bovate' or *'oxgang'. It was one eighth of a *carucate. [< L *bos* = ox]

Bow bells. The famous bells of the church of St Mary-le-Bow in Cheapside in London. They were sounded at night at *curfew, to call people in from the fields immediately outside London's walls. – *Cf.* CURIA DE ARCUBUS

Bower. The private rooms of the king or lord of a *burh, where he could be private and away from the hall, which was always public. Sometimes it was a small building physically separate from the hall, containing private rooms. More poetically, it was later a kind of summer-house wrapped in flowers and foliage for the ladies of the court. – *Cf.* BURTHEGN

Bowyer [bower]. A maker of bows; also a bowman.

Boy bishop. In the lead up to the *Feast of Fools, minor clerics and choir boys conducted services and other roles of senior churchmen. The boy bishop was the choir boy who was elected to be bishop on St Nicholas's Day, 6 December.

Boyst. *See* BOIST

Brabanters [Bragmanni]. The Brabant was conveniently placed for English expeditions against the French. It was also a unsettled region which supplied the terrifying *mercenaries Henry II used in 1174. They were also called *routiers*. Their appalling reputation was such that they earned the distinction of being condemned at the Third Lateran Council in 1179.

Bracer [brace]. The piece of armour protection for the upper and lower parts of the knight's arms. The word carries the sense of two, as in a 'brace' of pheasant. – *Cf.* VAMBRACE 1

Brachet [brach]. A hunting hound which hunted by scent, used in pursuit of deer or boar. – *Cf. next*; LYAM HOUND

Braconarius. That member of a royal or lord's household in charge of the hunting hounds. – *Cf. previous*

Bracton. This name is given to an immense work on common law, entitled *De Legibus et Consuetudinibus Angliae* (*On the Laws and Customs of England*). The Bracton referred to is the judge Henry Bracton (d. 1268). However, it is now thought that Bracton was not himself responsible for the text, but that it was the work of an anonymous clerk, much like the *LHP*.

Bragget [bragot, bracket]. Alcoholic drink somewhat like *mead, made from the fermenting of ale, sugar and honey; spice was also added. Its Latin form was *bragetum*.

Brand. A fire or flame; also a sword. From this the mark made by burning, as cattle are branded, as the result of punishment for vagrancy or forgery.

Brandones. Latin term for the first Sunday in Lent.

Brandreth. A gridiron; also a wooden framework.

Brasil. A bright red dye. A source was the tree found in Ceylon and India (*Caesalpinia braziliensis*); it was used in the English wool industry until the 15c. A later source was the Caesalpinia tree (*Caesalpinia echinata*) of South America. In later times, the dye gave its name to the country of Brazil. – *Cf.* SCARLET

Brattice. A defensive parapet or gallery built during a *siege; being temporary, it was made of wood. Among the Latin forms are *bretesha* and *brutaschia*. – *Cf.* BARTIZAN

Brehon law. Term for the law code of Ireland before it was occupied by the English. [< Ir. *breith* = judgement]

Brenagium. Rent paid to a lord in the form of bran (*brennum*), which formed part of his hunting hounds' feed. – *Cf.* BRACHET

Brenin. Welsh word for king, for which *rex* was the Latin equivalent. – *Cf.* ARGLWYDD

Breton lay. A brief narrative poem originally found in French but with Celtic origins.

Bretons. The Celtic people of Brittany, who fled from Great Britain to escape the advances of the Angles and Saxons in the 5c. Unlike the later Norsemen in the adjacent territory who adapted to their new surroundings, becoming Normans, the Bretons long maintained their own language and culture.

Bretwalda. Lit. 'ruler of Britons'. A title given to outstanding *Saxon kings before England was a unified, coherent political entity. In **ASC*, one MS uses *bretwalda*, others *brytenwalda* under the year 829. *Bretwalda* was used by Bede when he named kings ruling south of the Humber. The English *bretwalda* could be likened to the Irish **ard-ri*, or high king: one who claimed superiority over lesser kings. [< OE *bryten* = Britain + *walda* = ruler]

Breve [brieve]. Latin for a writ; also a letter of authority, given by king or pope. It was similar in kind to a brief, which word was also used of a summons.

Breviarium. Lit. 'abridgement or epitome'. A collection of decrees both moral and canonical made by Cardinal Atto of Milan (d. 1085). It was a part of the drive to provide the force of legality to the reforms of Pope Gregory, as well as strengthening the papal hand by making *canon law valid only when it had been approved by the pope.

Breviary. The service book containing the service for each day; the complete collection of divine offices, thus obviating the need for separate books of prayers and psalms. The *mendicant preachers and friars of the 13c were among the first clerics to make use of these useful items. – *Cf.* BOOK OF HOURS

Breviate of Domesday. Term used for an abbreviated version of **DB*. – *Cf.* *Abbreviatio*

Brewgabulum. Fee payable for a licence to brew ale. [< OE *breowan* = brew + L *gabulum* < OE **gafol* = payment] – *Cf. next*

Brewster. An ale-wife or female brewer; a home-brewer who brewed ale for a little extra money. [< OE *breowan* = brew + *-estere*] – *Cf. previous*; -ESTERE

Brice's Day Massacre, St. On St Brice's Day (3 November 1002) Æthelred the Unready ordered the killing of all Danes in England. However, just how many fell in the massacre is not clear.

Bricius, St. *See previous*

Bridale. Lit. 'bride ale'. Ale-drinking at a wedding. – *Cf.* Scot-ale

Brigandine. A coat of *mail, consisting of iron rings attached to a heavy-canvas garment; a jacket heavily padded and reinforced with metal plates.

Brimstone. Sulphur; colloquially, the fuel of hell's fires: the 'brimstone and fire' which destroyed Sodom and Gomorrah (Genesis 19:24). [< OE *brynstan, brunston < bryne* = burning + stone]

Brithem. A local judge in Ireland.

Britons. The Celtic inhabitants of southern Britain when the Romans first came; they were driven out to the west (Wales, Cornwall and Brittany) by the various invasions of the *Angles and *Saxons after the 5c. – *Cf.* Bretons; Welsh

Brocket. Male red deer in its second year. The 13c Latin form was *brokettus*. [< ME *broach* = a stag's first antlers] – *Cf.* Staggard

Brothel. A wretch, a worthless person; later, post-16c, a prostitute; only then, by transference, the place where prostitutes work. [< OE *breoðan* = waste away, decay] – *Cf.* Abbess

Bruch. A kind of undergarment worn by men in the 12c and later. [< OE *broc* = breeches]

Brudtoll. *See* Pontage

Brunia. Tunic made of leather, reinforced with metal rings or metal plate; so named because of the natural colour of leather. It was replaced by the *hauberk. [< L *brunius* = brown]

Brut. A chronicle or history, so called after Brutus, the supposed eponymous founder of Britain. For example, the Welsh *Brut y Tywysogion* = *Chronicle of the Princes*. – *Cf. next*

Brutus. Founder in legend of Britain. In Geoffrey of Monmouth's *Historia Regum Britanniae*, Britain was first settled by Brutus (whence its name), a refugee of Troy and great-grandson of Aeneas. In this task he was aided by Corineus, another Trojan, after whom Cornwall is named. Together they killed the giants living here, after which British history begins. Brutus was also credited with founding Troynovant (New Troy), i.e. London. After seizing the throne in 1399, Henry IV was referred to by Chaucer as 'O conqueror of Brutus Albion'. – *Cf.* Prydein

Brytenwalda. *See* Bretwalda

Buckler. A small round shield. [< OFr. *bocler* = boss (on a shield)] – *Cf.* Targe

Budge. Lambskin worn with the wool outwards. Budge was used to decorate the edges of gowns and other formal clothing. There is a Budge Row in London, near Cannon Street, where skinners and makers of budge once lived and worked. The Skinners' Company had its hall nearby.

Bugle. An ox; a horn of an ox (hence modern 'bugle'). [< L *buculum* = horn of an ox]

Buhurdicio. *See* Béhourd

Bull, papal. The seal of lead attached to a papal letter or edict. The actual phrase with the date is for instance *Per bullam pontificiam anni mccc*, i.e. 1300. Papal bulls were identified by their opening words or phrases, the **incipit*. – *Cf. next*

Bulla. A seal attached to documents; later by transference applied to papal edicts or letters sealed with lead or gold. – *Cf. previous*

Bulla cruciata. Lit. 'crusade bulls'. A special papal **bull first issued by Pope Alexander III in 1163 to those on crusade and fighting Moslems. It granted concessions and privileges. However, after the Moslem incursions and settlement in Spain, such bulls were usually only issued to Christian soldiers fighting there.

Bullion. Orig. a melting place, a mint; a large quantity of precious metal in a lump. The word is derived from the appearance of metal boiling in a liquid state. [< OFr. *bouillon* < L *bullio* = boil]

Bulmong. A mixture of oats and peas. – *Cf.* Maslin

Bulwark. A defensive rampart, fortification (*cf.* boulevard). [< OE *baulk* = mound, ridge, + work]

Bumbace. To quilt or stuff with cotton padding, i.e. bombast; bombazine; hence our use of bombast for puffed up or stuffed speech. [< L *bombacem* = cotton]

Burewarmot. The name of the court at, for example, Torksey and Lincoln in the 12c. It is a sign that the two were ancient boroughs, Torksey having been held in **demesne by Queen Edith (d. 1075) before the Conquest. [< OE *burgwara* + *gemot* = assembly of burgesses] – *Cf.* Witenagemot

Burga fife. The **Five Boroughs named in the **ASC annal for 942 as: Ligora ceaster (Leicester), Lindcylene (Lincoln), Snotingham (Nottingham), Stanford (Stamford), and Deoraby (Derby). – *Cf.* Fifburgingas

Burgage. Land and buildings in a city or town held in tenure of a lord for service or rent. Sometimes it is known as 'burgage tenure'. The Latin term is *burgagium*; this was also used of a *tenement within a borough. [< OE *burh* = borough] – *Cf.* BOROUGH

Burgensis. *See* BURHWARA

Burgess. A *borough dweller with full rights, a free citizen of a borough; later, in the 15c, a member of *parliament for a borough or university. [OE *burh* = borough]

Burghal Hidage. Document drawn up in the reign of Edward the Elder, *c*.916, which listed each *burh* fortified against the Danish *Viking armies. It was also a war plan, setting out arrangements for their defence. – *Cf.* DOMESDAY BOOK

Burgwara gemot. *See* BUREWARMOT

Burh [burgh]. Orig. a fortified *manor house or private stronghold. Before the Vikings arrived, *burh* referred to ancient hill camps, and remnants of Roman encampments. Later it was used of fortified towns (which may well have grown up around a fortified manor house); spelling changed to *borough and the word came to signify a municipal district. Alfred was responsible for the establishment of many fortified *burh*s, new towns in effect, as part of a strategy of defence against the Vikings. In Wessex, few places were further than 20 miles from a *burh*. Many placenames ending in '-bury' might well have been *burh*s. Often such places thrived because of their markets. However, *burhbot* applied only to walled towns and the fortified places established by Alfred. In the sense of a manor house, possession of a *burh* marked the graduation from *ceorl to *thegn. – *Cf. Burghal Hidage*; BURHWEALLES SCEATING; DUN; PORT

Burhbot. A levy or tax raised specifically for the repair or upkeep of a *burh's* fortifications. It is first mentioned in a charter of King Æthelbald in 749. It could also require men to work, as happened during construction of Offa's Dyke. It applied particularly to those fortified places established by Alfred as part of the general defences set up against Vikings. – *Cf. previous*; BOT 2

Burhmann. A townsman or burgher, as in *ASC. – *Cf. next*; PORTREEVE

Burhwara [burgwara]. An inhabitant of a *burh*, as in *ASC. In *DB the Latin term used for such a person was *burgensis*. Town-dwellers or countrymen, the *burhwaru* were still robust: in *ASC* 994, the *burhwaru* of London inflicted more harm and injury than Sweyn and his men had expected, driving them off. – *Cf. previous*; BUREWARMOT; BURGESS; WITENAGEMOT

Burhwealles sceating. A part of the *burh's* public revenue for the repair of its walls. [< OE *burh* + *weall* = wall + *sceatt* = shilling] – *Cf.* BURHBOT

Burnt Candlemas. 2 February 1356. A destructive campaign in Lothian conducted by Edward III. His intention had not been to confront a Scottish force, but was purely punitive and destructive. Similar campaigns conducted in France were known as *chevauchées.

Burse. A kind of holder or purse used after the 11c, which held the cloth or *corporal used during the *eucharist.

Burthegn. Lit. 'bower-thegn'. An attendant of the king in his chamber (*bower); a *chamberlain whose responsibility was the king's money-chest. He was a *thegn close to the king; an attendant with access to his lord's or lady's private rooms. It was a senior and trusted post. – Cf. HORDERE; HRÆGLTHEGN

Bushel. A unit of dry measure, used of grain. One bushel = eight gallons. While there was an *assize in every town to regulate measures and ensure accuracy, there was no standard, nationwide measure. However, by the 14c, when the crown issued instructions, the bushel measure used at Winchester was used as the standard. Also used to indicate a great deal of something. – Cf. CHALDRON; QUARTER 3

Bussellus. Latin word for a *bushel.

Butescarl. Lit. 'a boat carl'. A fighting sailor. Much like the *huscarl, the butescarl was a professional soldier but one who fought on a ship, as marines did in the 18c English navy. The term could also indicate the man was a mercenary. – Cf. LITHESMAN; SCIPFLOTA

Butt 1. Barrel or cask holding c.100 gallons. – Cf. HOGSHEAD

Butt 2. A small piece of land at the end or on the edge of a ploughed strip. – Cf. BAULK

Butt field. Place set aside for archery practice. A butt was the mound on which the target was set.

Buttery [butlery]. A store-room where food and wines were kept in large establishments. The word has no connection with butter. [< AN boterie < OFr. botelerie]

Buzone. In today's language a buzone might be termed one of the great and the good. They were knights with substantial holdings in a shire, perhaps 500 acres or more. Most had probably been called to parliament. *Bracton said that they were 'four or six or more of the greater men of the *county, who are called the buzones of the county and on whose nod the views of the others depend'. [< Fr. buzo = great] – Cf. AFFINITY 2; PROBI HOMINES

-by. Norse placename element, particularly in the East Midlands, and also in Cumbria, which indicates that in the 9c and 10c Danish Vikings settled there in numbers enough to name the place, often after a person. Thus Grimsby,

Thoresby, Salmonby in the east; also Kirkby in the north and north-west. [ON *by* = farmstead, settlement] – *Cf.* -ING

Byrlaw. Law and custom of a *manor; local law. This local law was used when transgressions such as trespass were settled. The term is probably the origin of bylaw. [< -*by* + law] – *Cf. previous*

Byrnie [brinie]. A chain-mail coat; a *hauberk or *lorica.

C

Caballarius. Latin term for a horseman or a horsed soldier; also the duty of escorting on horseback. The word has its Spanish descendant in *caballero* = a gentleman. [< L *caballus* = a horse; in classical Latin, a nag] – *Cf. next*; HENCH-MAN

Caballus. A pack-horse, a *sumpter horse. Such horses were generally limited to carrying *c.*200 lb. In Europe, a *destrier was broadly reckoned to be worth about three times the value of a humble *caballus*. – *Cf. previous*

Cabbage. *See next*

Caboshed. *Her.* Describes the head of an animal *sans* neck; in a *blazon the description would read, e.g. a bull's head caboshed. The word has a curious etymology, being derived from the OFr. verb *cabocher* = to cabbage, meaning to cut off an animal's head from close behind the ears, thus leaving the neck on the body. – *Cf.* COUPED

Cack. Excrement; from this, though much reduced, we have today cack-handed = clumsy. [< L *caco* = to defecate]

Cadastral map. Modern term used in discussions of land ownership for a map showing the *extent, value and ownership of a section of land. 'Cadastre' is sometimes used for a register of property. [< Gr. *katastikhon* = a register] – *Cf.* TERRIER

Cadaver tomb. Modern term for a tomb which bears on top a sculpture of a decaying corpse. They are one of the blacker elements of the late medieval imagination, the kind of *memento mori* which was also represented in the more familiar *Dance of Death. Such tombs carried epitaphs; one such began: 'For like as I am, right shall ye all be'.

Cadency, mark of. *Her.* A *charge whose purpose was to indicate the status of a son of the family. The eldest son and heir displayed a *label of three points on his father's arms, the next a crescent, the third son a *mullet, the fourth a *martlet, the fifth an *annulet, the sixth a *fleur-de-lys.

Cadet. Genealogical term for the junior branch of a family, i.e. the family and descendants of a younger son.

Caesalpinia braziliensis. Linnaean name for a tree native to the Middle East whose galls were used in the production of red inks and dyes. – *Cf.* BRASIL

Cain 1. The son of Adam, and the killer of his brother, Abel. For that crime he was banished, thus becoming a wanderer and archetype of pilgrims. However, the medieval person would also know that before his crime, Cain was 'the tiller of the land' (Genesis 4:2) while Abel was 'the keeper of sheep'. With Abel dead by his brother's hand, the land was cursed and barren: 'When thou tillest the ground, it shall not henceforth yield unto thee her strength; a fugitive and a vagabond shalt thou be in the earth.' – *Cf.* CAYME

Cain 2. Tribute of food and other produce in 13c Ireland and Scotland, which might also include for example an otter skin. Not to be confused with Adam's son and Abel's brother. – *Cf. previous.*

Caitiff. A prisoner; a cowardly, wicked person. [< OFr. *caitiff* = captive < L *captivus* = captive]

Calaber. Fur of a squirrel, used for decoration, so called for coming from Calabria. – *Cf.* GRIS; MINIVER; VAIR 1

Caladrius [charadrius]. A wholly white bird with the magical power of drawing illness out of a sick person; however, if one of these birds looked away from an invalid, that was a sure sign that death would soon follow. Having 'drawn out' the illness the caladrius flew towards the sun and the illness was burned out, though the bird itself did not catch fire. Its droppings were said to be a cure for blindness.

Calamus. Reed pen used in very early MSS, esp. before the 6c, when the quill began to be favoured for the most expensive commissions. – *Cf.* SHAWM

Calcei fenestrati. Lit. 'window shoes'. – *Cf.* PAUL'S WINDOW

Calciamenta hyemalia [calsiatura]. Lit. 'winter shoe allowance'. As part of their *livery, servants of the royal household were given money for clothing and shoes each year. How much money one received depended, of course, upon one's place in the household. For example, in 1287, a kitchen usher/doorkeeper received 2s 3d. There was a similar payment in the summer *calciamenta estivalis.* [L *calciamenta* = shoe allowance; *hyemalia* = of winter; also *estivalis* = of summer]

Calefactory. A container which held heat; sometimes it was shaped as a ball to warm the hands of a priest before the *eucharist, when it was known as a 'pome' (Fr. *pomme* = apple). Later, in the 16c, it was the heated room in a monastery. [< L *calefacto* = to make warm] – *Cf.* MISERICORD 3

Calendar. A system of tables displayed so as to show the days of the week and the months of the year successively. The word is also used less familiarly of lists of documents, and an index of documents, particularly of *rolls; a table of contents. [< L *calendarium* = an account book, also *calends* = the day debts were due to be paid]

Calsiatura. *See* CALCIAMENTA HYEMALIA

Caltrop 1 [calthrop]. Orig. a snare; then, a spiked iron ball thrown on the ground to cripple horses in battle. Its principal element is still to be found in use today as the spiked metal strip used by police forces to puncture the tyres of miscreant car drivers. It was named after a plant called the 'water caltrop' (*Trapa natans*), also known as 'water chestnut', which entangled legs in its underwater leaves and tendrils. Caltrops were also used by poachers to disable deer. – *Cf.* LAQUEUS

Caltrop 2. *Her.* A *charge showing a ball with four spikes.

Cambria. Wales. [< W *Cymru* = Wales]

Cambric. A fine, white kind of linen, made at Cambrai in Flanders. – *Cf.* SINDON

Cambridge University. The university emerged after the more sober elements at *Oxford fled the rowdiness there in 1209. The first college was Peterhouse, founded by the bishop of Ely. It was some time before its reputation became international with the arrival of Erasmus in 1511, who inaugurated the northern Renaissance there.

Camelopard. A giraffe, which a very small number of people in Europe would have seen. It was supposed to bear some resemblance to a camel, while its spots were likened to those of the leopard.

Camera Rosamundae. Lit. 'Rosamund's room'. A room or chamber so named after Rosamund Clifford, mistress of Henry II, many years after their deaths. The phrase was used as a euphemism for the rooms of the royal mistress.

Camlet. A luxurious material from the East, light in weight and used for cloaks; possibly of mohair (angora wool) among other materials. [< Ar. *kamlat* = nap or pile of velvet]

Campipartito. Latin form of *champerty.

Cancellaria. *See* CHANCERY

Candlemas. 2 February. This Church feast celebrates the purification of Mary and also Christ's presentation in the Temple. At the Temple, Simeon, after a revelation, lifted up the child, calling him 'a light to lighten the gentiles'. Candles are blessed during the service, hence the name. – *Cf. next*

Candles. An essential but expensive part of medieval Christianity, and in ordinary use for domestic lighting. For example, at the funeral of Henry V, 60 candles, each weighing 14 lb, were carried; 40 lb candles were not uncommon on other special occasions. – *Cf. previous*

Canfara. Ordeal by hot iron. – *Cf.* Ordeal, trial by

Canon 1. Member of an order in a *monastery or in the precincts of a *cathedral living according to a rule and so renouncing private property, accepting chastity, i.e. a canon regular; secular canons did not live according to a rule. – *Cf.* Minor canon

Canon 2. Orig. a list of books of the Bible considered genuine by the Church; later, a set of books considered to exemplify excellence. A set of rules to follow or decrees. Thus *canon law.

Canon law. Ecclesiastical law, as articulated in papal pronouncements and bulls. Gratian's *Decretum* (*c*.1140) is a collection of almost 4,000 texts concerned with every aspect of Church discipline and regulation. The Church dealt with a great many matters which today we would consider appropriate for secular courts. – *Cf.* Decretal; Ecclesiastical courts

Canon tables. A concordance of the Gospels created in the 4c by Eusebius of Caesaria. Passages in each *Gospel are numbered in the text and correspond to tables, arranged in columnar form, indicating the concordance of passages in the other Gospels. These tables were placed at the beginning of Gospel books, Bibles and New Testaments.

Canonical hours. A canonical hour is a fixed part of the office which the Church appointed to be recited at a particular time; all the prayers fixed for a certain day took the name of 'canonical'. This term was then extended to apply to the book containing these prayers, from which we have the expression *book of hours. The rule of St Benedict is one of the most ancient documents in which the expression 'canonical hours' is found, *omnes canonicas horas.*

Canopy. The covering above a seat found, for example, in the choir of a *cathedral. In time, canopies became extremely decorative. However, this did not alter their function, which was to shelter the monk in the seat from the downward draughts of the *clerestory above. In the 15c, the word was spelt 'canape'. [< Gk. *konopeion* = a mosquito net]

Canticle. Lit. 'a little song or hymn'. Used for example in reference to the Song of Solomon. *Cf.* Antiphonary

Canting arms. *Her.* Describes a *charge in a coat of *arms used to suggest the owner's name; somewhat like but not strictly a *rebus.

Cantle. The high part at the back of a knight's saddle. It was designed to offer him extra support on his *destrier*, absorbing the shock of his opponent's lance striking him.

Canton. *Her.* A square with a *tincture different from the field of a shield, less than one quarter its size, usually placed *dexter *chief.

Cantor. Clerk in charge of chanting in a monastery or church; other duties included care of the library. [L *cantor* = a singer]

Cantref [cantred]. Welsh term for a district with 100 townships. The Latin form was *cantredus/cantaredus* from the 12c. This word was carried to Ireland from Wales by English lords in the 12c, being used to indicate a small, administrative area or division of land. [< W *cantref* < *cant* = 100 + *tref* = town] – *Cf. next*; COMMOTE

Cantrefmawr. Lit. 'great *cantref*'. In Carmarthen, the stronghold of the princes of South Wales. – *Cf. previous*

Caparison. *Her.* A horse's *trappings.

Capeline. The iron skullcap much used by medieval archers. [< OFr. *capel* = hat]

Capella extra portas. Lit. 'a chapel outside the gate (of a monastery)'. These chapels were for the use of travellers and those not permitted inside a monastery, e.g. women. A more recent name is *ante portas* chapel. – *Cf.* CHAPEL

Capitagium. A *poll tax, i.e. a head tax. [< L *capitum* = a head] – *Cf.* CHEVAGE; PEASANTS' REVOLT

Capitolium. Latin term for a chapter-house; also a chapter meeting.

Capitular. Adjectival form of *chapter, as of a *cathedral chapter; thus a capitular library is a chapter library.

Cappa clausa. Lit. 'a closed cape'. Gown worn by a lecturer, always a *clerk, during lectures at universities in theology, arts and law. It was sewn closed in the front, except for a small opening which permitted the hands to emerge.

Caput honoris. Lit. 'head of the honour'. The main seat, or head, of the *honour of a lord holding several manors, on which there would have been many fiefs. It was the administrative centre of a widely distributed honour. When first used this term referred to that place within an honour which was considered the most important, such as a monastery which a lord had founded. The fitz-Walters, for example, who possessed Baynard's Castle in London, did not use it as their *caput honoris*, even though tenants paid for the castle guards. Instead the *caput* was at Little Dunmow. – *Cf.* HEAFODBOTL; RECEIVER; WARDA CASTRI

Caput jejunium. Lit. 'beginning of the fast'. The Latin term for Ash Wednesday, the first day of *Lent. – *Cf.* GENTACULUM

Caput mortuum. Lit. 'head of death'. Term used by alchemists for what was left after experiments in distillation or mixing various compounds. Often these dregs were an iron compound, the result of the search for a process to turn lead into gold.

Carectarius. Latin term for a carter or head-carter. These men were responsible for the safe and efficient movement of the royal household on its endless *itinerary through the realm. The *carectarius* is found in livery lists among the middle ranks, with the *nuncius regis* and minstrels. Cartage service was known as *opus carectarium*.

Carimauri. A rough coarse material used for clothing.

Carlovingian. The adjective used for the dynasty of Charlemagne; however 'Carolingian' is now preferred. [< L *Carolus* = Charles]

Carmelite. A member of the order founded at Mount Carmel in Palestine in the early 13c and approved by the pope in 1226. A *mendicant order which was known as the White Friars; its first members, however, were mostly *hermits. The first Carmelite house in England was founded at Aylesford, after 1240 and the failure of the *crusades. There was also an order of nuns modelled on the White Friars. Although only formally instituted in 1452, the sisters had first appeared in the 13c. In 1452, the Carmelite Second Order was organised and adopted the same rule as the Carmelite brothers.

Carol. Orig. a dance with accompanying song. In the 15c the carol was a form of lyric poetry, more like a popular song to be danced to than our familiar Christmas carols. They usually had refrains which contributed to group singing; they were as often humorous as they were religious in temper.

Carolingian. The Carolingian dynasty replaced that of the Merovingians in 751, when Pepin II became king of the Franks. The Carolingian Empire was created by and named after Charlemagne (771–814) in imitation of the Roman Empire: a Holy Roman Empire with the ambition of stretching from the North Sea to Italy. It was divided in 843, disintegrating soon after. The term Carolingian relates to the period from *c.*750 to *c.*900 in Western Europe. The court was admired and in some ways copied by Charlemagne's contemporary monarchs, e.g. Offa and Alfred.

Carpet knight [chamber knight]. The body of knights who attended the monarch in the more private spaces, rather than the public, communal hall; also, part of the transformation of the royal court from a military to a civil establishment. Later, it was a term of disparagement for a knight dubbed at court rather than on the field of battle; hence an idle man, a ladies' man.

Carr [car]. Fen land; boggy ground. [< ON *kjarr-myrr* = marsh, bog, with undergrowth]

Carraccio. A cart with a large pole or ship's mast firmly attached. Its purpose was to act as a rallying point with appropriate banners. It was used at the Battle of the Standard on 22 August 1138, and it was this which gave the battle its name, the *standard held high. Such a cart or wagon was used in Italy by the city states, the loss of which cart being a signal disgrace.

Carrack. Large merchant vessel which could also be used for military purposes. [< OFr. *caraque* < Ar. *qurqur* = merchant or cargo vessel]

Carrel. A small space with a bench for reading set into the walls of a *cloister for solitary study. Carrels are to be found in the libraries of modern universities, sometimes with doors.

Carta mercatoria. Merchants' Charter, 1303, granted by Edward I to alien merchants, permitting them to retail spices and *mercery; previously only the English had been able to sell such things.

Cartae baronum. Lit. 'records or returns of the barons'. A set of returns made to the *exchequer of Henry II by tenants-in-chief in 1166 concerning the knights enfeoffed on their lands. The questions asked concerned the number of enfeoffments each tenant-in-chief had made since 1135 (the first year of King Stephen's reign), and how many were retained in the household, i.e. in *demesne. Their names were also requested. Henry was trying to ensure that all knights had done *allegiance to him. Those who had not were to do so within a set period. Implicit in the latter instruction was the king's assertion that allegiance to him was of greater weight than the allegiance owed to tenants-in-chief by those holding fiefs of them. It is a useful document for giving a detailed record of the state of military feudalism in England in the last half of the 12c. – *Cf.* ENFEOFF

Carthusian. Order of monks (O. Cart.) founded in 1085 by St Bruno of Cologne. Although without a written rule – they followed that of St Benedict in their own way – its members lived austere, solitary lives of silence and fasting within the monastery. Their lives were spent in cells, for the order abjured both dormitories and common refectories. The monks would gather together for prayer at certain times of the week and also on Sunday for dinner. Their monasteries were called Charterhouses; the first was established in England in 1178 at Witham in Somerset; their tenth and last was established by Henry V in 1414 at Sheen. Their name is formed after the Latin

Cartusia, i.e. from Chartreux, near Grenoble, which was known as La Grande Chartreuse.

Cartulary [chartulary]. Book in which were kept copies of *charters and deeds and other legal documents. Such charters were important as proving entitlement, e.g. that a gift of land had been made. Monasteries frequently kept not only their own charters and deeds but also those belonging to landowners in the surrounding district.

Caruca. Latin term for a plough; usually of the heavy kind, requiring a team of eight oxen. – *Cf. next;* ELEEMOSYNA CARUCARUM

Carucage. Tax fixed on a *carucate of land, first imposed by Richard I in 1198; used only irregularly thereafter. The Latin form used in documents was *carucagium.* – *Cf. next;* -AGIUM

Carucate. Land which could be ploughed in one year with eight oxen. The OE term was *plogland.* [< L *carucata* < *caruca* = a plough] – *Cf. previous*

Casemate. A large room set into the thickness of the wall of a castle (**enceinte*) with several ports for firing guns from.

Castellan. The *constable or governor of a *castle. – *Cf. next*

Castellaria [castellatus]. A castlery or castellany was a block of territory attached to a *castle or within its jurisdiction. There were 14 named castleries in *DB*. A legitimate castle, licensed by the king, would have had around it knights' fiefs; these knights would have been distributed around the *honour, so as to provide **warda castri*. – *Cf. previous;* ADULTERINE CASTLE; LOWY

Castle. The question of how exactly to define the term 'castle' is a vexed one, and only a brief sketch can be given here. The great stone structures familiar today are late developments of the ditch surrounding a mound of earth on the top of which was a stronghold found in France in the 9c. The mound was known as a *'motte'; the stronghold or *donjon was within the *bailey. This *'motte and bailey' template became widespread in Europe in the 11c. There is some contention over the first appearance of a castle in England, centred on structures apparently built by Normans during Edward the Confessor's reign and on the nature of English lordly residences in the pre-Conquest period. The Normans began building castles in England after 1066; most were built of earth and timber in the first instance. William I was responsible for the Tower of London; orig. a simple enclosure but finished by William II towards the end of the 11c. Castles allowed a lord living accommodation while being able to dominate the surrounding area; they also, of course, provided a defence against enemies. They became the sign and military instrument of Norman lordship in England. Over the next two centuries building techniques improved, allowing ever greater and stronger buildings and *curtain walls.

Moats surrounded the *enceinte; *machicolation and *loopholes appeared allowing the defenders more fire-power. – *Cf. previous*

Castlery. *See* CASTELLARIA

Catel. Goods, property, wealth, cattle; hence goods and *chattels. The current word 'cattle' itself is a variant spelling of *catel*. The Latin form was *catallum*. – *Cf.* CHATTEL

Catenae. Lit. 'chains, series'. An anthology of comments and glosses on the Bible by Church Fathers and others. The first *catenae* appeared in the 6c, when a series of comments by various authors on a particular verse were gathered together, the chain being particular sentences or words of the scriptures on which were 'hung' the comments. Thomas Aquinas (d. 1274) edited one such known as *Catena Aurea = The Golden Chain*. Collections of *catenae* formed an important part of teaching in the 13c *cathedral and monastic schools, reflecting the importance attached by the medieval Church to the past and authority. The singular form, *catena* = a chain, which secured valuable books to a reading place. [< L *catena* = a chain, a series] – *Cf.* CHAINED; GLOSSA ORDINARIA

Cateran. A fighting-man from the Scottish Highlands. – *Cf.* GALLOWGLASS; KERN

Cathedra. A seat; specifically, a bishop's seat in his home church, i.e. *cathedral.

Cathedral. The crucial distinction of a cathedral church is neither its size nor its splendour but that it has a *cathedra*, i.e. the bishop's throne or chair of office. The first English cathedrals were built in the 6c and 7c, e.g. Rochester and (the first) St Paul's, but all AS cathedrals were demolished under the Normans. Today, the cathedral is one of the most visible parts of the Norman legacy. Cathedrals were no doubt an assertion of power on the part of the Normans, but such buildings also affirm a powerful faith. [< L *cathedra* = a (bishop's) seat]

Cattus. Latin term for a cat, a kind of shelter light enough to be moved and used by soldiers to shelter beneath while attacking a walled town or castle. *Cattus* was also used of the domestic animal, *Felis catus*.

Cayme. A medieval spelling of Cain. – *Cf. next;* CAIN; CAYMITICUS

Cayme's castles. Phrase used by John Wyclif (after 1382 and during his exile in Oxford) to describe the great churches of the Franciscan friars. Cayme is a medieval form of *Cain, son of Adam, killer of his brother, Abel. The reason for the hostile epithet is that the *mendicant orders, the wandering brothers, were supposedly founded by Cain, a fugitive on the earth after Abel's murder. An acrostic poem plays on an alternate spelling, CAIM, beginning succeeding lines with *Carmelite, *Augustinian, *Jacobin, *Minorite. This association between Cain and the friars emerged during the later part of the 14c. – *Cf. previous and next*

Caymiticus. Fratricidal; derived from *Cayme. – *Cf. previous*

Ceap. *See* CHAP 1

Ceaster. A fort or castle. The word was used of old Roman fortified towns, becoming the suffix in placenames derived from the Latin *castra* = a fort. It is found in many names today ending in '-chester' or '-caster'.

Celibacy. The compulsory celibacy of the *clergy was abolished in Protestant England in 1549. However, the Church of Rome had been trying for several centuries to impose it and was close to success when England defaulted. A *decretal issued by Pope Siricius in 386 confirmed earlier attempts to ensure all senior clergy should be celibate. The celibacy of monks in their monasteries was broadly adhered to in the early years, between the 7c and 9c; again during the reform years after 1000 the rule applied. The Lateran Council of 1139 declared all clerical marriages both unlawful and invalid. [< L *caelibatus* = unmarried, a bachelor]

Cell. A solitary monk or nun's single-room dwelling; also, a small *monastery under the charge of one larger, usually some distance away. As punishment, a monk might be sent to a cell far from the mother-house.

Cellarer. That *obedientiary of a *monastery charged with overseeing the supply of its food and wine. His responsibilities included matters such as the mill and brew-house, and ensuring that workers on *granges worked as they should and were not stealing. He was further charged with working with the abbot, e.g. attending to the sale of leases. [< L *cellarius, cellerarius*]

Cellarium. Latin for the cellar or storage space of a monastery or other large establishment. – *Cf. previous and next*

Celleragium. Cellarage; fee for storing wine in a cellar. – *Cf. previous;* -AGIUM

Celt. Name for one of the ancient peoples inhabiting NW Europe and southern Britain from before 700 BC, up till the time of the Romans – Caesar mentions Celts (though in a more restricted sense) – and after; forced out by *Saxons during their incursions in the 5c and later. The word was first used in this wide sense by William Camden (1607). [< L *Celta*]

Celure. Canopy of honour placed over the great *rood, or altar, to augment its dignity. In the 16c, the (draught-excluding) hangings around a bed. [< L *celum* = heaven; also, ceiling]

Cementarius. Latin term for a mason. Such men were recruited for campaigns in France. Most of their work involved the repair of bridges or castles taken after a siege. [< L *caementum* = stone, quarry stone]

Cena domini. Lit. 'the lord's supper or meal'. The term sometimes used to refer to the *eucharist. – *Cf. next*

Cenacle. The room in which Christ and the apostles had the Last Supper on *Maundy Thursday; the Latin form was *cenaculium*. That day was known in the Latin of the 12c and 13c as *dies cenae* = day of the meal/supper. – *Cf. previous*

Cenn fine. The head of an Irish kindred group. – *Cf.* Gwely

Censarius. A rent-paying tenant who was not obliged to perform week-work but could be called upon for *boon work. He might be obliged to do some mowing or lend his plough. A money rent was known as *censaria*. In the early 12c, rent could be 1s 6d per *bovata*. [< L *censura* = assess < *census* = tax, payment] – *Cf.* Cervisarius; Mellitarius

Cense. Income or tax paid to a lord by his tenants. An early 19c edition of *DB* was entitled *Libri Censualis* by its editors. The *censor* was the magistrate in charge of the *census*, a list of those who paid tax. [< L *censeo* = to assess (for tax)] – *Cf. previous*

Centener. An officer commanding 100 soldiers. (The Roman equivalent was the *centurio*; the English form is 'centurion'.) The term was also used of the *bailiff of a *hundred. [< L *centenarius* = numbering 100] – *Cf.* Decuria; Vintinary

Ceorl. A free man on the lowest rung but having land to farm. Like many terms of the period, *ceorl* defined a social status or *degree, without necessarily indicating financial worth: a *ceorl* might be well-off or poor. Nevertheless his *wergeld* was set at 200s. The *ceorl* would have had military obligations, as befitted a free man; he might even have had slaves. – *Cf.* Gebur; Thegn; Trimoda necessitas

Ceragium. *See* Wax-scot

Ceraint. Kin-group responsible for the payment and receipt of *galanas*, Welsh equivalent of *wergeld*.

Cere. *See* Crinet

Certiorari. An order or royal writ issued by the king's *exchequer demanding information about an earlier judgement or order. (A corrupt, mispronounced form of the word was 'siserary'.) These would be addressed to a bishop, e.g. concerning monies owed the crown by prebendaries within his diocese. If a prebendary had died owing money, the king's exchequer would demand information about the deceased's executors, issuing an order for his *chattels to be seized. Other complaints via the court of common pleas might concern unpaid pensions. The speed with which responses were expected might be surprising. It was not uncommon for *chancery or the *exchequer to write after 30 days demanding to know why no answer had been made. [< L *certioro* = to inform, apprise]

Cervèllaire [cervelière]. A skull cap worn beneath an iron helmet; also a metal cap which served as a helmet. [< Fr. *cervelle* = the brain]

Cervisarius. Tenant of land who paid for that land by supplying beer to his lord. The Latin word was also used to indicate a brewer. *Cervisia* was used of an ale feast, also of *boon work at which ale was provided. [< L *cervisia* = a kind of beer] – *Cf.* Censarius; Mellitarius

Cestui-que-use. *See* Enfeoffment to use

Chafe-wax. *See* Chauffer of Chancery

Chained. *Her.* Term used when a chain links two animals' collars. [< OFr. *chaine* < L *catena* = chain] – *Cf.* Catenae

Chaldron. Unit of dry measure, used of weights of grain. One chaldron = 36 *bushels; one bushel = 8 gallons. – *Cf.* Quarter 3

Chamber. One of the departments of the king's household which evolved from his chamber, that part of the palace or castle which contained his private sleeping quarters. Four knights would sleep immediately outside the door as bodyguards. (The rest of the household slept in the hall.) By the 13c, this chamber had become a busy office with its own clerks and close servants. The officer in change was the *chamberlain who had become in the late 14c one of the five senior officers of the crown or royal administration. The Latin word for a chamber was *camera.* – *Cf.* Chancellor; Constitutio Domus Regis; Familia regis; Privy seal

Chamberlain. Personal servant of a king or a nobleman; a *steward; later, the officer responsible for the daily running of the monarch's private establishment. [< ME L *camera* = room + -ling] – *Cf. previous*

Chambre coi. A privy or latrine. [< OFr. *coi* < L *quietus* = quiet, at rest]

Chamfron [chamfrain]. Protection for the head of a knight's *destrier. – *Cf.* Bard 1

Champaign. Open, level country. The English form is 'champion country'. [< OFr. *champaigne* < L *campania* = open country]

Champertor. A person who participates in *champerty; the Latin term for such a person was *cambiparticeps*.

Champerty. Legal term for an agreement with one side of a dispute to have a share in the property being disputed; this was clearly corrupt practice. Champerty was explicitly forbidden under statute by Edward III, as was *embracery. The Latin form is *campipartito*. [< AN *champartie* = a division, a lord's share of an estate's produce < L *campi pars* = part of the land] – *Cf. previous*

Champion. A fighting man; someone who fought in place of another: thus the king's and queen's champion. The title is hereditary and resides with the Dymoke family of Lincolnshire. At Richard III's coronation, John Dymock, splendidly arrayed on a charger with two attendants, arrived at the doors of Westminster Abbey to await the end of the coronation mass. When Dymock's nephew performed the role of champion on the occasion of Henry IV's coronation, he seems to have entered the king's hall in the course of the banquet fully mounted, and ready to sustain the king's right against any challenger. [< L *campus* = a field for military exercises] – *Cf.* DUELLUM

Chancel. That part of a church for the use of *clergy and choir and kept separate and concealed from the lay congregation. The two parts were separated by a screen, a *cancellus*. [< L *cancellus* = lattice]

Chancellery. *See* CHANCERY

Chancellor. The office emerged during the reign of Edward the Confessor (1042–66), who followed the procedures of the *Carolingian court. The title means secretary; the post in time acquiring power and authority. Until the 14c the chancellor was invariably a priest, serving as royal chaplain and king's secretary in secular matters; also keeper of the royal seal, or *great seal as it is known. He controlled the *exchequer. Because of his legal work in *chancery, the chancellor became the country's chief legal officer; at the same time he presided in parliament, a position which changed somewhat when parliament became bicameral and the chancellor sat in the House of Lords. [< L *cancellarius* = secretary or porter] – *Cf. next;* EXCHEQUER

Chancery. One of the two great offices of royal administration, the court of the lord *chancellor. Chancery was responsible for the writing of charters, and writs issued in the king's name. Orig. chancery formed part of the royal household; by the 13c, it had moved out of court, usually housed in the great hall at Westminster. All its documents were issued under the *great seal: these could be letters, writs or charters. It worked in association with the office of the *privy seal. Its documents were copied on a series of *rolls, among which were the *Charter, *Close and *Fine Rolls. Its senior official was the chancellor, who was often a bishop. The title comes from the Latin term *cancellus*, a screen marking off the space where documents were kept. – *Cf.* CHANCEL; CHANCERY DOCUMENTS; EXCHEQUER

Chancery, court of. The *chancellor began to hear pleas for legal redress which other courts could not deal with during the 14c, such as those against king's officers or the king himself. Its procedures were relatively informal and the chancellor was able to make speedy decisions. Those using this court were particularly the poor and those weak and without friends in government. This form of justice was known as 'equity'. – Cf. previous; ATTACHIAS; ENFE-OFFMENT TO USE

Chancery documents. *Chancery's records were recorded on *Charter Rolls, *Close Rolls, and *Letters Patent Rolls. In effect these rolls became the archive where copies of royal letters and writs were kept, a kind of public records office.

Chansons de geste. Lit. 'songs of (great/heroic) deeds'. Long narrative poems telling of heroic deeds in French history and legend. Roland was the hero par excellence.

Chant. See GREGORIAN CHANT

Chantry. Orig. the endowment of a priest to offer up prayers for a particular person after their death; later a chapel or altar endowed for the saying of prayers and singing of mass for its founder. They remained popular until suppressed in 1545 in the Dissolution. Some were dedicated chapels within a larger building; others were small and dedicated, set apart. [< OFr. chanterie < chanter = sing] – Cf. BENEFICE; OBIT

Chap 1 [ceap]. To buy and sell; to bargain or trade. [< OE ceapian = to buy, to bargain]

Chap 2. A fellow, a young man; abbr. of *chapman = a purchaser.

Chape. Decorative metal covering a sword's scabbard; later, that part of the scabbard covering the sword's point. [< OFr. chape = a hood] – Cf. CRAMPET

Chapel. Orig. the shrine with the cape (chapele) of St Martin of Tours kept by the kings of France. It was in the charge of a cappellani, or *chaplain, offering *sanctuary. Thus a place for private worship; also the equipment of a portable chapel. Such places were found in private houses or as side chapels in cathedrals. After the 13c such chapels were included in a cathedral's eastern walls during construction; some, long gone, are remembered in such places as Chapel St Leonards (Lincolnshire) and Whitechaple (E London). [< OFr. chapele < L capella = cape] – Cf. CHAPEL OF EASE

Chapel de fer. An iron cap shaped like a dome with a brow projecting all the way round. The 13c Latin form was capella de ferro. [< OFr. chape = hood + de fer = of iron]

Chapel of ease. A church founded in that part of a parish with a new population, or on *assarted land, the original church being distant from newcomers. Not all such chapels became permanent, having only temporary licences. The AS called them 'field churches'. Their continuation depended on the owner of the land and the prosperity of the new land. If successful, then a new endowment would be established. – Cf. CHAPEL; CHAPELRY

Chapel royal. A *chapel attached to a royal house or palace.

Chapelry. A part or division of a parish having its own *chapel. – Cf. CHAPEL OF EASE

Chaperon. A kind of cap or hood worn by women. – Cf. next

Chaperonne. Her. The small shield bearing a *crest displayed on the heads of horses at funerals. – Cf. previous

Chaplain. The priest of a particular *chapel; also a chantry priest; the priest who conducted services in the private chapel of a king or lord. Nunneries also had their own chaplain. [< L capellanus = chaplain]

Chaplet 1. A wreath of flowers worn on the head like a crown.

Chaplet 2. Her. *Charge showing a garland of leaves with four flowers placed equidistantly.

Chapman. A person who bought or sold; a merchant; a travelling salesman. [< OE ceap = goods, bargain + man] – Cf. CHEPE

Chapter. Orig. a section or chapter of the monastic rule, which was read daily to the assembly of the canons of a *cathedral or a *collegiate church; also the members of a monastic or knightly order. Later it came to refer to the assembly itself. The assembly met to listen to that reading and conduct other business. [< L caput = head] – Cf. next; CAPITOLIUM

Chapter house. Place where monks met each day to discuss business; cathedrals would also have a chapter house. Chapter houses are often superbly built, polygonal in shape. – Cf. previous

Chare. An alley way or narrow lane, still in use in Newcastle as a street name (Pudding Chare).

Charge. Her. An *honourable ordinary. As a verb, to add a charge to a shield of coat of *arms. When not specified, a charge was always placed at the fess point of a shield. For example, John de Wodehouse's arms were charged by a *chevron *or with *gouttes, i.e. spots, of blood, after the Battle of Agincourt (1415). The description of this latter would have been five gouttes de sang.

Charing Cross. The last of 13 *Eleanor crosses built by Edward I to mark the stopping places of the funeral cortège of Eleanor, his queen. It was where the statue of King Charles I can today be found (in Trafalgar Square), at the head of Whitehall. In the precinct of Charing Cross railway station is an elaborate cross but this is only a memorial of the original. Parts are copied from other crosses, also not extant. Initially, a wooden cross had been put up; later it was replaced by one of Caen stone. This was taken down in 1647 during the Civil War. – *Cf.* REGALIA

Charta. An alternative spelling of *carta*, often found in 19c historiography.

Charter. A document recording grants of land; also rights or privileges given e.g. by the monarch to a person, town, or borough; the document noting permission for the establishment of a town or a market in a town. A charter also recorded the grant of liberty to a serf; this was known as a *'charter of franchise'. The purpose of such a grant for a town was to gain independence from a lord or even the king. For instance, London paid King John £2,000 for its charter – then, a vast sum of money. Charters recorded a grant previously made; they were not the grant itself. Hence the Latin phrase *sciato me dedisse et hac carta confirmasse*, i.e. 'know that I have given and by this charter confirmed'. [< L *charta* = a record, a book] – *Cf.* CORAM POPULO

Charter of franchise. A *charter documenting the grant of liberty by a lord to a serf; it also applied to freedoms granted to the inhabitants of a town or borough. The issue of such a charter freed the town from servitude or obligation to its feudal lord, either the king or a local magnate. Such charters cost a great deal of money but were considered well worth it. For instance, a town would gather its own specified taxes, rather than have them collected or *farmed by an outside official.

Charter Rolls. A record of the grants or confirmation of grants of land and rights made by the king. Those surviving date from 1199. – *Cf.* PIPE ROLLS

Charterhouse. A *Carthusian monastery.

Chartophylacium. A chest for papers or files, for documents of a legal nature. [< L *charta* = a page or record + *phylacterium* = valuation of an estate]

Chase. A private forest, land reserved for hunting by a magnate. Such forests required royal permission, necessitating a substantial *fine. The citizens of London had rights of the chase in Middlesex and the Chilterns. – *Cf.* DISAFFORESTATION; FOREST, CHARTER OF THE

Chattel. The word is usually used in the plural, i.e. chattels. It indicated property which could be moved or transferred, as e.g. a lease could be transferred to another person, but not the land itself, which could not be moved. [< OFr. *chattel* = cattle] – *Cf.* CATEL

Chauffer of Chancery. The official in *chancery whose task was to heat the wax on the occasions when the *great seal was being used. A chafer was a

small grate which held fire for heating. Chauffer was known more colloquially as chafe-wax. [< OFr. *chauffer* = to warm]

Chausses. Mail leggings of the kind worn by the Normans at the Battle of
Hastings, 1066, and later.

Chaussier. A maker of shoes; possible source of Geoffrey Chaucer's surname.

Checky. *Her.* A *charge comprising small squares of an alternating *tincture
and *metal, i.e. *argent or *or; usually of seven squares at the top, diminishing downwards as size and shape of the *shield allowed. A minimum of 20
squares were shown.

Cheminage. Toll paid for passage through a forest. The Latin term was
cheminagium [< Fr *chemin* = road, path]

Chepe. Goods, merchandise; also, a bargain. The word also indicated the
place, Cheapside, where goods and bargains could be had. It is found in
placenames such as Chepstow = a market place. – *Cf.* CHAP 1; CHAPMAN

Chepen. To buy or sell, to transact business.

Chepilt. A female merchant or seller of goods. – *Cf.* CHEPE; CHEPEN

Chepynge [chepinge]. A market; such places are remembered in placenames
such as Chipping Camden and Chipping Norton. – *Cf.* CHEPE

Cherubim. Order of winged angels attending God and next below the *seraphim, who were the highest order. The word is the plural of the Hebrew
cherub.

Chester plays. A collection of some 25 *mystery plays, probably dating to the
14c but preserved only in MSS from the 16–17c. They were performed from
carts in the course of a procession through the city, over several days. – *Cf.*
MIRACLE PLAY; MYSTERY PLAY; WAKEFIELD PLAYS; YORK PLAYS

Chevage. Payment made by a *villein to his lord by way of poll tax; it was
also payment made e.g. for permission to live away from the manor, as a
*chapman travelling freely. The Latin word was *chevagium*, of which *capitagium*
was a synonym. [< OFr. *chef*]

Chevalier. A *knight on horseback; a term used to associate a knight with the
code of *chivalry. Chevalier remains the title of the lowest order of the French
nobility. [< AN *chevaler* < L *caballarius*] – *Cf.* CABALLARIUS

Cheval-trap. *Her.* Lit. 'a horse trap', synonymous with *'caltrop'.

Chevauchées [war-rides]. Term used for the marauding marches of Edward
III's armies in France, which were meant to cause alarm and despondency

and to destroy French resources, making life unpleasant for the French. The *chevauchée* was a strategy of attrition – of food and war matériel. Much medieval warfare was of this kind, set-piece battles being relatively rare. Battle was risky. While many battles were not decisive, some could be catastrophic to the loser, e.g. Stamford Bridge and Hastings (1066), Crécy (1346) and Agincourt (1415). [< Fr. *chevaucher* = to over-ride] – *Cf.* ROUTIER

Chevisance. Any kind of commercial exchange or bargain. By the 14c it signified *usury, as increasingly merchants were the great lenders of money after the expulsion of the *Jews in 1290. Protection by the pope (as formerly usury was condemned by the Christian Church) assured its 'legality' – the Church itself and its magnates were themselves all heavily in debt. The Latin form was *chevantia*.

Chevron 1. A V-shaped Norman architectural decoration; there are fine examples at Durham Cathedral. [< L *capreolus* = a pair of rafters, looking like a V]

Chevron 2. *Her.* An *honourable *ordinary shaped as an inverted V, i.e. a bent *bar, like a rafter. Chevronel is a small, half-size chevron.

Cheyne. *Her.* An old French term for an acorn. [< Fr. *chêne* = an oak]

Chichivache. Lit. 'a thin, meagre cow'. This was a creature of fable living on good and honest women. The animal was very thin, such women being supposedly rare.

Chief. *Her.* One of the nine *honourable ordinaries, being a band across the top of a shield or flag; also, the topmost part of a shield, often one fifth but no more than one third; used as in *dexter chief to indicate the top right. [< OFr. *chef* < L *caput* = head]

Childermas. Festival of the Holy Innocents, 28 December, which commemorated Herod's slaughter of the children. [< OE *cildamæssedæg* < *cild* = child + *mæsse* = mass + *dæg* = day]

Chirchethurl. A church-window; window in an *anchor-hold looking on the church's altar. [< OE *cirice* = church + *ðurl* = window, opening]

Chi-rho. Two letters of the Greek alphabet, being the first two letters of the Greek *Khristos*, which were used as a monogram for Christ.

Chirograph. Lit. 'written by hand'. The chirograph or *cyrographum* in the Latin of the records was an *indenture. Such documents were records of a transaction, e.g. of land changing hands. They were used by the AS, before seals replaced them, allowing all parties a copy of the transaction. The earliest surviving chirograph dates to the early 10c. Details were written twice on one sheet, the sheet then being cut in half, one piece going to each of the parties. In the case of fines, there were three pieces, with the third going to a safe place, like an abbey, or even the king's treasury. Later, rather than a straight line being used to cut the original sheet, an indented path was taken by the cut, hence our word indenture. This system was in principle very similar to the practice of the *tally stick. *Bracton refers to chirographs, noting their value as records. For instance, he affirms their use 'if one makes a gift by charter so that a fine and chirograph is made with every formality in the lord king's court'. He also states that a chirograph 'cannot easily be impugned'. The Latin used of the division was *in forma trium cyrographorum* = in the form of three chirographs. [< Gr. *kheir* = hand + *graphos* = something written] – *Cf.* FINAL CONCORD

Chivalry. Chivalry is as much about the skills and manners of a warrior class as with a literature derived from the deeds of those warriors, but presented in an idealised fashion which returned to define the manners of the warriors. Chivalry was a collocation of qualities made into a coherent ideal: skill and courage, and a craving for glory or fame acquired through knightly skills and its necessary courage. Tournaments were the place to acquire and hone skills. They were also places where a great deal of money could be made with sufficient courage and skill, as William Marshal and others did. Chivalry required that the knight be courteous and gallant towards ladies. He must be generous with a defeated enemy; his word must be his bond, for should he break his oath or parole, his name and glory would be fatally sullied. In October 1326, Sir Hugh Despenser was executed, having been one of the most influential men at Edward II's court; he was said to have dishonoured the order of chivalry. As part of his sentence it was ordered that Despenser be hanged in a *surcoat *quartered with his arms and that afterwards his arms should be destroyed for ever.

Chivalry, orders of. Chivalric orders were a 14c creation with, to a lesser or greater degree, King Arthur and his knights of the Round Table in mind. There is a case for stating that an order of chivalry was and is one in which the number of members is limited. For example, the Most Noble Order of the *Garter, created by Edward III *c.*1346, has no more than 25 members today, the original complement being 24. It is the highest civil and military honour in the gift of the monarch. Other associations or societies can be considered as confraternities if they have a corpus of statutes and hold meetings at regular intervals. A member's conduct was obviously important: he must not disgrace the order by being guilty of a reproachable offence or incurring dishonour or otherwise infringing the code of *chivalry. There must be no *fautes en armes*; he must remain *un chevalier sans reproche*. – *Cf.* REPROACH

Choir. The singers attached to a church or *cathedral whose rôle is to lead singing and responses; later, by transference, the word was attached to that part of a church where the choir sang. [< L *chorus* = singing in a play]

Chough. Member of the crow family (*Pyrrhocorax pyrrhocorax*) found on sea cliffs. One story has it that King Arthur's soul migrated into a chough. [< OE *ceog* = a chough]

Chrism. The oil used at ceremonies such as christening, consecrated by a bishop on Holy Thursday. Balsam was mixed into the oil, its invisible scent representing the holy spirit. [< OE *crisma* < Gr. *khrisma* = anointing oil] – *Cf. next*

Chrismatory. The vessel in which were kept the holy oils, e.g. *chrism. – *Cf. next*

Chrisom. Child's white christening gown which became a funeral shroud if the child died within its first month, such a child being known as a 'chrisom-child'. – *Cf.* CHRISM

Church courts. Church courts were introduced into England after the Norman Conquest to deal with heresy, marriage, sexual immorality and disputes over wills, and other disputes concerning the human soul. Generally these courts were held under the auspices of a bishop, or his archdeacon, but sometimes an archbishop or pope. Anyone who could prove the *benefit of *clergy came under these courts' jurisdiction.

Church haw. What today we call the church yard. The phrase was often used in wills, being specified as where a person wished to be buried. In particular, it appeared in some Lollard wills, as part of an expression of humility, since those entering the church would walk over the grave. [< OE *haga* = a piece of enclosed land] – *Cf.* HAGA 1

Churl. *See* CEORL

Cingle. A belt or girdle. The Latin equivalent was *cingulum militare*.

Cingulum militare. Lit. 'military belt'. The belt of knighthood, which carried the scabbard, given at the ceremony of knighting.

Cinnabar. Cinnabar, also known as *minium*, was employed to produce the reds and vermilion used by MS illuminators. Large quantities have been mined in Spain for two millennia; it is known to chemists as mercury sulphide (HgS). – *Cf.* BRASIL; LAPIS LAZULI

Cinque Ports. Five ports on the south coast of England: Hastings, Sandwich, Dover, Romney, Hythe; to these Rye and Winchelsea were later added. They provided the early English navy. This was most likely initiated by Edward the Confessor some time before 1066. Some 50 or more ships were maintained for the king in the 11c. The ports were granted *charters of privileges in late 1270s. The towns became particularly important as a first line of defence once possession of Normandy by the English crown had been lost. By the 13c, a part of the ports' ancient service due to the king was still the supply of ships, each with two dozen crew, for the customary 40 days each year. For Edward I this was the basis of his navy, under the command of an *admiral. As with many such dues and services, when they were commuted to cash payments the system fell apart. By the mid-14c, the king was paying the wages of the crews, not the ports. – *Cf.* Cog; Lithesman

Circaria 1. Term used for one of the regions or circuits into which *Premonstratensian abbeys were organised. In England, there were three: *Circaria australis* (southern circuit); *Circaria mediana* (middle circuit); *Circaria borealis* (northern circuit). There was also one for Scotland: *Circaria Scotiae.* The English form is 'circary'. – *Cf. next*

Circaria 2. Latin term for a round of visitations made by a bishop. – *Cf. previous*; Visitation

Circator. *Obedientiary whose duty it was to make a tour or circuit of the monastery and its buildings each night with a bright lamp to ensure that all was well. [< L *circo* = to go about]

Circumvallation. Raised-earth ramparts put up around a castle by those besieging it to prevent anyone getting in or out, while also protecting themselves from sudden attacks by the castle's defenders.

Cirice. A religious community; also a church. – *Cf. next*

Ciricsceat. Lit. 'church tribute or church *scot'. The *first fruits of grain payable to a parish church on the Feast of St Martin, 11 November; mentioned in a letter from King Cnut to the English people in 1027. – *Cf. previous*; Sceatta

Cissor. A tailor or cloth cutter who took his name from the tool of his trade, his scissors; 'tailor' from AN *tailleur* was also used. [< OFr. *cissoires* < L *cisorium* = cutting implement, scissors]

Cistercian Order. The monastic order founded in 1098 at Cîteaux (Latin Cistercium) by Robert of Molesme (d. 1110); a Benedictine reform. It was a strict, even puritanical order. The monks wore unbleached clothing, and undyed wool; they ate no meat, fish, or eggs. In their unheated cells they slept on bare boards. The lay brothers worked in the fields rather than studying in the *cloister. Cistercian churches were very plain, and undecorated, without stained glass or tower. Cistercians were the first to use the *conversus*, a lay brother who had left the world to serve God. However, *conversi* only did manual labour; their regime was fairly relaxed and they were not obliged to observe the usual religious requirements of the regular monks, so strictly observed by the Cistercians. The use of these *conversi* was adopted by other orders, such as the Premonstratensians. The order required its members to establish themselves away from other people and to work the land themselves; they would transform wilderness into arable or pasture. They established many granges and possessed large flocks of sheep – whose great value contributed to King Richard I's ransom. Their first house in England was at Waverley, founded in 1128; Rievaulx followed in 1132. By 1152 there were 50 Cistercian houses in England, all remote. In the 13c there were some 600 Cistercian houses, of which more than 70 were in England. The Cistercians preached the crusade against the Albigensians in 1209. Trappists are a late reform of the Cistercians. – *Cf.* CLUNY; PREMONSTRATENSIANS

Cittern. Stringed instrument somewhat like a *lute, played with plectrum. The gittern was a similar instrument but of later date.

Clamores. The word, meaning claims, is used in *DB* as heading for a section of entries found in several counties, placed as an appendix. These entries concern properties over which there were claims and disputes – about who held what and the size of holdings. In the *Little DB* which covered Essex, Suffolk and Norfolk, this section was titled *Invasiones* = annexations. There is a similar section for Huntingdonshire but this is untitled. In the *Liber Exoniensis*, the claims are referred to as *terrae occupatae* = appropriated lands. For the Yorkshire and Lincolnshire entries *clamores* is used. [< L *clamo* = call aloud, to complain]

Clap-dish. Alms-dish made of wood whose lid clapped to draw attention to the beggar or *mendicant.

Clarenceux. *Her.* The second (English) King of Arms, whose jurisdiction lies south of the Trent. – *Cf.* GARTER KING OF ARMS; NORROY AND ULSTER

Clas. The mother church of a Welsh district, served by abbot and canons. Such a district was often a *cantref.

Claustral prior. An abbot's second-in-command, responsible for the internal life of the monastery. [< L *claustrum* = cloister]

Clausura. Lit. 'closed (off), enclosure'. This word refers to the practice of barring members of the opposite sex from a monastery or nunnery. – *Cf.* DOMUS FENESTRAE

Clavus. *See* CLOVE

Clerestory. The upper portion of a large church with rows of windows, above the aisles, so as to allow light into the central parts of the building.

Clergy. Orig. the word meant learning or scholarship; later, by transference, it was applied to the clerics, as they were supposed to be literate, able to read and know Latin. [< L *clericus* = a clerk] – *Cf. next*

Clerk. A man of the secular *clergy, i.e. not a monk or *canon of a religious order. In 12c England perhaps five per cent of the male population were clerks. Such men were not permitted to marry. Clerks were supposed to be educated, and were given a Latin text to read as proof. However, this could easily be memorised – at a time when many were illiterate, and much depended on the memory of local custom, memory was of signal importance. [< L *clericus* = a clerk] – *Cf. previous*

Clerk of the market. Whenever the king's household was on the move, the clerk of the market was required to ride in advance of the royal party, securing all necessary supplies. As part of his authority he declared the *assize of bread, wine and ale, and oats to ensure their quality. This assize would apply to every market within the *verge for whatever time the royal household remained in the district. A further duty was to ensure that prostitutes were kept away from the court. At this time, the court was an all-male institution. These duties came under the purview of the *Marshalsea. – *Cf.* DOMUS REGIS; INTRINSECUS; ITINERARY; PURVEYOR

Clermonia. A *clerk's Latin term for the gathering together of the canons of a *cathedral. It was also used colloquially and somewhat tongue in cheek to indicate sobriety.

Cleyed. *Her.* With tusks (of a boar); it is a form of 'clawed'. – *Cf.* SANGLIER

Cloister. Orig. a place of seclusion or a monastic house; an open quadrangle with a covered colonnade for walking within a *cathedral or college. [< L *claustrum* = an enclosure] – *Cf.* GARTH

Close Rolls. Records of letters, mandates, and other writs of a private nature, which were addressed to individuals in the king's name and were closed, then sealed on the outside with the *great seal (hence close roll). Many of these would have been summonses issued to barons to attend *parliament. When folded these letters could become small enough to fit in the hand and could even be swallowed *in extremis*. – *Cf.* FINE ROLLS; LETTERS PATENT ROLLS; PIPE ROLLS

Clouges. Money paid to a *herald at a *tournament, deriving its name from the time when it was the herald's duty to nail a knight's shield to a tree on which all the challenges were to be found. [< Fr *clou* = nail] – *Cf.* TREE OF HONOUR

Clove. Measure of weight = 7–8 lb (*c*.3.5 kg) used of wool and cheese. [< L *clavus* = a weight]

Cluny. A reform of the Benedictines, which grew out of the abbey of Cluny, in Burgundy, in 910. The Cluniacs' organisation was more centralised than the Benedictines': daughter-houses, established as priories, remained dependent upon the mother-house, whose *abbot had control over all other foundations. This arrangement allowed for uniformity both of practice and observance. Cluniacs used a more elaborate ritual than did the Benedictines, and their architectural ornamentation was distinctly lavish; even their vestments were more expensive than those of other orders. St Bernard, a *Cistercian, said of them, 'Oh ye professors of poverty, what does gold do in a holy place?' Learning and scholarship was the centre of their way, rather than labour in the fields. Their first English house was founded at Lewes in 1077. – *Cf.* ALIEN PRIORY

Cniht. *See next*

Cnihtena gild. Lit. 'guild of knights'. The OE word *cniht* = a youth or young retainer, including military retainers. In the reigns of both William II and Henry I the privileges of the London *cnihtena gild* were confirmed; however, this was an association of the most prominent burgesses. There were other such associations of the same name in Winchester and Canterbury, the latter being referred to in a charter during King Æthelberht's reign.

Co-aration. Lit. 'co-ploughing'. Modern term for the practice of AS settlers of working together in groups larger than the family. A plough-team of eight oxen was too costly for one family to own and maintain; the heavy plough itself, the *caruca*, was also expensive. Thus, although large fields were divided up, they were worked co-operatively. [< L *aro* = to plough]

Cockatrice [basilisk]. *Her.* Two-legged monster or dragon with barbed tongue and cock's head; a reptile/serpent with fatal halitosis and equally fatal stare, from which basilisk-stare is derived. Its feet were those of a cockerel (whereas a *wyvern's were those of an eagle). It was thought to come from a cockerel's egg, being hatched by a serpent. While its breath could kill, it could itself be killed by a weasel. Later, it was a term for 'whore'.

Codex. Term used for a MS in book form, a format which superseded the MS roll *c*.7–8c. The leaves of the MS were sewn on one edge, much as books today are sewn or glued. [< L *caudex* = tree bark; also an account book]

Coenobite. A member of any monastic community who observes the shared life of the community, as opposed to a hermit or idiorhythmic monk (who follows his own rules of living). [< L *coenobita* = a monk]

Cofferer. Orig. a craftsman who made chests, usually covered with leather. These chests in time gave their name to the post of the officer who kept money in them, i.e. a cofferer. One of the treasurers of the royal *household; he ranked third in the hierarchy of the *king's wardrobe. The title was also borne by an officer of the *Green Cloth. [< L *cofferarius* = cofferer]

Cog. A broad cargo vessel with blunt prow and stern; cogs formed an important part of Edward III's navy. – *Cf.* CINQUE PORTS

Cognisance. A sign by which to be recognised, i.e. the heraldic badge or emblem or *crest worn by the retainers of a particular lord, or noble house; part of the *livery. Before *heraldry became an art and science, knights would put signs or simple cognisances on their shields as an easy means of identification in battle or *mêlée.

Coif. A skull cap worn under a helmet, known sometimes in the contemporary French as *coyfe de Chartres*.

Coins and coinage. *See* FARTHING; MONEYERS; NOBLE; PENNY; SOLIDUS

Cóir Anmann. *Fitness of Names.* An etymological collection of Irish tribal and personal names in two versions. The earlier and shorter is 14–15c, the later 15c. In all there are *c*.300 names whose meanings and origins are described.

Cokeneyes. A small fowl or cockerel; ultimate source of Cockney.

Cokini. Grade of king's messenger junior to the *nuncius regis* and who travelled on foot. The term was first used in the *rolls *c*.1251. Initially, they were simply a spare pair of hands from the kitchens, used as casual messengers. Later, they were recognised as a group known as *cokini* or *coquini*. Being casual labour, they cost less than the full-time *nuncius*. Their pay was 2d a day, and they were not initially included in the annual distribution of *livery. On occasion, when they were in the company of a *nuncius*, a horse might be used. They came to be known as *cursores* when the association with the kitchens was felt undignified; the name *cursor* [L = a runner] also had the advantage of suggesting speed and proficiency. Some *cokini* remained in service for 10 or 20 years; others were promoted to *nuncius*. Their numbers varied greatly from year to year, e.g. depending on whether there was a war being fought, in which case their numbers might increase to 40 or so. In time, they were given new cloaks and shoes annually: working for the king meant wearing his livery. [< L *coquinus* = things to do with cooking, also a market where cooks were hired] – *Cf.* KITCHENER

Colibertus. A group of men who were not slaves but were not wholly free, ranking below the free *villein; known also as *quolibertus*. They were found in Wessex as reported in *DB*; their rare occurrence elsewhere indicates only that other commissioners – for whatever reason – did not report them. – *Cf.* CULVERTAGE

Collation. A small meal or snack in a monastery. After *vespers and before *compline in a Benedictine monastery, the monks gathered in the *cloister to listen to a reading and take refreshment such as a stoup of beer. [< L *collatio* = a collection]

Collaud. Acclamation by the populace, i.e. the citizens, of a king; particularly the citizens of London for which there was ancient precedent. This was taken into account during the deposition of Richard II in 1399, and the search for legitimate grounds for Henry IV's claim to the throne. [< L *col-* = together + *laudo* = praise]

Collect. A short prayer said before reading in the *eucharist. – *Cf.* COLLECTAR

Collecta. The term used by middlemen in the wool trade of the clip collected from many small-scale producers. This happened during the great time of sheep farming in the 13c. These middlemen could be magnates or abbeys such as those of the Cistercian order, who contracted to supply so much from their own flocks, but also agreed to supply a specified number of sacks, collected from the surrounding area. [< L *collectum* = something collected] – *Cf.* ARRA; SACK OF WOOL

Collectar. A book of *collects, i.e. a collection of short prayers said during a service.

College of Arms. *See* ARMS, COLLEGE OF

College of Heralds. *See* HERALDS, COLLEGE OF

Collegiate church. A church, not a *cathedral, endowed for a *chapter of canons or prebends. These establishments were served by groups of secular *clergy, forming an association or college. They were known in the AS period as *minsters. Some became *chantries of a very costly kind; some became parish churches or were dissolved; others were taken over by the new orders of the 12c, e.g. the *Augustinians. Those at Westminster and Windsor, St George's Chapel, survived until the 1530s.

Collier. A charcoal maker; only later did the word come to mean one who sold coal, as well as charcoal.

Colloquium. In 1226 writs of summons were sent out, calling four knights from each *county to gather at Lincoln for a special assembly, a colloquium or conference. It was called to resolve various practical problems involved in the implementation of *Magna Carta. Such men as these knights were known as *'buzones'.

Collying. *Her.* Falconer's term used by *heralds to indicate the head of a bird erect in preparation for flight.

Columbine. *Her.* A flower (*Aquilegia vulgaris*), which was used as the *badge of the house of Lancaster.

Combatant. *Her.* Describes two animals facing each other, poised to fight, each *rampant.

Comes. Title used in documents and chronicles for the holder of office in a shire or *county; the Latin word from which the title count derived. In its original use, *comes* was used of a companion of the emperor, or someone who had specific duties in the imperial court, e.g. *comes stabuli*. Later, in England, the count had charge of a county, responsible, in the king's name, for law and financial matters, as well as military affairs. [< L *comes* = an attendant or companion] – *Cf.* COMITAL; CONSTABLE

Comes stabuli. Lit. 'count of the stables'. From this title *'constable' is derived. – *Cf. previous*

Comet. There are several comets mentioned in the *ASC*. In the annal for 891, there is a reference to 'the star that men in book-Latin call *cometa'*. Another appeared in 975, at the time of a great famine. The most famous is *Halley's comet, which appeared on 24 April 1066, and was visible for the next week. This was seen as an ill omen, as indeed it proved for the English in the Battle of Hastings later that year. [< L *cometa*] – *Cf.* FEAXEDE STEORRA

Comital. Modern term denoting anything relating to a count or an earl. [< L *comes* = an attendant or companion] – *Cf. next*; COMES

Comitatus 1. Latin word = company, used to refer to the close companions of a lord or king. The usage is a 19c reapplication of the word *comitatus*, taken from the description in *Germania* by Tacitus (d. 120) of the Germanic warrior band loyal to their lord. Such loyalty is exemplified later in the OE poem *The Battle of Maldon*, which relates the struggles of the household warriors and their loyalty to their *ealdorman* in the battle of 991, also mentioned in *ASC*. A further example was at the Battle of Hastings, in 1066, after the death of King Harold II. Harold's family and their closest retainers were all killed, refusing to leave the body of their dead king and wanting to avenge his death. – *Cf.* DOMUS REGIS; FAMILIA REGIS

Comitatus 2. After the Conquest, this word was used as the Latin translation of 'shire', i.e. the modern *'county'. – *Cf.* TOTUS COMITATUS

Comitiva. Term used of a member of a king's or lord's *comitatus*. He was a retainer and companion in arms. – *Cf.* MEINIE; RETINENTIA

Commendam. *See* IN COMMENDAM

Commendation. Term used to describe the relationship between man and lord. *DB assumed everyone had a lord, even the king, who was subject to God. At its heart was the idea that a man placed himself under the protection of his lord. The practice began in the dangerous 8c. It merged into what we call *feudalism and vassalage. The contemporary Latin term was *se vertere* = to submit to, translating the OE *gebugan* = to bow to. [< L *commendatio* = entrusting] – *Cf.* VASSAL

Commensalis. Latin term (English 'commensal') used of the sons of noblemen and gentry who were placed in the charge of a monastery for education in the 15–16c. Another and earlier practice was to place the son in the house of a great ecclesiastic or other magnate to learn the ways of a great house and how to be a gentleman. It was not uncommon for them to serve at table. Fees were paid, esp. if the boy was sent to a monastery. [< L *com-* = with + *mensa* = table; thus to eat at the same table] – *Cf.* CORRODY; VALETTUS

Commilitones. Brothers-in-arms. The term was used of the fighting men, not retainers, who accompanied the household knights when they were summoned to war by the king. [< L *commilito* = to soldier together]

Commise. The penalty – the confiscation of his fiefs – imposed upon a *vassal for a serious breach of expected conduct. One great instance was that imposed by King Philip VI of France upon Edward III for giving aid to Robert of Artois, then enemy of the king of France. Philip proceeded to confiscate both Aquitaine and Gascony, which Edward held of Philip. This was the formal occasion of the beginning of the *Hundred Years' War. [< L *commissa* = fine, penalty]

Common Pleas, Court of. Established by Henry II in 1178, it comprised five members of his own council (the *curia regis*) specifically to hear pleas – civil suits not involving the crown. However, this court was not wholly independent until *Magna Carta determined the need for a specific place for civil cases, i.e. in Westminster Hall. By 1272 it had acquired a chief justice. – *Cf.* CERTIORARI

Commons, House of. *See* PARLIAMENT

Commote [commot]. English form of the Welsh *cymyd*, term for a division of land less than a *cantref*. In the late 11c, Welsh commotes were areas under Norman control yet subject to Welsh law and custom. The commotes were west of Offa's Dyke and, in general, they represented recent Norman-English advances into Welsh territory. – *Cf.* RAGLER

Commune concilium. Lit. 'general council'. Latin term for the assembly of all the tenants-in-chief of the king; its origin is in the early years of Norman rule in England. It was the Norman equivalent of a *witan. From it evolved the *privy council. – *Cf.* WITENAGEMOT

Communitas regni. Lit. 'the community of the realm'. The term for the nation in parliament, or its representation in parliament.

Commutation. The conversion of a labour service into a sum of money payable to a lord.

Company. Companionship or fellowship. [< L *com-* = with + *panis* = bread, i.e. those who break bread together]

Compass. *Her.* A compass was used in the insignia of the Company of Carpenters, and also in the Company of Masons, whose arms were granted in 1473, and later by the Freemasons. – *Cf. next*

Compass, master of the. A stone-mason of the highest rank and skill. The compass was the mason's indispensable tool which ensured the accuracy of his work.

Compensation. AS law, carried over into the *LHP*, contained detailed rules and schedules of compensation for injury, from the loss of a finger-nail at 4s, to a *thegn*'s death at 1,200s. If a man was rendered impotent by a wound then 80s were payable, while the loss of a big toe warranted 20s.

Comperta. Lit. 'discovered or ascertained'. Term used of wrongs found during a bishop's *visitation requiring further action or being sent to trial. – *Cf.* DETECTA; SECRETE ET SINGILLATIM

Compline. *See* HORARIUM

Compony. *See* GOBONY

Compurgation. At the heart of AS law and custom was the oath which was considered sacred. Compurgation involved the accused person swearing his innocence; at the same time he had to produce a number of other people willing also to swear to the accused's assertion of innocence. [< L *com-* = with + *purgo* = to purge]

Computus. The science of calculation or computing, usually of the calendar for a Church festival, e.g. Easter. An early such work was produced at the Vivarium of Cassiodorus in 562. This was the first document of the medieval world to use the Dionysian mode of date reckoning we still use and which defined the Christian era.

Conductor. The Latin term for one of the two men who worked an eight-ox *plough-team. The *conductor* guided the plough itself; the other, known as the *fugator*, drove the oxen. [< L *conductor* = a guide, leader]

Confiteor. Lit. 'I confess'. Opening word of the prayer, *Confiteor Deo Omnipotenti* (I confess to Almighty God), which was the confession of sin made by priest and congregation at the beginning of the mass.

Conflictus Gallicus. Lit. 'the Gallic (French) way of fighting or combat'. The *tournament first emerged in what today we call France. The term was used by chroniclers such as Ralph Diceto and Roger of Wendover, while Ralph of Coggeshall used the phrase *more Francorum* (in the way of the French). From *c.*1130 France was the place to go for a young man keen to make a name and money for himself. Indeed, there was almost a professional circuit on which it was possible to make a fortune, and many Englishmen travelled across the Channel for just that reason. – *Cf.* HASTILUDE; TOURNAMENTS

Confraternity. An association with a church, signifying the claim on the spiritual benefits and remembrance in prayers of a monastery by a benefactor or founder. To the lay population this round of prayer was crucial to a monastery's existence.

Congé d'èlire. Lit. 'permission to elect'. AN term for the king permitting the chapter of a *cathedral and its dean to elect a bishop. The constitutions of Clarendon of 1164, issued by Henry II, set down the procedures for the election of a new bishop or archbishop.

Congius. Old Roman measure of liquid, amounting to six pints. It was used in late ME documents, which set down the allowances of members of the royal court, who were entitled to *bouche en court*. – *Cf.* CONSTITUTIO DOMUS REGIS; SEXTARY

Conjury. Someone who has taken an oath, e.g. William Caxton (d. 1400) said of himself: 'I am citizen and conjury of London.'

Conrois. Closely packed cavalry formation of between 20 and 30 men. Norman knights fought in such tactical units.

Consistory court. The court of a bishop for hearings concerning ecclesiastical offences; a diocesan court.

Constable. Chief officer of a royal household, also the governor of a castle. The development in meaning of this word from senior in a stable to a royal officer of high rank is similar to that of *marshal. [< L *comes stabuli* = a count or chief officer of the stables] – *Cf.* COMES; MARSHAL; STALLER

Constabularia. Unit of the feudal host comprising 10 knights.

Constance, Council of. 1415. At this council John Wyclif was declared a heretic; at the same time it was ordered that his body be 'ungraved'. Earlier, in 1410, some 300 proposals had been found and condemned in his writings. – *Cf.* DE HAERETICO COMBURENDO

Constitutio Domus Regis. Establishment of the King's Household. This document was drawn up a short while after the death of Henry I in 1135, by the bureaucracy of the new king, Stephen, describing the arrangements and conditions of the household in the last years of Henry's life. It sets out the pay, allowances and living conditions of those who served the king, beginning with the *chancellor. The chancellor was to have 5s a day, with itemised food – *simnel bread – and specified quantities of wine and candles and so on. The description then passes through the ranks from master-butler to various *stewards, dispensers, naperers, cooks, and concludes with the *marshal. The keeper of the cups received three halfpence a day. These lower-paid workers had no food allowances specified; rather they were said to live in the household, meaning that 'customary food' was provided. – *Cf.* CURIA REGIS; SEXTARY

Consuetudinarius. Latin form of the *consuetudinary used in a monastery. By the 13c this Latin word had acquired another meaning, as an infrequent synonym of *custumarius*. [< L *consueo* = to be accustomed] – *Cf.* CUSTUMARIUS

Consuetudinary. The household books of a monastery in which are found its customs and those of its surrounding area. The Latin form was *consuetudinarius*. [< L *consueo* = to be accustomed] – *Cf.* CUSTOMARY

Consuetus. *See* CUSTUMARIUS

Contemptus mundi. Lit. 'contempt for the world'. An attitude prevalent throughout monastic communities (13–15c), which went beyond mere disdain and contempt for the delights of physical existence. The passage of time itself was seen as a process of decline, and the process of 'civilisation' moving westwards, away from Jerusalem (the centre of the world) was both part of and sign of that decline. Bernard of Cluny (*fl.* 1140–60) wrote a poem entitled *De Contemptu Mundi* in which he castigated the morals of the times.

Contenement. Property required by a man to maintain his position, i.e. to be able to live according to his rank. Ranulf de *Glanville (d. 1190) stated that when a man inherited he should not make demands for *relief on those who held of him which would jeopardise their contenement. The Latin form is *contenementum*. [< L *con-* = with + *tenementum* = tenure]

Contract captain. In the mid-14c, the feudal system of summoning by writ knights to fight for the king was disappearing fairly rapidly. In its place, two systems of recruiting fighters were emerging: hiring by contract and volunteers. Contract captains, who were knights, were charged by the king to recruit set numbers of men, for set periods of time; the contract for fighting being with the captain, not the king. The standard period of contract was for 40 days, the quarantine. The daily rates of pay, during Edward III's reign (1327–77), for various ranks were as follows: an earl, 6s 8d; banneret, 4s; knight, 2s; man-at-arms, 1s; mounted archer, 6d, unmounted, 3d. The recruiting captain of volunteers usually found his men in the prisons. In usual circumstances, as many as 10 per cent of an army were ex-prisoners, released on condition of serving in the army. There were also *mercenaries recruited in Flanders and elsewhere. – *Cf.* ARRAIATOR; ARRAY, COMMISSION OF; REGARD

Contrafactum. Modern term for a piece of music where a different text is set to the notes from that originally intended; e.g. an English text might be set to an originally Latin motet. An example would be the recasting of the lines (originally in Latin) 'Now at the beginning of the day/ to God as suppliants we pray' as the following, 'Now at the dawning of the day/ We must start drinking straight away'. Later, when friars began their mission to travel and preach to people outside the church, they used popular tunes, changing the words to suit their purposes. This use of music known to the general populace was why St Francis called his followers *joculatores Dei*, God's minstrels. [< L *contrafacio* = to imitate, to counterfeit]

Contraiz. A term for a crippled or otherwise damaged person.

Contrarients. Name adopted by supporters of Queen Isabella and Mortimer in the rebellion against Edward II in the 1320s.

Convent [nunnery]. The place of a community of Christians living together according to the rule of the religious order to which they belong (the term is not confined to women religious). [< L *conventus* = assembly] – *Cf.* CONVENTUALIS; MONASTERY; OBLATE

Conventio. Lit. 'an agreement'. During the 11c and the 12c, the barons of England and France/Normandy were almost continuously in dispute. These were private wars of the kind William I had forbidden in England after 1066 but which were not so susceptible to one authority across the Channel. The Church also sought to limit these eruptions, e.g. the *Truce of God. However, these quarrels did not always spill over into violence; likely enough, one of the two sides simply wished to agitate and secure an agreement – *conventio* – which might favour him slightly.

Conventiones. Latin term for payments to the crown which were not *amercements, but were rather like the *relief paid on succession to an estate. *Scutage also would come under this category of royal income. [< L *conventio* = agreement, agreed payment]

Conventualis. Latin term indicating that a monastery had sufficient members to make it viable, that number being the apostolic 12. Fewer than 12 meant that the rule was unlikely to be adhered to and discipline would fall away. St Bernard was very conscious of this likelihood. 'Conventual' is the adjectival form of *'convent'.

Conversatio. Lit. 'conversation'; used of behaviour. The phrase *de male conversacionis* = bad behaviour, implying sexual impropriety of (usually) a woman. This links with the phrase 'criminal conversation' = adultery, sexual misconduct. 'Converse' had the sense 'to be intimate with'.

Conversus [lay brother]. A lay member of a monastery who entered late in life, perhaps with a *corrody. They were so named for being 'converted' from the secular world. They were often illiterate and not permitted to become monks; monks from wealthier families tended to be literate and were known as 'fathers'. The main purpose of the *conversus* was to do the manual labour of a foundation, making the worldly wealth needed, as the religious worked for the soul. The Cistercian order had more *conversi* than other rules. For example, at Rievaulx, when Ailred was abbot (*c.*1150–60), there were 140 monks and 600 *conversi*. The better able were sent to the monastery's outlying farms and *granges; however, a great many were found to be unreliable and much was stolen. By the time of the *Black Death, granges and farms had been let out on commercial terms; after this, there were scarcely any *conversi*. – *Cf.* NUTRITUS

Coopertus. Lit. 'covered'. Word used of a knight in the phrase *cum equis coopertis* = with covered horse, i.e. the horse was *barded. During the reign of Edward I the vast majority of knights on the king's payroll rode armoured horses; horses described as *discooperti* (uncovered) were very scarce. Such men with their horses could be described as 'heavy' cavalry. – *Cf.* BARD 1; DESTRIER

Copyhold. Land held of the lord of a *manor but according to local custom – custom being defined and recorded in the manorial court records. The copy referred to the manorial record of which a copy might be held; or referral could be made to the original. By the late 14c, services owed by villeins had been commuted into money payments.

Coquini. *See* COKINI

Coram populo. Lit. 'in the public presence'. Term used when the transfer of title was made in public, that being the occasion of legal seisin, of which a *charter was a record and not title.

Coram rege. Lit. 'in the presence of the king, the king's bench'. This court travelled with the king wherever he went; it tried cases involving magnates and those entitled to a hearing before the reigning monarch. It was precursor of the high courts which deal with common law. – *Cf.* CURIA REGIS; EYRE

Corbel. A raven or crow; later a projection from a wall designed for something to hang from, named for its likeness to the raven's large beak. 'Corbie' was the 15c Scottish form. [< OFr. *corbel* = raven]

Cordelier. A *Franciscan observant, so called because of the knotted cord around the waist.

Cordwain. A fine quality goatskin leather, originally made at Córdova, in Spain, after which it is named. In 1367, shoes of cordwain cost 6d, boots 3s 6d; cowhide shoes cost 5d, boots 3s. – *Cf. next*

Cordwainer. A leather worker, shoemaker. The title cordwainer applied not only to the maker of leather goods but also to the merchant who imported cargoes of Spanish leather. Some of these men achieved prominence in London: e.g. Gervase the Cordwainer was the king's chamberlain of London in 1227, becoming *sheriff in 1237. – *Cf. previous and next;* CORVEISERIA

Cordwainers, Ordinances of. 1272. Ordinances drawn up in the last year of King Henry III's reign, which specified and limited *cordwainers' activities. Fees for an apprentice were set at 40s at least, with 2s going to the commonality. Cordwainers were not to interfere with tanners and vice versa. At fairs, tanners had to set up with tanners and cordwainers with cordwainers under penalty of a 40s fine; nor were they allowed to work at night. Strangers were not permitted to sell footwear in London save in wholesale quantities. Selling in the streets was allowed only between two named streets and this before dinner; but on the eve of a feast day only after dinner.

Core. Measure of wheat equal to a quarter. – *Cf.* QUARTER 3

Coriarius. A leather worker; currier; artisan who worked on leather, improving it, after the tanning process. The Latin words *corarius* and *coralius* were synonymous with *coriarius*. – *Cf.* PELLETARIUS; TANNER

Corn. The grain of a cereal plant; in England the most widely planted was wheat.

Cornagium. Cornage; a rent paid for grazing rights, esp. in northern England.

Coronal. The crown-like end of a lance used in a peaceful joust. The idea was that several points would distribute the thrust wider than a single-pointed lance. [< L *coronalis* = like a wreath or crown] – *Cf.* JOUST OF PEACE; JOUST OF WAR; ARMS, STATUTE OF

Coroner. District officer whose duty was to look after royal property in his district. The title comes from the last word of the Latin title, *custos placitorum coronae* = guardian of pleas of the crown.

Corporal. The cloth used at *eucharist on which the cup and paten or plate were placed during the eucharist. – *Cf.* BURSE

Corporal acts of mercy. Charitable acts which aided the giver towards salvation. They were: feeding the hungry, providing drink for the thirsty, clothing the naked, visiting the sick and prisoners, taking in the traveller and burying the dead.

Corrody [corrodier]. Pension paid to a monastery for the maintenance of someone. Such an arrangement was often used as a way of dealing with awkward members of a family; as a noble woman also was put into a nunnery if her marriage might prove politically unwelcome. – *Cf.* CONVERSUS; OBLATE

Corvée. Forced, and unpaid, labour, commanded by a lord from a *vassal.

Corveiseria. The Cordwainery, the name of the 13c London ward, near St Mary-le-Bow. – *Cf. next;* CORDWAINER

Corveser. A cobbler. [< OFr. *courveis* = leather < L *Cordubensis* = Córdova] – *Cf. previous;* CORDWAINER

Cotagium. Latin term for the land attached to a small dwelling or cot. – *Cf.* -AGIUM; COTLAND

Cote. A small house or cottage; it is found in placenames, e.g. Somercotes (Lincolnshire).

Cotland. Land attached to a cot or small dwelling, perhaps five acres, belonging to a *cotsetla*. – *Cf.* COTAGIUM

Cotsetla. An 11c *ceorl*, a free peasant, owing his lord a day's labour a week with *boon work at harvest time. In return he had a small dwelling place or cottage and farmed a small share of the common. – *Cf. previous;* COTAGIUM; -SETLA

Couchant [couched]. *Her.* Describes an animal lying down with its head held up.

Coucher. A large book, such as a *breviary or *book of hours, usually too large to be carried with ease, left upon a lectern; the word was also used of a *cartulary.

Council of Fifteen. On 11 June 1258, at Oxford, a council of barons resolved to rule the country in conjunction with King Henry III, who was deemed to be mentally incapable. This was prompted by a variety of reasons. The previous year's weather had been bad, with poor harvests and *murrain. The ordinary people of England were also suffering greatly from the expenses of war. Before the council, another was formed, which drew up the Provisions of *Oxford. Henry's foreign advisers were extremely unpopular; indeed it was thought they were favoured above the English and their wealth was much disapproved of. Feeling was such that they then decamped; their land and castles were immediately confiscated and distributed. However, the council began internecine squabbling.

Council of the North. A council created by Richard III, instructed to protect England's northern border marches with Scotland. Ordinances were drawn up in 1484. The post of warden of the marches was created. Defence was put into the hands of the Percy family in the east; the Nevilles were charged with defending the west.

Counter-castle. Siege works set up on a scale equal to that of the castle under attack. Built at the beginning of a siege, it contained a garrison whose function was to prohibit access to a castle and limit the defenders' activities; assaults could also be launched from such a building.

Counter-couchant. *Her.* Describes two animals lying beside each other but with their heads away from each other. – *Cf. next*

Counter-passant. *Her.* Describes two animals passing each other in opposite directions. The word 'counter' is used in hunting to indicate the direction opposite to that of the game. – *Cf. previous and next*

Counter-potent. *Her.* A T-shape or crutch. The term refers to one of the heraldic *furs shown alternately as azure or *argent patches arranged so as to resemble a crutch, i.e. in opposite order to *potent.

Counter-salient. *Her.* Describes two figures leaping away from the other. [< L *salio* = to leap] – *Cf. previous*; SALIENT

Counter-vair. *Her.* One of the chief *furs alternating *argent and azure bell shapes, i.e. in opposite order to *vair.

County. The court held under a *sheriff which dealt with *shire matters; the territory of a count; later, by transference, county came to apply to the area of land discussed at such meetings. [< AN *counté* < L *comes* = count] – *Cf.* PALATINE

Couped. *Her.* Cut off, e.g. a figure couped at the shoulders showing only head and shoulders. – *Cf.* CABOSHED

Courage. One of the essentials of a knight, rated higher than prowess, it being a moral quality and thus superior to the merely physical. Raymon Lull (d. *c.*1315) said of courage that 'no man may more honour and love *chivalry ... than that dieth for love and for to honour the order of chivalry'. It required no skill to die. As originally used, courage indicated more disposition and purpose than the bravery we associate almost exclusively with the word. [< L *cor* = heart, mind, spirit + *-age* associating a quality] – *Cf.* PROWESS

Courant. *Her.* Running (of an animal).

Courser. A fast-running horse. [< OFr. *courseur* < L *cursor* = a runner]

Court baron. Court held before a *manor's freemen that dealt with services owed to the lord by tenants; also for the recovery of debts of less that 40s. However, the court had no power to imprison. Somewhat strangely, it appears that the court baron has not been abolished by parliament. – *Cf.* CURIA REGIS

Court leet. Court of record for which a royal *charter was required, usually held once or twice a year, to examine members of the *hundred and to punish misdemeanours. – *Cf.* LEET

Courtly love. Modern term popularised by C. S. Lewis to describe the various kinds of love between man and woman described in the works of *troubadours and others between the 11c and the 13c. The range of feeling ran from the dutiful respect owed a lord's wife, to the adulterously sexual. One relationship was excluded, that between husband and wife. The genre first appeared in Provence and then spread through Europe. Appearing at much the same time as Arthurian tales, the two created a potent and memorable mix of *chivalry and romance. The French phrase *amour courtois* is a 19c coinage. – *Cf.* AUBADE; PASTOURELLE

Couter. That part of a suit of armour which protected the elbow. Originally they were rounded, but became conical in shape through decoration. After becoming articulated, they comprised three pieces.

Coward 1. Someone without courage. On the battlefield, the *thegn* was expected to fight and, if necessary, die with his lord – one reason for the loss of so many of the AS nobility, or *comitatus*, at Hastings, in 1066. Cowardice was the lowest of qualities in the chivalric world where physical courage counted as much as physical prowess. A coward was a soldier who turned tail and ran. In old hunting terms a hare was referred to as *la coward ou la court cowe*, i.e. the coward or the short-tail. *Coart* was the name of the timid rabbit in *Roman de Renart*. [OFr. *coe* = tail < L *cauda* = tail] – *Cf. next*

Coward 2. *Her.* Describes a lion with its tail between its legs. – *Cf. previous*

Crakow. *See* POULAINE

Cramoisy. Crimson; used esp. of cloth. [< OFr. *crameisi* < Ar. *kirmiz*] – *Cf.* SCARLET

Crampet. The *chape of a scabbard; also used as a heraldic charge.

Cranage. The payment made for the use of a crane to handle goods. The Latin form was *cranagium*.

Crannequin. The rack and pinion mechanism, or crank, used to cock a steel *crossbow. This procedure was markedly quicker than by hand, allowing the *arbalester or trained bowman to fire three times a minute.

Crannock. A unit of measure of wheat; used also of fish; equiv. to 37 gallons. [?< Ir. *cran*]

Craven. Lit. 'overcome'. The cry of the defeated man, concluding a duel. From this we have our use of the word as an adjective qualifying coward. [?< OFr. *cravanter* = to overcome, overwhelm] – *Cf.* DUELLUM; ICTUS REGIS; RECREANTIA

Creance. Lengthy cord attached to a falcon during its training, long and light enough to permit flight without escape. – *Cf.* FALCONRY

Credo. Lit. 'I believe'. The first word of the Creed, the statement of Christian belief formulated in the early Church.

Credo ut intelligam. Lit. 'I believe that I may understand'. The scholastic phrase made famous by Anselm of Bec (d. 1109).

Crémaillère. The inside zig-zag of a *parapet.

Crenellate. To *embattle or provide embattlements and *embrasures to a building e.g. castle; cathedrals might also be fortified, e.g. by King John at Lincoln in 1216. A licence from the king was required to crenellate a castle (which itself was licensed).

Crenellé [crenel]. The space between *merlons, the indentation where soldier or archer had some protection; the gap of the gap-toothed look. [< OFr. *crenel* = a notch < L *crena* = a serration, notch] – *Cf.* AJOURÉ

Cresset. A container of light-giving oil or coals; often suspended from a pole. [< OFr. *cresset* < *craisse* = grease, oil]

Crest 1. A plume of feathers worn atop a helmet; an identifying mark, such as coloured rings beneath the feathers of an arrow; something worn as a *cognisance. [< L *crista* = a plume or tuft] – *Cf.* FLETCH

Crest 2. *Her.* A figure or image on a coronet or shield or helmet.

Cresten. Christian.

Crime. AS law evolved an elaborate collection of monetary penalties for all manner of offence. The intention was *compensation for the aggrieved. Medieval society was violent. For example, in Lincoln in 1202 there were 114 murders, 89 violent robberies and 65 fights in which there were serious woundings. However, there were as a result of that year's mayhem only two executions. Rather than go to the expense of keeping criminals in prison, they were exiled or else hanged or mutilated: hands, ears and feet were cut off either singly or in various combinations. But these brutalities emerged during the reign of Henry II, under reforms intended to solve the 'crime wave'.– *Cf.* PILLORY; SANCTUARY

Crined. *Her.* Term indicating the hair of a human being or the mane of a horse is of a different *tincture from that of the body. [< L *crinis* = hair] – *Cf.* ANIMÉ; BEQUE; MEMBERED; RAMÉ; UNGULED

Crinet. Small feathers growing at the base of a hawk's beak, that part being known as the *cere*. [< L *crinis* = hair; *cere* < L *cera* = wax] – *Cf. previous*

Crinière [crinet]. The armour pieces or heavy padding used to protect the neck and throat of a knight's horse.

Crockard. The crockard was a foreign coin which appeared in England during Edward I's reign, the result of a shortage of coin in the country. He instituted a reform of the coinage in 1279–80, intending to fund his Welsh campaigns. However, it was too successful: good English coins left the country, although prohibited, for use in Europe. The shortage remained, even when European rulers and princes produced their own imitations of the English coins. These latter were usually lighter and less valuable than the English and were known as 'crockards', flooding in during the 1290s. There was an attempt to demonetise these coins in 1300 but fluctuations in the supply of coin in the first decades of the 14c caused grave problems. – *Cf.* POLLARD

Crocket [crotchet]. Leafy decorations or curls, e.g. on the top of capitals or other surfaces, often in high relief. These are very distinctive of Gothic architecture, so called for their likeness to a crotchet = a hook.

Croft. A smallholding or piece of land with a house. – *Cf.* TOFT AND CROFT

Crosier. Staff carried by a bishop as the sign of his office. Its symbolism, being shaped like a shepherd's crook, betokens his rôle as guide and protector of his flock.

Cross cramponée. *Her.* A cross with a bend at the end of each limb; a swastika. – *Cf.* FYLFOT

Crossbow. Form of bow used to fire arrows with a bow much smaller than the traditional *longbow, being drawn or cranked by a handle with a trigger release; it was so called because it somewhat resembled a cross (probably the single most potent image of the time). The crossbow was easier to handle than a longbow because of its use of a crank. However, this was also its great disadvantage, since it took longer to reload than the longbow. The crossbow had a range of up to 250 yards and was used best at relatively close quarters. However, in the mid-15c a steel crossbow emerged, with a range of up to 450 yards, and powerful enough to unhorse an armoured knight. The user was known as an *'arbalester'. – *Cf.* ARCHERY; CRANNEQUIN

Crosslands. Land in Ireland in the possession of monasteries and churches, or of prelates. These lands were subject to intervention by the *county *sheriff in guarding the crown's rights, even if within a *franchise or liberty.

Crosslet. *Her.* Term for a small cross or cross-like object.

Crowde. A wheelbarrow. [< OE *crudan* = to push]

Crown glass. The medieval method of making glass involved spinning molten glass on a pointed iron rod so that it was spread by centrifugal force, creating a sheet thickest at the centre. The familiar thick-set centre is called a 'bull's eye'. – *Cf.* GROZING

Cruciform brooches. Cruciform brooches tended to be Angle in origin; round brooches tended to be Saxon.

Crucisignatus. Latin term for 'signed with the cross', i.e. crusaders. They wore a tunic of white with a cross in red on the chest. – *Cf. next*

Crusades. The crusades made up the sequence of expeditions mounted in Europe with the intention of freeing the Holy Land from Islam, and imposing Christian rule. The crusading movement is striking testimony to the influence of the pope throughout Europe, esp. in the late 11c. For all the mercenary impulses which were attached to later crusades, the first came from a genuine enthusiasm for a holy war against the infidel. The first such military adventure was preached by Pope Urban II in 1095. The nominal purpose was to free the Holy Land from the Muslims. This was achieved when Jerusalem was taken in 1099. Jerusalem then became a kingdom with its first king, Baldwin (1100–18); several other crusader states were also created. There were other expeditions in the 12c, again aimed at the Muslims in the Holy Land and also those in Spain. The Second Crusade was preached in 1145. However, Jerusalem was retaken in 1187 by Saladin. This was followed by the Third Crusade, in which King Richard I played a significant part. The kingdom of Jerusalem lasted precariously until 1291, when Acre fell, despite the efforts of countless crusaders and nobles seeking war and glory. Crusades took place also in other areas, e.g. the Baltic. [< OFr. *croisade* < L *crux* = a cross] – *Cf. previous*

Crutched friars. The English name given to members of the military-religious orders; they were canons regular, for example the Order of the Holy Cross (*Fratres Cruciferi*), founded in 1211. 'Crutched' is a garbled version of 'crouched', a 'crouch' being a cross. Members of these orders might carry a cross in their hands, or have a cross sewn on the chest of their *habit. [< OE *cruc* < L *crux* = a cross]

Cubit. Measure of length based on the length of a man's forearm. – *Cf. next;* YARD 2

Cubit arm. *Her.* An arm severed at the elbow. – *Cf. previous*

Cuck-stool. A stool or chair in which miscreants were confined and subject to ducking and public shame. Perhaps given the source of the word cuck, it was not vegetables which were thrown at victims; it was also referred to as *cathedra stercoris* = the chair of excrement. It is found in Chester, in the 11c and later, e.g. for the brewers of bad ale: the monetary penalty was 4s, as specified in the city's entry in *DB – more than a brewer could afford. [< ON *kúkr* = excrement] – *Cf.* PILLORY

Cuirass. Piece of body armour, orig. of leather; somewhat like a waistcoat, protecting chest and back. Later it was made of *mail. [< OFr. *cuir* = leather] – *Cf. next*

Cuir-bouilli. Leather boiled in water, then moulded into shape, which, when dry, hardened sufficiently to be carved for use as cheap armour. In 1278, Edward I held a *béhourd* in which all the armour was *cuir-bouilli*. The only distinctions were that the noblest jousters were permitted golden *helms, while the lesser wore silver. [< OFr. *cuir* = leather + *bouillir* = boil] – *Cf. previous;* BATON 1; BULLION; JOUST OF PEACE

Cuisse. A piece of metal armour or *cuir-bouilli*, used to protect the thigh. [< OFr. *cuisse* = a thigh]

Culdee. Member of an Anglo-Scottish order of ascetics.

Cultiva terra. Arable land; land which can be cultivated. – *Cf. next*

Cultura. Term used in Latin documents for cultivated and *demesne land. – *Cf. previous*

Culverin. Early kind of hand-held gun, though later the word was applied to a cannon with a particularly long barrel. In heraldry, 'culverin' was always used of a cannon with a wide, out of scale, bore.

Culvertage. The demotion or abasement to the status of a freed *serf. [< OFr.. *culvert* = villein] – *Cf.* COLIBERTUS; NITHING

Curate. A *clerk who tended a church and did the work for another who actually held the *benefice. In England, the curate is an assistant to the parish priest. In France, however, the *curé* functions as the parish priest himself, not as the curate. [< L *curo* = to take care of, to attend to] – *Cf.* CURE

Curator. Latin word used of a lawyer or attorney who served in the ecclesiastical courts. [< L *curo* = to take care of, to attend to] – *Cf. next*

Cure. The complete phrase is 'cure of souls'. It refers to the priest's responsibility for the souls of his parishioners; from which *curate. [< L *cura* = care] – *Cf. previous*

Curfew. Borough regulations required fires to be covered; for this reason people had to be home and off the street by a certain time to ensure this was done. Houses of wood were highly flammable; fires spread with ease and rapidity. Hence the necessity of a curfew bell. [< OFr. *cuevrefeu* = covering of the fire] – *Cf.* BOW BELLS; DAYBELL

Curia de Arcubus. The Court of the Arches was the court of the province of Canterbury. It acquired this name from the church where it sat, St Mary de

Arcubus, i.e. St Mary-le-Bow (the church with the well-known *Bow bells). [L *arcubus* = a bow, an arc; *curia* = court]

Curia regis. Lit. 'the king's court'. The successor of the AS *witan*, this court saw the meetings of the king's tenants-in-chief, i.e. the *baronage and the Church. William I, the Conqueror, held this court three times a year, at Christmas, Easter and Whitsuntide. The *curia regis* was the forerunner of what we would recognise as the court in all the splendour and magnificence at the king's disposal. It became the centre of government and the gathering place of the country's magnates. From it evolved the various departments which were established and maintained as need arose. – *Cf.* CONSTITUTIO DOMUS REGIS; COMMON PLEAS, COURT OF; CORAM REGE

Curiales. Term used of the men working in the royal bureaucracy, the professional, career civil servants, whether or not they were clerks. [< L *curia* = (royal, papal) court]

Curialis. Courtly. An 11c term indicating a change in ways of thinking. Although the court remained a military institution, ideas about knighthood, politeness and diffidence were coming into focus. – *Cf.* ELEGANTIA MORUM

Currier. *See* CORIARIUS

Cursitor. The clerk in *chancery who did the department's writing and copying. The post continued until the mid-19c. [AN = *coursetour*] – *Cf. next*

Cursiva anglicana. The cursive script used in *chancery; it was adopted as a book-hand in the 13c. – *Cf. previous and next*

Cursive. Term used of handwriting in which the pen does not leave the paper between letters: the result is joined letters. – *Cf. previous*

Cursor scaccarii. Lit. 'exchequer courier'. A collector of rents for a monastery, usually based in the mother-house of the order and answerable to the order's bursar. – *Cf.* EXCHEQUER

Cursores. These men were sometimes also known as *viatores*, i.e. travellers or wayfarers; but they should not be confused with the *nuncius regis* or *cokini. They were freelance messengers, making a living by obtaining writs in the king's *chancery on other people's behalf.

Curt. Abbreviated, short, cut short, mutilated; only after the 17c does the word acquire its modern sense of abruptness in manner. [< L *curtus* = cut short] – *Cf.* CURTAL

Curtain wall. Usually the free-standing outside wall of a castle running between two towers.

Curtal. An early, short-barrelled gun; soon, a horse with docked tail; thus anything docked. [< L *curtus* = incomplete, circumcised, castrated] – *Cf.* CURT

Curtal axe. *See* CUTLASS

Curtana. The blunt sword carried at the coronation of the monarch symbolising justice without vengefulness: having no point was a sign of mercy. It is sometimes referred to as the sword of Edward the Confessor. [< L *curtus* = cut short] – *Cf.* ARMES COURTOISES; CURT

Curval [curvent]. *Her.* Curved or bowed.

Custom house. A house or shop which beggars used to visit in hope of alms; these became their customary or usual stopping places.

Customary [custumal]. Legal document itemising such things as the duties of a *reeve on a particular estate; also those of other manorial officers. Such documents were closely associated with the estate's *extent. Cathedrals also had such a document; this was referred to as a *consuetudinary. The Latin form *custumarium*.

Custos armorum regis. Lit. 'guardian of the king's arms'. Phrase used in the records as the title of the clerk charged with the administration of the king's armouries.

Custumarius [consuetus]. Latin term for a customary tenant who was able to supply a man or more to perform those labour services required from his lord. – *Cf.* CONSUETUDINARIUS

Cutlass [curtlace, curtaxe]. A short, heavy sword, curved, somewhat like a machete, used by sailors; particularly apt for slashing or close fighting on a ship's deck.

Cuvata [cofata]. Latin form of cuve = a cask/quantity of beer. [< L *cupa* = vat, cask]

Cwalstow. A place of execution. These were designated, as were all highways, as being wholly within the king's own jurisdiction, rather than, say, a sheriff's. The Latin = *qualstowa* is found in *LHP.

Cyfraith Hywel. Lit. 'the law of Hywel'. Hywel Dda, king of Dyfed, later also of Gwynedd and Powys (d. 950), is credited with the codification of Welsh law. The earliest extant text is a 13c Latin version.

Cygnet royal. *Her.* A swan with a coronet around its throat, i.e. *gorged. A chain also hangs from the coronet.

Cymorth. Payments made by Welsh tenants of the English marcher lords; such payments were made in cattle.

Cymyd. Welsh word for a *commote.

Cynebot. The penalty or compensation for the death of a king. [< OE *cyne* = king + *bot* = compensation] – *Cf.* BOT

Cynedom. The king's dignity, his kingliness; kingly rule or government.

Cynges geneat. Lit. 'the king's companion'. A leading member of the royal household, with a *wergeld* the same as a king's *thegn*. – *Cf.* COMITATUS; GENEAT

Cyning. OE for king. Its ON cognate *konungr* is found in such placenames as Conington (Cambs), Conisborough and Coningsby.

Cynocephalus. Creature much like a human being save for its head, which was that of a dog. Such monsters decorated the margins of *illuminated MSS. – *Cf.* BABEWYN; BESTIARY

D

Dagger. The knife we know but in the 14c the word was slang, 'a word of the vulgar tongue'. Henry Knighton (d. 1396) described in quiet shock the appearance of several ladies at a *tournament, all dressed brightly as men, with daggers 'across their bellies in a pouch'. [< OFr. *dague* = a long point]

Dalmatic. Vestment of a bishop with distinctive wide sleeves; also worn by monarchs; part of the *regalia of royalty established by the Holy Roman Emperor, using the Church as an authenticating power. [< OFr. *dalmatique* = (made of wool) from Dalmatia] – *Cf.* ORB; SCEPTRE 1

Damask. An elaborately decorated silk fabric. Orig. used of materials from Damascus.

Dame. French title ascribed to a knight's or baronet's wife; the female equivalent of *sieur* or Sir; a title of rank and dignity. Later the title was given to the wife of a man of lower rank than a knight: a respectable woman of modest means, the mistress of a house, e.g. used by an apprentice of his master's wife. The French used the word for the Virgin, i.e. Notre Dame. Chaucer uses the word 'Of the Emperor's daughter, dame Custance'. – *Cf.* DAMOISELLE

Damoiselle. Old French title for an unmarried woman, and also for the wife of a *squire, the rank immediately below that of a knight. The word has been anglicised as 'damsel'. Less familiar is *damoiseau*, the male equivalent of *damoiselle*: a young man of good birth, not yet a knight's *esquire. – *Cf.* DAME

Dance of Death [danse macabre]. An allegory expressed in literary and visual representations showing death taking the high- and the low-born in procession towards the grave. The idea was probably given impetus by the *Black Death of 1348.

Danegeld. In the late 11c and 12c, the term for the pre-Conquest *heregeld, levied 1012–51 to pay the *lithesmen of the king's fleet. After 1066, the term was used of a general tax. 'Danegeld' is also used in modern history for the tribute paid to *Viking armies, esp. those paid by Æthelred II (the Unready). Huge sums of money were paid: in three payments, Æthelred handed over something like 94,000 lb of silver. (On one occasion some 20 million silver coins were handed over by Cnut to his army.) In 1155–6 Henry II collected the last Danegeld. – *Cf.* UNRÆD

Danelaw [Danelagh, Denalagu]. That part of England (roughly) north of Watling Street subject to Danish invaders from the 9c to 954. This comprised the kingdom of York and the *Five Boroughs where Scandinavian legal customs were in force.

Dapifer. Word used for a senior servant or *steward in a royal or baronial household. He would be known in the records as e.g. *dapifer regis* = king's steward. A 12c dapifer was a senior member of his lord's household, present at councils and meetings involving the *manor or *honour. Royal duties were in the king's hall, which at this time was the central room of the household (as with magnates' establishments) where most time was spent and meals were taken. – *Cf. next;* PINCERNA; SEWER; STEWARD

Dapiferatus. Latin word for stewardship. – *Cf. previous*

Darrein presentment. In the 12c, *canon law provided that if a benefice were vacant for six months, the bishop could place someone without consultation. The *darrein* writ summoned a jury to determine who had the *advowson and had nominated the last holder of the *benefice. [< AN *darrein* = last]

Daub. *See* WATTLE

Dauphin. Title of the eldest son of the king of France, heir to the French throne; used from 1349. [< *Dauphiné* = province of SE France, centred around Vienne on the Rhône.]

Daybell. During the 13c and 14c, a bell was sounded to indicate the opening of the market. – *Cf.* CURFEW

De donis. Lit. 'concerning gifts'. One of the chapters of the Second Statute of Westminster, 1285. It was an attempt to prevent land which had been given to younger sons or daughters being alienated. It stipulated that this could happen only after the third generation. Should they not survive until the fourth, the land reverted to the main line of inheritance. – *Cf.* ALIENATION; ENFEOFFMENT TO USE; QUIA EMPTORES, STATUTE OF

De haeretico comburendo. Lit. 'on the burning of heretics'. This statute of 1401 determined that heretics, having been convicted of heresy by a spiritual court and subsequently refusing to recant, were to be handed over to the secular authorities to be burned at the stake. It was inspired by the authoritarian Archbishop Arundel; few were actually burned at the stake, however. Between 1401 and 1485 there were only 11 such cruel executions. – *Cf.* CONSTANCE, COUNCIL OF

De intendendo. Lit. 'to be attended to, to be observed'. A writ of *chancery issued in the king's name on the appointment of a bishop. It was addressed to a see's tenants informing them of the restoration of *temporalities to the bishop – which in the hiatus between bishops would have been taken by the crown.

De Legibus et Consuetudinibus Angliae. *Concerning the Laws and Customs of the English*. This work is ascribed to Henry *Bracton (d. 1268) and has as distinguished a place in English law as the *Tractatus de Legibus*. There are some 50 MSS extant.

De mutuo faciendo. Lit. 'about obtaining loans (of money)'. During Henry VI's reign the crown was heavily in debt; indeed it owed twice its annual revenue. Commissions *de mutuo faciendo* were despatched around the country to raise money from those thought to be wealthy enough to oblige the king, which might be as many as 400. During Henry VI's reign 17 such commissions were sent out. However, they rarely raised much.

De scutagio habendo. Lit. 'concerning receipt of *scutage'. A writ authorising a lord to take scutage money from the knights holding of him by way of recompense for the money he, the lord, had paid the king by *servitium debitum*.

Deal. A division or part; also a share of something. [< OE *dæl*] – *Cf.* FARTHINGDEAL

Death's head. *Her.* Term used of a human skull when placed over the coat of *arms of a man who had died and was last of his line.

Debased. *Her.* Turned upside down.

Decania. Latin term for a *tithing or *frank-pledge group.

Decimation. Orig. a punishment imposed by the Romans in which one in 10 was killed. A word used of the extravagant distribution of 10 per cent of his lands by King Æthelwulf in 854 to the Church and his *thegns before going on pilgrimage to Rome. Kings were expected to be generous; they also expected something in return, usually loyalty. Decimation was also used in referring to *tithes. – *Cf.* DIME

Decrescent. *Her.* Term used of a crescent whose horns point towards the *sinister.

Decretal. Document or epistle issued by the pope concerning a specific issue or point of doctrine; also a collection of decrees. The best-known such gathering of the time was Gratian's *Decretum.* – *Cf.* CANON LAW

Decuria. A group of 10, sometimes known as a 'decurion', a term used of people and soldiers. Bede used the word when referring to *decuriae* of *slaves. – *Cf.* CENTENER; VINTINARY

Deer-leap. A ditch around a forest or hunting-ground which prevented animals from escaping.

Degree. A man's degree was his rank or station in the medieval world. Magnates disputed precedence at the highest level in the king's household, when the higher ranked had better access to the king. Degree determined where one sat at the king's table – if one sat there at all. At the beginning of the General Prologue of the *Canterbury Tales* Chaucer says that he will describe his pilgrims' 'degree and condition'. He apologises if he has not described them in the 'degree . . . as that they should stand'. – *Cf.* THREE ORDERS

Dei gracia. Lit. 'by the grace of God'. A phrase used in the style of English monarchs in writs and charters. It was first used by Henry II in 1172.

Demesne. Property owned freely; land held for the lord's own use rather than let or leased. This land would have been worked for the lord by his serfs, occupying between a fifth and a third of the land available. It was likely that this *manor was the *caput honoris.* Held by a lord of the manor, such property could be passed on to descendants. It is another way of spelling *domain. [< L *dominus* = lord] – *Cf. next;* MESNE

Demesne farming. Particularly common in the 13c, the phrase refers to the practice of a lord farming his land himself, using his villeins, rather than renting it out. A *bailiff would be responsible to his lord for all profits of a *manor. When prices were high, such self-management was advantageous, esp. with free labour; however, at times of uncertainty, a fixed annual sum had merits. – *Cf. previous*

Denarius. Orig. a Roman silver coin; its name was revived by Pepin *c.*755. It was adopted by the English, and named a *penny; the d abbreviation was retained in English coinage until decimalisation (1971). – *Cf.* SOLIDUS

Dene [denn]. A small valley, wooded and with a small stream. Such woodland was used as pasture for swine. In time some became villages as swineherds built themselves wooden shelters, cutting timber for fuel. The forest of Dean is a modern use of the word.

Denizen. Term applied to an *alien *priory in England independent of its mother-house overseas, i.e. in France.

Deo gratias. Lit. 'thanks be to God'. A phrase frequently found in the Latin liturgy. In Benedictine houses, *Deo gratias* was said by the gatekeeper whenever a visitor was given entrance. Sometimes the abbr. DG is found.

Deorhege. Lit. 'deer hedge'. The service owed by a *thegn of maintaining the hedge-fence around a royal residence. It was to ensure that deer did not stray but remained in the forest for the king to hunt.

Derring-do. Lit. 'daring to do'. The phrase is perhaps taken – and slightly misused – from a line in Geoffrey Chaucer's *Troilus and Criseyde*.

Destrier. The war horse or charger used by knights, who might campaign with as many as four *destriers*. They were large beasts, strong enough to carry a man in armour. *Destriers* were trained not to shy when jousting at a *tilt, nor in a full charge against a real enemy. A fully trained *destrier* lost in battle would be worth £20 or more in *restauratio equorum*. Superior mounts could be worth as much as £100. For example, a grey bought for Edward III in 1331 cost £120, while Richard II rode to his coronation on a charger worth £200. The Latin term for such an animal was *dextrarius*. [AN < L *dexter* = right-hand side; the knight's *squire led the war horse with his right hand.] – *Cf.* CABALLUS; COOPERTUS; PALFREY; ROUNCY; SOMIER

Detecta. Lit. '(things) detected'. *Detecta* were wrongs found during a bishop's *visitation. – *Cf.* COMPERTA; SECRETE ET SINGILLATIM

Detractari. Dry clerk's Latin term for a grim mode of execution: each of the victim's limbs was attached to one of four horses, which were driven in different directions, pulling the victim apart. [< L *de* + *traho* = to draw, to pull]

Device [devise]. A person's will or intention. – *Cf.* DEVISE

Devise. To distribute or divide, used in particular of property in a person's will. Thus an inheritor is devised land in another's will. The word is used in the rather sad will of Edward VI (d. 1553), which is headed 'My devise for the succession' and opens with the words 'For lakke of issu (masle) of my body' [< L *divido* = to divide] – *Cf.* DEVICE

Dexter. *Her.* The right-hand side. In *heraldry, left and right are determined from the holder of a shield's point of view, not from the onlooker's. Thus dexter is the viewer's left. – *Cf.* DESTRIER; SINISTER

Dialogue of the Exchequer. *See next*

Dialogus de Scaccario. *Dialogue of the Exchequer.* A description of the exchequer in the 12c, written *c.*1179 by Henry II's treasurer, Richard fitz-Nigel. It is the earliest first-hand work showing the functioning of medieval administration.

Diaper. The diamond or square patterning frequently used as background in medieval design, e.g. in stained glass; also incised or cut in low relief. The term derives from a textile woven in such a way as to produce a recurring diamond pattern.

Dicker. A gathering of 10 skins or gloves. In the 14c, the Latin *decenna* = a group of 10. [< L *decuria* = group of 10] – *Cf.* DIME

Dictatus papae. Lit. 'dictates of the pope'. A list of brief statements by Pope Gregory VII (1073–85), being papal claims of authority. They asserted that the spiritual authority of the pope was greater than that of temporal kingship.

Dies cinerum. Lit. 'day of ashes'. Latin for 'Ash Wednesday'.

Difference, marks of. *Her.* These are the same as marks of *cadency.

Diffidatio. Lit. 'defiance'. A statement in which allegiance to a lord was renounced and that renunciation justified. Such a statement was the only way by which the break from a lord could legally be accomplished. In 1138, Robert, earl of Gloucester, sent his *diffidatio* to King Stephen 'according to ancient usage, [and] renounced his fealty and friendship, and annulled his homage'. Gloucester was breaking with Stephen for the latter's breach of promise and oath to acknowledge Matilda as true heir of Henry I, as Henry demanded before his death (1135). At the deposition of Edward II in January 1327 Sir William Trussell verbally renounced all homage and allegiance to Edward in person, *ex parte tocius regni* (on behalf of the whole realm). The *steward of the household, Sir Thomas Blount, broke his staff of office, declaring the royal household defunct. – *Cf.* HOMAGE 1

Dime. A tenth part. Edward III was granted a dime and a fifteenth by parliament in 1332, as was Richard II in 1398. The word was spelt *disme*, reflecting the pervasive French influence in English. [< L *decima* = tenth] – *Cf.* DECIMATION

Diocese. The district over which a bishop has jurisdiction and for which he is responsible to an archbishop. This term is taken from its use during Diocletian's reign (284–305), when the Roman Empire was divided into 12 dioceses. [< L *dioecesis* = a governor's jurisdiction]

Dirige. First word of the Office of the Dead: *Dirige, Domine, Deus meus, in conspectu tuo viam meam* = 'Direct my path, Lord, my God, in your sight'. The English form is 'dirge'. – *Cf.* PLACEBO

Disafforestation. The removal of the legal status of land as forest. Although

Henry II was still afforesting land, this changed in his reign's latter years. Permission was given to change land's legal status for a *fine. Henry's sons, Richard I and John, both allowed extensive changes – for suitable fines. Indeed, it was not uncommon for groups of freemen and knights to come together and contribute to the king's fine for large tracts of land. In 1204 Cornwall and Devon were disafforested; Middlesex followed in 1227, while in 1230 it was the turn of the forest of Kesteven in Lincolnshire. All were freed for suitable fines. – Cf. AFFORESTATION; CHASE

Disarmed. *Her.* With no teeth or claws (of an animal) or lacking a beak (of a bird). – Cf. MORNE 2

Discthegn. Lit. 'dish-*thegn*'. An AS *steward. One of the many ranks and degrees of *thegn* which had developed by the end of the AS period. [< OE *disc* = a dish or bowl + *thegn*] – Cf. SENESCHAL

Disour. A storyteller or minstrel. [< Fr. *disant* = talking]

Disparage. A marriage between unequals in rank was disparaging; such a marriage involved dishonour and/or disgrace. *Bracton says of an heir in wardship: 'A lord may give the heir in marriage when and where he wishes, provided [the heir] is not disparaged.' Later, *Magna Carta states explicitly: 'Heirs shall be married without disparagement'. [< OFr. *desparage* < *dis-* = a negative lack + *parage* = equality]

Disseisin. The act of dispossessing someone of their goods. – Cf. DISTRAIN; SEISIN

Distaff. Orig. a stick or staff with a V cut in one end from which flax or wool would be drawn in the spinning process. From this, the distaff became a symbol of women's work, and of women in general. – Cf. PER COLOS; TOW

Distemper. An imbalance of the bodily *humours, resulting in a harmful state; in human beings illness.

Distrain. To force a person to do something or act out an obligation under threat of being dispossessed. – Cf. *next*; DISSEISIN, DISTRESS; DISTRINGAS

Distraint of knighthood. The attempt, introduced by Henry III, to compel the holder of land worth £20 or more to accept a knighthood. Edward III did the same in 1278. It was a means of increasing royal revenue. However, many sought to evade the ordinance. It also resulted in a diminution of the chivalric ideal of a knight by making qualification a matter of money. – Cf. *previous and next*

Distress. The seizing of a person's *chattels in order to force payment of a debt or obligation; this legal sense is also known as 'distraint'. – Cf. *previous*; DISSEISIN

Distringas. Lit. 'thou shalt distrain'. The first word of a writ for a sheriff to *distrain someone.

Dock. Bakers were required to mark every loaf they baked with a mark, or *hallmark, known as 'dock'. The mark or sign was issued by the Bakers' Guild, as goldsmiths were issued with a hallmark.

Dole. Orig. a portion of something divided, a person's share of something; thus a part of a common field; later, in the 14c, also the distribution of charity, i.e. the doling out of charity.

Dom. Doom, judgement, opinion. – *Cf.* Domboc

Domain. Land or property which could be inherited. Eminent domain = the monarch's sovereignty over all property within the realm. [< L *dominus* = lord] – *Cf.* Demesne; Dominion directum

Domboc. Doom book, i.e. book of laws. This term is sometimes used of the laws of Alfred the Great, now extant only in 12c compilations of OE law. – *Cf. Leges Henrici Primi*

Domesday Book. Compiled from the records of royal commissioners who in the summer of 1086 toured England to discover for King William I just what he had conquered and how much it was worth. The decision was made at Gloucester during the Christmas court of 1085. To its makers *DB* was known as *Descriptio*, a description. Sometimes it was referred to as *Liber de Wintonia*. It listed land and possessions: who owned what and what tax or dues were paid in 1066 (the end of Edward the Confessor's reign) and at the time of examination. All information was given on oath. However, it was by no means inclusive of every place in England. The findings were set out *county by county, though the north-east (later Northumberland and Durham) and much of the north-west (later Cumberland and Westmorland) were not surveyed; only parts of the border country of Wales were examined. Furthermore, several large towns were not included, e.g. London, Winchester and Bristol. The descriptions of Norfolk, Suffolk and Essex appear in a separate volume, *Little Domesday*. When finished *DB* had 382 folios, making 764 sides of writing; it had required the skins of 200 or more sheep. *Little Domesday* had 450 folios. *DB* was sometimes referred to as *liber hidarum* = the book of hides (the *hide being the basic unit of land used in its compilation). The name *Domesday Book* is to be found in the *Dialogus de scaccario*: 'This book is called by the natives Domesday; that is, by metaphor, the day of judgement . . . when the book is appealed to its sentence cannot be scorned or avoided with impunity.' – *Cf. previous*; TRE

Dominica in albis. Lit. 'the Lord's day in white'. On the first Sunday of Easter, it was customary for the newly baptised to be dressed in white. [< L *dominicus* = a lord, thus God + *in albis* = in white] – *Cf.* Chrism; Whitsun

Dominicans. The order founded by St Dominic (1170–1221) in 1215, named the Order of Friars Preachers. They were known as the Black Friars or the preaching friars. Some Dominicans were mendicants, dedicated to evangelical preaching. They were very active in combating heresy. They also placed emphasis upon learning, which they considered necessary to preach intelligently and for rational theological debate, always preferring to convert by persuasion. In 1219 King Alexander of Scotland met St Dominic in Paris and requested him to send some members of his brotherhood to Scotland. However, they came first to England in 1221. Their emphasis on education meant the Dominicans were deeply involved in the growth of universities.

Dominion directum. Lit. 'direct lordship or direct *domain'. The ownership of property without having use of it. This was the relationship of the king to land held by his barons: all land was the king's but others had tenure and use. [< L *dominus* = lord + *directum* = direct, immediate]

Domus fenestrae. Lit. 'the house of windows or the window house'. This building in a *Gilbertine double monastery was between the male and female houses, intended to keep the sexes separate. It contained windows through which they communicated. – *Cf.* CLAUSURA; FENESTRA PARVULA; MAGNA FENESTRA VERSATILIS

Domus regis. Lit. 'household of the king'. The officer core of the *familia regis*, also that at the heart of government. It members comprised the *chancellor, *constable, *chamberlain and master-marshal. Other members were barons and those who followed royal instructions without having titles. Some of these would be known as *princeps militiae* = leader of the knights. *Domus regis* = household of the king, as does *familia regis*, but *domus* carries the more personal sense of home; its officers being in closer touch with the king. – *Cf.* COMITATUS; PENTEULU

Dona. These gifts were extracted as extras by the *exchequer from some towns and boroughs, the larger towns in most counties. [< L *donum* = gift]

Donatus. A child whose parents have promised him to a monastery at a later date. – *Cf.* OBLATE

Donet. A book of elementary instruction of e.g. *Latin, or other subjects. The term is derived from Aelius Donatus, author of *Ars Grammatica*, a 4c Latin grammar.

Donjon. A well-defended tower, or tower-like structure placed centrally within a castle, designed for strength in defence; the *keep of a castle, from which comes dungeon.

Doom. A law, ordinance or statute; then a sentence pronounced; also the Last Judgement. [< OE *dom* = a law, ordinance or statute] – *Cf.* DOM

Dordrecht bonds. In 1337 Edward III, in an attempt to raise funds for his war with France, sought to create a monopoly for the export of all wool from England. To this end, he created a syndicate of merchants through which the demand for English wool on the continent might be satisfied, while gaining revenue for himself. One result was the reduction in exports, another the expansion of cloth making in England itself. The scheme disintegrated in failure in 1338. At Dordrecht, Edward took control of all the wool stored there, offering the merchants bonds as a means of temporary compensation, before settlement at a later date. However, the merchants sold their bonds at a discount and relations between king and wool merchants deteriorated. A combination of greed, need and bad faith sabotaged the scheme wrought in the king's desperation for amounts of money beyond the country's ability to expend on war.

Dormant. *Her.* Term used of the figure of an animal lying with head on paws.

Dormitorii necessaria. *See* RERE-DORTER

Dormitorium. *See* DORTER

Dorse. The cover of a *codex; the beginning part of a *parchment roll; also the back of a parchment sheet, hence 'endorsement' = [something written] on the back. [< L *dorsum* = back]

Dorter [dortour]. The dormitory in a monastery.

Dottrell. A small plover, one of the water fowl favoured by 15c and 16c nobility.

Dower. That portion of a dead man's property left to his widow; customarily one third. A dower house was a small house built on an estate for a widow, e.g. when the son had inherited and his mother moved out of the main house. This use of 'dower' is not to be confused with that of the late 15c for a rabbit's burrow. – *Cf.* JOINTURE

Dragetum. *See* DREDGE

Dragium. *See* DREDGE

Dragon. *Her.* The dragon was an imaginary heraldic animal, much used, but not so often as the *griffin. It was always shown *rampant, with the head of a serpent and forked tongue; it also had ears, which snakes do not possess. Dragons' bodies and legs were always scaled; wings were webbed, like those of a bat; feet were taloned. – *Cf.* BESTIARY; OPINICUS

Dredge. A mix of grains sown together, i.e. oats and barley. Latin forms include *dragium* and *dragetum*.

Dreng. Term for a lord of a small *manor, who was free except for some duties of military service; it was used primarily in Northumbria. [< ON *drengr* = brave man] – *Cf.* SOKEMAN

Dromond. Large medieval ship, used in peace for trade but also serviceable in time of war. It was the largest sailing vessel of the 14c.

Dryhten [drihten]. An AS lord or war-lord; also used of God.

Dub. The action of conferring a knighthood by the touch of a sword; to invest with a dignity or a new title. The ceremony was part of the world of homage and lordship, the dubbing being done by a lord. At the ceremony, the new knight was given the arms and weapons appropriate to his new status. The AN word for the ceremony was *adoubement. [< OE *dubbian* = to knight by tapping the shoulder; OFr. *adouber* = to equip with armour and accessories] – *Cf.* CINGULUM MILITARE

Ducking-stool. Although descriptively apt, this may be a rhyming euphemism and polite form of *cuck-stool.

Dud [duds]. Coarse woollen cloth distributed to the poor. From this we have our sense of something worthless or unsatisfactory.

Duellum. The duel between *champions was introduced into England by the Normans; before then the Church in England had sufficient authority to prevent it. The *duellum* was the final recourse of two sides unable to resolve an argument. (This civil duel was far from the duel of honour, which persisted in Europe until the 19c.) Abbeys were not averse to hiring a champion; some even paid a man a nominal retainer to stay on the books. *Tirones* were also used for such occasions. The champion would have agreed a contract with his employer – this after the 12c, when champions were supposed to be witnesses of the cause they fought for. Such drastic solutions were a last resort in the certainty that God would not permit the party with justice on its side to lose. Thus the *duellum* was a *judicium Dei*, an ordeal subject to God's judgement. For a champion to be killed was not unknown; however, after *ictus regis*, the sides might come to an agreement to end the duel (*concordia per finem duelli*) before bloodshed or loss of life. Eventually, all came to agree duels were unseemly and undignified, for both churchmen and laymen. By the 14c, all such civil disputes were being settled in the courts of law. – *Cf.* CRAVEN; RECREANTIA; TRIAL BY COMBAT

Duguth. Mature warriors who had served in their lord's household and been rewarded with land on which to establish their own household. – *Cf.* GEOGUTH

Duke. A chief or ruler, after Roman usage, which referred to a military commander as *dux*. Now it is the highest rank of hereditary title of nobility, next below a prince (who is next below the monarch). The title was used in France, e.g. William I was duke of Normandy. The first English duke in this sense was Edward the Black Prince, created duke of Cornwall in 1337. The creation of the title was part of an imitation of the French court and its elaborate peerage. Four more dukes were created by Edward III, all members of the royal family. By the beginning of the 16c there were some 45 dukes. [< L *dux* = leader] – *Cf.* Dux; GARTER, ORDER OF THE

Dulcimer. A musical instrument played by striking its strings of differing lengths with a hammer. [< L *dulcis* = sweet + *melos* = a song or melody] – *Cf.* PSALTERY

Dun. An Irish fortified dwelling. – *Cf.* BURH; PELE TOWER

Dunce. The word is formed after the name of John Duns Scotus, 13c theologian. His views fell into great disfavour in England during the Reformation, esp. his defence of the papacy. The epithet 'Dunsman', first used by William Tyndale (d. 1536), became in time 'dunce', a word of abuse, suggesting ignorance and stupidity. The word's vector from scholar to ignoramus is intriguing.

Dux. This was the usual Latin term for the OE *ealdorman*. – *Cf.* DUKE

Dwale. An analgesic potion used to render a patient insensible. It was a mixture of henbane, hemlock and opium, each of which could have been fatal if unskilfully administered. Most hospitals and infirmaries had herb gardens and traditions of use were passed down. – *Cf.* EMPIRIC

Dyling. The practice of dividing large fields into strips of arable or pasture by wide ditches.

E

Eaffor. Tenant's obligation to perform carrying services for the king; also a draught horse. – *Cf.* AVER; GENEAT

Eald Seaxe. The old, continental *Saxons.

Ealdorman. Noble of the highest social rank in AS England, appointed by the king to govern a *shire.

Earl 1. A nobleman of the highest rank, until the title of *duke was created. [< OE *eorl* = noble] – *Cf.* EORLCUND

Earl 2. A Scandinavian commander; royal officer equivalent to *ealdorman*; the title replaced that of *ealdorman* in the 11c. [< ON *jarl* = nobleman, leader]

Earl Marshal, Court of the. The Court of the Earl Marshal of England was by the 14c a court with jurisdiction over a wide range of military matters, such as discipline in the army, treason, also prisoners of war and disputed heraldic arms. What remains is the jurisdiction over heraldic arms according to the law of arms. The title of Earl Marshal is now hereditary in the line of the dukes of Norfolk.

Easement room [chamber of easement]. A privy or latrine. Euphemisms are perennial: today an American equivalent of 'easement room' is 'comfort station'. – *Cf.* LONGAIGNE; STOOL-ROOM

Easter. The most solemn Christian festival, which celebrates the resurrection of Jesus Christ. It is a movable feast: its date each year is determined by the phases of the moon, i.e. the first Sunday after the first full moon of the vernal equinox. There had been controversy about its determination, dividing the Celtic (i.e. Irish) and Roman churches, but this was settled for England at the *Synod of *Whitby in 664. [< OE *Eostre* = goddess of spring] – *Cf.* TONSURE

Easterlings. The word was first used of coins *c*.13c. Later, the name was given to merchants of the Hanse in London. – *Cf.* HANSEATIC LEAGUE; -LING; STERLING

Ecce homo. Lit. 'behold the man'. Pontius Pilate's words on presenting Christ to the crowd, after which Christ was whipped and scourged. The moment is to be found in John 19:5: 'Then came Jesus forth, wearing the crown of thorns, and the purple robe. And Pilate saith unto them "Behold the man!"' It became a moment frequently depicted in medieval art.

Eccles. A church. Its Celtic use indicates a Christian population and some survival in Derbyshire and elsewhere. [< L *ecclesia* = church]

Ecclesiastical courts. Civil, common law and canon law were different legal systems co-existing uncomfortably; some way had to be found to permit co-existence. From the 12c, the *clergy had a privilege of belonging to the jurisdiction of the ecclesiastical courts. By the 13c, these courts had come to exercise jurisdiction over a great range of matters we might consider the province of civil law. For instance, the ecclesiastical courts had jurisdiction over marriage and legitimacy, and in the matter of wills and church land outside the feudal system. They also had the power to interpret bequests of personal estates and to settle disputes over wills, and to impose punishment of mortal sins and breaches of faith. Grants of probate and even the behaviour and actions of executors were under these courts' purview. Furthermore these Church courts dealt with any member of the Church, from the lowliest deacon or clerk, who committed an offence. Conflict between crown and Church over these courts arose from the fact that offenders in Church courts were deemed not properly punished: a murderer in a royal court would be mutilated or heavily fined, in a Church court a cleric would be defrocked – that being the severest penalty an ecclesiastical court could impose. – *Cf.* BENEFIT OF CLERGY; CANON LAW

Échorcheurs. Lit. 'skinners'. One of the bands of *mercenaries or ex-soldiers who, during the last period of the *Hundred Years' War, plundered and ravaged France. – *Cf.* ROUTIERS

Écranché shield. A kind of shield used in *jousts of peace, rather than of war when the shield was triangular. The *ecranché* was oval with a portion removed on its right to limit hindrance to the lance, which was held by the right arm across the body.

Eels. Eels were an important part of the fenland economy, being bred in ponds attached to monasteries and caught in rivers. At Wisbech, fishermen rendered 37,000 eels to the abbot of Ely, Bury, Ramsey and Crowland. They are the origin of Ely's name. [< OE *æl* = eel] – *Cf.* STICHA

Eigne. *See* AYNE

Eisteddfod. Assembly of minstrels and poets in competition; the first recorded such assembly was in 1176 at the castle at Cardigan. It is uncertain whether this event was inspired by similar meetings under the patronage of Eleanor of Aquitaine. Norman influence in Wales by this time was sufficient to have been a conduit for such ideas.

Eleanor crosses. King Edward I's queen, Eleanor of Castile, died at Harby, in Nottinghamshire, in December 1290. Over the following three or four years, the journey from Harby to her burial place in Westminster Abbey was marked by 12 stone crosses the king caused to be built at each place the cortège had rested. They were at Lincoln, Grantham, Stamford, Geddington, Hardingstone, Stony Stratford, Woburn, Dunstable, St Albans, Waltham, West Cheap, *Charing Cross. Sadly, only three are left: at Waltham, Geddington and at Hardingstone (Northampton). At Waltham the cross is of Caen stone, finished by a crocketed spirelet and cross, and is supposed to have been designed by Pietro Cavallini, a Roman sculptor.

Eleemosyna carucarum. Lit. 'plough alms'. The penny given at Easter for each plough within a village. – *Cf.* CARUCA

Elegantia morum. Lit. 'elegance of manners, fashion'. The term points to those qualities necessary for a courtier and a sophistication of manners and behaviour: conduct should be moderate and affable, self-effacing but always competent. These qualities first appeared in Germany after Charlemagne's reign in the 8c: that example was admired and much copied, as Charlemagne himself had been. It was incipient *chivalry, a style established at court but widely copied beyond. – *Cf.* CURIALIS

Elements. In the ancient world there were four elements: earth, water, air, fire. In alchemy the three basic elements were salt, sulphur and mercury. – *Cf.* HUMOURS

Elixir. Something which alchemists believed would turn metals to gold; also *elixir vitae* = the elixir of life. [< Ar *al-iksir* = a powder for wounds, used as a desiccant] – *Cf.* QUINTESSENCE

Ell. A standard length of 45 inches, used of cloth; a ruler of that length was known as an 'ell-wand'. This measure applied only in England; in Flanders the equivalent measure was somewhat over half the English, i.e. 27 inches. – *Cf.* AULNAGE

Embattle. To make ready for a battle or war; to take up battle positions; to fortify a town; later to provide or add battlements to a castle, to *crenellate. It is a specific form of fortifying.

Ember days. Four groups of three days in the Church calendar during which fasting was observed, i.e. Wednesday, Friday and Saturday following the first Sunday in Lent, *Pentecost, Holy Cross Day (14 September), St Lucy's Day (13 December). Ember Week was one in which Ember days occurred. [< OE *ymbren, ymbryne* = course, anniversary]

Emblazon. *Her.* The description of a coat of *arms. As a verb it means to display armorial bearings, also to decorate something, such as a shield, with arms. – *Cf.* BLAZON

Emblem. *See* COGNISANCE

Embowed [flected]. *Her.* Bent, e.g. a man's arm, often used also of dolphins.

Embracery. The attempt to influence a jury or a member of a jury illicitly. Bribery was a form of embracery. [< AN, OFr. *embraseor* = instigator] – *Cf.* CHAMPERTY

Embrasure. The space or gap between *merlons which widens towards the outside, thus a V without the angle.

Emerald. *Her.* English equivalent of the *tincture *vert. – *Cf.* SMARAGD

Empiric. A doctor learned his trade empirically, without using either Hippocrates or Galen. He might be a cleric, monk or layman, perhaps even a barber-surgeon. – *Cf.* DWALE

Emption. At first, the act of buying (1461) was correlative of *venditio* = the act of selling; later, a tax levied on bullion and plate sold in the king's exchange.

En arrière. *Her.* The formal term used of a charge shown flying away from the viewer, wings spread.

Enarmes. Straps on the back of a shield by which it was held in place. – *Cf.* GUIGE

Enceinte. The enclosed main space of, or the wall which encloses, a fortified place. 'Enceinte' is also used of that area of a town enclosed by its walls. Thus, while the Tower of London was within the city of London's walls, the palace of Westminster was well without the enceinte. [< L *incingo* = to gird]

Endemot. A term specific to the Scottish border country, Cumberland and Westmorland. It was a military obligation to fight the Scots which excluded any other military duty.

Endole. *Her.* The vertical divider of a shield, one eighth of a *pale, also one quarter.

Endorsed. *Her.* Term referring to the wings of a bird or hybrid animal which are thrown back, the tips of which are almost touching. The term 'sepurture' is a synonym.

Enfeoff. To put a person in possession of land in *fee simple. Thus a *tenant-in-chief would enfeoff subtenants (this was known as *'subinfeudation') who would be required to provide the knightly services which the tenant-in-chief was in turn required to bring to the king, as a part of his tenure. – *Cf.* FEUDAL-ISM; VASSAL

Enfeoffment to use. A legal procedure by which a landowner granted land to another person on the understanding that the grantee would do what the original owner instructed. It was a means of bypassing legislation which under certain circumstances restricted the bequeathing of freehold property, e.g. *entail. 'Enfeoffment to use' came under the purview of the *chancery. The phrase was sometimes abbreviated to 'in use' or 'the use', while the procedure itself was also known as *Cestui-que-use*. – *Cf.* ENTAIL; JOINTURE

English. From the time of the Conquest, England was a tri-lingual country. French was the language both of court and of the baronage, while French and Latin were used among the literate and educated clerics, Latin being the language of records and documents. English continued to be used by the majority of the population. During the *Barons' War, an English party emerged, resenting non-English favourites at court, and English was used for administrative purposes. However, without French, there was no possibility of advancement, social or political. But during the middle years of the 14c things began to change. John Trevisa said in 1385 'children leave French and learn in English'. The first piece of parliamentary English is a petition of the *mercers to parliament in 1386. English was the first language of Henry IV, who took the throne in 1399. Henry IV's will is the earliest king's will in English since the Conquest. Its first words are, 'I, Henry, sinful wretch'. In turn, Henry

V conducted all business in English: he used it in much written correspondence. His letters are also the earliest letters of a monarch in his own hand to survive. A note in the London Brewers' Company's records sets down their future use of the *vernacular, rather than French, following the king's (Henry V's) own use and insistence. They noted that English had begun 'to be honourably enlarged and adorned'. – *Cf.* FRANCIGENARE; PLEADING, STATUTE OF

Englishry. The English as distinct from the Normans, esp. in law; also later, the English inhabitants of Ireland. – *Cf.* FRENCH

Engoulant. *Cf. next;* VORANT

Engouled. *Her.* Used of a *charge entering a mouth, e.g. a cross being swallowed by an animal. – *Cf.* VORANT

Engrailed. *Her.* Describes the pattern of indentations on a *bar across a shield; this pattern looks like a series of the letter U, with sharp upward points. The Latin form was *engrallatus*. – *Cf.* INVECTED

Engrallatus. *See previous*

Engross 1. Orig. to buy up a large quantity of goods, preventing others from buying, thus to 'corner a market'. This was regularly forbidden in *assizes.

Engross 2. Orig. to make a copy in a large fair hand. Later, to make a copy of record, or to enter a formal document.

Enhanced. *Her.* A *charge shown higher on the shield than usual for such a charge, such as a *bendlet.

Enrolment. Term used for the practice of registering all documents which left *chancery; a practice instigated by Hubert Walter, *chancellor to King John.

Ensign. *Her.* To make a sign; to mark a shield with a distinctive badge, as a bishop might use a mitre.

Entail [fee tail]. The settling of property, i.e. a landed estate, on a descendant in such a way that the land could not be broken up subsequently when passed on again. It was the epitome of a landed aristocracy's interest: to maintain its great estates intact through primogeniture. – *Cf.* ENFEOFFMENT TO USE, FEE TAIL; JOINTURE

Eorlcund. Lit. 'earl-kind, earl-born'. The AS nobility, its warrior caste. [< OE *eorl* = earl + *cund* = kind, born into (i.e. the class of *eorls*)] – *Cf.* EARL; GESITH

Epicière. A spicer. The servant responsible for carrying spices to his lord's table; also a container or small vase for holding spices.

Epistle side. That place in a church from which the Epistle is usually read, i.e. south end of the altar.

Epistolary. A liturgical book containing the Epistle readings for mass arranged according to the liturgical year.

Equitatio. A knight's service of riding with his lord, as an escort, between various places. The equivalent service in French was *chevalchia*. In the 10c, St Oswald used the phrase *equitandi lex* – law of riding – in a letter to King Edgar. Men granted Church lands were required to provide riding services for the bishop. – *Cf.* AVERA; GENEAT

Erber [arber]. When used in the hunter's phrase 'to make the erber' it meant to begin disembowelling what had been hunted down. Also common term for 'garden'. [< OFr. *herbier* = rumen]

Eremite. A hermit. [< L *eremita* = hermit]

Ermine 1. The stoat (*Mustela erminea*). The fur is reddish-brown during the summer, but turns wholly white in the winter except for a black tip on the tail. Much used as trimming on clothing for royalty and nobles. In 1074 the Scots' King Malcolm gave William I gifts, among which were many '*pyleceon* (i.e. *pelisses) of marten-fur . . . and ermine-fur'. It was known in medieval Latin as *mus Armenius*, i.e. the Armenian mouse. [< OE *hearma* = ermine; *cinnen* = ermine skins] – *Cf.* FOIN 1

Ermine 2. *Her.* *Tincture showing the animal's white skin with black spots. – *Cf.* ERMINOIS

Ermine Street. The ancient way which runs from London to Lincoln, leaving the city through the 11c Bishopsgate. Another of a similar name, spelt 'Irmine', runs from Silchester to Gloucester. [< OE *Earninga stræt* = road of the Earningas, i.e. Earn's people] – *Cf.* –INGAS

Ermines. *Her.* A *fur, the reverse of *ermine, i.e. white spots on a black ground. – *Cf. next*

Erminites. *Her.* A *fur similar to *ermine, but with the addition of red hair on each side of the spots. – *Cf. previous*

Erminois. *Her.* *Tincture showing gold (*or), with black (*sable) spots. – *Cf. previous*; ERMINE 2

Erne. An eagle. The name of the Shropshire village Earnwood = eagle's wood.

Error. *Canon law considered incorrect or false judgement to be error when such a judgement was not based upon ignorance. Such an error might be opinions or judgements made by Lollards or more specifically John Wyclif.

Among the errors attributed to Wyclif were the following: that it was against Holy Writ for clerics to have temporal property; that it was lawful for anyone to preach, even though they were neither deacon nor priest; that a *friar who begged after giving a sermon was simoniacal. – *Cf.* HERESY; LOLLARDY; SIMONY

Escalade. The taking of a town by scaling its wall with ladders. The 15c Latin verb was *escalo* = to scale. [< L *scala* = a staircase]

Escambium. Latin term for an exchange of a particular legal kind related to *warranty. When a man paid *homage to a lord, the lord took on the obligation of defending the man whom he had seised and what he, the lord, had granted, i.e. with land or a *tenement. This act carried a warranty. Were the lord for some reason unable to defend the tenant's right to the land, the tenant having been disseised, he was obliged to provide the tenant with an *escambium*, i.e. an exchange, to replace what had been lost. *Bracton had this to say: '[the lord] makes a gift for homage and service, . . . to homage belong warranty and defence and *escambium* if he cannot warrant'. – *Cf.* DISSEISIN; SEISIN

Escheat. The reversion of land to a lord on the death of a tenant without heir. Ranulf de *Glanville was clear: 'The ultimate heir of any person is his lord.' Land might also revert through felony or *treason, e.g. when a *tenant-in-chief was *attainted. [< OFr. *eschete* < L *excido* = fall away] – *Cf.* PRIMER SEISIN; SCACCARIUM AARONIS

Eschipre. A Norman ship-owner or the master of a ship.

Escrol. *Her.* A ribbon-like scroll which supported a *crest while displaying a motto.

Escuage. Service owed as part of land tenure, usually 40 days in a year. [< L *scutum* = shield] – *Cf.* SCUTAGE

Escutcheon. The shield-like area upon which a coat of *arms is portrayed or emblazoned; this shield is typically heart-shaped.

Eskippa. *See* SKEP

Esnecca. *See* SNECCA

Esplees. What could be obtained from land, i.e. its crop, rents and services, or the 'issues of the land'. *Bracton said that 'the taking of esplees [added] nothing to *seisin' except where they made the seisin 'clearer' or 'evident'. He adds, 'the seisin of the *proprietas* [ownership] ought not to be so momentary that esplees are not taken'. In the case of vacant seisin the esplees were not taken.

Esquire. A young man who attended a knight. An esquire ranked immediately below a knight; but he was of gentle birth. The esquire was referred to in Latin as *scutifer*. [< OFr. *esquire* < L *scutarius* = shield carrier] – *Cf.* COMMENSALIS; SQUIRE

Essoin. An excuse given for not attending a court. Illness, absence in the king's service or being on *pilgrimage were common and acceptable reasons, since an essoin prevented a case from continuing.

Essoin Rolls. These *rolls recorded the excuses offered for not attending a court when summoned.

Essorant. *Her.* Describes a bird standing but with wings spread, as if about to take flight.

Estate. One of the words used in this period for the broad category in society a person belonged to. Today we use 'class'. Other words of the time were *degree and condition. These were considered to be clear and defined, as were the various monastic orders. Although movement upwards was very difficult, nigh impossible for the ordinary *villein, there was enough flexibility for wealthy merchants to become ennobled, e.g. the de la Poles of Hull in the 14c.

-estere. A suffix indicating a female. – *Cf.* BEGGESTERE

Estoile. *Her.* A *charge in the form of a star with wave-like rays. [< L *stella* = star] – *Cf.* MULLET

Estovers, rights of. The ancient right to take reeds, heather and bracken; also to cut and take wood. – *Cf.* RIGHTS OF COMMON

Estreat. An exact copy of the record of an *amercement, entered on a court's *roll, which was to be levied by a *sheriff. [< L *extraho* = to extract]

Estrif. A form of poem, popular in the 13c particularly, which took the form of a debate, often between unlikely pairings. For example, *The Owl and the Nightingale, The Thrush and the Nightingale, The Fox and the Wolf*. They were popular in France and also in England, where they were also known as 'strif'. Such dramatic dialogues can be seen as precursors of English drama and theatre in the 16c. [< OFr. *estriver* = to strive, quarrel, argue]

Estrinland. Eastern land; far, distant and unknown, except in fantasy and dubious travellers' tales, e.g. those of Sir John Mandeville.

Eubonia. The Isle of Man.

Eucharist. A central part of Christianity, the sacrament in which bread and wine are consecrated; also known as 'holy communion'. It is referred to by St Paul in I Corinthians 11:23.

Eulogia. The host, consecrated bread, dispensed after the mass. [< Gr. *eulogia* = praise, blessing]

Evensong. The English equivalent of the Latinate *vespers. [< OE *æfensang* = even[ing] + song]

Ewerer. The servant responsible for taking water to guests at table for the washing of hands. He was also responsible for drying the king's clothes if they got wet while hunting or travelling, and for the king's bath. Whenever the king took a bath, the ewerer was paid 4d each time, except on the three great festivals of the year – Easter, *Whitsun and Christmas – when the king bathed *gratis*.

Ex cathedra. Lit. 'from the chair'. Orig. an official statement issued with the authority of the pope, i.e. from his throne. [< L *ex* = from + *cathedra* = chair] – *Cf*. CATHEDRAL

Exchequer. The department which dealt with all aspects of the revenues of the crown; the department responsible for collecting and making secure all royal monies. Receipts were dealt with in the lower exchequer, handling expenditure and collection of royal revenue. The exchequer of account, the upper exchequer, audited all returns made by government agents. The department took its name from the chequered cloth spread on the table around which the officers sat: *ad scaccarium*, anglicised as 'exchequer'. Calculations were made by adding and subtracting counters set on the chequered cloth. Officers of the exchequer, known as 'barons', met twice each year with the sheriffs and other royal-revenue collectors to record revenue and expenditure; these were enrolled on the *Pipe Rolls, kept at the treasury, along with *DB and other royal records. – *Cf. Dialogus de Scaccario*

Excommunication. A sentence of the Church forbidding a person to celebrate or receive the sacraments, much as an *outlaw was placed outside the law and its protection. – *Cf*. INTERDICT

Exennia. Customary gifts of produce from a monastery's estates to the archbishop at Christmas and at Easter.

Exercitus. Lit. 'an army, infantry'. The Latin word used of a military expedition, also the army involved in such an expedition. In the 13c, the word was used in conflicts with Scotland; in the 14c, it was used for the 'expeditions' sent against France. From it we have our modern use, e.g. a military exercise. [< L *exerceo* = to exercise, to train] – *Cf*. EXPEDITIO; FYRD

Exon Domesday. *See Liber Exoniensis*

Exorcist. One of the *minor orders of the Church. Although the exorcising of evil spirits was never confined to this order, they assisted in this process. They also poured out water at the mass.

Expeditio. Latin term for the obligation of a tenant to follow his lord to war. The word was also used, synonymously with *exercitus*, for a military force or expedition. [< L *expeditio* = expedition, campaign] – *Cf.* FYRD

Explicit. Lit. '[here] ends'; used to conclude a roll or book and other texts. [< L *explico* = to set forth] – *Cf.* INCIPIT; LECTIONARY

Extent. An extent was a survey of the lands possessed, e.g. by a monastery. It would give the boundaries, and name the tenants; there would also be sizes of buildings, rents and services due. Sometimes an extent would also include a *customary. – *Cf.* TERRIER

Eyot [eigt, ety]. A small island or islet in a river, e.g. Chiswick Eyots in the Thames; pronounced 'eight'. – *Cf.* WICK

Eyre. The circuit travelled by a judge moving from *county to county; hence *justice-in-eyre. [< OFr. *eire* < L *iter* = journey] – *Cf.* BRACTON; CORAM REGE

F

Fableor. Successor of the wandering minstrel, the fableor told stories without musical accompaniment. [< L *fabulor* = to talk, tell a story] – *Cf.* GLEOMAN; TROUBADOUR

Fabliau. A bawdy medieval verse tale; a French form used by Geoffrey Chaucer in *The Miller's Tale* and *The Reeve's Tale*. – *Cf.* REEVE

Fair. The gathering of sellers and traders at set intervals at particular places under a licence or charter granted by a lord – for which he was paid. Such occasions took on the character of a local holiday. A few still exist, e.g. the annual Nottingham Goose Fair.

Faits d'armes. Lit. 'deeds or feats of arms'. The phrase used by Jean Froissart throughout his work for many kinds of knightly combat, e.g. the *hastilude and *tournament, also of the genuinely hostile combat during war.

Falchion [fauchart, faussart]. A curved broad sword, sharp on the outer or convex side; a billhook. It was sometimes used to despatch a stag at the end of a chase. [< OFr. *fauchon* = sickle]

Falconer. Both kings and nobles being avid sportsmen would have had falconers. King Harold II is shown in the *Bayeux Tapestry with hawks and dogs. The Latin term for the falconer was *accipitrarius*. – *Cf. next;* ACCEPTOR

Falconry. Like other forms of hunting, falconry was the sport of kings and one requiring great skill. It was a particular favourite of Henry II. There were many kinds of hunting birds: gerfalcons (*Falco rusticolus*) came from Norway, Iceland and Greenland; these were reserved for use by the king. The peregrine was the bird of earls; the goshawk of yeoman, the sparrow hawk of priests. Merlins were used by knights. [< L *falco* = a falcon] – *Cf. previous;* CREANCE

Faldage. Rent paid for a sheep fold; also, a lord's right to have a tenant's sheep graze on his land and fertilise it. Frequently the tenants' sheep were pastured with the lord's flock. It was also customary for the shepherd to fold his lord's flock on his own small piece of land for 14 days over Christmas, also for fertilising. The Latin form was *faldagium*. [< OE *fald* = a fold] – *Cf.* FOLD SOKE

Faldstool. A seat used by a bishop or other senior ecclesiastic when not using his bishop's throne. It was a portable item without arms, for use when a bishop was in another's church. [< OE *fald* = fold + stool]

Faldyng. A coarse wool cloth.

Familia regis. Lit. 'king's household'. In the AN kingdom, this was basically a military establishment, because from before the Normans and long after, as the king was commander-in-chief, his household was necessarily military. It functioned both as the fighting and the administrative heart of the king's army and the realm. Senior army officers were often also senior government officials. In William I's case the army was the means by which he had acquired the throne, and certainly the means by which he, and later his sons, held, maintained and defended it. Usually referred to as the *familia*. – *Cf.* CONSTITUTIO DOMUS REGIS; DOMUS REGIS; *Leges Henrici Primi*

Familiaris. An individual member of the *familia regis*.

Famulus. The *famulus* was one of an estate's full-time workers. No estate or *manor of any size could have been worked relying on the week-work owed by villeins who earned their living on their own plot of land. The *famulus* earned his living by working for his lord. [L *famulus* = a slave or servant]

Fane. A flag, or pennant. In time it became the vane in 'weather-vane'.

Fardel 1. A small pack or bundle; also from bundle the word came to indicate a burden of sin. The first sense is found in a phrase in the Paston Letters: 'some money came trussed in some fardel'; the second is found in Hamlet's question, 'Who would these fardels bear?'

Fardel 2. A fraction or part of something; also more precisely one quarter. [< fourth + deal] – *Cf. next*

Fardel-holder. Holder of a quarter of a *virgate; consequently, one of the poorest of villeins. – *Cf. previous*; FARTHINGLAND

Farm. A fixed sum of money due annually, e.g. tax, rent or something in kind. Later, the sum paid for the licence to collect monies, e.g. taxes from a city. Moneyers had the farm, in their case for minting coins. It was a gathering in of plenty, which in usage became the agricultural farm as we use the word. [< L *firma* = a fixed payment; OE *feorm* = rent in kind, tribute] – *Cf.* FEORM; FIRMA BURGI; MONEYERS, ASSIZE OF

Farmery. *See* FERMERY

Farthing. A coin worth one quarter of a *penny, first minted at the recoinage of 1279. [< OE *feorðing* = fourth part] – *Cf.* GROAT; HALFPENNY; SCEATTA; THRYMSA; FERDING

Farthingdeal. One quarter of an acre. [< OE *feorðing* = a fourth part + *dæl* = a division] – *Cf.* DEAL

Farthingland. Term used in Somerset for one quarter of a *virgate; however elsewhere the term covered any area of land up to 30 acres. [< OE *feorðing* = a fourth part] – *Cf.* FARDEL-HOLDER; FARTHING

Fastness. A stronghold or fortress. [< OE *fæstan* = make fast = make secure; *fæsten* = a fortress]

Fat fish. The designation is unclear; whale or dolphin may be meant.

Fauchart. *See* FALCHION

Faulds. The hoops of steel in a suit of armour, placed so as to protect the hips and lower back.

Fautor [fauctor]. An accomplice, associate; the AN form was *fauteur*. [< L *fautor* < *faveo* = to favour] – *Cf.* AFFINITY 2; MEINIE

Fealty. A *vassal's oath of fidelity to his lord; also the duties of service and aid. [< L *fides* = oath, faith; L *fidelitas* = loyalty] – *Cf.* HOLD OATH; HOMAGE 1; IMMIXTIO MANUUM

Feast 1. The day on which an anniversary of religious importance is celebrated; also, a village festival occurring on the feast day of the patron saint of that village's church. [< L *festa* = festival, festive holiday]

Feast 2. A large festive meal for a grand occasion. One such was on the marriage of Margaret, daughter of King Henry III to Alexander III of Scotland in

1252. Then 1,000 knights attended dressed in silk, while some 60 oxen were eaten.

Feast of Fools. A custom of the 10c and later following the Feast of the Nativity. On the *triduum*, or three days, following the Nativity, minor clergy and others were permitted to undertake divine service, with the exception of the mass. On St Stephen's Day (26 December) the deacons took service, followed by priests and choir boys on succeeding days. These occasions were taken in a holiday spirit and often became riotous. They were condemned by the pope in 1207, and in England in 1236; a further prohibition was made in 1390. It was for the far from sober conduct that these occasions were named variously *festum fatuorum* = feast of fools and *asinarium festum* = festival of asses or donkeys. Christmas in the Middle Ages was a secular feast as much as it was religious; in the Feast of Fools the two merged.

Feaxede steorra. Lit. 'hairy or long-haired star'. Most famously *Halley's comet in 1066, seen later as the ill-omen which preceded the Battle of Hastings . The phrase was also used in *ASC in 892 and 995. [< OE *feax, fax* = hair; still to be found in Fairfax and Halifax]

Fee 1. Livestock, movable property; also money. [< OE *feoh* = cattle]

Fee 2. *See* FIEF

Fee simple. Tenure of a heritable estate in land for ever and without restriction to any particular class of heirs; an estate so held; equivalent to freehold. [ME *simple* = without duplicity or complication] – *Cf. next;* ENTAIL; SUBINFEUDATION

Fee tail. This was tenure of property which could be inherited by or willed to a lineal descendant only. If there were no descendants 'of the body' upon the death of the tenant, the land reverted to the lord. Such land was thus *entailed. – *Cf. previous;* ENTAIL; ESCHEAT

Feet of Fines. *See* FINAL CONCORD

Feld. Open or cultivated land, esp. in forested country. From *feld* derives 'field'.

Fell-monger. *See* PELLETARIUS

Felony. In feudal law, any serious violation of the relation between lord and *vassal was a felony, to be punished by forfeiture of his *fief; used also of treason, the gravest of crimes. Later, the word was assimilated into common law to encompass crimes against the king's peace. – *Cf.* ESCHEAT

Femme sole. During this period a woman was usually not considered independent: before marriage she was in her father's charge; on marriage, in her husband's. But a widow, esp. one left with money or property, was accepted as being independent. If she carried on her husband's business she was accepted as a *femme sole* = a woman alone. – *Cf.* HUCKSTER

Fenestra parvula. A small window through which nuns and canons of a *Gilbertine double house communicated and made confession etc. Another similarly small window enabled nuns to speak to their family when permitted. [< L *fenestra* = window + *parvula* = small, very small] – *Cf.* ANCHORITE; DOMUS FENESTRAE; MAGNA FENESTRA VERSATILIS

Feodary. *See* FEUDARY

Feoffment. The process of assigning property to a person under feudal law, for which military service was due. – *Cf.* ENFEOFFMENT TO USE; FEE 1; LIVERY IN SEISIN

Feorm. The AS version of a *farm was in effect a food-rent, latterly commuted for money. As with other kings, the AS kings had several manors, which the surrounding area was required to supply with food in specified quantities. Thus a group of hides would have to send certain amounts of bread, ale, cattle, cheese, honey etc. These are sometimes known as 'food renders' or 'renders in kind'. – *Cf.* GWESTFA; HIDE

Ferding. Unit of land, being a quarter of a *virgate; also, one of four parts of a *shire. [< OE *feorðing* = fourth part] – *Cf.* FARTHING

Feretory. A small shrine, often portable, in which were kept the relics of a saint; a small chapel set aside to contain such shrines and relics. Often the chapel was set close to the main altar. [< OFr. *fiertre* < L *feretum* = a bier]

Feria una. Lit. 'weekday one'. In this period, days of the work were referred to in Latin, and were named, as today, after pagan gods or the moon and sun. Church writers, sensitive to these pagan references, sometimes preferred to use a neutral nomenclature, which was to number the days of the week. Thus there was *feria una* for day one, i.e. Sunday, *feria secunda* for day two, i.e. Monday, and so through the week. – *Cf.* NOON

Fermerer. The fermerer's duty was to tend the sick in a monastery and prepare those who had died for burial. The elderly and infirm were also housed in the *fermery, where those who had been bled recuperated for three days. – *Cf.* BLOOD-LETTING

Fermery. The infirmary of a monastery; its *obedientiary was the *fermerer. [< L *infirmaria*]

Ferratus. Term used of an iron-clad soldier, i.e. one in some form of armour. [< L *ferrum* = iron]

Fertinus. *See* FARTHINGLAND

Fess. *Her.* One of the nine *honourable ordinaries, being a *bar or stripe across the middle of a shield, comprising one third of the space. [< L *fascia*] – *Cf.* ENGRAILED; INVECTED; ORDINARY 2

Fess point. *Her.* The exact centre of a shield. – *Cf.* ABYSS; CHARGE

Feud 1. Antagonism, hostility, hatred; intense hostility between factions or families, fed by revenge and tit-for-tat killings. (This word has nothing to do with 'feudal'.) [< OE *fæhðu* = enmity] – *Cf.* WERGELD

Feud 2. *See* FIEF

Feudal incidents. Modern term for the various obligations of a man who held land by knight service. These incidents provided a large part of any lord's income, great or small. – *Cf.* AIDS; CONTENEMENT; PRIMER SEISIN; RELIEF

Feudal levy. The summoning of an army by the king. The *fyrd* came together as a result of the king's summons. After the Conquest, *servitium debitum* answered the king's need for knights; the great lords with their retinues also responded, though they may well have been at court when such a decision was made. By the 14c, the emergence of paid service and the use of *mercenaries became increasingly common, and a more reliable source of troops, equipped as knights or not. Those knights answering the levy who were part of a lord's *servitium* were among other such groups, producing a rather disorganised force. *Scutage also presented problems; even the collection of the money liability of scutage proved difficult. Recruiting by *indenture and payment made organisation and administration easier and more predictable. Ordinary foot soldiers were still supplied by the boroughs and the shires. The very last summons of the feudal levy was issued by Richard II in June 1385. – *Cf.* ARRAY, COMMISSION OF

Feudalism. A term of tortuous elusiveness. Broadly, the word is used of the system of land-holding, administration and relations between vassal and lord in England after 1066. At its heart is the assumption that everyone had a lord, from the lowliest *servus* to the king, who had the sternest and most powerful lord of all, God. This relationship had superseded the familial or kin relationship of the old Saxon world. However, before the Conquest there were clear duties owed to the king by *thegn and *ealdorman, and the importation of the system by the Normans as something wholly new is itself disputed. Feudalism was in effect a combination of two relationships: material and personal. The material is found in the kind of tenure the tenant had and in the way he paid for the land he held of his lord: with service – in the fields or militarily – until the late 14c, after which the incidence of monetary payment increased, i.e. after the *Black Death and concomitant labour shortages. So long as all dues were met the tenure was heritable. The personal relationship derived from the tenant's place in the social ladder and the kind of dependence or protection the lord could provide. The word is first recorded in 1635, long after the period it now relates to. [< OFr. *feu* < L *feudum* = heritable estate, heritable land.] – *Cf.* BASTARD FEUDALISM; FEE SIMPLE; FIEF

Feudary [feodary]. A *vassal or feudal tenant; one who held land of a lord on the condition of services. The Latin form was *feodarius*. – *Cf.* FEUDALISM; FIEF

Feudum. Latin word used in *DB for land held of a lord, i.e. a *fief or fee. – *Cf. previous*

Feudum loricae. A *hauberk *fief; known in AN as a *fief de haubert*. It was also known as a *fief loricae*. Orig. the Norman term for a knight with a *mail hauberk – a term of distinction, as not all Norman knights had one. In England the distinction was unnecessary: all enfeoffed knights were required to possess a hauberk. *Feudum loricae* and *feudum militis* (a knight's fief) were effectively one and the same. [< L *feudum* = a fief + *lorica* = mail] – *Cf.* ENFE-OFF

Fewterer. A keeper of greyhounds. [< AN *veutrier* = hound]

Fidelis. Latin word for a retainer who remained faithful to his lord. [< L *fidelis* = faithful]

Fief [fee]. Land which was held of a superior lord in return for which service – mostly military – and *homage was offered. This chain of homage and service reached upwards to the monarch. Such land became heritable by the 12c. Our sense of the word 'fee' as payment comes from its extension to offices which received payment. The Latin form in *DB = *feudum*. [< OE *feoh* = cattle, money, chattels in general] – *Cf.* BOOK OF FEES; FEOFFMENT; FEUDALISM; HON-OUR

Fief de haubert. The 11c French term equivalent to a knight's fee. So named from the *hauberk of *mail each knight was required to have and wear when his services were called upon. – *Cf.* FEUDUM LORICAE; SERVITIUM DEBITUM

Fief loricae. Synonymous with *feudum loricae*.

Fief militum. Lit. 'fief of the knights'. – *Cf.* FEUDUM LORICAE; FIEF

Fiefs-rentes. Members of the king's household guard, successors to the *huscarls* of pre-Norman England, provided with fiefs for their support. Such payments were not necessarily made in coin; food and wine were also given, being known as 'money fiefs'.

Field. *Her.* The surface upon which a *charge is blazoned.

Fieri facias. Lit. 'cause to be done'. Common-law writ issued, e.g. for the collection of a debt. Such writs were addressed to a *sheriff for execution; he would seize goods and *chattels to the value of the judgement. In Latin documents the abbr. *fi. fa* was used.

Fifburgingas. Term used in the 11c for the inhabitants of the *Five Boroughs.

Fighting season. The fighting season lasted generally from St Hilary's day, 13 January, until *Michaelmas, 29 September. – *Cf.* TRUCE OF GOD

Fihtwite. A fine, i.e. a *wite*, for fighting. In *LHP*, the Latin was *fightwita* and was considered a relatively minor offence, punishable by the offender's lord. – *Cf.* FORSTEAL; LEYRWITE

Filbert. Fruit of the hazel tree; so named as it ripened close to St Philbert's day, 22 August.

Filiatio. Latin word for the obedience required of the monks in a monastery. [< L *filiatio* = sonship] – *Cf.* ABBOT

Fimbriation. *Her.* When two colours (metals) are adjacent an edging is added to prevent their touching; this edge or border is the fimbriation.

Final concord. The legal documents recording a private transaction, usually concerning the transfer of property, made before the king's justices. The form continued in use until the 19c. Such a document was a *chirograph, being cut into three pieces, one for each party, the third for the court. Seals were not used as most people did not have one, their use being largely confined to king and magnates. From the late 12c, these were enrolled as Feet of Fines.

Fine. A sum of money paid at the end of something, e.g. a set period of time, like the end of a lease, or on the death of the holder of land. Then the best beast might be paid to the lord with something to the incumbent priest, over and above regular payments. Later, a fine was paid by the incoming tenant. (The phrase 'in fine' with the sense of 'in the end' continues the sense.) [< OFr. *fin* < L *finis* = end] – *Cf. next*

Fine Rolls. Rolls recording payments of money, i.e. fines, made to the king for charters, privileges, writs and pardons, for favours and grants, e.g. of land. Here 'fine' is used in the sense of payment. These rolls also contain the appointments of sheriffs and other officials. These documents were also known as 'oblata rolls', where the Latin *oblata* meant an offering, an *oblate of money. The Latin form of the name was twofold: *rotuli oblatorum* or *rotuli finium*. These records begin in 1199. – *Cf.* CHARTER ROLLS; PIPE ROLLS

Firma burgi. Latin term for a borough farm in which a town, e.g. Cambridge in 1186, acquired the right to pay all dues in an agreed lump sum, the town collecting all payments. This gave the town a significant autonomy, restricting interference from the lord. – *Cf. next;* FARM

Firma unius noctis. Lit. 'one night's *farm'. Payment or assessment of the money or produce needed to support the king and his travelling household for one night. – *Cf. previous*

First. *Her.* Used as in 'of the first', indicating a similarity with the *tincture first mentioned in a *blazon.

First fruits. Latin word for this term is *annates*. This gratuity was paid by the new holder of an ecclesiastical post to his superior, which was ultimately the pope. Such offices were lucrative and these monies amounted to the annual revenue of the *benefice or see in question. These payments, which appeared in the 11c, were first made only to bishops and abbots; however, from the 14c popes also began to receive them. This closely resembled *simony, which was at times rampant, though severely and universally deprecated by the Church.

Fisc. A modern term for a king's or prince's private affairs and finances, his properties. [< L *fiscus* = a money bag or purse, the imperial exchequer]

Fitch. *See* FITCHEW

Fitché. *Her.* Term used of a cross with a pointed lower limb.

Fitchew [fitch]. A polecat; also its fur. [< OFr. *fissel, fissiaulx, fissau*]

Fitz. AN patronymic. It was also used as we would use 'son'. For example, on the night King Edward I arrested his mother's lover, Roger Mortimer, she called out to Edward, 'Bel fitz! Bel fitz!' – urging gentleness on him. (*Bel* as a cognomen meant 'fair', as in 'handsome'.) Later, *fitz* was used of the illegitimate sons of princes. When names incorporating *fitz* were expressed in Latin, the translation was straightforward. Thus William fitz-Ralph became *Willelmus filius Radulphi*, i.e. William, son of Ralph (*Radulphus*). [AN < OFr. *fiz* < L *filius* = son] – *Cf. next;* BASTARD

Fitzroy. Name given to the *bastard child of the king, where *fitz* signified illegitimate and *roy* = king.

Fiufé. AN for enfeoffed. – *Cf.* ENFEOFF

Five Boroughs. Derby, Leicester, Nottingham, Lincoln, Stamford. The word *fifburgingas* was first used in 942 when the English under King Edmund I took over the towns from the Danes of York. They were within the *Danelaw.

Flancart. That piece of armour used to protect the thighs of a knight. His *destrier* was also protected on its flanks by a similar piece known as the *flançois*. [< OFr. *flanc* = side, flank]

Flançois. *See previous*

Flected. *See* EMBOWED

Fletch. To put feathers on an arrow. [< fledge = of young birds becoming feathered] – *Cf. next*

Fletcher. An arrow-maker; one who sold arrows. Fletchers used a gum made from bluebells to fix feathers to their arrows. – *Cf. previous;* ATTILLATOR

Fleur-de-lys. The heraldic lily. When adopted as the French king's device gold lilies were placed on a blue field. By the 13c, the number of lilies was set at three. Other senses: the royal arms of France until 1789; the French royal *standard; later the pattern of a brand applied to criminals in France; a mark of *cadency on the arms of a sixth son. It was adopted on the English king's coat of *arms by Edward III, as a sign of his claim on the French throne, which was abandoned finally by George VI. – *Cf.* FLEURY

Fleuron. An architectural, flower-like decoration.

Fleuronnée 1. Elaborate penmanship, with ample flourishes. [< Fr. *fleurir* = to blossom, bloom]

Fleuronnée 2 [flourished]. *Her.* Highly decorated, e.g. with *fleur-de-lys or trefoils. [< Fr. *fleurir* = to blossom, bloom] – *Cf. next*

Fleury. *Her.* Decorated with *fleur-de-lys. – *Cf. previous*

Florin. English form of Latin *florenus*, a gold coin first issued at Florence in 1252.

Focage. Hearth-money. A tax paid on the number of hearths in a house. [< L *focus* = hearth, fire] – *Cf. next;* FOUAGE

Focaria. Lit. 'a hearth-girl or kitchen maid'. The term was used of women living with priests who were meant to be celibate; though it could mean, in other circumstances, a concubine. – *Cf. next*

Focarius. Lit. 'a kitchen boy'. The English term was 'hearthman'. The servant of the royal household, indeed of all the great houses, responsible for the fire in the great hall between *Michaelmas and Easter. He was paid 4d a day. [< L *focus* = hearth, fire] – *Cf. previous*

Foin 1. Fur of the *marten, also known as 'stone' or 'beech marten' (*Martes foina*); also trimmings made from this fur.

Foin 2. Fencing term for a thrusting or stabbing attack with a sword.

Folcland. Lit. 'folk land'. A term which through its infrequency eludes precise definition. However, it is taken to indicate land which was not immune to the various rents and services owed for the king's maintenance. It was probably ordinary land, i.e. land held under common law, being restricted in terms of inheritance within the family or *alienation outside the family. Such land is remembered in placenames like Faulkland in Somerset and Falkland. – *Cf. next;* BOCLAND

Folcriht [folkright]. This might be called AS common (*folc*) law (*riht*). It was the collective understanding of rule and custom (not necessarily written down) which could be appealed to – that appeal being immediately understood. – *Cf. previous*

Fold soke. The relationship between tenant and lord which tied a man's sheep to his lord's fold. The purpose was to ensure that the lord's land was manured by the sheep. It was termed a consuetude, a custom – one most frequently found in East Anglia – which a lord could extract from a free man. The Latin term was *consuetus ad faldam* = tied to the fold, where *consuetus* meant something stronger than simply custom: an obligation, but one owed by a free man. – *Cf.* CUSTUMARIUS; FALDAGE

Folgere. A household retainer. A freeman who did not possess a house of his own and worked for another, being entitled to the produce of two fields, one of which he had to sow himself. [OE *folgere* = follower, attendant]

Folio. A leaf of *parchment or paper; in a post-Gutenberg book, a sheet of paper folded once to produce two leaves; a bifolium, i.e. four pages.

Folkmoot. A general assembly (*moot) of the people (folk) of a town in King Alfred's time; but esp. of London where it was (probably) the city's oldest institution and its first in dignity. It was summoned by ringing the great bell of St Paul's Cathedral. Sessions were held at *Michaelmas, Christmas and Midsummer – save for occasions of emergency. It was the place for declarations of outlawry. The meeting was in open space a little to the north-east of St Paul's Cathedral. [< OE *folcgemot*] – *Cf. previous;* GEMOT; SAINT PAUL'S CROSS

Football. The chronicler-monk who wrote the *Miracles of King Henry VI* described (*c.*1365–70) football in these terms: 'The game . . . for common recreation is called by some the foot-ball-game. It is one in which young men, in country sport, propel a huge ball not by throwing it into the air but by stroking and rolling it along the ground and that not with their hands but with their feet. A game, I say, abominable enough, and, in my judgement at least, more common, undignified and worthless than any other kind of game, rarely ending but with some loss or accident or disadvantage to the players themselves.' The breathless indignation concerning the doings of the young still rings fresh.

Foot-cloth. A highly decorated piece of cloth displaying a knight's arms and large enough to cover a horse. A foot-mantle was a large cloak-like garment worn by women when riding. – *Cf.* TRAPPINGS

Foragium. Latin word used of forage, also for the obligation to provide it, as part of customary dues. – *Cf.* PANNAGE

Foreath. Lit. 'a fore-oath', one taken before the beginning of a legal suit.

Forelock. Clasp beneath the chin which secured a knight's helm.

Forest. An area of land to which certain specific legal rights pertained, such as hunting. A forest was not necessarily wooded – a bare mountain could be a forest, provided the legal status applied to it.

Forest Assizes. 1184 and 1198. Punishment for taking animals from the king's hunting grounds was fierce: castration and blinding were almost customary, while it was not unknown for the culprit to be executed. Crown lawyers sought to establish ancient custom for the king's prerogatives in the *forest, resorting to forgery in the case of a code said to date from King Cnut's reign. During Henry II's reign, there were some 69 forests, estimated to cover perhaps one third of England. These were constantly watched over by foresters and agistors, while courts dealt with petty offences every six weeks. Offences involving venison were dealt with by special courts. A great deal of money flowed into the crown's coffers from those who broke forest laws. However, mutilation and the death penalty were abolished in 1217. *Magna Carta, clause 47, stated: 'All forests that have been created in our time shall be disafforested immediately.' – *Cf. next;* HAMBLE; SWANIMOTE

Forest, Charter of the. *Charta de foresta*, 1217. Until this charter the penalties imposed by the crown for infringement of forest law were severe and horrible: mutilation and/or death. In the 1217 charter these penalties were repealed. However, 10 years later, Henry III reimposed them; by 1250 large parts of the country, esp. around London, were being treated as if *forest. It was said the forest had its own laws based not on the common law of the realm but on arbitrary legislation by the king. – *Cf. previous;* REGARDER

Forestallers, Statute of. *Statuta de forstallariis*, 1390. Forestalling was deemed to evade the *assize and was prohibited. The practice involved buying up goods before a market, for example, thus 'cornering the market' in a particular item. Trading times of markets were strictly regulated: anyone meeting those coming to market and buying early was deemed a forestaller and subject to public exposure. The statute specified that 'names shall be presented distinctly and openly, and they be amerced for every default, or be judged to the *tumbrel, if they forestall contrary to the statute'.

Forestel. Assault carried out on the king's highway; an ambush on that highway. It was one of the offences reserved to the king's judgement. The penalty was a fine of 100s. In the Latin records the offence was described as *prohibitio itineris* = hindrance of a journey. [< OE *foresteall* = hindrance (of justice), ambush] – *Cf.* FORSTEAL; HAMSOCN; MUNDBRYCE

Forinsec. Term used for the service one owed to the lord from whom one's own immediate lord held his land, thus 'outside' the local *manor. This use survived in the Dorset placename Ryme Forinseca. However, it can still be found in the anglicised Rye Foreign. [< L *forinsecus* =on the outside] – *Cf. next;* INTRINSEC

Forinsecus. Title of the king's outer marshal, known also as the *earl marshal. His first duties were the dispositions of the king's army on the field before battle. (It is from this the title 'field-marshal' is derived.) In times of peace, his responsibility was to select where to halt – castle, monastery etc. – during the king's endless *itinerary. He would also ensure all known malefactors in the *virgata regis*, i.e. district, or *verge were under lock and key during the king's stay. [< L *forinsecus* = on the outside] – *Cf. previous;* INTRINSECUS; VIRGATE

Forma. The 12c Latin term for a *misericord, i.e. the ledge on the underside of a seat in the choir. – *Cf.* FORMULA

Formariage. *See* MERCHET

Formula. In the 12c, Latin term for the kneeling board in the stalls of a church or *cathedral. – *Cf.* FORMA

Fornagium. Latin term for payment to a lord for the obligation to use his oven; it was also a payment for the right to use one's own oven. The anglicised version of *fornagium* is 'furnage'. [< L *furnus* = an oven] – *Cf.* BANALITY

Forsteal. An offence mentioned in *DB* relating the laws of the city of Chester. It meant violent affray in the streets. The penalty was a fine of £4 if committed on a feast day or a Sunday; on other days the fine was 40s. – *Cf.* FIHTWITE, FORESTEL; HAMFARE; HENGWITE

Fortunium. *See* VENTURE

Foss Dyke. The navigable canal between the Rivers Witham (at Lincoln) and Trent, thought to have been first cut by the Romans to drain the marshes. [< L *fossa* = ditch] – *Cf. next*

Fossarius. A builder of ditches and dykes. [< L *fossa* = ditch] – *Cf. next*

Fossatores. The forward part of an army responsible for cutting roads through woods, broad enough to preclude an ambush. They were much used by Edward I during his campaigns in Wales, c.1296–1300. – *Cf. previous*

Fosse. A ditch or trench; a defensive structure, thus a moat is also a fosse. – *Cf. previous and next*

Fosse Way [the Foss]. A road built by the Romans, running from south-west

England to Ilchester, then Bath, Cirencester and Leicester, reaching *Ermine Street near Lincoln. It was known originally as 'the Fosse' because there was a (defensive) ditch on both sides; 'Fosse Way' is post-15c. Bishop Latimer said in 1553: 'I live within half a mile of the Fossway and you would wonder to see how they [pilgrims] come by flocks out of the west country to [see] many images [and shrines].' [< L *fossa* = ditch] – *Cf. previous*

Fouage. *Hearth tax imposed by Edward, prince of Wales and Aquitaine, in 1364. – *Cf.* FOCAGE; FUMAGIUM

Foumart. A polecat (*Mustela putorius*); also a foumart-dog, which was used for hunting.

Four banal. The community oven in France but common in English villages, where the bread was baked not as well as it could be. This bread was called 'banal' as it came from something of common use – from which we have our use of the word 'banal' = ordinary or commonplace. Banal is derived from the *ban*, which was the lord's power to punish in everyday matters. [< Fr *forn* < L *furnus* = an oven] – *Cf.* BANALITY; FORNAGIUM

Fraellum. *See next*

Frail. Rush basket used for carrying and packing raisins in particular; also the weight of raisins carried, approx. 70 lb. The Latin form is *fraellum*.

Franchise [fraunchyse]. Local justice in this period was exercised by a lord. Franchise is sometimes referred to as a 'liberty', as it allowed a lord some immunity from royal officials, such as the *sheriff. For instance, a writ could only be delivered within a franchise, not executed. (The Latin term for this was *retorna*.) Within his franchise, a lord was possessed of a part of royal power, which permitted him to judge and punish in his manorial court through *sake and soke and *infangen-theof. A town might also be granted various liberties and privileges, which were called a 'franchise', for which considerable sums of money were given to the king. A further use of the term was involved with the *guilds. A guild member who offended his fellow members could ultimately be disenfranchised and thus lose the freedom to pursue his craft or trade. Also *Magna Carta (1225) offers a defence in these words: 'If anyone has been disseised of or kept out of his lands, castles, franchises or his right by us without the legal judgment of his peers, we [the king] will immediately restore them to him.' The Latin term was *franchisa*. [< OFr. *franche* < L *francus* = free] – *Cf.* DISSEISIN; FIERI FACIAS; FRANKLIN; WRITS, RETURN OF

Francigenare. Lit. 'to become French'. Latin term for those who tried to 'Frenchify' themselves after the Conquest. Accommodating the new Norman power in the land, they hoped to advance themselves. – *Cf.* FRANKLIN; PLEADING, STATUTE OF

Franciscan. A friar or nun of the order founded by St Francis (d. 1226) in 1209; also known as Grey Friars or Friars Minor. It was the least intellectual of the monastic orders, with members taking vows of poverty and preaching in emotional ways on the sufferings of Christ.

Franciscan observant. Member of a branch of the *Franciscan order which followed a stricter regime than others. They were known colloquially as 'Cordeliers'.

Frankalmoign. The term for tenure of land held in perpetuity by a religious body in return for prayers for the donor's soul and his/her descendants. The land was free of all obligations bar the *trimoda necessitas*. Fealty was not owed to any lord. This was the tenure by which the majority of monasteries held their land. [< *frank* = free + *almoign*] – *Cf.* OBIT

Franklin. Free man who held land but not of noble birth, a peasant immigrant; also known as *francigena* and *francus homo* in *DB*, i.e. Frenchman, a free man. The term derives ultimately from the Germanic tribes known as *Franks. – *Cf.* FRANCIGENARE; VAVASOUR

Frank-marriage. Tenure by man and wife of land given by the wife's father; the land was directly heritable for four generations with only *fealty owing. Few families survived three generations, let alone four, in direct line of male heirs – one reason why the family name of so many earldoms did not persist.

Frank-pledge. Members of a *tithing were responsible for each other's actions – if one was fined, all were responsible for part of that fine; thus a potent kind of neighbourhood watch grew up in which the liability to a share of a penalty ensured attentiveness. Members were also obliged to report one who committed a crime. A number of tithings were organised into a *leet or ward. The sheriff held a 'view' of the frank-pledge twice a year, fining those not within it. *Bracton has this to say: 'Every [male] who has reached the age of 12 years must take an oath at the view of frank-pledge that he does not intend to be a thief nor a party to thieving. All who hold land and house, who are called householders, ought to be in frank-pledge, and also those who serve them, who are called followers.' Women could not be outlawed because they were not within a frank-pledge, nor could a boy younger than 12.

Franks. The Germanic tribes who invaded Gaul, what is today France, after the collapse of Roman rule in the 5c; particularly successful was Clovis I during the years 484–507. Their dynasty was named Merovingian, which lasted until the 8C, when it was displaced by the Carolingians under Pepin. They gave their name to France. They were so named after their favoured weapon, OE *franca* = a javelin.

Frater. The dining room or hall of a religious house; a refectory. [< OFr. *fraitur* = refectory] – *Cf. next*; RECREATION

Fraterer. The *frater or refectory was the fraterer's sphere of influence. He saw to it that tables were laid, that tablecloths were clean and repaired; he kept a count of cups and spoons. He was also meant to keep the wash-room (*lavatorium*) clean and supplied with towels. [< OFr. *fraitur* = refectory < L *refectorium*] – *Cf.* OBEDIENTIARY

Free man. In *DB, *liber homo* indicates a free man with land who was not noble. The phrase was sometimes used of a *thegn*.

French. From the Conquest in 1066, all English kings down to Henry IV spoke French before English. French was the language of court, the law courts (with Latin) and the new aristocracy which William I created. A linguistic curiosity which remains is the wording of the monarch's assent to a bill from parliament: kings sign *Le Roi le veult*; queens *La Reine le veult*. – *Cf.* ENGLISH; FRANCIGENARE

Friar. Member of one of four (male) *mendicant orders who lived in the world, outside the monastery, whose purpose was to preach, living off donations. This was resented by some who thought such money should more properly be given to the local parish church. By living in the world they were bypassing the earlier idea that monks should be of fixed abode. In time they became rich, receiving gifts from wealthy sinners, losing their moral edge, even though they were not burdened by the extensive properties as monasteries were. The Franciscans (first arrived in England in 1224) and Dominicans (first arrived in England in 1221 at Oxford) were evangelists from *c.*1220, esp. in the towns. [< Fr *frère*, *fredre* = brother] – *Cf.* AUGUSTINIAN; AUSTIN; CARMELITE; LIMITOUR

Frith. Safety, security, peace; later, a deer park or forest; also a place where fish were kept. The word is still to be found, e.g. in Chapel-en-le-Frith (Derbyshire) or Frithville (Lincolnshire). As a verb, *frith* = to fence something in (and to protect).

Frithborh. A *frank-pledge. – *Cf. previous*

Frithsoken. A *sanctuary or an asylum. – *Cf.* FRITH; SOKE

Frithstol [fridstool]. A peace-stool, i.e. a refuge, or sanctuary; a seat near the altar of a church where sanctuary was found. It should be noted that not all churches had such power, which was carefully regulated. – *Cf.* FRITH; SANCTUARY

Frontlet. A band worn by women across the forehead and secured beneath the chin. It often formed the basis of headwear. During the 15c black became an increasingly fashionable colour, perhaps by way of contrast when framing a white forehead and face. – *Cf.* ATOUR

Fructed. *Her.* Bearing fruit. [< L *fructus* = fruit]

133

Frumenty. A dish of wheat, hulled or husked, then boiled in milk with spices such as cinnamon and sugar. Venison with frumenty is one dish of the period.

Fugator. Two ploughmen worked a plough and team of oxen. *Fugator* was the Latin term for the man who drove the eight oxen; the other, known as the **conductor*, handled the plough itself. The *fugator* would usually carry a long stick and whip with which to encourage his charges. *Fugator* was sometimes also used of animal drovers and of hunters, i.e. a horse for hunting. A hunter was also known as a *fugatorius*. [< L *fugo* = to chase or drive] – *Cf.* PLOUGH-TEAM

Full. The process of cleaning and giving body to cloth, originally by treading on it in a trough. This process was called 'cloth walking'. By the 13c the procedure had changed and feet were replaced by wooden bars. – *Cf.* FULLER'S EARTH; FULLERY; TUCKER; WALKER

Fuller. A person who fulled cloth for a living. – *Cf. previous;* WALKER

Fuller's earth. A fine-grained clay used as a cleaner in the process of fulling cloth. – *Cf. next;* FULL

Fullery. A place for fulling cloth; a fulling mill. – *Cf. previous;* FULL

Fulwite. Lit. 'the full fine'. The Latin equivalent is *plena wita*. When imposed for an offence, it indicated the maximum fine was being imposed; however, on some occasions it could mean twice the normal fine. This penalty was incurred when there was resistance to paying church dues. This was payable in English districts in the 12c. In the Danelaw the offence was known as **lahslit*. – *Cf.* WITE

Fumagium. A hearth-tax, used in **DB*. It was also known as ***'reek-silver'. – *Cf.* FOCAGE

Fur. *Her.* Animal skins; a **tincture representing tufts of fur. There are eight main furs: **ermine, **ermines, **erminois, **pean, **vair, **counter-vair, **potent and **counter-potent.

Furlong. Length of a furrow in a field of the kind ploughed by a team of eight oxen. It was 40 perches or 220 yards in length. This made one part of the measure of an acre, the other being 22 yards in width. This was the area of land deemed ploughable by a team in one day. The Latin term used in **DB* is *quarentina* = 40. [< OE *furh* = furrow + *lang* = long] – *Cf.* ACRE; ROOD 1

Furnage. *See* FORNAGIUM

Fusil. *Her.* A **charge in the shape of a long lozenge.

Fuster. A maker of saddle-trees, which were the skeletons or frameworks of saddles.

Fustian. Fabric made from a mix of flax and cotton; later, used of pompous, bombastic language or speech. – *Cf.* BUMBACE

Fylfot. Pattern like a swastika; also known as a *'cross *cramponée'*. [< *fylfot* = fill-foot = design to fill the foot of a stained-glass window.]

Fyrd. Lit. 'a military expedition', hence host. Before the Norman Conquest, the *AS militia or military host. *Fyrd*-service formed a part of the *trimoda necessitas* owed to the king. Failure to present oneself was subject to heavy fines: a *thegn* was liable to forfeiture, while a retainer would owe his lord 40s for not attending. In Henry I's reign the fine was 120s. – *Cf.* EXERCITUS; EXPEDITIO; HERE 1; SCUTAGE

Fysilver. Lit. 'fish silver'. Cash payment to a lord replacing the supply of fish to meet the lord's requirements during Lent, or on Fridays, when meat could not be eaten.

G

Gabion. Wicker basket filled with earth and stones, reinforced by metal bands and used to plug gaps and breaches in damaged castle walls. [< Ital. *gabbia* = a cage]

Gafael. Land held by a family group or *gwely*. Its application varied throughout Wales; in some districts the *gafael* was a small unit within the larger *gwely*.

Gafol [gavel]. Tribute, rent, payment to a superior; also interest on money. The word was used also of corn cut and waiting to be formed into a sheaf. Latin forms include *gabulum* and *gavelagium*. – *Cf. next*; GAVELKIND

Gafolbere. Barley paid to a lord as payment of rent. [< OE *gafol* = rent, tribute + *bere* = barley] – *Cf. previous*

Gafolgerefa. A tax gatherer. – *Cf.* GAFOL

Gage. A pledge or surety, which could be property or a person. Later, the term applied to a glove or gauntlet by way of challenge, as a gage of battle, or surety of that challenge. Thus the gauntlet came to be thrown down. – *Cf.* GAUNTLET; WEDD

Galanas. System of compensation paid to the *gwely* or kindred of a victim by the *gwely* of the killer: the Welsh equivalent of *wergeld. It was an elaborate system, which was falling out of favour in Gwynedd in the 13c, although it persisted in other parts of Wales until the 15c or even the 16c.

Galilee. The large porch of a *cathedral forming part of the route of the Sunday procession. The reference is symbolic of Christ's going into Galilee after the Resurrection.

Galley ha'penny. An unauthorised halfpenny coin from Genoa, introduced into England via London by Genoese merchants in the 14c. It was somewhat thicker than the English coin; some continued in use till the 16c. It was called a 'galley ha'penny' because the Genoese were known as 'galley-men', being based in Galley Quay on the Thames.

Gallowglass. Bands of *mercenaries, foot soldiers, from Scotland, who went to fight the English in Ireland. They wore a light armour, with distinctive helmets, their weapon of choice being a *poleaxe. They were often attended by two squires. Later the word was used of the soldiers retained by the Irish kings or chiefs; a household soldier. [< Gaelic *galloclach* < *gall* = foreign + *oclach* = a young man] – *Cf.* CATERAN; HOBELAR; KERN

Gambeson. Jacket or tunic of *cuir-bouilli* or heavy cloth worn as protection by a knight. – *Cf.* ACTON

Gang. Gang Week, a period of processions in the street at important times of the agricultural year, e.g. first ploughing, when crops were growing, harvest. Gang Day was one of the three days before Ascension day, during *rogation. [ME *gang* = travelling, moving about] – *Cf.* PLOUGH DAY

Gannet's bath. Phrase used in *ASC* (975) of the sea when referring to invaders from Europe, i.e. Vikings, or rather their absence in England during the reign of Edgar the Peaceful. The phrase is apt: gannets are famous for their greed, thus those who crossed the gannet's bath also were greedy. The term used for this kind of compound synonym is *kenning*.

Garbe. *Her.* A wheat-sheaf. When other kinds of grain were used heraldically, the name of that grain needed to be specified. Thus, barley-garbes were used in the *blazon of the Brewers' Company.

Garbler. Official who visited shops and warehouses to check the purity of spices. [< ME *garble* = to sift, to remove dross] – *Cf.* AVERIA DE PONDERE

Garçons. In *sumptuary regulations issued in 1363, workers on the land were referred to in French as *garçons*, as were those worth less than 40s. – *Cf.* GENS DE MESTERE

Gardein. AN term for one of the clerks of the *marshalsea who was guardian of the royal *baggage train on its travels. It was his responsibility to ensure the carts were functional and the animals fit and ready.

Garderobae armorum. Latin term for armouries, e.g. those found at the Tower of London.

Garderobe. Small room for keeping robes and clothing. Later, it was used euphemistically of a privy or latrine; these were sometimes built into a thick wall, directly above a *moat. – *Cf.* Torche-cul

Garde-visure. *Her.* The visor of a knight's helmet.

Gargoyle. A grotesque figure, e.g. on the gutter of a roof, through whose mouth rainwater spouts; a distinctive feature of *Gothic architecture. [< OFr. *gargouille* = throat; thus the passage of water from the mouth] – *Cf.* Babery; Blemmya

Garret. A turret or watchtower. [< OFr. *garite* = watchtower]

Garter King of Arms. *Her.* Chief King of Arms in the College of *Arms. – *Cf.* Clarenceux; Norroy and Ulster

Garter, Order of the. Founded in 1348 by Edward III, the purpose of the order was to honour the king's most trusted companions. The order's motto is well known: *Honi soit qui mal y pense.* Originally there were 24 members with the king and prince of Wales. The induction ceremony was almost mystical, involving a vigil in a church through the night, and the taking of a bath to wash the knight's sins away. The blue of the robes was the blue of the French crown, which Edward claimed. They were made of wool, a way of affirming the importance of the wool trade to England. – *Cf.* Chivalry, orders of

Garth. Enclosed yard in the precincts of an *abbey, round which lodging for the worshippers might be found. Although open at first, these were later covered, with a *pentice roof, for some protection against the northern climate. They were attached to the main church building, the roof creating an enclosed space for walking. They came to be known as *'cloisters', in the form of a square with the garth surrounded by the four walkways. [< OE *geard* = an enclosure or yard]

Gate 1. An opening or entranceway in a wall. [< OE *gæt* = an opening]

Gate 2. When used in placenames or street names, 'gate' does not always mean gate as an opening or entrance; rather it means a street or way. This is esp. so in the north of England. [< ON *gata* = road] – *Cf.* Port

Gaud. A piece of showy ornament; a bauble. [< L *gaudeo* = to rejoice] – *Cf.* Bead

Gauntlet. Armoured glove lined with cloth or leather; by the late 14c a flared cuff had been added, which was decorated with extra metal plates. A gauntlet or *gage was thrown as sign or token of a challenge. [< OFr. *gant* = glove + -*let* as a diminutive]

Gavel. *See* GAFOL

Gavelkind. Kentish form of land tenure for which rent was paid rather than service due, under which the land was distributed equally between sons on their father's death, rather than all going to the eldest.

Gaveloc [gavelock]. A javelin or long dart; also, later a crowbar. [< OE *gafeluc* = spear]

Gebugan. *See* COMMENDATION

Gebur. An AS peasant before the Conquest; his land, a *virgate, reverted on death to his lord upon whom he was dependent. The *gebur* is mentioned in Ine's laws of the late 7c. The following details are from *Rectitudines Singularum Personarum*, a treatise on such things, dating from the early 11c and written most likely in Mercia. He owed both week-work and casual work: three days a week in harvest, also from *Candlemas (February 2) until Easter, then two days a week at all other times. If he had carrying to do, then he need not do the week-work while using his horse. He was required to plough an acre a week from start of ploughing till *Martinmas (November 11), then a further eight acres, two of which were his payment for pasturage. He also paid 10d rent. He was further required to render barley, hens, a lamb; and give some loaves to the swineherd. When first taking the land, the *gebur* would have had his land already sown, and would also have been given stock, implements, and even utensils for the house. However, everything returned to the lord on the *gebur*'s death. – *Cf.* CEORL

Gedælland. Common meadow or other land divided into shares by *ceorls; this land was usually fenced off to keep stray animals out. [< OE *dælan* = divide, share + *land*] – *Cf.* HAW; WORTHIG

Gemel. *Her.* Paired or coupled with something else. [< L *gemellus* = twin]

Gemot. A meeting or assembly; a *moot. – *Cf.* BUREWARMOT; WITENAGEMOT

Geneat. Lit. 'companion'. A free tenant with various duties, including *eaffor. He paid rent and offered a pig each year for pasture rights; he might have acted as *hayward. The *geneat*'s most important duties were to ride in his lord's retinue and attend him at the hunt. The name indicates a retainer in a lord's household. – *Cf.* AVERA; CYNGES GENEAT

Gens de mestere. Lit. 'people/men of the *mystery'. The term used in *sumptuary regulations of 1363, applied not only to those belonging to a trade *guild but also to town burgesses and merchants. – *Cf.* GARÇONS

Gentaculum [jentaculum] Latin word used for breakfast; an alternative might be *primum cibum* = first meal. [< L *jejunium* = fasting, hunger; *jento* = to breakfast] – *Cf.* CAPUT JEJUNIUM

Genuillières. The knee-guards as part of a suit of armour. At one time made of *cuir-bouilli*, they were later made of jointed steel. [< Fr. *genou* = knee]

Geoguth. Lit. 'youth, the young'. Household fighters who had not been rewarded with a gift of land. Although notionally young men, *geoguth* was used of any retainers without a grant of land. – *Cf.* DUGUTH

George, St. Patron saint of England (shared with Portugal, Lithuania and Aragon). He was martyred in Palestine in the 4c; his association with the dragon is late, emerging only in the 12c. Moscow also claims St George as its patron saint, as do lepers, Boy Scouts, saddle-makers and Venice.

Gesith. Lit. 'companion'. The *gesithcund* were men of aristocratic rank in the following of the king. *Gesithas* had their own households, sometimes on land given by the king in return for services. Ine's laws (late 7c) allow a *gesith* who moved from his land to take with him his *reeve, smith and children's nurse. The term *thegn* replaced *gesith* in the late 9c. – *Cf.* EORLCUND; GEBUR

Gilbertine Order. The order founded by Gilbert of Sempringham *c.*1131 was unusual in being the only one which originated in England. Sempringham is in Lincolnshire, where Gilbert's family were wealthy landowners. His order was also distinctive for its establishing double monasteries, i.e. for men and women, in which the canons served the nuns. The rule of St Augustine was observed by the canons, while the nuns observed the rule of St Benedict. The first house was built *c.*1131. By the time of Gilbert's death in 1189, there were some 700 canons and 1,500 sisters. At the Dissolution there were 26 Gilbertine houses.

Gild. *See* GUILDS

Gildhalda Theutonicorum. Lit. 'guild hall of the Teutons'. The guild and the hall of German merchants in London during the 13c. – *Cf.* HANSE

Ginetes. The Castilian light cavalry encountered by the Black Prince during his expedition into Spain in 1397. [< Ar. *Zanata* = tribe of horsemen]

Gioguth. *See* GEOGUTH

Gipon. A shortened *surcoat, perhaps padded and worn under a *hauberk, designed to be less awkward for the knight fighting on foot. – *Cf.* JUPON

Gisarme. Kind of *halberd with a sharp spear point, an axe at the base of that point, often with a second spike opposite the axe.

Gisement. Cattle taken to land for keeping and feeding at a fixed rate per head. [< AN *gister* = to lodge] – *Cf.* AGIST

Giwerie. A Jewish quarter or district.

Glaive. Weapon comprising a long handle, to which was attached a sharp metal point or blade.

Glanville. *See Tractatus de Legibus et Consuetudinibus Regni Angliae*

Glazier's nippers. *See* GROZING

Glebe. Land, cultivated land; more commonly, glebe-land was used of land within a parish assigned to support its priest. A glebe-house was the incumbent's house; a parsonage. *Gleba spiritualis* was the Latin form of glebe-land. [< L *gleba* = land, a field] – *Cf.* TEMPORALITIES

Gleoman. A musician; often used specifically of a musician who performed on a harp. The anglicised form 'gleeman' came to indicate a minstrel. The word came later to refer to a part-song. [< OE *gleo* = entertainment, music + *man*] – *Cf.* FABLEOR

Glomerellus. A schoolboy, esp. one studying *grammar. – *Cf. next*; MAGISTER GLOMERIE

Glomerie. Grammar. – *Cf. previous*; MAGISTER GLOMERIE

Glossa Ordinaria. Lit. 'regular or standard gloss'. The *Glossa* of the *Vulgate was begun in the school of Laon under Anselm of Laon (d. 1117) and added between the lines of text. However, it drew upon earlier collections which had been used since the 7c. Bede laid the foundation for the gloss with his work on the Acts. The *Glossa* contains both marginal and interlinear comments. It was drawn almost exclusively from the works of the fathers and was finished by the mid-12c. – *Cf.* CATENAE

Gobony. *Her.* A row of squares with alternating tinctures. This was also known as 'compony'. When there were two rows, this was known as 'counter compony'. Thus one might find *bend gobony and bend counter compony.

Gog and Magog 1. The names of the two nations which will seek to destroy the kingdom of God, according to the Book of Revelation (20:8): 'Satan shall be loosed out of his prison, and shall go out to deceive the nations which are in the four quarters of the earth, Gog, and Magog, to gather them together to battle, the number of whom is as the sand of the sea.' During the 1240s, the Tatars were moving across Eastern Europe causing horrors and creating such fears that they became easily identified with Gog and Magog, the ferocious hordes of the biblical Apocalypse. Medieval legend had it that Gog and Magog had been locked up by Alexander the Great behind a gate in the Caspian mountains, as is depicted for example on the Hereford *mappa mundi*. At the end of time they would break free, as Revelation described. – *Cf. next*

Gog and Magog 2. Two large wooden figures in the Guildhall in London; they are said to represent the giants destroyed by *Brutus, legendary founder of Britain and London. This legend is unrelated to the nations of the same names found in the Book of Revelation. – *Cf. previous and next*; TRINOVANTUM

Gogmagog. According to Geoffrey of Monmouth, Gogmagog was the giant which lived in Cornwall and was killed by Corineus, who threw him from the top of a cliff. – *Cf. previous*

Goldsmiths, Company of. An act of 1300 gave the company the right to assay gold and silver. The metal was given a mark to denote its standard. The term *'hallmark' arose from that mark having been given in Goldsmiths' Hall. The company is now known as the Worshipful Company of Goldsmiths.

Goliard. Generic name for satirical jesters and jokers, well educated, usually clerks, and thus able to write Latin verse, esp. in the 12c and 13c. As a class they were found in Europe as well as England, taking their name from a mythical bishop, Golias. They were known as tellers of tall stories by the time of Chaucer and William Langland. The best known collection of such writings today is to be found in the 13c *Carmina Burana* (Songs of Beuern, a village in Bavaria with a monastery). The songs were drinking songs, their subject-matter licentious for the times, but acceptable in taverns, as was their ribaldry.

Gomphus [gomph stick]. A curved stick supplied in the *longaigne* and used as we use toilet paper; an alternative to the *torche-cul* also supplied in a basket.

Gonfanon. A small flag carried on a lance, which indicated its bearer was a commander. [< OE *guðfana* = a war banner, an ensign]

Gong-hus. Lit. 'going-house'. An outhouse, latrine. – *Cf.* LONGAIGNE

Gore 1. A piece of land in the corner of an asymmetrical field. [< OE *gara* = a corner or point of land]

Gore 2. *Her.* A *charge comprising two curved lines, one drawn from a *chief point, the other from the base point and meeting at the *fess point.

Gorged 1. *Her.* Falconers used the term for the contents of the crop of a hawk. [< OFr. *gorge* = throat]

Gorged 2. *Her.* A figure with a ring around its neck. [< OFr. *gorge* = throat]

Gorget. That piece of a suit of armour which protected the throat. – *Cf.* ARMET

Gospel. Orig. the *godspel* = good news announced by Christ. This was a translation of the Latin *bona annuntiatio* and Greek *evangelion*. Later, the first four books of the New Testament, recounting Christ's life. – *Cf.* BIBLE 1

Gothic. Term for a style of European architecture in the 12c to the 16c, most familiar in cathedrals with flying buttresses and pointed windows; broadly, the distinctive medieval style; the term is 17c and was then intended to be derogatory, as the Goths (3c to 5c German tribes) were considered to have been uncouth barbarians.

Gouttes. *Her.* Drops, e.g. of blood. When used as a *charge they were distinctly pear-shaped.

Gradual. Pair of verses, from the Psalms, after the Epistle in the mass; a book containing the choral parts of the mass; an *antiphon sung between the Epistle and the *Gospel at the *eucharist.

Grail. The cup or plate used by Christ at the Last Supper. Variant definitions include a dish with some kind of supernatural properties, which made its first appearance in the *Conte du Graal* of Chrétien de Troyes. Later it was identified as the chalice used at the Last Supper; also the dish of the paschal lamb or the basin used by Pilate when he washed his hands. A further suggestion had the grail as the container in which Joseph of Arimathea caught the blood of Christ on the Cross. [?< L *gradalis* = dish]

Grain. Unit of weight; derived from a nominal average of grains taken from the middle of the ears of wheat. Some 7,000 grains = the pound avoirdupois, and 5,760 grains = the apothecary's troy pound. One grain = 0.0648 grammes.

Grain of paradise. The seeds of *Aframomum melegueta*, a member of the ginger family found in West Africa. It was used as a spice and in medicine. The phrase is sometimes used of cardamom seeds.

Grammar. Teaching grammar in medieval schools meant teaching the classics, e.g. Virgil. The works of Donatus, a 6c grammarian, were also used. Ælfric (d. 1010) composed a Latin grammar in OE in the 11c. Grammar became the core of the curriculum in succeeding centuries. – *Cf.* GLOMERELLUS; MAGISTER GLOMERIE

Grange. A granary; a farm some way from its feudal lord or the monastery to which it was attached or belonged.

Gravamina. Lit. 'grievances'. Latin word used by the Church when placing grievances before parliament. These frequently concerned taxes and tithes, such as the clerical tenth. Church liberties were also complained of, as was the freedom of Church courts. The basis of these grievances was lay and/or royal encroachment on Church prerogatives. – *Cf.* BENEFIT OF CLERGY

Great Sea. The Mediterranean.

Great seal. The seal first appeared in its developed form in England during Edward the Confessor's reign. The great seal was double-sided (unlike other English royal seals) and usually showed the monarch seated, as well as the royal insignia. Henry I's showed him on the obverse seated on the throne with orb and sword, while on the reverse he was mounted with sword and shield as duke of Normandy (*dux Normannorum*). In time it was augmented by other, smaller seals as the central administration expanded, then by the *privy seal, the keeper of which was a minister of state. Literal possession of the seal conferred immense power on its bearer; it gave and affirmed authority of sovereign and state. – *Cf.* CHAUFFER OF CHANCERY

Greave. The piece of armour for the leg below the knee.

Green Cloth. Used as in 'Officer of the Green Cloth'; a department of the royal household, dealing with financial and legal matters, overseen by a lord steward. Essentially the department dealt with all matters related to below stairs. It was so named for the green cloth on the table around which its meetings were held. The steward's post was well worth having: remuneration was £100 a year plus 16 dishes with every meal. It was held by a succession of powerful earls and dukes. The board of the Green Cloth persisted into the 19c, as a branch of the lord steward's department. Today it still meets in Buckingham Palace.

Gregorian chant. The Gregorian chant of monks singing in unison is so distinctive as to be instantly recognisable. The one or more notes sung to each syllable of the text of the service form the archetypal sound of pre-Dissolution Christianity. (One to four notes per syllable is termed neumatic; unlimited notes, melismatic.) Until the 9c the Gallican chant, used in Gaul, was used. However, during the reign of Charlemagne as Holy Roman Emperor, the Gregorian form was imposed throughout the West, as part of his policy of standardisation. It is so named after Pope Gregory (590–604) under whose tutelage the music was codified. What we are familiar with today is most likely a blend of Gallican and Gregorian chants. [< L *cantus* = song] – *Cf.* PLAINSONG

Gresuma [gersuma]. Latin term used in a lord's book of accounts for the entry *fine paid by a tenant, which usually carried the privilege of family inheritance.

Greyhound. The greyhound was much used for hunting, esp. hares; they hunted by sight not scent. In 1389 an ordinance decreed that no priest nor clerk was permitted to own a greyhound or other hunting dog, if his income was less than £10 a year. The Latin is *leporarius*. They were also known as *canes currentes* = running dogs. [< OE *grighund* = greyhound] – *Cf.* FEWTERER; LYAM HOUND

Grieve. Northumbrian form of *reeve, used of the overseer of an estate. [< OE *gerefa* = steward, officer]

Griffin. Creature of fable with the head and wings of an eagle and the body of a lion, already familiar to the Greeks around 1400 BC. In medieval symbolism, this creature was said to represent Christ, who was two natures in one, i.e. God and man. In heraldry it was the most frequently used of the imaginary creatures. The lower part of the body, tail and ears were a lion's; the fore-legs and talons were an eagle's, as were the wings. When displayed, the griffin was always shown *segreant – which was the synonym of *'rampant'. – *Cf.* Bestiary; Opinicus

Griffin seal. One of the royal seals. This seal was that of the king's chamber which, during Edward III's financial troubles in the 1340s, acquired the lands of royal wards and the estates of alien priories; other kinds of escheated land also went into the chamber. This practice ceased after October 1349, when the *exchequer took such lands and estates.

Gris. (Grey) fur of a squirrel. – *Cf.* Purfle

Grithbreche. Breach of the peace, but a lesser offence than a breach of the king's peace, e.g. a shire's *earl's peace. [< OE *grið* = peace + *brece* = a break or breach]

Groat. Coin first issued at Edward I's major recoinage of 1279, with the half-penny and the *farthing. It was worth 4d, weighing 89 grains (0.2 ounce). It was not a success, being poor quality with its weight out of proportion to its value, while its design facilitated clipping. It was reissued successfully by Edward III in 1351, accompanied by a half-groat valued at 2d. [< Fr gros = large] – *Cf.* Penny

Grocer. Trader or merchant in a variety of goods who dealt in wholesale goods. Only later did the term come to mean the shopkeeper who was a retail trader dealing in many items. [< AN *grosser* < L *grossarius* = an engrocer < L *grossus* = great, a large quantity] – *Cf.* Pepperer

Grozing. A grozing-iron was used to manipulate and shape glass with its hooked end. It was also known as 'glazier's nippers'.

Gryllus. A fantastic monster of unusually awkward anatomy: its face was between its legs. [L *gryllus* = grasshopper] – *Cf.* Babewyn; Bestiary; Blemmya; Cynocephalus

Guardant. *Her.* Term used of an animal seen in profile or looking out of the shield.

Guard-penny. *See* Ward-penny

Guerdon. A reward.

Guige. Strap attached to a shield allowing it to be carried over the shoulder. – *Cf.* ENARMES

Guild of St Nicholas. *See* NICHOLAS, GUILD OF ST

Guilds. Trade or craft associations, much like trade unions, but usually confined to a town. Most towns had craft guilds. The merchant guilds sought protection from foreign traders, as well as agreement between their associates as to behaviour and prices, for example. Craft guilds also sought to regulate practice, to ensure others were not working more hours than others, or charging higher prices. They also endeavoured to control quality of goods. Many were religious and social, e.g. the Guilds of Corpus Christi, putting on short plays or interludes on their saint's feast day. A great number of these disappeared in the *Black Death and were not revived. Trade or craft guilds lasted better and survived and even thrived after the plague, due to the shortage of labour. The practice of taking apprentices and the rôle of masters continued long after this period. The European equivalent organisations were: France: *corps de metier*; Flanders: *ambach*; Italy: *arte*; Germany: *Zunft*. [< OE *gyld, geld* = payment, render] – *Cf.* JOURNEYMAN; MASTER; MIRACLE PLAY

Gules. *Her.* The *tincture red. [< AN *goules* < L *gula* = red-dyed fur] – *Cf.* MINIUM

Gusset. *Her.* A *charge in the form of a line drawn from its top left or right (*sinister or *dexter *chief) to the central point of the shield, then continuing straight downwards. It is a mark of *abatement. If the line emerges from the shield's sinister chief it indicates adultery, from the other it indicates drunkenness. – *Cf.* FESS POINT

Gwely. Extended Welsh family group or kindred, all of whom were descended from a common ancestor. They would share ownership and rights in their land in *gwelyau*, partnership. The term was also used of the land which they shared. The term for this tenure was *tir gwelyog* = land in partnership. – *Cf.* GAFAEL; GALANAS

Gwestfa. A food render owed by a freeman to his king. – *Cf.* FEORM

Gynaeceum. The women's part of a house, rooms set aside for women-only meetings or as a place of work, e.g. weaving and making wool. – *Cf.* DISTAFF

Gyron. *Her.* A triangle whose apex touches the *fess point of a shield. – *Cf. next*

Gyronny. *Her.* Term for a shield divided into six triangular segments, i.e. gyrons, by lines which radiate star-like from the *fess point. – *Cf. previous*

H

Habergeon [haberioun, haburjon]. A sleeveless jacket or short tunic of mail or flexible scale armour. [< OE *healsbeorga* = a neck defence] – *Cf.* HAUBERK

Habillé [habited]. *Her.* The figure of a man shown clothed. It was also used of a ship whose sails were differently tinctured.

Habit. Ground-length garment characteristic of monks, its colour indicating the order.

Hackbut. An early *harquebus.

Hackney [hakenei]. Orig. a place near London where horses were pastured; by transference the horses kept there for hire. They were also used as pack-horses. Such horses would be used by king's messengers. Since then the word has become familiar in the 'hackney cab', once pulled by a horse. – *Cf.* BAG-GAGE TRAIN; NUNCIUS REGIS

Hafod. Lightly constructed shelter built in the Welsh upland pastures for use during summer. – *Cf.* BOOTH; HANDREF

Haga 1 [hegge]. A piece of land enclosed within a hedge (*DB*); the purpose was to keep forest and other animals out. – *Cf. next*; HAW; HAYWARD; MES-SUAGE

Haga 2. As well as an enclosure, *haga* was used when referring to a hall or meeting place, being enclosed. *Haga* was also a plot of land within a *bor-ough. – *Cf. previous*

Hagiography. The writing of saints' lives and the modern study of such writings. – *Cf. next*

Hagiology. The body of literature concerned with lives and legends of Christian saints; also a collection of saints' traditions, e.g. Eusebius's stories of the martyrs of Palestine in the 4c, or Pope Gregory's *Dialogues*, which recount stories about St Benedict and others in the 6c. – *Cf. previous*

Hagioscope [squint]. An opening in a wall (through which one 'squinted' – hence its colloquial name of 'squint') enabling the congregation to see the elevation of the host during mass, which – strictly – was intended only for *clergy.

Hair shirt. An uncomfortable and irritant under-shirt worn as a penance, either permanently or during Lent. Thomas Becket wore one, which was found, after his death, to be infested with lice. [< OE *hære* = hair-cloth, sack-cloth]

Hakenei. *See* HACKNEY

Halberd. A long-handled weapon with an axe and spike on the end. – *Cf.* GISARME; POLEAXE

Halfpenny [ha'penny]. A coin first issued in Edward I's recoinage of 1279. – *Cf.* FARTHING; GROAT; PENNY

Haligdom. A state of holiness; a holy place, i.e. a sanctuary or chapel. The *haligdom* was the place where *AS kings kept their relics, of which they were great collectors. It was also where their important documents were kept. [< OE *halig* = holy + *-dom* = state or condition]

Haligwerfolc. The 'people of the holy man', i.e. St Cuthbert, meaning the dwellers between the rivers Tyne and Tees.

Halimote. *See* HALLMOOT

Halley's comet. The appearance it is perhaps most famous for, that of 1066, is noted in *ASC, where it is referred to as 'the star called comet', as it had been when visible in 955; it was also called the 'long-haired comet'. Although the *Bayeux Tapestry shows the comet at Harold I's coronation, soon after Edward the Confessor's death on 5 January, it was in fact visible in England only in the last week of April, 10 days after Easter. The comet appeared also in June 1456. Then it was taken as a sign of the return of King Arthur, who would replace the hapless King Henry VI. As in 1066, the comet was seen as harbinger of a change of dynasty. – *Cf.* FEAXEDE STEORRA

Hallmark. *See* GOLDSMITHS, COMPANY OF; BAKERS, WORSHIPFUL COMPANY OF

Hallmoot. The *manorial court, held in a *manor's hall; a court of customary and ancient law. Minor, local, offences were dealt with and the only capital offences considered were those involving *infangen-theof. Later, hallmoot was used also of the court of a trade *guild. [< OE *mot* = moot, assembly]

Halsfang. *See* HEALSFANG

-ham. Placename suffix = home village. – *Cf.* HAMM

Hamble. To maim the feet of a dog by cutting its pads, thus preventing it from hunting, at a time when, in much of England, hunting was jealously reserved to the king. – *Cf.* FOREST ASSIZES; LAWED

Hamfare. The crime of breaking into a house to rob. It is mentioned in the *DB entry for the city of Chester, in the section where its laws are itemised. For *hamfare*, the penalty was a fine of £4 if committed on a Sunday or feast day, while 40s was payable for other days. – *Cf.* FORSTEAL; HAMSOCN; HENGWITE

Hamm. A piece of pasture or meadowland, particularly one enclosed, e.g. by a ditch. – *Cf.* -HAM; -ING

Hammer 1. Heavy weapon with a shaft and a hammerhead, used on foot or one-handed on horseback. [< OE *hamor*]

Hammer 2. *Her.* Hammers were often used as a *charge, usually with claws. Not unnaturally, smiths' and hammermen's companies used the hammer.

Hamsocn. The offence of forcible entry into another's house, or following him inside and assaulting him there. This was one of the offences reserved to the king's judgement. It would seem there was little real difference between *hamsocn* and *hamfare. The Latin was *hamsocna*. – *Cf.* FORESTEL; HUSBRECHE; MUNDBRYCE

Hanap. An elaborately decorated drinking vessel. – *Cf. next*

Hanaper 1. The basket used by a *nuncius regis* to hold bulky items. Later, a basket for hanaps or expensive plate. From this we have our picnic 'hamper'. – *Cf. next*

Hanaper 2. *Chancery department into which were paid the fees for sealing charters; such fees were then paid into the *exchequer. – *Cf. previous;* CHAUFFER OF CHANCERY

Hand-fast. A marriage or betrothal contract; a sign of a committed relationship with no religious ceremony. Such a relationship had existed between Edith (Eadgyth) 'Swan-neck' and Harold before he became king in 1066.

Handref. A substantial house of the Welsh valleys, which provided real shelter during the winter. – *Cf.* HAFOD

Hangwitha. Fine imposed for wrongfully hanging a criminal; also a fine for letting a criminal escape.

Hanse. *See next;* HANSEATIC LEAGUE

Hanse of Cologne. In 1157, Henry II and Emperor Frederick Barbarossa agreed a treaty which permitted merchants from Cologne to establish themselves in London. They were granted royal protection and privileges, e.g. to sell wine. In 1194, they purchased from Richard I freedom from various tolls in England and were allowed their guild hall in London without the payment of the customary 2s.

Hanseatic League [the Hanse]. The commercial and political league, established in the 1240s, of north German towns, centred round Lübeck from the

13c. The London Hanse had a fortified hall and wharf on the Thames (it was known later as the Stahlhof, the Steelyard, which was a misreading of the German *stahl* = a sample of goods + *hof* = courtyard); it adequately protected the German merchants in 1381 when elsewhere in London Flemish merchants and Lombards were massacred. During the 15c there were Steelyards also at Boston and King's Lynn. The London Steelyard was demolished in 1863; Cannon Street railway station now occupies the site. [< OHG *hansa* = a company, a troop] – *Cf.* EASTERLINGS; GILDHALDA THEUTONICORUM

Harbinger. Name given to an official of the royal household who went on ahead of the itinerating royal party to secure lodgings for all who would need them. – *Cf.* DOMUS REGIS; ITINERARY

Hards. *Tow, coarse portions of flax or hemp. [< OE *heorde* = tow, hards] – *Cf.* HAIR SHIRT; HERE 2

Harley lyrics. The collection of Middle English lyrics found in British Library MS Harley 2253. It originally belonged to the Harleian library. Recent work has shown that it was made by a professional scribe in Ludlow, Shropshire, working in the 1340s. Other lyrics in the MS are in Latin and French; their subject matter is both secular and religious. It is the largest such collection to survive.

Harquebus. Early kind of gun which used a tripod or a V-shaped rest to support the unwieldy barrel. They were quicker to learn to use than a *longbow or *crossbow.

Harrying of the North. 1069–70. In response to rebellion in Northumbria in mid-1069, which was assisted by Danes who wished to reclaim the kingdom of York, William I acted to lay waste much of Yorkshire. The king's assault lasted over the winter, until he and his army returned south in spring 1070: the policy was to destroy all means of life and thus of resistance to his rule. Although Yorkshire was the most damaged, Cheshire, Nottinghamshire and Derbyshire also suffered greatly.

Hart. Male red deer, older than five years. It was often used as decoration or part of a *livery, e.g. of Richard II. A white hart represented purity, sometimes the solitude of a hermit. [< OE *heorot*]

Harvest handful. One of the customary dues allowed a serf. According to the *Rectitudines Singularum Personarum* he was entitled to a sheaf of corn from each acre of the estate. – *Cf.* SERF

Haslet. Pig's fry; the viscera of pig or sheep, served cold in a meat loaf, still relished in Lincolnshire. [< OFr. *hastelet* = roast meat]

Hastellarius. Grand Latin title for the lowly kitchen worker who turned the spit; a turnspit. [< L *hasta* = a spit, spear]

Hastilude. Jousting in a *tournament, not necessarily with hostility or intention to harm, although it remained very dangerous. It was carried on as a serious sport at which *prowess was displayed and applauded. In 1388, Henry Knighton (d. 1396) recorded in his chronicle that during the *Merciless Parliament, four French knights sent a challenge to four English knights to fight a hastilude at Calais. In this case, the Frenchmen offered to fight 'in the form of war' or *joust of war. Although he mentions only two of the Englishmen by name, he says they returned with 'great renown', which was all any knight really wanted. [< L *hasta* = spear, spit + *ludus* = play] – *Cf.* CONFLICTUS GALLICUS; JOUST OF PEACE

Hatch. A small gate, a wicket gate; a gate or door with upper and lower parts, which could be opened independently. [< OE *hæcc* = a grating or half-gate]

Hatchment. *Her.* Armorial device or *escutcheon; a painted board displaying the arms of a person who had died, set on their house or in a church.

Hauberk. A long coat of mail reaching below the knees; the most important piece of protection worn defensively. In the 11c a hauberk might be worth about 30s. These coats were obviously subject to rust. The solution was a kind of varnish which gave the metal a yellow tinge, known as *hauberc saffré*. When the varnish had been removed through use and battle, the coat was abraded with sand, after which another coat was applied. Colour could be added to the varnish as the owner wished. – *Cf.* BRUNIA, BYRNIE; HABERGEON

Haurient. *Her.* Term for a fish shown as if reaching up for air.

Havoc. The cry given up permitting an army to break order and search out spoil and plunder; but it was given only when victory was clear and the enemy no threat. To cry 'Havoc' during battle was liable to invite defeat and was thus punishable by death. Shakespeare uses the word somewhat anachronistically in *Julius Caesar*: 'Cry Havoc, and let slip the dogs of war.' Elsewhere he uses it as we do for confusion and disorder. [< OFr. *havo* = pillage, plunder]

Haw. Fence or hedge enclosing a piece of land or dwelling place; also used of what the fence enclosed, an enclosure. It is from this that the *hawthorn gets its name: it functions well as a hedge. Thorns create an effective barrier, while flowers in spring provide a visible boundary. [< OE *haga* = hedge] – *Cf.* HAGA 1; WHITEBEAM

Hawking. *See* FALCONRY

Hawthorn. *Her.* The hawthorn was used as his badge by Henry VII; it was shown with a crown. When used elsewhere it was often *fructed and with white may-blossom. – *Cf.* HAW

Haybot. Material for the repair of fences; the right of peasants to take wood from their lord's estate to make the repairs. – *Cf.* BOT 2; RIGHTS OF COMMON

Hayward. The person designated to see fair distribution of hay for village animals during the winter months. He also ensured no animal broke into a hay or corn field, or anywhere it should not be. For this reason he was also known as the 'hedge-ward', a corruption of OE *hægweard*. [< OE *hæg* = meadow, hay; *hege* = hedge; *weard* = warden, ward] – *Cf.* HAGA 1; WARD

Hazard. A game of dice with complicated rules; also a term used in Real Tennis. Like all gambling, hazard was disreputable and condemned by the Church. [< OFr. *hazard* < Ar. *az-zahr* = the dice]

Heafodæcer. The strip of land, an acre in size, at the head of a field. [OE *heafod* = head + *æcer* = field]

Heafodbotl. This term was translated into the Latin of English law as *capitale mesuagium* = a chief *messuage. It was a broad term which referred to the hall or home of a *thegn; certainly, someone of higher status than his neighbours. It was used also of an ancestral home. In time, as English and Norman usage blended, this term was replaced by *manor. [OE *heafod* = head, chief + *botl* = building, place] – *Cf.* CAPUT HONORIS

Heahgerefa. *See* HIGH REEVE

Healsfang. An instalment of *wergeld. In the case of a *thegn this amounted to one tenth of 1,200s and was, according to *LHP, to be paid within 21 days. For lesser folk, the instalments varied from 12s 6d upwards. As well as an instalment payable by a due date, the term was used of that proportion of the man's *wergeld* which was to be paid to the nearest relatives of the man who had been killed; following which the dead man's *manbot had to be paid. The *healsfang* was also used in the late 7c Kentish law as the sum a man who had sacrificed to devils should pay. In *LHP*, the Latin equivalent is given as *apprehensio coelli* = seizing by the neck. [OE < *heals* = neck + *fang* = taking]

Hearth-tax. Household tax determined by how many hearths there were. The Latin term in *DB = *fumagium < *fumus* = smoke. – *Cf.* FOCAGE

Heaume. A heavy helmet used in the 12c and later by jousting knights. Being heavy and well padded, it offered the head extra protection. Also, the eye-slot or visor did not move, which further served against injury should it move when struck by a lance.

Hebdomadary. The *canon whose duty it was to celebrate mass for a week; the rôle was taken in rotation among a cathedral's canons. [< Gr. *hebdomas* = week]

Heckle. A wooden implement armed with long spikes through which beaten flax would be drawn, so as to straighten the linen fibres already exposed by water and beating.

Hedge-ward. *See* HAYWARD

Hell. The place of the dead, the underworld in Germanic mythology; to Christians the place of torment.

Helm-show. The occasion before a *tournament when contestants displayed their crests and achievements to the heralds and judges.

Henchman. A *squire who attended a monarch, or great lord, orig. on horseback; in time, loosely, a companion or associate. For example, the tomb of Thomas, the second Howard, duke of Norfolk, declares him to have been 'hencheman to Kyng Edward the iiij'. This refers to his having fought with Edward IV at Barnet in 1471. [< OE *hengest* = stallion + *man*]

Hengwite. Offence mentioned in a section of *DB* dealing with the laws of the city of Chester. *Hengwite* was failure to raise the *hue and cry. An ordinary citizen was liable to a fine of 10s, while an *earl or king's *reeve had to pay a fine of 20s. – *Cf.* FORSTEAL; HAMFARE

Hennin. The tall, cone-like headwear worn by the fashionable women of Burgundy in the 15c. A veil was often suspended from its peak. – *Cf.* ATOUR

Heptarchy. The seven kingdoms of England (7–8c) before the *Viking invasions, i.e. Wessex, Mercia, Kent, East Anglia, Essex, Sussex, Northumbria, of which Wessex, Mercia and Northumbria vied for supremacy. [< Gr. *hepta* = seven + *arkhia* = government]

Herald [herald of arms]. The court official who actually voiced the monarch's proclamations, e.g. at state occasions, at jousts and tournaments; also, the officer of the College of *Arms who decided who was entitled to arms. Heralds were also important on the occasion of a judicial duel. For instance, if the battle between two knights concerned treason, heralds were positioned so as to have a clear view and be ready to act if need be, e.g. if rules were infringed. As a reward, heralds took possession of all the weapons and armour left in the field, broken or whole, of both men. The lists and barriers were given to the marshal who had overseen the event.– *Cf.* ARMIGEROUS

Heraldry. The work and art of a *herald: blazoning armorial bearings; the determining of those entitled to such arms.

Heralds, College of. *See* ARMS, COLLEGE OF

Herbage. That which can be grazed in a forest, e.g. beech mast for pigs, which was considered separate from the land itself; later, the right of such grazing on another's land. – *Cf.* AGIST

Herbergage. Lodging, accommodation. [< OFr. *herberge* = an encampment] – *Cf. next*

Herberger [herbergeour]. Official responsible for the allocation of lodgings to members of the royal household, the **familia regis*. A regulation of 1318 specifically forbade the presence of wives, presumably to limit the numbers of mouths to be fed. Since the court was peripatetic, its more lowly members were provided with clothing through *livery, and with food, with their job. Lodging – herbergage – was more difficult. The king's messengers, **nuncii regis*, had stabling allocated for their horses; it is probable the messengers themselves slept in warm stables. Likely enough, it was a combination of mad scramble and favours given which determined who slept where. [< OFr. *herberge* = an encampment] – *Cf. previous*

Hercarius. Latin term for a horse used for harrowing fields; also for the man who guided the horses, the ploughman.

Herce [herse]. Term used by Froissart when referring to a particular formation of English archers on the battlefield, e.g. at Crécy (1346). The phrase he used is *à manière d'une herce* = like a *herce*. Unfortunately there is no evidence for just what that formation was as Froissart assumed his reader knew what he meant. OFr. has *herce* or *herse* = a harrow. But it may be derived from the Greek *herkos* = a fence. *Herse* was used in French heraldry of both the harrow and of a *charge looking like a portcullis. – *Cf. previous*

Here 1 [heer]. An army or host. The OE word was applied to the Danish *Viking invaders of the 9c, while the English defenders were named **fyrd*. In AS law a *here* was a band of robbers, 35 or more strong, a sense which was transferred to the force of Danish invaders. In Edgar's law code of 962, the word *here* had come to apply to inhabitants of the Danish settlements in general, without military connotation.

Here 2. Hair-cloth, a *hair shirt. [< OE *hære* = hair-cloth, sackcloth] – *Cf.* Hards

Hereditament. That which could be inherited. As it suggests, corporeal hereditament was something physical, such as land or goods; incorporeal hereditament was intangible but real, e.g. a right to something; as *Bracton says, 'an incorporeal thing does not admit of *livery'. [< L *heredito* = to inherit]

Hereditario jure lagaman civitatis. Lit. 'hereditary lawmen of the city'. This part-Latin phrase refers to the 12 men who were the hereditary jurors of e.g. York in the early 12c. – *Cf.* Lawman

Heregeatu. Lit. 'war gear'. Military equipment in general. – *Cf.* Heriot

Heregeld. Lit. 'army geld'. Tax imposed by Æthelred the Unready and his successors to pay for the lithesmen who manned the ships in the king's service. It was discontinued in 1051 by Edward the Confessor but reimposed by

William I. At the time it was the only national tax in all Europe. – *Cf.* HERE 1; LITHESMAN

Heresy. *Canon law considered heresy to be the obdurate denial by a Christian of one of the fundamental tenets of Christianity. For example, among the heretical judgements of John Wyclif were the following: that the substance of the bread and wine remained in the sacrament after consecration, i.e. there was no transubstantiation at the altar; that Christ was not present in the sacrament at the altar in any form; that to someone who was truly contrite confession to a priest was neither needful nor necessary. At times the heretic might be subject to fierce punishment, such as burning at the stake. [< Gk *hairesis* = choice] – *Cf. next;* ERROR

Heretic. Someone whose belief was considered unorthodox and unacceptable to the Church; only later, post-11c, was the term used also of non-Christians. [< Gk. *hairesis* = choice] – *Cf. previous;* LOLLARDY

Heriot. Feudal service due a lord on the death of one of his men, namely the return of military equipment; later, heriot consisted of giving the lord the best beast or a sum of money. Latinised as *herietum*. [< OE *heregeatu* = war gear] – *Cf.* HEREGEATU; RELIEF

Hermit. A person living in solitude for religious reasons; later, also a vagabond. Ideas about hermits were not hard and fast: they could be good men or rogues. The romances of the 13c often portrayed hermits sympathetically, particularly aiding wandering knights. In 1412, a statute was issued ordering the punishment of *pillory and whetstone (suspended from the neck) for anyone pretending to be a hermit. [< L *eremita*] – *Cf.* RECLUSE

Herse. Term for a kind of *portcullis, i.e. a door heavy with spikes, which could be dropped in front of another to hinder and further dismay attackers.

Hibernagium. Latin term used for the time from Michaelmas (29 September) to Christmas: this was the sowing season. The word was also used for winter itself. [< L *hibernus* = of winter, wintry]

Hidated. Modern term used of land divided into hides. – *Cf. next*

Hide. The area reckoned to be sufficient for one family and/or ploughable by an eight-ox plough team in a year. The term was used for taxation purposes, notionally comprising an area of up to 120 acres. In Berkshire, however, the hide was approx. 40 acres; there was much variation. The five-hide group became the basis of payments for the support of local members of the *fyrd. In *Historia Ecclesiastica* Bede used the phrase *terra unius familiae* = land of one family. When his work was translated into OE the word used was *hid*. The Latin word is *hida*. – *Cf. previous; Tribal Hidage;* VICTUM VEL STIPENDUM; VIRGATE

High reeve. In Northumbria, a high-ranking nobleman, below an **ealdorman* but equivalent to a **hold*; in southern England, a royal official (L *summus praepositus*) exercising some of the functions of an *ealdorman*, but without the rank. – *Cf.* REEVE; SCIR-REEVE; WICGEREFA

Hilary. Name of a university term; also a session of the English High Court, both beginning in January (the feast of St Hilary is 13 January).

Historiated. Modern term for the sometimes highly decorated initial letters found at the beginning of chapters or sections in illuminated MSS.

Hithe. Place of shelter for boats; a mooring or landing place on a river; hence its use in placenames, e.g. Hythe and Smallhythe.

Hlafordswice. Betrayal of or treachery towards a man's lord. Such a betrayal by a **thegn* in the AS world dominated by lordship and the imperatives of loyalty was a great crime, since all members of a lord's household were bound to him by mutual oaths. [< OE *hlaford* = lord, master + *swice* = treachery, deceit]

Hobelar. Term used of lightly armed horsemen, as opposed to heavily armed and armoured knights, who were sometimes cumbersome and slow. It is thought these hobelars were the precursors of archer-horsemen; and that they were brought from Ireland, where they were known as *hobinos* (Ir. *obann* = quick, nimble). Their horses were lighter than the **destrier* and also cheaper. – *Cf.* GALLOWGLASS

Hock-day. The Tuesday after Easter Sunday; important as being one of the days on which rents were to be paid. Money was also collected for parish use. It was the occasion for games like catch, when those caught had to buy their freedom ('hock' themselves) for a small sum, which was added to the parish collection.

Hodden grey. Undyed homespun cloth worn by peasants and land-workers. They wore caps of very similar material. Illustrations in MSS show ploughmen wearing a cap with its peak turned back – much as baseball caps are worn today. – *Cf.* Hoo; SUMPTUARY REGULATIONS

Hogshead. Measure of wine = *c.*52 gallons. – *Cf.* BUTT; TUN

Hold 1. Name for a high-ranking Scandinavian leader, equivalent to a northern **high reeve; it is found in placenames such as Holderness = a promontory or headland of the *hold*. – *Cf.* REEVE

Hold 2. Defence, a place of support; also, a place of refuge; from which later, property held.

Hold oath [hyldath]. AS oath of allegiance. A man taking the oath swore to be faithful and true to his lord; however, like all such oaths, it was conditional upon the lord reciprocating with his obligations to the man. [< OE *hold* = loyal, faithful + *að* = an oath] – *Cf.* DIFFIDATIO; FEALTY; HOMAGE 1

Holiday. Lit. 'holy day'. By the 14c, a holiday had become a day of leisure; it follows the same trajectory of debasement as *seely. [< OE *haligdæg* = holy day]

Holm. Small island in a river or close to the mainland. [< ON *holmr* = island]

Holmgang. A fight between two opponents on a small island from which neither could move without losing the contest; supporters watched from the banks of the river. Such encounters were generally fought to the death. [< ON *holmgangr* = going to the holm, i.e. an island]

Holograph. MS in the hand of a named person; used of manuscripts and letters by the well known and figures of importance. Thus the Book of Kells might strictly not be called a holograph, whereas it could be safely used of Bede's own MS of his *Historia Ecclesiastica*. The term relates to letters and MSS of the work of a poet or novelist, esp. post-1600, when the term was coined. The letters of Henry V are certainly holographs. Apart from their intrinsic interest, his are the earliest extant letters in a monarch's own hand. [< Gr. *holos* = whole + *graphos* = writing]

Homage 1. Formal acknowledgement of a *vassal's allegiance and *fealty to his lord. Thus the young King Edward III did homage in June 1329 to Philip, the new king of France. But Edward did this as duke of Aquitaine, not as king of England. *Bracton said: 'The *nexus* between a lord and his tenant through homage is . . . so great and of such quality that the lord owes as much to the tenant as the tenant to the lord, reverence alone excepted.' [Fr. *homme* = man < L *homo* = a man + *-age* = sense of attachment] – *Cf. next*; HOLD OATH; IMMIXTIO MANUUM

Homage 2. The phrase 'the homage' was used as a collective noun, as when all men of a *manor acted in concert for some particular end. For example, consent of the homage was required for the enclosure of land. – *Cf. previous*; VILLATA

Homines lunares. Lit. 'Monday men'. Monday was the day of the week when those so obliged worked on their lord's land. – *Cf.* FERIA UNA

Hommes de lignage. Lit. 'men of lineage'. This French term was used of men of noble birth fallen on hard times and unable to live as splendidly as they wished and their ancestors had. – *Cf.* FRANCHISE; LIGNAGE

Homo ligeus [homo ligius]. A *liegeman. – *Cf.* LIGEUS

Honi soit qui mal y pense. Lit. 'let it be a dishonour to him who thinks badly of it'. The motto of the Order of the *Garter, founded by Edward III, perhaps on St George's Day in 1348, after victories at Calais and Crécy (1346). The origin of the order's name and its motto is reputed to have come from the occasion of a ball given by the king to celebrate his victories in France. A legend first recorded a century and a half later has it that after the countess of Salisbury dropped her garter while dancing, the king picked it up and tied the ribbon around his knee. Those who saw the king's action laughed in jest but the king responded gallantly, *Honi soit qui mal y pense*.

Honour. A group of manors or fiefs held by one lord; a lordship. The honour had its own court at the lord's *caput honoris*. *LHP makes it clear that a tenant would have to go to his lord's *caput* from wherever he held land, even if in another *county. The word as first used indicated an estate which gave its holder dignity and status, i.e. honour. England was the king's honour. – *Cf.* CAPUT HONORIS; TENANT-IN-CHIEF

Honourable ordinary. *Her.* One of the nine main ordinaries known as honourable: cross, *chief, *pale, *bend, *bend sinister, *fess, *bar, *saltire, *chevron.

Hoo. A head-covering; a cap. [< OE *hufe* = covering for the head] – *Cf.* HODDEN GREY

Hoodman blind. Name used in the 15c for the children's game we know today as 'blindman's bluff'.

Horarium. Latin word for a *book of hours; English = horary. The word was also used to indicate a timetable, for example, that of a monastery: Matins: 2–3 am winter, 1–2 am summer; Lauds: 6–7 am winter, 4–5 am summer; Prime: 7–8 am winter, 5–6 am summer; Terce: 9–10 am winter, 7–8 am summer; Sext: 12–1 pm winter, 11–12 am summer; None: 1–2 pm winter, 2–3 pm summer; Vespers: 4–5 pm winter, 6–7 pm summer; Compline: 6:15–6:30 pm winter, 8:15–8:30 pm summer. [< L *hora* = hour]

Hordere. Lit. 'the hoarder, keeper of the hoard', i.e. the king's treasurer. He had charge of the collection of monies and was based in Winchester, where AS kings kept their treasury. Monasteries also had their hoarder or storekeeper, known in Latin as *hordaria*. – *Cf.* BURTHEGN

Horse-thegn. Member of the royal household, acting as a bodyguard. – *Cf.* KING'S HOUSEHOLD; THEGN

Horsweard. Warden or protector of the king's horses. One such is mentioned in King Æthelberht's laws of the early 7c. He was responsible for all aspects of the horses' treatment and management: tending and organising the wild horses, as well as the stud. The legal definition of a herd of horses was 50 mares. The rôle changed little but the title did over the years. During John's reign he was Chief Keeper; in Henry III's reign he was King's Farrier; later still he was Master of the Horse. [< horse + OE *weard* = warden]

Hospitaller. *See next*

Hospitarius [hospitalarius, hostillarius]. The *hospitarius*, i.e. hospitaller, was the monk in charge of arrangements for guests at a monastery. [L *hospitarius* = a host, one in charge of billeting arrangements]

Hospitium. The small select group, the inner trusted circle, of the king's household servants. [< L *hospitium* = lodging] – *Cf.* MEINIE

Hostages. From the time of Alfred to that of Cnut and later, hostages were taken and given. They were intended to be a sign of good faith regarding a treaty; their death resulted from any breach. A hostage could be a child or a knight of some importance. Some were treated well, others were not. Some were killed; others were mutilated and then returned.

Hostiarius. *See* OSTIARIUS

Hosticum. Part of the **familia regis* but that part which served as the king's own close bodyguard. This sense is found in **LHP*. It was also used of an army or military force.

Hostillarius. *See* HOSPITARIUS

Houpelande. Tunic with exaggeratedly long-sleeves, reaching the floor, sometimes with a train, and designed to be worn at court and to be impractical.

Hours. *See* BOOK OF HOURS

Housecarl. *See* HUSCARL

Housel. Holy communion; the administration of the consecrated host at the **eucharist.

Hræglhus. A vestry where vestments were kept. [< OE *hrægl* = clothing + *hus* = house, building] – *Cf. next*

Hræglthegn. Keeper of the king's wardrobe. One of the AS king's most trusted **thegns*, who maintained close contact with him. The Latin term for this office was *vestiarius*. [< OE *hrægl* = clothing] – *Cf. previous;* BURTHEGN; KING'S WARDROBE

Huckster. A petty trader, with a small market stall; a street hawker. Women were often forced to make a living in such trading, esp. when widowed without property. – *Cf.* FEMME SOLE; REGRATOR

Hue. To shout, as when hunting or in battle. [< OFr. *huer* = to shout] – *Cf. next*

Hue and cry. The general call to chase a miscreant; also the pursuit itself. Raising a hue and cry was usually done to alert people in the immediate area to a recent crime; public support in the pursuit and arrest of the criminal was obligatory. Pursuit could go into a neighbouring *vill if need be. To ignore a hue and cry rendered one liable to punishment under *frank-pledge. In writing about murder, *Bracton said that as it was secretly done, 'no public hue and cry immediately pursues [the perpetrator]'. – *Cf. previous*; JURATI AD ARMA

Hulk. Large sailing vessel used for cargo in the 13c. Only later did the word come to mean the hull of an abandoned ship. [< OE *hulc* = a vessel]

Humours. The physiological determinants of health and character. They were four in number: blood, *phlegm, choler, and melancholy or black bile.

Hundred. AS administrative district within an English *shire from which representatives met each month; such a district had its own judicial court. The term was also used in the north for a subdivision (12 carucates) of the *wapentake.

Hundred Years' War. A 19c phrase for the conflict between England and France from 1337 to 1453. Edward III laid claim to the French throne in 1337, adopting the title in 1340, but other issues fuelled the conflict. At first successful in battle, his fortunes were reversed in the second phase, which began in 1369. England regained superiority under Henry V at Harfleur and the Battle of Agincourt in 1415. At the Treaty of Troyes in 1420, Henry's right to the French throne was acknowledged, affirmed by his marriage to Catherine of Valois. England was in control of northern France until 1435; however, this control was weakened in succeeding years, until Normandy was lost in 1450 and Gascony in 1453.

Hurdle. Basket used for hauling earth, e.g. during the construction of a mine; used as well for the sledge on which a traitor was dragged or 'drawn' through the town on the way to execution. It was also a portable section of fencing, used for example for constructing sheepfolds.

Hurdy-gurdy. Musical instrument which produced a droning sound like a bagpipe; it was played by turning a handle, which then played on the drone-strings, leaving the other hand free to play a small keyboard.

Hurling time. Phrase used in the *Brut or Chronicle of England* of the *Peasants' Revolt of 1381. Hurling = fighting, strife and violence.

Husbonda. The householder; master of the house, whence modern 'husband'. [OE *hus* = house + *bonda* = a freeman, householder, occupier of soil] – *Cf. next*; BONDA

Husbonde. The mistress of a house. – *Cf. previous*

Husbote. The right of tenants to take wood from their lord's land for the repair of their houses. [< OE *hus* = house + *bote* = a good or advantage, a use]

Husbreche. An attack on a dwelling, which, like arson and murder, *LHP* states could not be compensated for by a money payment, unlike e.g. *strætbreche*. – Cf. BOTLEAS; HAMFARE; HAMSOCN

Huscarl [housecarl]. Household retainer, esp. a military retainer; used particularly of the retinues of the Danish kings of England and their successors. – Cf. THEGN

Hushe. 15c hunter's term for a group of hares. The term for dislodging a hare from its hiding place was 'moving' it.

Husting. Assembly of his men called by a lord; later a court, specifically one of the courts at London, dating perhaps from the 11c. Its use probably arose from commercial exchanges between Londoners and Scandinavians. In time it became the place of authority for commercial matters in the city of London – the place where matters of debt and disputes over land were settled and cases involving foreign merchants. Its importance was such that it met during the 12c in the Guildhall on every Monday. Suitors were seated on four benches – a relic of a much older proceeding where justice was sought before a lord. [< ON *húsþing* = house assembly]

Hydgeld. *Fine paid by a *serf to avoid corporal punishment; this was usually 30d. [< OE *hyd* = skin + *geld* = money] – Cf. PRETIUM CORII

Hyldath. *See* HOLD OATH

I

Icknield Way. Prehistoric track which connected the Wash with Salisbury Plain. The meaning of 'Icknield' is unknown.

Ictus regis. Lit. 'king's strike or blow'. The formal exchange of blows at the beginning of a duel between individual combatants, e.g. *champion and challenger. – Cf. CRAVEN; DUELLUM

IHS. *Iesus, hominum salvator* = Jesus, saviour of mankind. These initials were often used in images and paintings of Christ.

Illumination. Term applied to the practice of applying gold and silver to initial letters in MSS in this period. The term is now used to include colours, often red, but strictly should refer only to gold and silver. – Cf. RUBRIC

Immixtio manuum. Lit. 'mixing of hands'. During the ceremony of *homage, the *vassal placed his hands between those of his lord; this was followed by the oath of *fealty.

Impale. *Her.* Term used when two coats of arms were displayed on the same shield, separated by a vertical line (*pale). When a woman's family's arms were impaled upon those of her husband they were placed on the *sinister side. Arms which were not impaled indicated they were those of an unmarried man. – *Cf.* ARMS, COAT OF

Impeachment. Form of criminal trial which emerged in the 14c, falling from use after the mid-15c. Such trials were begun in the House of Commons with the lords serving as judges. [< OFr. *empecher* < L *impedico* = to catch]

In capite. Lit. 'in *chief'. Latin term indicating land was held 'in *chief' of the king, as a *tenant-in-chief would.

In chief. Phrase used of land held directly of the king. Such lords and magnates were known as 'tenants-in-chief'. The Latin = *in capite*.

In commendam. Lit. 'in trust'. Latin phrase used when a *benefice was given to a layman temporarily until a permanent appointee could be found. [< L *commendo* = to deposit, to entrust]

In curiam. *See* IN PECUNIA

In denario. *See* IN PECUNIA

In domus. *See* IN PECUNIA

In paragio. Lit. 'in line'. Joint tenure of an estate through inheritance; or, tenure between *parceners. This form of tenure ensured an estate's unity, the senior partner being responsible for all estate obligations. The English form is 'parage'.

In pecunia. Lit. 'in money'. Phrase used in account books for a sum paid in coin, rather than in kind, e.g. grain, eggs, honey. *In denarii* was also used of payments in cash; *in argento* was used when silver coins were proffered; *in auro* for payment in gold. For a payment made in the *manorial court, *in curia* was used; in the house, *in domo*; in the *exchequer of a large establishment, *in scaccario*; *in aratro* was used if the collector found the payer at the plough.

In scaccario. *See* IN PECUNIA

In use. *See* ENFEOFFMENT TO USE

Inblanch. Term used of payments made in assayed coin, rather than in goods or produce. – *Cf.* ALBA FIRMA; BLANCH FARM

Incensed. *Her.* Angry (of an animal), with fire bursting from mouth and eyes.

Incipit. Lit. 'it begins, here begins'. MSS lacked title pages as we know them; instead the texts they contained were referred to by their opening words or words in lists or catalogues of books. (A papal *bull was known by its opening words.) However, there were times when a monastery possessed several copies of one text. In such cases, the words *secundo folio* (= second folio) prefixed the first word or words of the second leaf for use as identification. Few if any copies of a text were likely to have the exact same number of words written by the beginning of the second leaf. – *Cf.* EXPLICIT

Incontinence. A word much used in medieval times, meaning a failure of will to control fleshly passions. It is stronger than synonyms such as 'intemperance', being deemed a sin for which one would be punished. Dante placed the incontinent in an upper part of the *Inferno, it being less serious than deliberate wickedness. – *Cf.* NICOLAITISM; VIRTUE

Incumbent. The holder of a Church *benefice.

Incunabulum. Term for a book printed before 1501. This word was used by 19c booksellers needing categories and descriptions for their catalogues. [< L *in* + *cuna* = cradle]

IND. *In nomine Domini* = in the name of the Lord; also *In nomine Dei* = in the name of God.

Indenture. Orig. a legal document exchanged between two or more people with its edges indented, so as to be easily identifiable. Later, the agreement by which an apprentice agreed to work under a master for a set period of time, usually seven years. – *Cf.* CHIROGRAPH

Indiction. A period of 15 years; as a fiscal period it was instituted by the Emperor Constantine in 313. A particular year within that period was referred to by a number, as regnal dates are indicated, e.g. 7 Henry I.

Indulgences. At first indulgences were limited to 40 days, and were remissions of punishment and of sin and a specified quantity of penance. Purgatory came to be thought of as the place where penance was performed after life; a place in time, rather than eternal like heaven. Thus an indulgence would limit the time the sinner spent in purgatory. Pilgrimage might be undertaken as expiation of particularly serious sins. When preaching the First Crusade, Pope Urban II granted a *plenary indulgence, saying all those who went might count that journey in lieu of all penance. It may be that the very first text printed using movable type was an indulgence issued by Pope Nicholas V in 1454. [< L *indulgentia* = leniency, concession.] – *Cf.* JUBILEE; PENITENTIAL PILGRIMAGE

Inescutcheon. *Her.* A small shield shown within a larger.

Infangen-theof. The right of a lord to pursue and hang a thief caught in possession of stolen goods, i.e. red handed. Before the Norman Conquest, OE kings did not permit the growth of private justice. [< OE *infangen*= caught + *ðeof* = thief] – *Cf.* FRANCHISE; MAINOUR

Inferno. Hell: the place of eternal fires and the destination of sinners. [< L *infernum* = below]

-ing. Suffix of placenames indicating the followers of a person and their chief settlement, thus Reading = Reada's people. It also functioned as a patronymic, or suggested the bearer possessed certain qualities, thus *Ætheling = son of a noble, or one possessed of noble qualities. – *Cf.* -BY

Ingenium. A contrivance, an engine; used of poachers' traps. Their construction is uncertain but withies were used, sometimes in conjunction with a *laqueus*. Sharpened stakes were referred to as *ingenium*.

Inland. The area within a *manor devoted to its lord's own use, rather than being let to another. Latinised as *inlandia*. – *Cf.* BEREWICK

Inning. The reclaiming of fenland; later, the enclosure of land.

Inns of Court. Institutions in London responsible for legal education: Lincoln's Inn, Gray's Inn, Inner Temple and Middle Temple. The benches, their governing bodies, had the exclusive right to admit or not persons to practice: they are formally called to the *bar. English law was studied, not Roman. By the mid-13c, common law had increased by practice and become intricate, requiring lay professionals. The clerks who worked in the *chancellor's offices seem to have taken students and trained them.

Innsi Gall. Phrase employed by Irish chroniclers for the islands off the west coast of Scotland following the Vikings' attack on Iona in 795. *Innsi Gall* = islands of the foreigners. These were Norwegian Vikings, or Norsemen. To these Vikings, the Western Isles were known as Suthreyjar = the southern islands. – *Cf.* MAN, ISLE OF

Inquest of Sheriffs. Orig. the *sheriff was appointed by the king; his duties included financial and judicial matters. He collected money annually for the *exchequer and presided at the *county court. After the *Anarchy of Stephen's reign, sheriffs no longer acted as agents of the crown, but of their local magnate. This corruption grew worse as sheriffs began also to abuse powers which had been granted by the Assize of Clarendon, e.g. the power to seize the property of criminals, and to collect taxes. Therefore, in 1170, Henry II attempted to correct abuses by instituting this Inquest of Sheriffs. It was designed to take securities and pledges from sheriffs and the local barons and magnates, reclaiming crown authority.

Inquisition post mortem. An enquiry held after death. A writ was issued so that local people could be questioned to determine whether or not an heir was of age and able to inherit. Local people would be asked to confirm dates of birth and baptism.

INRI. *Iesus Nazarenus Rex Iudaeorum* = Jesus of Nazareth, king of the Jews: the text placed on the Cross on which Christ was crucified. John 19:19 ascribes the wording to Pilate: 'And Pilate wrote a title, and put it on the cross'.

Inspeximus. A charter which confirmed that an earlier charter had been examined, and reaffirmed it. [L *inspeximus* = we have inspected]

Insular. Style of calligraphy which emerged in Britain following the departure of the Romans. The Insular half-uncial was used by both Irish and English book writers. It evolved from the standard *uncial but showed some very elegant cursive features in its ascenders (b, d, f, h, l), and descenders (g, p, q), as well as the loops between letters. – *Cf.* MINUSCULE; TEXTURA

Insular French. Anglo-Norman French, as spoken in England, particularly in and after the 12c, when it was beginning to lose contact with continental French. It was sometimes known as Marlborough French, a phrase used by Walter Map.

Interdict. One of the weapons in the papal armoury. Sentence of interdict excluded a district, country or person from all privileges and benefits of the Church. In effect, this barred a person from receiving the host in holy communion, or from confession. If the ban was placed on a district, only baptism and extreme unction were permitted. It was imposed upon England in 1207 by Pope Innocent III, during the reign of King John (1199–1216). John's *excommunication followed in 1209. [< L *interdico* = to forbid by decree]

Intrinsec. Services and dues owed a lord. They are called *intrinsec* as they were deemed to be within the *fief and engaged no one outside it. This use survives in the Dorset placename Ryme Intrinseca. [< L *intrinsecus* = on the inside, within] – *Cf. next;* FORINSEC

Intrinsecus. The king's inner marshal. His duty was to watch over and guard the inner parts of wherever the king was in residence, and to ensure that courtesans (those with attachments to a courtier) were not too intrusive or conspicuous. [L *intrinsecus* = on the inside, within] – *Cf. previous;* CLERK OF THE MARKET; FORINSECUS

Introit. The *antiphon sung at the beginning of mass. [< L *introitus* = entrance] – *Cf.* REQUIEM

Invected. *Her.* Describes the scalloped pattern on a stripe or *fess across a shield. – *Cf.* ENGRAILED

Inward. The duty to provide a bodyguard for the king when he was in the *county. Should the king not visit in any particular year, a *fine was payable.

Irish Remonstrance. The remonstrance of the Irish princes was sent to the pope in 1317, setting out the ancient lineage of the Irish and the illegal nature of the papal grant, in 1155, of Ireland to England made by an English pope, Adrian IV (Nicholas Breakspear, d. 1159). The remonstrance protested the subjugation the Irish had endured because of the Norman invasion and occupation of Ireland. It detailed the usurpation of Church lands and dispossession of the Irish, the disregard of Irish law, and the closure of the English royal courts to those of Irish blood. It was a 14c claim to the ancient freedoms and independence of the Gael, while associating Gaelic Scotland with Ireland; it asked for Edward Bruce as king, claiming he was a descendant of Irish ancestors, and would thus be an Irish king, not a foreigner.

Iterans justitiarius. Lit. 'a travelling justice'. A justice on circuit; but known as a *'justice-in-eyre'. [< L *itero* = to journey; *justitiarius* = a justice]

Itinerary. The medieval court was constantly on the move, travelling between castles, towns, estates and monasteries, consuming great quantities before moving on. Frequently, the king travelled on to a favourite forest to hunt, with hounds or kestrel, or to a magnate's castle. Henry II attempted to make the process a little more predictable and easier to administer by announcing the route a month in advance. This made matters easier for a *purveyor. Edward I changed residence 78 times in one year late in his reign. King John changed place two or three times a fortnight; it was a great event for him to settle anywhere for a month. However, during the later part of Edward III's reign (1327–77) such removing was dramatically limited to three or four favourite places, all within easy reach of London, i.e. Havering, Woodstock, Windsor and Sheen. – *Cf.* CLERK OF THE MARKET; FORINSECUS; HARBINGER; INTRINSECUS; VERGE

J

Jacobin. Uncomplimentary word applied to *Dominican friars. – *Cf.* CAYME

Jacobipeta. A pilgrim going to St James of Compostella, *Jacobus* being the Latin form of 'James'. [< L *peto* = to make for] – *Cf.* ROMIPETA; THOMIPETA

Jambeau [jamb, jamber]. Protection for a rider's legs, extending from the saddle. [< OFr. *jambe* = leg]

Jazerant [jazerine]. Coat of armour made from small, light pieces of metal, which were then attached to a coat of heavy leather to make a complete piece. The word is probably of Saracen origin.

Jess. One of the straps attached to each of a hawk's legs, with a *varvel to serve as link to a leash.

Jessant. *Her.* Describes a plant emerging from the ground or from the mouth of an animal. [< Fr *gisant* = lying down]

Jews, Charter of the. Charter confirmed on 10 April 1201, its first sentence reading: 'John, by the grace of God, &c. Know that we have granted to all the Jews of England and Normandy to have freely and honourably residence in our land.' Section VII of the charter reads: 'And we order that they be free through all England and Normandy of all the customs and tolls and modiation [measurement] of wine just as our own *chattels. And we order you to guard, to defend, and to maintain them.' This charter was very similar to one granted by Richard I, and another even earlier by Henry I. Like all charters, this one cost money, being confirmed on due payment. Here, 4,000 marks were paid over two years, with 1,000 marks to be paid on succeeding *Michaelmas Days and Easters.

Jews, expulsion of the. 1290. The Jews in Britain, most of whom arrived during the 11c from France, had long acted as bankers to the ruling and business classes (being permitted to lend money at interest whereas Christians were not). In Henry III's reign, the Jews had provided the king with much needed finance. However, in 1275, a statute was issued by Edward I forbidding this practice. He had developed a new system of banking using Italian cash advances by 1275 and no longer needed to protect the Jews. Strong anti-Semitic feeling continued, many Jews being made scapegoats for England's difficulties. In 1287, Edward imprisoned and ransomed 3,000 of their number. The ransom was paid, but in 1290 an edict was issued expelling all Jews from England. – *Cf.* BARDI; USURY

Jinetes. *See* GINETES

Joculator. A showman or joker who performed at court; the acts were of the kind we associate with a circus. [< L *joculor* = to joke or jest]

Jointure. Legal term for land held jointly by man and wife. This form of tenure ensured that should the husband die first his wife could enjoy the estate until her death, rather than being subject to the whims of the heir. This could mean a long-lived widow frustrating the heir for many years. A further advantage of jointure was that it delayed, at least, the superior lord's right of *wardship. – *Cf.* DOWER

Journeyman. A craftsman, no longer an apprentice, not yet a master; one qualified to work on his own and to be paid by the day. [< Fr *jour* = day; journey = a day's travel 13c; a day's work 14c]

Joust. The joust was the familiar fight between knights on horseback with lance and shield. It evolved from the *hastilude and *mêlée, becoming an exhibition but one using real skills, with a genuine threat of serious injury or death. Unlike the mêlée, the joust was an individual affair and much of the elaborate stage setting was as much influenced by chivalric literature and romance as it was by the real world. These emerged in the late 13c. [< OFr. *juster* = to bring together < L *juxta* = close to, near] – *Cf. next*

Joust of peace. Some tournaments took place with the intention of limiting the threat of serious injury or death. For example, in 1278, a Tournament of Peace was held at Windsor. None of the weapons were made of metal: swords were bone, shields wooden, the armour *cuir-bouilli*. – *Cf. next;* BATON 1

Joust of war. In the 13c and 14c England was frequently at war with both France and Scotland. Such wars rarely involved full-scale pitched battles; rather, there were skirmishes and much plundering of the countryside. From this came a variation of the sport of jousting: hostile combat or jousts of war. On these occasions men were killed. However, afterwards a *herald announced winners, or those who had jousted best on each side. During sieges, which could be very tedious, knights from the two sides used convenient open spaces for hostile jousting. They are known as 'tourneys *à outrance'* = to the bitter end, or to the death. – *Cf. previous*

Jubilee. Year in which the penalties of sin may be remitted for those going to Rome under conditions set by the pope. Such years were usually granted every 25 years. The term is from Mosaic law, where the interval was set at 50 years. – *Cf.* INDULGENCES

Judicium. Lit. 'judgement'. A legislative act, of the kind given by a *county court.

Jugum. Measure of land equiv. to *c.*60 acres. Four *juga* = one **sulong*, approx. two hides. – *Cf.* WAND

Jupon. Short padded garment worn under a *surcoat and *hauberk. The *jupon* was also worn over the suit of armour, being decorated with its wearer's coat of *arms. – *Cf.* GIPON

Jurat. Lit. 'a sworn man'. Someone sworn to do something, i.e. carry out a duty on oath; someone sworn to give information at a court. The term was also used of the *burgess in English towns who swore to advise faithfully. In Sark, a jurat was one of the island's magistrates, elected for life. The Latin form is *juratus*. [< L *juro* = to swear] – *Cf. next*

Jurati ad arma. Lit. 'sworn to arms'. Armed townsmen. Although in social terms the *jurati* ranked below the ordinary foot-soldier, they were not much use in battle, being best suited for guarding the coast and keeping watch for hostile shipping. Anything more military than police work, e.g. supporting bailiffs, or as part of a *hue and cry, was beyond their skills. – *Cf. previous*

Jus. Latin law term referring to custom which became the basis of common law. – *Cf.* LEX

Jus gentium. Lit. 'law of the people'. Bracton said: 'the authority of . . . lords [is] sanctioned by the *jus gentium*; it once extended to life and death but is now restricted by the civil law . . . life and member are in the king's *potestas'.

Justice-in-eyre. One of the justices, i.e. judges, on the *county circuit, hearing cases at local courts. These justices ensured that criminals with local influence and able to intimidate local courts were subject to the king's justice, which was not to be imposed upon. The Latin for justice-in-eyre is *justicarius in itinere. – Cf.* EYRE

Justice of the Peace. These officials emerged from the keepers of the peace in the 14c. Local knights and lords of the *manor, they held courts in place of the *eyre. Four times a year they held quarter sessions with jury trials and these courts had capital powers. The justices largely replaced sheriffs and also the old *hundred courts.

Justiciar. The officer who acted as king's regent or viceroy. He presided at the king's court, during the time of the Norman and early Plantagenet monarchs, when the king was in France or Normandy. The office lapsed in 1261. Its Latin form is *justitiarius*.

Juvenes. Young men at tournaments, often the younger sons, for whom a father could not provide; young men who would become squires. [< L *juvenis* = a young man]

K

Kaernia. Latin collective term for a band of kerns, the Irish foot soldiers who attached themselves to the households of English lords in Ireland. [<Ir. *ceithearn* = band of soldiers] – *Cf.* GALLOWGLASS; KERN

Keep. The central part of a castle; the *donjon. It was built defensively as a position of last resort, the inner stronghold.

Keeper of the Peace. Usually a local lord or knight responsible at first for the *hue and cry. The keeper evolved into the *justice of the peace.

Kenilworth, Ordinance of. May 1326. One of the amendments undertaken during the last year of Edward II's reign, withdrawing the wool *staple status from foreign towns, giving it to towns in England. In 1326, it was further ordained that persons worth less than £40 a year were forbidden to wear anything made from imported cloth, as a kind of protection of the wool industry.

Kenning. Modern term for periphrastic phrases characteristic of Old Norse verse, sometimes also applied to Old English, e.g. *gannet's bath (*ganotes bæð*) was used for the sea. Other examples are: *heathorlinde* = war-lime = wooden shields (made of lime or linden wood) and *hamora lafan* = hammer's leavings, i.e. metal weapons.

Kern [kerne]. In the 13c, 'kerns' signified those who attached themselves to the establishments of English lords in Ireland. They were considered idlers and spongers. Later the term was used of a fighting man from Ireland, a foot soldier without armour. When fighting at close quarters the kern used a battle-axe much like that used by the Vikings. The Latin form was *kernus* or *homo de kerne*. [< Ir. *ceithearn* = band of soldiers] – *Cf.* CATERAN; GALLOWGLASS; KAERNIA

Kid. A bundle of wood or brushwood, twigs, for kindling.

King's household. Medieval government was conducted by the king himself. The members of his household inevitably had a rôle in government; they were chosen for this purpose, or, like the magnates, their power demanded their participation. All medieval departments began as a part of that household. Some of these went out of court, and thus ceased to be part of the household, by acquiring permanent offices at Westminster, no longer travelling with the king. However, they were always subject to his direct authority, which was often prescribed by statute. These departments included *chancery, the *exchequer, the courts of law and the office of the *privy seal. The king's household varied in size between 400 and 700 men and women, including servants, clerks and officials. Officials had their own servants and hangers-on. Most worked to provide the food and drink, the stabling, even music and medicine; there were also chaplains. Each department was required to keep and render its accounts. – *Cf.* DOMUS REGIS; FAMILIA REGIS

King's messenger. *See* NUNCIUS REGIS

King's peace. The state of civil order within the realm, backed by the king's authority; also that special protection attached to certain people on royal business, e.g. the king's messengers. – *Cf.* MUND; NUNCIUS REGIS; WITE

King's vert. All the greenery within a forest which provided food for deer, i.e. all trees and shrubs such as hawthorn, holly, blackthorn. – *Cf.* VERT AND VENISON

King's wardrobe. The king's wardrobe was involved with more than his clothing, although that had been its origin. It became an administrative department which dispensed money and kept accounts, handling domestic expenses of the court; for example, the king's messengers were paid from the wardrobe. It was run by a keeper and his subordinates, the controller and *cofferer. The keeper was responsible for receiving money for the household's expenses, for checking the accounts of its departments and for rendering these accounts in the *exchequer. The controller kept a duplicate set of accounts by way of a control on the keeper. The cofferer was the official charged with the care of the coins themselves. The privy wardrobe was based at the Tower of London, where military supplies were also kept. The Great Wardrobe, near Barnard's Castle, was responsible for civilian supplies, from furs to imported spices. – *Cf.* SIGNET SEAL, OFFICE OF THE

Kitchener. The *obedientiary who was overseer of all things pertaining to the cooking and serving of food in a monastery. He saw to it that supplies were maintained by those under him, with food ready on time and cooking utensils cleaned. The Latin form was *coquinarius.* – *Cf.* COKINI

Knave. A boy child; a servant-boy or a menial; later applied to a man as a rogue or scoundrel. [< OE *cnapa* = boy]

Knight. Orig. a boy or young man; the military servant of someone of high rank; a feudal tenant holding land for which he owed military service; a man raised by king or queen to an honourable, high rank; in courtly romance and lyric sometimes used for an acknowledged suitor or lover. [< OE *cniht* = a young boy, hence warrior, servant] – *Cf. next;* KNIGHT'S FEE

Knight bachelor. The full title of a gentleman who had been knighted; the lowest order of *knight. He was a knight without a *fee. Frequently a younger son, trained in the skills of war, such men earned their living fighting for a lord. – *Cf. next;* BACHELOR

Knight of the shire. One of the two knights of a shire or *county elected to be its representative in parliament. Their election was overseen by the *sheriff in the county court, in response to the king's summons. – *Cf.* MAINPERNOR

Knight's fee. That area of land required for the service of one *knight. This was the essence of the obligation of military service in the 12c and 13c. Land was granted by a *tenant-in-chief to a knight, who would answer the king's summons to provide a certain number of men. Their customary obligation was to serve for 40 days each year without pay. In the 12c, *scutage appeared, by which the king raised money in lieu of military service. – *Cf.* FIEF

Knights Hospitaller. One of the military orders, originally founded to tend the sick and injured of the Crusades; their chief house was the Hospital of St John at Jerusalem. Expelled from the East after the fall of Acre, they moved first to Rhodes and thence to Malta; hence they were also known as the Knights of Malta. – *Cf. next*

Knights Templar. The Knights Templar derived their name from having been the occupants of part of the place where Solomon's Temple used to be. (They were known first and fully as the Poor Knights of the Temple of Solomon.) The order was founded by Hugues de Payns in 1118 after the taking of Jerusalem. A military and religious order, its purpose was to protect pilgrims to the Holy Land. Their rule was written by St Bernard. The Church recognised the order in 1128; it was suppressed in 1312. – *Cf. previous*

Koran. The sacred scriptures of Islam. Although there had been previous contact and conflict between Christians and Muslims, the Koran was not translated into a Western language until the 12c. The first translation into Latin was commissioned by an abbot of *Cluny, Peter the Venerable, in the 1140s. His purpose was to study it and by study refute and deny it. For a long time in the West it was thought that Islam was a heretical form of Christianity, rather than a new religion.

L

Label. *Her.* A band across the top of a shield with usually three or five points depending from it. It signified the eldest son of the family and was displayed only during the life of the father, after whose death the son would inherit. – *Cf.* CADENCY, MARK OF; MULLET

Laboratores. *See* THREE ORDERS

Labourers, Ordinance of. 1349. The king issued this ordinance to set maximum wages. It required labourers to finish their contracts before looking for another job. It failed largely because of economic pressures after the *Black Death of 1348: the problem of a shortage of labour could not be legislated away. It did, however, manage to control the rise in wages somewhat. This ordinance and the Statute of *Labourers were both reissued between 1360 and 1362.

Labourers, Statute of. 1351. This statute's purpose was to give oversight of the Ordinance of Labourers of 1349. It began, 'Because a great part of the people and especially of the workmen and servants has now died in that pestilence, some, seeing the straits of the masters and the scarcity of servants, are not willing to serve unless they receive excessive wages'. It concluded, 'because many sound beggars do refuse to labour so long as they can live from begging alms, giving themselves up to idleness and sins, and, at times, to robbery and other crimes, let no one, under the aforesaid pain of imprisonment presume, under colour of piety or alms to give anything to such as can very well labour, or to cherish them in their sloth, so that thus they may be compelled to labour for the necessaries of life'. – *Cf. previous*

Lactagium. Latin term for a fee or rent paid on dairy cows; also the term for dairy produce, e.g. when the rent was paid in kind. [< L *lac* = milk] – *Cf.* CERVISARIUS

Lady. Early use of the word referred to the mistress of a private household, the OE *hlæfdige*; it was also the female equivalent of a lord and title of the king's wife in the 10c and 11c. Later, 'lady' acquired the poetic sense of a woman who was the object of chivalric attentions, the object of *courtly love in the songs of troubadours. Its origin is less refined, as the OE word *hlæfdige* < *hlaf* = a loaf + *dæge* = a female servant; a lady was one who kneaded bread dough. – *Cf.* LORD

Lady chapel. A chapel in either a church or *cathedral dedicated to the Virgin Mary. They are often found east of the high altar.

Lǣcecrǣft. Lit. 'leech-craft'. The art of traditional medicine based on ancient recipes and practical experience. It was replaced by the more consciously rational 'physic', based upon knowledge of *physica*, i.e. nature. – *Cf.* BLOOD-LETTING

Lænland. Lit. 'loanland'. The most important characteristic of *lænland* was that it was not hereditary; rather, it was granted for a fixed time, usually the life of the grantee and that of his widow and heir. At the end of the term it reverted to the granter. *Lænland* implied service to the granter for the fixed term; in this, and in not being hereditary it resembles the *benefice. – *Cf.* BOCLAND; FOLCLAND

Lagaman. *See* LAWMAN

Lagan. Wreckage lying on the sea bed. One of the rights in the Charter of the *Cinque Ports granted in 1155 was title to such wreckage. It is not to be confused with flotsam = wreckage floating on the sea, or jetsam = goods and wreckage on the beach. – *Cf.* SCIPBRYCE

Lahslit. Orig. a breach of the peace. In time, by transference, *lahslit* came to indicate the penalty for an offence. It was used in the laws of Cnut (1020–3) for offences committed in the *Danelaw. [< OE *lagu* = law + *slitan* = tear] – *Cf.* FULWITE

Lame. A thin piece or plate of metal. [< L *lamina* = veneer, a thin sheet] – *Cf.* SPAULDER

Lamia. Monster of mythical status, with the body of a woman, whose diet comprised human flesh and the blood of infants. [< Gr. *Lamia* = female, child-eating monster]

Lammas land. Land released or unenclosed to permit animals to graze, after harvest until the next spring. Lammas day was 1 August, on which there was a harvest festival, celebrated with bread made from the first new grain. [< OE *hlafmæsse*, *hlaf* = loaf + *mæsse* = mass]

Lance 1. Lances varied in length between 10 and 14 feet (3–4.2 m). They were

made from ash wood; in war they were tipped with iron or steel. – *Cf.* Coronal

Lance 2. A unit of armed men supporting a *knight on the battlefield, i.e. a
*squire, some foot soldiers, and archers. The numbers would depend on the
financial resources of the knight.

Lancet 1. A small *lance.

Lancet 2. An 18c word for a slender window (lancet light) with a pointed or
tapered apex resembling a lance.

Landboc. Lit. 'land book'. This was the written charter which recorded a
grant of land, i.e. *Bocland*. – *Cf.* Folcland

Landgabulum. The Latin form of *landgavel* or *landgafol*.

Landgafol [landgable, landgavel]. Land tax payable each year, akin to ground
rent; payable to the king or in some circumstances a local lord. The rate was
1d per *messuage. [< land + OE *gafol/gavel* = tax, tribute, rent] – *Cf. previous*

Langue d'oc. Modern term for the dialect of Provence, known also as
Provençal and Occitan; so named for using *oc* = yes. – *Cf. next*

Langue d'oïl. Modern term for the language of medieval France, north of the
River Loire; so named for using *oïl* = yes, in contrast with *langue d'oc.

Lapis lazuli. Laboriously extracted from rock, lapis lazuli was brought with
difficulty and danger from Afghanistan and Persia to provide a rich blue,
known sometimes as azure, or ultramarine (i.e. beyond the sea, where the
lapis came from), for scribes and painters of illuminated MSS. Its value was
indicated by being used only for significant parts of an image, e.g. the blue of
the Virgin's cloak. [< L *lapis* = stone + *lazuli* < Persian *lazward* = lapis lazuli] –
Cf. Cinnabar

Lappet. Small pieces of a suit of armour which flap or overlap, somewhat
like fish scales, thus giving flexibility with protection.

Laqueus. Latin word for 'snare', as used by poachers in forests; made from
horsehair or cord, or sometimes withies. – *Cf.* Caltrop 1; Ingenium

Last. Unit of measure used for items such as wool and grain. It was the equivalent of 12 sacks of wool; a last of grain = 10 quarters of grain or 80 bushels.
[< OE *hlæst* = a load] – *Cf. next;* Sack of wool

Lastage. The tax paid on goods and merchandise such as wool or grain which
were sold in units of lasts. The Latin form is *lastagium*. – *Cf. previous*

Lathe. Term for the seven districts into which Kent was divided: Aylesford,

Milton, Sutton (West Kent), Borough, Eastry, Lympne, Wye (East Kent). All were centred on royal vills. [< OE *lǽð* = landed property] – *Cf.* RAPE 1

Latimer. A translator. Latin forms were *latinarius* and *latimarius* (11c), *latimerius* (13c); from which came the AN form and English family name. [< L *Latina* = Latin language]

Latin. Language of the Romans; known in the **ASC* as 'book language'. It was the common language of scholarship, learning and teaching in England and Europe. – *Cf.* BOCLÆDEN; VULGATE

Latronissa. A female robber or brigand. [< L *latrocinium* = robbery, brigandage]

Latten. An alloy somewhat like brass used for adding refinements to suits of armour; also for making ornaments in a church and the ornamental brasses commemorating local worthies.

Lauds. *See* HORARIUM

Lavatorium. A place for washing, a container of water for washing; a row of basins. Such a room was to be found adjacent to the **frater. [< L *lavo* = to wash] – *Cf. next;* RERE-DORTER

Laver. Conduit running through a **lavatorium which carried water for washing. [< L *lavo* = to wash]

Lawed. Dogs, esp. those near royal forests, were lawed, i.e. had their claws removed, to prevent them from chasing the king's venery. – *Cf.* HAMBLE

Lawman. Scandinavian institution imported by settlement in the 9c and found afterwards at Lincoln, Stamford, Cambridge, York and other places in the **Danelaw. (The Latin term for the 12 jurors of York, described as hereditary lawmen, was *hereditario jure lagaman civitatis*.) Referred to in documents as *judex* and *judices*, also in **DB as *lagaman*, these 12 men gave judgement on cases, while also remembering and passing on local customs. Their persistence to the time of *DB* and after is a sign of heavy Scandinavian influence. As they expounded custom, it appears the office may have passed from father to son. In 1086, it would seem that some lawmen of Lincoln were sons of men who had been lawmen in Edward the Confessor's reign. Indeed, in the late 13c there are still lawmen to be found at Stamford. Another way of describing them might be as judgement-finders. Twelve remains the set number of jurors in an English court of law.

Lazar. A person with **leprosy; often used in general of the very poor and diseased. A lazar-house was a place cut off from the world for lepers to live in isolation. [< Lazarus in John 11:1]

League. A measure of distance lacking precision but thought to be about three miles; this was variable, according to where in England it was used. [< L *leuca, leuga* = a league]

Leaning staffs. In the 11c and 12c it was forbidden to sit down in a church or *cathedral. However, it was realised this posed problems for elderly or ailing monks. They were therefore permitted to use leaning staffs or *reclinatoria*, which were crutches fitting under the armpit. These staffs are mentioned in the *customary of Lincoln Cathedral. – *Cf.* CONSUETUDINARY; MISERICORD 2

Lectionary. A collection of biblical extracts to be read at the mass; these were sometimes to be found in the *missal. Bible texts were at one time marked with an *incipit* (beginning) and *explicit* (ending). [< L *lectio* = a reading]

Leet. A group of tithings organised for the administration of *frank-pledge and breaches of the peace. The leet had a court but was limited in the punishments it could administer to amercements alone.

Legerwite. *See* LEYRWITE

Leges Henrici Primi. *The Laws of Henry I.* This compilation, based on the law-codes of the AS kings, was made some time between 1110 and 1120. Surviving MSS date from *c.*1201 and the early 14c. It was by no means exhaustive. It opened with Henry I's Coronation Charter; one chapter dealt with ecclesiastical law; the remainder is wholly concerned with secular law. – *Cf.* CURIA REGIS; FAMILIA REGIS

Lent. Spring. The OE word was applied to the Christian period of fasting through the coincidence of time. [< OE *lencten* = spring time] – *Cf.* CAPUT JEJUNIUM

Leporarius. *See* GREYHOUND

Leprosy. A well-known disease, now treatable, but which when untreated caused horrible disfigurement; it was much feared in medieval times when leper colonies were established in out of the way places. Those infected were considered unclean; most feared contagion, though it is not highly contagious. Lepers (also referred to as lazars) were known as 'Christ's special sufferers', like the insane, who were also thought to have been specially touched. – *Cf.* SEELY

Letters Patent. These were royal letters, sent open with a seal and pendant attached. Their contents were not considered to be secret. Such letters authorised an action or instructed e.g. a sheriff to act. They date from 1201. [patent < L *pateo* = open]

Letters Patent Rolls [L = *Rotuli litterarum patentium*]. Rolls recording the letters patent issued under the *great seal, dealing with matters such as wardships, grants of land; the legal affairs of widows also came under this heading. The *alienation of land was dealt with in this manner. Also enrolled were grants of offices and the *temporalities of bishops and other ecclesiastics; and also letters regarding the creation of peers and various other licences. [patent < L *pateo* = open] – *Cf. previous;* CLOSE ROLLS; FINE ROLLS; PIPE ROLLS

Levant et cumbens. Lit. 'rising and laying down'. Legal term used of cattle which were put out both night and day. The phrase was also used of tenants of an estate. – *Cf. next*

Levant. Legal tern used of stray animals. An animal was said to be levant if it had been away for a day and a night; after this time it could be distrained, i.e. held by the owner of the land it was found on. – *Cf. previous*

Lex. Latin term for the statute law (rather than common law) which grew out of the legislating powers of the king. – *Cf.* JUS

Lex mercatoria. Lit. 'mercantile law'. Although sounding a formal promulgation, *Lex mercatoria* was a largely unwritten set of customs of the merchant community. Public courts recognised it; part of its expression appeared in the *Piepoudre courts. – *Cf.* OLÉRON, LAWS OF

Leyrwite [lairwite, leyrwite]. The fine and/or offence of fornication. In *LHP* the offence is known in Latin as *legerwita* and is considered one of the minor offences (*minora forisfacta*) like *fihtwite. The jurisdiction for such offences was with the offender's lord, assuming the person had escaped from the scene. From *leyr* derives 'lair'. [< OE *leger*= lying (down), a bed + *wite* = a fine]

Libel. A statement or declaration made by the plaintiff in a suit. Only later in the 17c does the word acquire its present sense of being derogatory or defamatory. [< L *libellus* < *liber* = booklet, document]

Liber Exoniensis. MS preserved in the library of Exeter Cathedral, containing Exon Domesday, from which the account of the five south-western shires in *DB* was compiled. Only Cornwall, Devon and Somerset survive in full, with about a third of Dorset and just one Wiltshire *manor.

Liber Feodorum. See Book of Fees

Liber judiciarius. Lit. 'the book of judgement'. The name given to *DB* by Richard fitz-Nigel *c*.1179, saying it was so named because it was not possible for any reason to depart from its judgement.

Liber Provincialis. A commentary upon the ecclesiastical decrees enacted in English provincial councils presided over by the archbishops of Canterbury. Commonly known as the *Provinciale*, it is a gloss upon all English legislation which supplemented the common law (*jus commune*) of the Church. It represents views accepted among English *clergy of his day upon a wide variety of subjects. Its author was William Lyndwood, bishop of St David's and the greatest of English canonists. He said that he finished the work at *Pentecost in 1430. He died in 1446.

Liberate Rolls. Rolls recording authorisation for payments to be made by the *exchequer. They run from *c*.1200 to the middle of the 15c. [< L *liberate* = release (of funds)]

Liberationes. Latin word, sometimes meaning liveries, sometimes money. The liveries were given annually, as lengths of cloth to be made up appropriately. Sometimes money was given in lieu. However, even if money, it is not quite the same as *solidata*, the term for wages. The difference in use lies in the class of persons being paid: the first, household servants; the second, soldiers.

Libertinus. A freed man, one who was manumitted from lawful bondage. *Bracton is clear: 'A *libertinus* is so called because he is liberated from bondage.'

Libri memoriales. Lit. 'memorial books'; also known as *libri vitae* = books of life. These books recorded the names of all who had made donations to a monastic house and for whom obits were to be said; such benefactors being received into the fraternity of the house. However, donations themselves were not recorded.

Lichewake. The watch or wake held over the body of the dead overnight. [< OE *licham* = body + *wæcc* = watch]

Liege. A liege was a lord's lord. The English king was the liege of everyone in England. – *Cf. next*

Liegeman. A man who owed allegiance and service to a *liege lord. – *Cf.* LIGEUS

Ligan. *See* LAGAN

Ligantia. Allegiance; the allegiance owed by a *vassal to a lord. [< L *ligo* = to tie, to bind] – *Cf. next*

Ligeus. Loyal, owing allegiance. [< L *ligo* = to tie, to bind] – *Cf. previous*; HOMO LIGEUS; LIGANTIA

Lignage. Lineage, line of descent, ancestry; the family line of someone nobly born. Lineage was at the heart of nobility and *chivalry in the medieval period: if a man's honour was offended, so was that of his family. The word was sometimes used in a phrase such as *la noblesse de lignage* and *honneur du lignage*. – *Cf.* HOMMES DE LIGNAGE

Limitour. A *friar who had exclusive begging rights within a specified area;

sometimes known derisively as procurators, a reference to the king's *purveyors or procurers, who were also very unpopular. (The *procurator* was also a Roman tax gatherer.) Their activities simply added another group of men going round the country *begging, however worthy the cause might once have been. Langland, in *Piers Plowman*, refers to a limitour as a losel, i.e. a vagabond.

Limner. An illuminator of manuscripts; later, one who drew or painted; a portraitist. [< L *lumino* = illuminate, brighten with colour]

Lind [linden]. The lime tree (*Tilia vulgaris*); also a shield.

Lindsey survey. Lindsey is a division of Lincolnshire. The survey was conducted during the reign of Henry I; two others, of Leicestershire and Northampton, were made a little later, between *c.*1125 and 1130. There is a contemporary text of only the Lindsey survey. Unlike *DB, this survey is organised by *riding and by *wapentake, allowing land belonging to separate fees to be gathered together. It is the source for the knowledge that land was assessed in the northern *Danelaw on a duodecimal system.

-ling. Suffix which gives the sense of belonging or being connected with, e.g. 'hireling', or having a particular quality, e.g. in diminutives like 'foundling' or 'halfling'. – *Cf.* LYNGHOUSE

Ling. Unit of length sometimes equal to a *perch, sometimes to 16½ feet. [< OE *lang* = long]

Linsey. A coarse material made of cheap wool and linen.

Lionced. *Her.* Describes a cross with a lion's head at the end of each of its four arms.

Lithesman. One of the warriors, mostly Danish, who manned the standing fleet maintained by English kings from Æthelred to Edward the Confessor. They were paid by means of the *heregeld*, and were stationed at London. [< ON *lið* = a fleet + man]

Litster. A dyer. [< ME *lit* = colour, stain, dye]

Littere de intendendo. *See* DE INTENDENDO

Little hours. *See* HORARIUM; NONE; SEXT; TERCE

Livery. Orig. the distribution of food and clothing by a lord to his retainers. This giving of food or clothing was a regular occurrence, e.g. clothing being given annually. Food, too, might be given regularly, for example wine at Christmas. *Bracton says that livery 'is the transfer of a corporeal thing, one's own or another's, from one person to a second . . . a voluntary transference from one's own hand or another's, as that of a procurator, provided the transfer has his lord's consent'. In time 'livery' came to signify the clothing itself. At first, colours were simple russet or blue. Then, livery became part of the colour coding that evolved in medieval courts, which became increasingly wealthy and stratified. The coding had clerks wearing blue, knights green and *squires striped cloth, as did household servants; hence, later, part of the absurdity of Malvolio's wearing yellow stockings in *Twelfth Night*. Trade *guilds or misteries had their own liveries. [< Fr *livrer* = dispense < L *libero* = to give] – *Cf. next;* Usucapion

Livery in seisin. The action of giving or transferring land or property, i.e. the *feoffment, done in a public manner, usually on the land itself.

Liveryman. A member of a trade *guild or *mistery. Liverymen tended to be the more successful members of their guild; indeed they were members of an inner circle within the guild, often formally associated. – *Cf. previous*

Living. *See* Benefice

Llwyth. Welsh tribal group where all were related to each other, living within a rural township and surrounding area. The *llwyth* was composed of a number of *gwelys or clans within which all were descended from the same male ancestor. – *Cf.* Agnate

Lode [load]. A journey or way; also guidance; later, a watercourse or open drain in fen country. The word is still found in names such as Whaplode in Lincolnshire.

Lollardy. Name given to beliefs considered heretical in the late 14c, held by John Wyclif and his followers. Lollard was not intended to be a complimentary name. Their complaints against the Church were wide-ranging. They disliked the subjection of the English Church to Rome, the doctrine of transubstantiation, clerical celibacy, temporal rule by the *clergy, the consecration of physical objects, masses for the dead (obits), going on *pilgrimage, and the veneration or worship of images. In 1401 the edict *De haeretico comburendo* was passed, allowing for the burning of Lollards. Fierce suppression continued through the reign of Henry V. [ME < Du. *lollaerd* = mutterer] – *Cf.* Twelve Conclusions

Long cross. *See* Short-cross penny

Longaigne. A latrine in a castle or keep, usually opening directly into a ditch below. However, being always open to the outside, they were a weak point of defence during a siege, through which entrance could be and was made. Straw, known as *torche-cul*, was used as we use toilet paper. – *Cf.* Easement room; Rere-dorter

Longbow. The longbow was a weapon with a lethal range of 250+ yards; the best bows were made of yew. Experienced archers could loose up to six arrows a minute. Its potential when used in large numbers was recognised by King Edward III. [< OE *boga* = bow] – *Cf.* ARCHERY; CROSSBOW

Loophole. A hole in the wall of a castle or other fortified building through which an archer fired his arrows; that for a crossbow or arbalest was also known as an *arbalestina* or *balistraria*. Only later by vague extension does the word become a way of escape or means of evasion. – *Cf.* ARBALESTER; LONGBOW

Lord. Today a title of rank, but originally a description of function, as well as status. The lord was head of a household for which he provided sustenance, receiving service in return. [< OE *hlaf* = loaf, bread + *weard* = protection, guardian] – *Cf.* LADY

Lorica. A coat of chain mail; synonymous with *'byrnie'. The word was also used of knight service, as when the phrase *fief loricae* was used in place of *fief militum.*

Lorimer [loriner]. A maker of the metal pieces of a horse's bridle and stirrup irons; also one who made small pieces of iron-work. [< OFr. *lorenier* < L *lorum* = a leather strap] – *Cf. next*

Lormery. Ironwork made by a *lorimer.

Losengier. Term found in courtly poetry for the faithless friend of two lovers; later, used of a betrayer or deceiver.

Lowy. The area around a castle or town under its jurisdiction; such an area might extend to about three miles. – *Cf.* CASTELLARIA

Lubber. *See* ABBEY LUBBER

Luce. A pike; the fish *Esocidae lucius*. A pike as a heraldic *charge is called a 'lucy'.

Ludens. A 14c term for a player, most likely a wandering minstrel, rather than an actor. [< L *ludo* = to play]

Lunellum. Crescent-shaped knife used for scraping a sheet of *parchment in its preparation. [< L *luna* = moon]

Luparius. A wolf-hunter or -catcher. In the 12c and 13c, there were still wolves enough in England for the king to have full-time wolf-hunters. During the first quarter of the 12c, these men had packs of running hounds and *greyhounds. There was a bounty of 5s for the killing of each wolf. Some men were clearly professionals, with names like Richard Luverez and William de Leveriz.

Lushbourne. English word for inferior silver pennies. They were said to have come from Luxembourg, Lushbourne being its garbled form. These coins were first minted by the blind King John of Bohemia, who adopted the odd spelling of his name EIWANES. This was done to confuse English merchants, hoping they might mis-read EIWANES as EDWARDVS and accept the coins as legitimately issued in the name of Edward III. Henry Knighton (d. 1396) refers to them in his chronicle, saying that so many were circulated in 1347 by both English and foreign merchants that many were drawn and hanged in London that year.

Lustrum. Latin term for a period of five years.

Lute. Arabic instrument much favoured by medieval minstrels. Its body was somewhat pear-shaped and it was played by plucking its strings. In the 13c returning Crusaders brought it to Europe via Spain. [< Ar. *al-oud*] – *Cf.* CITTERN

Lyam. *Her.* A *charge representing the leash of a dog. [< L *ligamen* = a string or fastening, ligament] – *See* LYMER

Lyam hound [liam, lyam, lyme]. A bloodhound. It was so named after the lyam or leash used by its handler during a hunt. The lyam hound was used to track game, e.g. deer or boar, by scent. – *Cf. previous;* BRACHET; GREYHOUND; LYMER

Lyke-wake. *See* LICHEWAKE

Lymer [lyam]. The leash of a hunting dog or hound; by transference the hound itself. In a hunt these animals were handled by a *varlet des chiens* on horseback. – *Cf.* AIDE DE LA VENERIE; LYAM

Lymphad. *Her.* One-masted ship shown with sails fluttering. It was based on a type of ship which used oarsmen.

Lynchet. The strip of unploughed land between two fields; the terracing on sloping land. [< OE *linc* = rising land] – *Cf.* BAULK; BUTT 2

Lynghouse. A kind of detention cell or small prison at Durham used to punish monks. The offender might have had to sit in chains for up to a year. He would not be permitted to speak to or see anyone but the abbot, who let down food on a cord. At Ely, the equivalent place was called, appropriately, 'helle'.

M

Mace. Short metal weapon with a heavy club end to which spikes were sometimes added. – *Cf.* MAUL

Machecole. Synonym of the verb 'machicolate', i.e. to add or create machicolations. [< OFr. *machecoller*]

Machicolation. An opening between the corbels which support a projecting parapet, or in the vault of a portal, through which molten lead, hot oil, stones, etc. could be dropped on attackers below. This is an 18c word formed from *machecole.

Madder. The plant *Rubia tinctorum*, a source of reds and reddish yellows for dyeing cloth. – *Cf.* CINNABAR

Magister glomerie. The official at Cambridge University in the 15c responsible for the teaching of *grammar. The post was in the gift of the bishop of Ely. – *Cf.* GLOMERELLUS; GLOMERIE

Magister scholarum. That clerical officer of a diocese, usually the bishop's archdeacon or chancellor, whose licence was required before a school could be opened or a person could teach. [L *magister* = master + *scholarum* = of schools] – *Cf.* MAGISTER GLOMERIE

Magna Carta. Lit. 'Great Charter'. The first version of this document of June 1215 had 63 clauses. Magna Carta (first known as the Articles of the Barons) emerged out of King John's dispute with rebelling barons. John saw it as a means of placating his opponents; they saw it as a means of controlling the king. The document was agreed at Runnymede and the following temporary peace is sometimes known as the Peace of Runnymede. A copy of Magna Carta was sent to every sheriff in England to be read out at the shire court. But that peace lasted a few months only. On the fresh outbreak of hostilities, the French king, Louis VIII, was invited to come to England and take the crown. Magna Carta was effectively forgotten. However, on the accession of Henry III, after King John's death in October 1216, it was reissued, somewhat modified. A third version was produced in 1217. Finally in 1225 it reached its fourth and final form. This is the version usually referred to, unless otherwise specified. Famously, it proclaimed in chapter 35 that 'no free man shall be seized or imprisoned, or disseised [i.e. dispossessed of property or rights] . . . except by the lawful judgement of his peers'. Another clause, equally important, states 'To no one will we [the crown] sell, to no one deny or delay right or justice'. Copies of the 1215 version remain in existence: one at Lincoln Cathedral, one at Salisbury Cathedral, while the British Library has two. It has come to represent a statement of basic liberties, though many of its provisions, such as those dealing with forest law, are now irrelevant. – *Cf.* DISSEISIN; JUSTICE-IN-EYRE

Magna fenestra versatilis. The large revolving shutter in a *Gilbertine double monastery through which food was passed from the monks' side to the nuns'. It was ingeniously constructed so that neither side was able to see the other. – *Cf.* DOMUS FENESTRAE; FENESTRA PARVULA

Magna garderoba. Lit. 'the great wardrobe'. In fact, the phrase was used of the network of castles and depots in which the king stored his weapons strategically around the kingdom. The term was used by the royal clerks in their records. – *Cf.* Custos armorum regis

Mail 1. Shirt-like piece of armour made from linked metal chains or rings. It was very flexible, unlike the suit of armour, but was vulnerable to a sharp thrust, being best at deflecting a slashing sword. [< L *macula* = mesh]

Mail 2 [mal]. A rent or other money payment or tax; e.g. rent for a farm. From this we have today 'blackmail', a 16c formation, referring to money which was extorted by way of protection. – *Cf.* Malman

Mail 3. A trunk of the kind used by merchants in their travels; also a travelling bag. [< OFr. *malle* = trunk]

Maindefer. Lit. 'hand of iron'. A plate gauntlet; a piece of special armour for use at a *tournament only; being rigid, its use in a real battle was limited. [< Fr. *main* = hand + *de fer* = of iron]

Mainour. Something found in the hands of a thief when caught. [< AN *main* = hand + AN *our* < *oeuvre* = work, thing] – *Cf.* Infangen-theof

Mainpernor. The person who guaranteed an elected knight's attendance at parliament, the guarantee being provided in the sheriff's *county court; also, a person who assured a criminal's attendance at court on the due date. [< OFr. *main* = hand + *prendre* = take; thus to take in hand] – *Cf. next*

Mainprize. To make oneself legally responsible for another person's completing an undertaking; to stand surety. [< OFr. *mainpris* < *mainprendre*] – *Cf. previous*

Maison dieu. Lit. 'house of God'. An alms house; a house of refuge for the poor.

Major orders. The higher ranks of the *clergy were the three orders: bishop, priest and deacon. – *Cf.* Minor orders

Maletolt. A burdensome and/or unjust (export) tax; applied esp. to exports of wool during the reign of Edward III. There were frequent occurrences of conflict and bad feeling in the Commons concerning the imposition of this tax, largely needed to finance Edward's wars. [< L *mala* = bad; *tolt* = tax]

Malman. A tenant who was exempt from services to his lord because he paid a money rent. [< OE *mal* = rent] – *Cf.* Ad malam; Mail 2

Malmsey. Sweet wine from Spain, of a kind originally from Greece. [< Gr. *Monemvasia*, town in the Peloponnese]

Maltese cross. A cross with arms broadening outwards. The ends are indented so that there are eight 'points', each of which symbolises one of the eight Beatitudes. It was used by the *Knights Hospitaller as their sign.

Manbot. The *wergeld* payable to the lord of a *villein who had been killed. Some 200s shillings were payable to the man's family, while 30s went to the lord. By way of contrast, a slave was worth only 40d to his family and 20d to his lord. – *Cf.* HEALSFANG

Manche. *See* MAUNCH

Manchet 1. A small loaf, of the kind served at breakfast. – *Cf. next;* TRENCHER

Manchet 2. – *Her.* A small round loaf used as a *charge. – *Cf. previous*

Manciple. The steward of a community of lawyers, their chambers; the servant of a college or monastery responsible for its provisioning. [< L *manceps* = an agent]

Mancus. AS term referring to one eighth of a (monetary) pound, i.e. 30d or 2s 6d; it was a unit of account, not a coin. It was used in England from the late 8c.

Mangonel. Military device for throwing stones and rocks. The purpose was crude and simple: to batter castle walls and frighten and kill defenders. The mangonel derived its power from twisting rope, which pulled down the throwing arm. [< Gr. *magganon* = engine of war] – *Cf.* SPRINGALD; TREBUCHET

Manor. An estate comprising the lord's *demesne (including the land of his dependent peasantry) and other tenements let out for rents and services. [< L *manerium*, OFr *maneir*] – *Cf. next;* CAPUT HONORIS; HEAFODBOTL

Manorial court. From the 12c each *manor usually held its own court every three weeks or so. It regulated the manor's agricultural affairs, while also enforcing its by-laws, labour services, transfer of manorial land, petty offences within the manor and against the servile dues, election of a *reeve. Theoretically, there were two types of manorial court, the court baron for free tenants, and the court customary for servile tenants; in practice though one court served all purposes. This was presided over by the lord's steward. If the lord of the manor had a *franchise, then other, more serious cases might also be dealt with.

Mansus. Latin term for estate or *manor. Those who worked on the land were known as *mansus serviles* = serfs of the manor or *mansus liberi* = freemen of the manor. From *mansus* derives 'manse'.

Mantel [mantelet]. A mobile shelter used to cover the activities of those besieging a castle or other fortified place. Its sense of covering remains in its use in 'mantelpiece'.

Manticore. A fabulous beast, which possessed the body of a lion and head of a man, while it was also provided with a porcupine's quills and a scorpion's stinging tail. – *Cf.* BESTIARY

Mantle 1. A sleeveless cloak or cape, usually worn by women.

Mantle 2 [mantling]. *Her.* Decoration rising from a helmet in the shape of acanthus leaves.

Manupast [mainpast] – Term for a household, also a member of another's household. In legal terms one belonged to a mainpast, as one belonged to a *frank-pledge or *tithing. [< OFr. *meynpast* < L *manupastus* < *manus* = hand + *pastus* = fed] – *Cf.* MEINIE

Manuscript. A document written by hand; MSS were intended to survive and last a long time and did so if *parchment was used. [< L *manus* = hand + L *scriptus* = written]

Mappa mundi. Lit. 'map of the world'. Maps of this period showed the world within a circle (the perfect form) with Jerusalem at its centre. In addition, there was a surrounding text and imagery depicting e.g. Christ as judge, which linked the worldly realm of history and people with the Last Judgement. Such maps did not simply offer a depiction of the physical world; rather they were attempts to display a moral universe in which man, his world and the creator were shown within the circle of being. The greatest surviving *mappa mundi* is to be found at Hereford Cathedral. – *Cf.* T/O MAP

Marcassin. *Her.* A *charge depicting a young boar, sometimes with a limp tail.

March. A mark or boundary; the land on or along a border, e.g. that between England and Wales, known as the Marches. – *Cf.* MARCHER LORDS; MARK 2; MIERCE

Marcher. Someone possessing land adjoining a border. – *Cf. previous and next*

Marcher lords. Name applied particularly to Norman landholders on the Welsh borders or marches. The term was also used later of the lords in Northumbria and Cumbria, on the troublesome Scottish border, esp. in the 14c. – *Cf. previous;* MARCH

Marined. *Her.* A body with the bottom half like that of a fish. It is a form of mermaid. [< L *marinus* = sea born]

Maritagium. Latin term for a woman's marriage portion which was given in land. However, by the end of the 13c such gifts were being given as money. But heiresses and wealthy widows who married again had different arrangements. – *Cf.* ENFEOFFMENT TO USE

Mark 1. In origin, a Danish unit of account, of 8 *ore*, introduced into England after the *Viking settlements. The Danish *ora* was reckoned at 16 English pence, giving a mark of 10s 8d. But the *ora* of 20d, making a mark of 13s 4d (i.e. two-thirds of a pound) was more common. Many payments were assessed in divisions of this unit, e.g. 6s 8d, 3s 4d, etc. There was also a gold mark = 6 English pounds (8 *ore* of 15s each). Neither the mark nor the *ora* was a coin; both were units of account. – *Cf.* ANGEL 2; NOBLE

Mark 2. A boundary or frontier. [< OE *mearc, merc* = margin, border] – *Cf.* MARCH; MIERCE

Mark 3. A *banner or *standard; also, a target.

Market. The gathering together of people for the purposes of trade, thus the licence of a lord to hold such an event from which he made money. On market days all shops within a set radius were required to be shut so that there was no competition. The Latin phrase used for a market in the records was *venalis locus* = a place for selling. [< L *mercatum* = a meeting for trade, a fair or market]

Marlborough, Statute of. 1267. A statute which signalled the conclusion of the *Barons' War. Under the Provisions of *Westminster Henry III had surrendered control of government to a baronial council with an agenda of institutional reform. The provisions were revised and reissued by the king in 1263, and a further revision in 1267 produced this Statute of Marlborough. – *Cf.* OXFORD, PROVISIONS OF

Marshal. Orig. a servant of the king's household who worked as keeper of the king's horses; in time the position acquired authority as many in the king's household did. This position progressed, becoming the king's leading military office, known as 'earl marshal'. – *Cf.* DOMUS REGIS

Marshalsea. The court of the *marshal at which cases involving the king's servants were heard; as were cases which fell within the *verge. From this, there was the prison known as the Marshalsea, where such a court was to be found in Southwark, under the control of the marshal. During the king's travels around the country, or across the channel, the marshalsea would oversee many of the arrangements necessary for moving such a great organisation. – *Cf.* CLERK OF THE MARKET

Mart. A cow or ox fattened for slaughter; Latin = *bos saginatus*. – *Cf.* MARTINMAS

Marten [marter]. A bushy-tailed mustelid; a weasel-like animal valued for its fur. The European marten is known as the 'baum' (tree) or 'sweet marten'. – *Cf.* CALABER; FOIN 1; GRIS

Martinet. A water-mill used for providing power to an iron forge.

Martinmas. 11 November. The feast day of St Martin of Tours (d. 397), a soldier, then monk and bishop and patron saint of France. The middle of November was the time for salting meat slaughtered for winter – there being insufficient feed until the following year. An alternate form is Martlemas; the *mart element = a slaughtered ox or cow. Falstaff is referred to as a martlemas in 2 *Henry IV*. New wine was also tested at this time.

Martlet 1 [martinet]. Indiscriminately a swallow, swift or (house) martin. – *Cf. next*

Martlet 2. *Her.* A bird without legs or feet, used as a *charge; the *cadency of a fourth son. This notional bird is shown without feet or legs because the swift and swallow were thought never to perch as they supposedly lacked the feet to do so. – *Cf. previous*; ALERION

Mascle. *Her.* A *charge in the form of a lozenge whose centre was empty or 'voided', showing the field behind.

Maslin. Kind of bread made from a mix of rye and wheat grain. [<OFr. *mesteillon* < L *mistus* = mixed] – *Cf.* BULMONG; MIXTIL

Master. A craftsman qualified and experienced enough to take on and train apprentices; one who worked for himself. A 'master-piece' was the piece of work requiring the greatest skill by which a man proved himself a master of his craft.

Matins. *See* HORARIUM

Matutinal altar. The altar where monks celebrated the first mass of the day.

Maul. A wooden club; also a *mace.

Maumet [Mahomet]. An idol or false god; later a doll. The incorrect medieval belief held that Mohammed himself was worshipped by Muslims. – *Cf. next*

Maumettrie. Idolatry; mistakenly applied to Mohammedism, i.e. Islam. The use of the word 'Islam' began in English in the 17c. – *Cf. previous*

Maunch. Long sleeve worn by both men and women, esp. fashionable in the 14c. They are to be seen in many illuminated MSS and were frequently inveighed against by preachers as excess of vanity. Various *sumptuary regulations also sought to circumscribe their use. This sleeve was also used as a heraldic *charge.

Maunciple. *See* MANCIPLE

Maundy. The ceremony in which the feet of the poor are washed by royal or ecclesiastical dignitaries, remembering Christ when he washed the disciples' feet; distribution of food, clothing and/or money came afterwards. Maundy Thursday is now celebrated by the monarch with the distribution of specially minted silver coins. [< OFr. *mandé* = commanded < L *mandatum* = commandment]

Mazer. Maple wood; also, a bowl or drinking cup made of such wood.

Mead. Alcoholic drink made from fermenting honey and water. [< OE *medu*, cf. Gr. *methu* = wine] – *Cf.* MEDARIUS

Meadow. A vital piece of land for any farming community, being kept in grass to provide hay when mown. It could be more valuable than arable; although this may be due to the increasing shortage of land in the 12c and 13c as population expanded, there can be little doubt that it was a prime asset in earlier centuries as well. Such land was often found beside a river. The Latin was *pratum*. [< OE *mæd* = meadow, mead]

Meadowsweet. A plant (*Filipendula ulmaria*) once used to flavour *mead; found in fenland and wet meadowland.

Medale. A festival or party with ale held to celebrate the successful mowing of the lord's *meadow. [< OE *mæd* = meadow + ale] – *Cf.* SCOT-ALE

Medarius. That *obedientiary responsible for a monastery's *mead.

Meinie [meignie]. AN word for retainers or liveried dependants of a lord or magnate; the retinue or members of a household. The queen would also have her *meinie*, composed largely of women. – *Cf.* FAUTOR; MANUPAST; RETINENTIA

Mêlée. A kind of mock battle between sides of armed horsemen. Such mêlées took place in the 12c and were held in open spaces and to all intents and purposes were pitched battles. There was no set area of conflict; the open fields between villages were used. They were seen as realistic practice and training for war; they also served for the successful as a source of income. As they were fought realistically, so those captured would be ransomed, their equipment also being a source of money. Mêlées had fallen out of fashion by the 14c and were replaced by the *hastilude and *joust. – *Cf.* CONFLICTUS GALLICUS; TOURNAMENTS

Mellitarius. Latin term for a tenant who proffered honey to his lord in payment for his land. [< L *mel* = honey] – *Cf.* ALVEARY; CENSARIUS; CERVISARIUS

Membered. *Her.* Term used to describe a bird whose legs were tinctured differently from its body. – *Cf.* ANIMÉ; BEQUE; CRINED; RAMÉ; UNGULED

Men-at-arms. Below the ranks of great lords, knights and bannerets on the field of battle were the men-at-arms, a term which encompassed a shifting group of men. Esquires below the rank of knight could be considered men-at-arms and when fighting in the 14c for Edward III would have been paid 12d a day. They would probably have been accompanied by a mounted archer. A man-at-arms might have been well born and aspire to a knighthood, or he could have been one of his shire's or borough's levy. This broad group, known in Latin as *homines ad arma*, was, however, distinct from the general rank and file, always on foot, known as *homines armati*.

Mendicant. One who lived on alms; a mendicant *friar belonging to of one of the three orders, *Franciscan, *Dominican, *Carmelite. Their members lived on alms while travelling in the world beyond their monastery on the look out for and preaching against heresy. [< L *mendicus* = beggar < L *mendum* = a blemish or fault]

Menever grossus. Lit. *'miniver whole'. This was the whole fur of the belly of the miniver with the grey hair left in place. – *Cf. next*

Menever puratus. Lit. *'miniver pured'. The white fur of the belly of the miniver from which the grey hair had been removed. – *Cf. previous;* MENNER

Menial. Someone within a lord's *meinie*, i.e. a man who performed household duties for his lord. These men were soldiers or officials. The tasks they performed would not have been degrading. The current sense is a dilution of the original meaning, applied only to lowly tasks. – *Cf.* MEINIE

Menner. Alternative English word for *miniver, a corruption of the AN *menuver*. – *Cf.* MENEVER GROSSUS

Menologium. An ecclesiastical calendar in verse found in the C MS of the *ASC. [< Gr. *men*= month + *logos* = account, relation]

Mentonière. That part of a suit of armour protecting neck and chin but attached to the breast plate. [< AN *menton* = chin]

Mercatores de lenna. Lit. 'wool merchant'. *Lenna* is medieval Latin for 'wool', corresponding to classical *lana*. [L *mercator* = merchant]

Merce. *See* MIERCE

Mercenaries. Soldiers of fortune, either officers or foot soldiers, were widely used throughout Europe and England. During the 13c many mercenaries were recruited from Flanders and were variously outlaws, criminals, erstwhile priests, and prisoners released for the purpose. When they were not paid, as often happened, they continued their pillaging regardless of whose side their victims were on. [< L *merces* = reward] – *Cf.* ROUTIER; TRAILBASTON

Mercer. A dealer of fabrics such as silk and velvet; orig. a dealer in small items of all kinds. [< L *merx* = commodity, goods] – *Cf. next*

Mercers, Worshipful Company of. The company's earliest ordinances date from 1347; its royal charter was granted in 1394. At first they worked from a row of shops – small open warehouses – in Cheapside beside St Mary-le-Bow. – *Cf. previous*

Mercery. A *mercer's goods in general; used also in 'the Mercery' = the Mercers' Company. – *Cf.* MERCER

Merchant Taylors, Worshipful Company of. This company was granted its first charter in 1327. Its early wealth came from the making of tents and *acton. In time its power and influence increased as it acquired the authority to check measures of cloth at fairs and at places like Cheapside in the city of London. In its earlier days the company was less respectable and worthy. A dispute with the Goldsmiths in 1267 got out of control and a number of people were killed: the leaders were arrested, tried and executed.

Merchants Adventurers. Incorporated in 1407, this was a trading company, which by the mid-16c controlled three-quarters of English foreign trade and had superseded the *Hanse. Its first continental centre was at Bruges; it moved to Antwerp in 1446, and Calais in 1493, then back to Antwerp in 1496. The company transferred to Hamburg in 1567, and acquired a Dutch base in the 1580s. It was attacked and resented for exercising a monopoly and finally lost its charter in 1689. – *Cf.* STAPLE 1

Merchants, Statutes of. *Statuta de mercatoribus*, 1283 and 1285. The first statute made provision for the collection of monies owed by merchants. In 1283 the mayors of London, York, Bristol, Lincoln, Winchester and Shrewsbury were empowered with the *sheriff to seize goods to the value of the debt. This did not work as intended and the second statute of 1285 was issued, with somewhat different provisions. This time, debts were enrolled and the mayor would act if the debt were unpaid on the due date. Defaulting debtors were imprisoned and their property and land could be seized and sold if necessary.

Merchet. A *fine paid to a lord for permission for a daughter to marry; its value was variable, according to the wealth or poverty of the father. The lord needed recompense for the loss to his *manor of the daughter's future children and their potential for work on his estate. The Latin was *merchetum*. [< late OE *markett* = place where things were sold]

Mercian Register. Annals covering the period 902–24, relating the deeds of Æthelflæd, lady of the Mercians. Much of the register was incorporated in the B and C texts of *ASC and the chronicle of Henry of Huntingdon (d. *c*.1158).

Merciless Parliament. On 3 February 1388, at the initiative of Thomas of Gloucester, Henry, earl of Derby, Richard of Arundel, Thomas of Warwick and others, this so-called Merciless Parliament convicted a number of the young King Richard II's advisers of treason; as a result many were executed, or dismissed from the court. The intention was to destroy the king's inner circle and thus isolate him. The occasion arose from the defeat of the king's 'friends', led by Robert de Vere, at the Battle of Radcot Bridge, shortly before Christmas 1387. De Vere and others fled the country. After this, the lords who had opposed the young king ruled until May of the following year, 1389. That month Richard declared himself of age to rule personally and did so for the next few years, which were peaceful.

Merlon. Part of an embattled parapet, the tooth-like projections between which a gap affords a soldier or archer some protection. – *Cf.* CRENELLÉ

Merton, Council of. In 1236 there was a clash between common law and *canon law over the matter of illegitimacy. Common law said that illegitimacy could not be undone by marriage; that bastards had no rights of inheritance over children born in wedlock. Canon law affirmed that marriage was potent enough to legitimise bastard children. At this council the earls and barons ignored ecclesiastical pressure and did not change common law.

Mesne. A kind of land tenure. Used as in 'mesne lord', indicating a lord holding land of another who was superior. This arrangement was known as *'subinfeudation'. [< *mesne* = intermediate, between, i.e. neither a great lord nor a serf.] – *Cf.* DEMESNE

Messenger, King's. *See* NUNCIUS REGIS

Messor. The man who superintended teams of reapers at harvest, i.e. reapreeve. He was a kind of lesser *reeve who supervised sowing and the ploughteams; he may also have had a rôle in the *manorial court. [< L *meto, messui* = to reap]

Messuage. That area of land taken up by a house and its associated buildings and land; the whole plot of land; also used of plots of land within a *borough. *Bracton refers to a messuage in discussing a widow's dower. He says that a widow should be permitted to remain in her late husband's 'chief messuage for forty days after his death . . . [unless] the house is a castle . . . [in which case] let a suitable house be provided for her'. In some circumstances, although a widow might inherit the chief messuage, she could have a house built for her to the value of one third of that messuage. – *Cf.* LANDGAFOL

Metal. *Her.* The *tinctures *or (gold) and *argent (silver).

Mete. A boundary stone or marker. The word was used in the phrase 'metes and bounds', which referred to the duties of a *regarder. [< L *meta* = a boundary]

Metheglin. A kind of drink based on *mead to which were added various spices; it was used medicinally. – *Cf.* Bragget

Metropolitan. Bishop with authority over a group of adjoining dioceses and their bishops.

Meurtrière. A murder-hole. An opening in the roof of an entry passage to a castle or fortified building with the same purpose as *machicolation: it offered protection to defenders firing down onto the enemy. It was also useful as a way of pouring water onto any fires the enemy might have set to destroy the door. The *meurtrière* would have been used only as a fallback, when the outer gate had been breached.

Mew. A cage used for hawks and other hunting birds, particularly when they moulted. Later a secret place or a hidden den. There are still today many *mews in London, near places where kings once hunted. – *Cf.* Acceptor

Mews. Royal stables at *Charing Cross, constructed where the monarch's hawk mews had once been. Also, the generic word for stabling built around an open space. – *Cf. previous*

Micel here. Lit. 'large army'. Term used in *ASC* for the Vikings' Great Army of 866, which occupied York in November that year. – *Cf.* Here 1

Michaelmas. Feast of St Michael (the Archangel), 29 September. One of the *quarter days in England on which accounts were customarily settled.

Michaelmas goose [stubble-goose]. A goose fattened on the fallen grain in fields and stubble and slaughtered on *Michaelmas, 29 September, when all such free-range food was gone.

Mierce. The Mercians. [< OE *merc, mearc* = border, limit, march, realm] – *Cf.* Mark 2

Milites feoffati. Lit. 'enfeoffed knights'. Term used in the records for the knights holding of a lord who owed him military service. They were the knights of an *honour.

Mill. Mills were a source of revenue for lords of the *manor. In *DB* some 5,000 are listed but there is no indication of their age. The first were watermills, dating perhaps to as early as the 8c. In many places, the mill's render to the lord was made up of the *ora, i.e. combinations of 16d. In fact, 2s 8d was not uncommon, while 8d, half one ora, is also found. Both Latin words *molendinum* and *molinum* were used for a mill; a miller = *molendinarius*. [< OE *mylen* < L *mola* = millstone] – *Cf.* Salt-pan

Minium. Latin term for *cinnabar or vermilion; also the heraldic *gules; the colour of a *rubric. The artist who used *minium* was known as a *miniator*; 'miniature' refers to his work.

Miniver. Fur used as decoration or trim on ceremonial dress. The animal usually used was the red squirrel. Miniver was permitted, under 14c sumptuary regulations, to those not allowed ermine. [< *menu* = little + *vair* = fur] – *Cf.* MENEVER PURATUS; SUMPTUARY REGULATIONS; VAIR 1

Minor canon. One of the *clergy, assisting at services, not a member of the *cathedral chapter; also petty canon. – *Cf. next*

Minor orders. Those belonging to the minor orders were tonsured and members of the *clergy. Among their ranks were porter and lector, also *acolyte and *exorcist. – *Cf. previous;* MAJOR ORDERS

Minorites. *Franciscan friars who were also known as Grey Friars from their *habit. Like other friars they were subject to severe criticism during the 14c and later.

Minster. In modern usage, a community of *secular clergy, with extensive parochial rights; these were being eroded from the 10c by the foundation of single-priest churches on individual manors, the latter forming the basis for the later system of parishes. Consequently, many minsters disappeared, though their former presence can be detected in placenames ending in '-minster', e.g. Charminster and Beaminster. Before 1066, the word was used both of secular and monastic communities, but always with the sense of a superior church. [OE *mynster* < L *monasterium* = monastery]

Minstrel. Orig. a servant or handyman with specific functions; later, a person hired by a court or its lord to make music and sing, also to act and clown. In the 12c they were condemned in *canon law by Gratian (d. 1159), and later in the decretals of Pope Gregory IX, 1227–41. [< OFr. *menestral* = entertainer]

Minuscule. A cursive script, as opposed to the more formal *uncial. Frankish writers in the 8c and 9c developed a script known today as Carolingian (Caroline) minuscule. It was imported into England in the mid-10c, where it became the norm for Latin texts, whereas the native insular minuscule continued to be used for *vernacular texts, e.g. *ASC. – *Cf.* TEXTURA

Minutor. *See next;* BLOOD-LETTING

Minutus. Latin term for a monk who had been bled, something which was done regularly. The *minutus* was permitted to rest in the infirmary for two or three days, where there was both warmth and better food, i.e. meat. [< L *minutus* = diminished, decreased < L *minuo* = to lessen] – *Cf.* SANGUINATI

Miracle play. In strict usage, a play about saintly or eucharistic miracles; also used more generally for biblical drama and *mystery plays. – *Cf.* MORALITY PLAY; NICHOLAS, GUILD OF ST

Mischening. A fine imposed upon a litigant who when giving evidence departed from the original declaration. As part of his coronation oath Stephen swore 'entirely [to] do away with all exactions, mischeningas, and injustices'. [< OE *miscenning*, *mis* = error + *cenning* = perception]

Miserabiles personae. Lit. 'pitiable or wretched persons'. Term used by the Church for the unprotected, such as widows and orphans, who had a special claim to charity and aid. In theory, this was the class of person the chivalric knight was sworn to protect.

Miserere. Lit. 'have mercy'. One of the penitential psalms, Psalm 51, whose opening word – in the Latin text – is *Miserere*.

Misericord 1. A knife or dagger used to deliver a coup de grace; the word was also used for a particularly slender knife designed specifically to pass through the gaps in a knight's visor. [< L *misereor* = to have pity] – *Cf.* OCULARIUM

Misericord 2. In pre-11c English churches, it was forbidden to sit down: there were no seats in the part of the church or *cathedral for the lay congregation; nor were there any for monks or canons. However, this practice eased during the 12c. Initially, *leaning staffs were permitted for the frail. Later, seats were added to the stalls. In time a further act of mercy was allowed by adding to the underside of the raised choir seat a small ledge, which gave some support. Misericord in this context was taken to mean an 'indulgence seat'. The earliest surviving misericords are to be found at Exeter Cathedral, dating from 1255–79. [< L *misereor* = have pity]

Misericord 3. Monks were forbidden meat, except in the infirmary. By the 13c, a kind of half-way house emerged between *frater and infirmary where meat could be eaten, i.e. the misericord or chamber of mercy. At Peterborough it was called the 'seyny house' (*seyny* < *seynen* = to make the sign of the cross, to bless). Later, this arrangement was further amended so that half the members of a monastery were permitted meat and the others not. It marked the waning of the fervour of the original revival of faith and the softening of the order's rules. – *Cf.* CALEFACTORY

Misprision. Wrongdoing, esp. misconduct by a public servant; a failure in duty. [AN *mesprisioun* = an error, wrongdoing, wrong speech] – *Cf.* SCANDAL

Missal. Book containing the service of mass; a book of prayer, which was frequently illuminated. [< L *missalis*, adjectival form of *missa* = mass]

Mister. *See* MYSTER

Mitta. Measure of salt equal to six or eight bushels.

Mixtil [maslin]. A mixture of wheat and rye grown together as one crop. During the 13c it began to replace a crop of pure wheat on manors in fen country. [< OFr. *mesteillon* < L *mixtus* = mixed] – *Cf.* MASLIN

Moat. One of the most familiar features of a castle's defences: a ditch filled with water which surrounded the building. They were often stocked with fish, a source of fresh food in winter; perhaps also ducks and swans. (However, the **garderobe* would have been directly over the moat.) A moat was also useful in offering a serious impediment to attackers wishing to mine beneath a castle's walls.

Modius. Old Roman measure of corn, roughly equal to a *peck; used in this period to indicate a *bushel.

Moiety. A half of something; later, a part or small portion. [< OFr. *moité* < L *medius* = middle]

Molendinarius. Latin word for a miller. – *Cf.* MILL

Monastery. The place where a community of monks lived their lives according to the rules of their order. They lived within the confines of their community's buildings, not going into the world. In the 8c and 9c, many monasteries were founded by aristocratic converts, who also became abbots; similarly with nuns in nunneries. The younger children of aristocrats or gentry might also enter monasteries. [< Gr. *monasterion* = monastery, *monos* = alone] – *Cf.* CONVENT; MONK

Monetagium. Lit. 'mintage'. In his coronation oath Henry I abolished *monetagium*: 'The common *monetagium*, which has been collected throughout the cities and counties, and which did not exist in the time of King Edward [the Confessor], I utterly abolish for the future. If anyone, whether a *moneyer or someone else, is taken with false money, let right justice by done thereof.' It seems to have been a levy intended to ensure that the king did not lose money through false coin or depreciation. [< L *monetarius* < L *moneta* = a mint]

Money fief. A source of income given to a knight which was not land. – *Cf.* FIEFS-RENTES

Moneyer. A licensed coiner or striker of coins. Mints, of which there were many in England at any one time, were run by private individuals experienced in metalwork, under royal control. Payment was one penny in every £1. Moneyers were liable to mutilation, having a hand chopped off, castration (which happened in 1124), or death, if coins were found to be debased. Dies were supplied by the crown; recoining was one way for the monarch to extract money from the populace by reducing the proportions of silver or latterly gold. This obviated the need for a tax. [< OFr. *monnier* < L *monetarius* = striker of coins] – *Cf. next*

Moneyers, Assize of. This *assize was called at Christmas 1124 at Winchester. All moneyers were summoned and questioned about their activities, being required to offer satisfactory accounts. Those deemed to be at fault for issuing inferior quality coins were mutilated, i.e. one hand or both cut off, nose and/or ears cut off, castration, even blinding. This assize was occasioned by poor-quality coins sent to Normandy in 1124. – *Cf. previous*

Monk. Member of one of the communities of Christian men who lived according to an order or set of rules established to ensure a life of devotion and prayer. [OE *munuc* < L *monachus* = monk < Gr. *monos* = alone] – *Cf.* MONASTERY

Moot [mot]. A meeting or gathering of people; also, the place of the meeting, namely moot hall and moot hill. [OE *mot* = assembly, society, court] – *Cf.* GEMOT; WITENAGEMOT

Morality play. These 15–16c plays usually had a central, allegorical figure, representing humankind between the personified opposing forces of vice and virtue. There was often a principal comic character. – *Cf.* MIRACLE PLAY; MYSTERY PLAY

Mormaer. Scottish word for its English equivalent of steward or *high reeve, the OE for which was *heahgerefa* and the Latin *summus *praepositus*. [< Gaelic *mor* = great + *maer* = bailiff] – *Cf.* REEVE

Morne 1. Term used to describe the head of a lance which had been blunted for safer use in tournaments. [< OFr. *morner* = to blunt] – *Cf. next;* CORONAL

Morne 2 [morné]. *Her.* Describes a lion without teeth or claws, figuratively blunted. [< OFr. *morner* = to blunt] – *Cf.* DISARMED; MORNE 1

Mort d'ancestor. A writ issued by *chancery which sought to establish the rightful heir of a property. The case was decided by a jury assembled by the *sheriff and held before one of the travelling justices or *justice-in-eyre. The question to be answered was whether or not the claimant's father had had rightful possession of the property and whether the claimant was heir. By specifying the claimant's father in the claim, the *assize sought to step back to before Stephen's reign and the disruption of that time. – *Cf.* EYRE; NOVEL DISSEISIN

Mortalité des enfants. Phrase used at the time for the *plague which struck England in 1361–2. It was distinctive for carrying off children, the offspring of many of those who had survived the first great outbreak, the *Black Death of 1348.

Morterel. A dish for peasants made from pieces of cake or bread boiled in milk.

Mortmain, Statute of. 15 November 1279. This statute determined that no more land could be given to the Church without royal agreement. Donating land had the effect of reducing royal tax revenues and also revenues to the baronage, since ecclesiastical land – held in perpetuity, the Church being an immortal institution – paid no reliefs. The phrase used in the statute was 'the services which are due of such fees . . . are unduly withdrawn'. It was a measure which the king, Edward I, and the barons both agreed upon. The *mortmain* (dead hand) of the statute's title referred to the Church, which being immortal could not relinquish what it possessed. Indeed, a duty of archbishops and bishops was to preserve and protect the *temporalities of their dioceses. – *Cf.* QUIA EMPTORES, STATUTE OF

Mortuary. Payment or *fine elicited by the church on the death of a parishioner. There were various degrees of payment, depending on the poverty or otherwise of the deceased. – *Cf.* SOUL-SCOT

Mortuary roll. List of names of the dead for whom prayers were to be said in a monastery at set anniversaries. Such prayers had been paid for in the dead person's will or by the family. The medieval belief was that only saints went directly to heaven. Everyone else had to wait until the day of judgement. Thus prayers said or addressed to a saint were felt to be esp. beneficial. – *Cf.* OBIT

Motte and bailey. Type of castle built by the Normans in England: a fort was built atop a motte, i.e. a raised mound of earth, surrounded by a *bailey.

Mould-board. That part of a plough which turned earth over and broke up the soil, rather than just scratching a furrow in the field as older ploughs did. It was an important technical advance from *c*.10–11c. [< OE *molde* = earth]

Mount. *Her.* A small hill or mound, usually found at the base of the shield. It is sometimes known as a 'mount-vert' when shown as green. – *Cf.* VERT

Mouvance. Lit. 'changing, shifting'. Modern critic's term for the changeability of medieval texts, particularly literary texts.

Movable feast. Term given to feast days determined by the date of *Easter, which itself is movable, taking place on the first Sunday following each spring's first full moon. Such feast days are: Ash Wednesday, Lent, Ascension Thursday, *Pentecost, Trinity Sunday and the Feast of Corpus Christi.

MS. Abbr. of 'manuscript'; plural = MSS.

Muid. Measure of liquid employed in France but familiar in England = 270 litres, i.e. *c*.59 gallons or 475 pints. When used of grain it represented a *quarter, i.e. eight bushels. In the *Constitutio Domus Regis* the bakers, given a muid of corn, were required to produce 40 superior simnels, 140 salt simnels and 260 loaves. – *Cf.* SIMNEL

Muldefang. *See* SLITCH

Mulierculae. The 'little women' whom students at Oxford *c.*1250 were forbidden to have or keep in their lodgings. – *Cf.* BEGUINE

Mullet. *Her.* A five-pointed star; it was a *charge used as a mark of *cadency which indicated the third son of a family. – *Cf.* ESTOILE; LABEL

Mummer. Actor of short entertainments, often of traditional style, and often disguised or wearing a mask; their shows might be mute or unscripted, though court mumming was the more formal entertainment. [< OFr. *momer* = act mutely, without words]

Mund. The *king's peace or protection. – *Cf. next*

Mundbryce. A breach of the king's protection; a breach of duty to guard or protect. [< OE *mund* = trust, protection, peace + *bryce* = breach, infringement] – *Cf. previous and next;* GRITHBRECHE

Mundbyrd. The giving of protection, e.g. the king gave protection to the realm, known as the *'king's peace'. The word was also used of a breach of protection owed. Others, such as a *sheriff, also had the right give the peace in the king's stead. Breaches of the latter, though serious, were liable to a lesser fine. [< OE *mund* = trust, protection + *byrd* = a duty, a charge] – *Cf. previous;* BAN; WITE

Murage. A tax or toll levied to pay for the cost of defensive town walls, both for their building and repair. The Latin word used in the documents was *muragium*. It would be imposed on strangers entering the town. However, it was not a permanent tax. To impose murage required a licence from the king in which the length of time it could be collected was specified. [< L *murus* = a wall] – *Cf.* TRIMODA NECESSITAS

Mural gallery. A gallery built into the *curtain wall of a castle but below the parapet, which was provided with loopholes. [< L *murus* = a wall]

Murdrum. Murder. After the Conquest, William I ruled that any unidentified murder victim was to be assumed to be Norman – for which the *hundred in which the crime occurred was to be fined – unless he was proved to be English. In the *Dialogus de Scaccario*, Richard fitz-Nigel said that *murdrum* also meant the murder was hidden and intended to be kept so by the perpetrator. By fitz-Nigel's own time distinctions between Norman and Englishman were blurring. One of the rights granted in a charter from Henry I to the citizens of London was exemption from the *murdrum* fine. Nevertheless, in

LHP the penalty for *murdrum* was fixed at 46 marks. The whole idea of a distinct difference between Englishman and Norman having become obsolete, *murdrum* was abolished by statute in 1340. [< OE *morð* = death, destruction, murder] – *Cf.* WERGELD

Murrain. Pestilence or plague. The word was used of the diseases of sheep in particular. It was most likely babesiosis, an infection carried by ticks. There were several severe outbreaks between 1315 and 1322. Lore had it that murrain appeared every seven years. [< AN *moryn* < OFr. *moraine* = pestilence < L *mors* = death] – *Cf.* BLACK DEATH

Murrey. The dark purple-red of the mulberry fruit's juice; the range of colour carries from purple to a reddish brown. The word was also used of cloth and stained glass so coloured. [< L *morum* = mulberry, fruit of the mulberry]

Musket. A male sparrowhawk.

Mynstermon. Lit. 'minster man'. One of the four kinds of monk, as described in an AS version of the rule of St Benedict. The *mynstermon* was the monk who lived in a monastery under a rule and under an *abbot. – *Cf.* SYLFDEMA, WESTENSETLA; WIDSCRITHUL

Myrce. *See* MIERCE

Myster [mister]. Handicraft or trade. Members of such trades would join together in *guilds. The Latin form is *mistera*. [< OFr. *mestier* < L *ministerium* = occupation, work] – *Cf. next;* MYSTERY PLAY

Mystery [mistery]. An occupation or trade or specialised handicraft of the kind which formed protective *guilds. [< 13c *mister* = a handicraft < AN *mester* < L *ministerium* = occupation, work] – *Cf. previous and next*

Mystery play. These plays, associated esp. with the feast of Corpus Christi, were called 'mystery plays' because they were put on by the *mystery, i.e. members of a *guild. They may have developed from liturgical drama acted within the church, or from religious processions through the city streets. They typically dramatised the whole of salvation history from the Fall of Lucifer to the Last Judgement, though not every cycle was so inclusive; some towns played only a Passion series, though no texts survive. The most characteristic form of staging was on pageant wagons that were moved from point to point through a city, as at York or Chester. They lasted from the late 14c to the Reformation; Kendal's play was still being acted at the start of the 17c. – *Cf.* MIRACLE PLAY; MORALITY PLAY

N

Naiant. *Her.* Swimming horizontally (of a fish).

Naif. A peasant or villein attached to a vill or settlement. – *Cf. next*

Naifty, writ of. Writ issued by *chancery allowing a manorial lord to reclaim his runaway peasant, or *naif* (AN). The Latin term was (*homo*) *nativus* = a native. [< AN *naif* = peasant or villein attached to a *vill or settlement]

Nail. Unit of measure of cloth = 2¼ in.

Naperer. That member of the king's household responsible for the linen. He was also known as the 'napier' (hence the surname 'Napier'). [< OFr. *nappe* = a tablecloth] – *Cf.* Steward

Natalis dies. Lit. 'birth day' (of Christ), Christmas Day.

Nativi. *See* Naifty, writ of

Ne in dubium. Lit. 'lest in doubt'. Without admitting any direct involvement in Thomas Becket's death (29 December 1170), Henry II nevertheless acknowledged his responsibility. *Ne in dubium* was the document in which Henry's purgation and penances were set down. His reconciliation with the Church took place within and outside the *cathedral at Avranches on 21 May 1172. This was repeated at Caen nine days later, ensuring news of the event was widely disseminated.

Nebuly [nebulé]. *Her.* A wavy line meant to look like the outline of clouds. [< L *nebulatus* = clouded]

Necrology. Register kept by a monastery recording the names and date of death of everyone connected with it, e.g. monks and those who gave gifts of money or land. Such a register kept by the *Cluniac order contained some 48,000 names. [< Gr. *nekros* = a dead person] – *Cf.* Obit

Negotia regni. Lit. 'the business of ruling (the kingdom)'. A phrase encountered in discussions of the relationship between king and the magnates; it is an abstract of all the problems of kingship from William I to Henry VIII.

Neudd. Long, wooden hall which served on the *demesne of a Welsh prince as did the *manor or *caput honoris* in England.

Nicholas, Guild of St. In the 14c, this *guild composed of parish clerks gave performances of miracle plays in the streets of Clerkenwell, near the Skinners' Well. Boys from the school of *St Paul's Cathedral also played their parts.

Nicolaitism. The practice of priests in being married or having a mistress, i.e. concubinage. It was one of the twin evils to be overthrown in the eyes of the reform movement of 11c Rome, inspired by Pope Gregory VII. (The second evil practice was *simony.) Being sexually active was considered to sully the priest and thus make him unworthy to perform the sacraments. Another anxiety was the prospect of churches and even bishoprics being handed down from father to son. Around 1100 it was not uncommon for rich prebendal churches of St Paul's Cathedral to pass from father to son, e.g. All Saints at St Paul's Walden in Hertfordshire. The term is derived from Nikolaos, a member of the early Christian Church who advocated pagan worship. Revelation 2:15 refers to 'the doctrine of the Nicolaitans, which thing I hate'.

Nicole. After the Conquest, Lincoln is referred to in AN documents and *rolls as 'Nicole' or 'Nycol' (but in Latin documents correctly as 'Lincolnia').

Nigra moneta. Lit. 'black or dark money'. This phrase referred to copper coins. – Cf. ALBA FIRMA; INBLANCH

Nigredo. Alchemical term for the state of disintegration metals must go through before their resurrection as something else. Mid-winter followed by spring was a sign of this process in the natural world.

Nisi prius. Lit. 'unless previously'. A writ to the *sheriff instructing him to provide a jury at the court of Westminster on a set day, unless the assize judges came to the *county.

Nithing. An outlaw or wicked person was declared 'nithing'. The term was used by William Rufus in 1088 when summoning the *fyrd to support him during a rebellion engineered by Odo of Bayeux. He requested all to present themselves, unless they wanted to be considered nithing. [< OE nið = enmity] – Cf. CULVERTAGE

Noble. First minted in 1344, under Edward III, this was an English gold coin initially worth one third of a pound, 6s 8d, or half a *mark; it was replaced by the *angel in 1464, when it was worth 10s and known as a *'ryal' or 'rose noble'. Edward III rejoiced in an extra title, King of the Sea, after his successes with naval battles; as a reflection of this, the noble showed Edward holding sword and shield in the *cog, *Thomas*, in which he had sailed and won the Battle of Sluys, June 1340.

Noblesse de cour. Lit. 'nobility of the court'. Before the 14c those who surrounded the king were of the nobility, whose position and power were somewhat independent of the crown. In many ways they were his companions. However, as the court and its attendant administrative functions increased, laymen or clerks were required for specialist rôles, and the most important of these officials were ennobled. The distinction also carried the implication that their rank was not conferred on the battlefield.

Nock. The notch at each end of a *longbow which held the string; these were usually small pieces of bone fitted to the stave. Later, the word was used for the cleft in the buttocks.

Noke. Measure of land equal to a quarter of a *virgate.

Nonage. Term used, esp. in legal documents, for someone under the legal age. [< AN *non* = not + *age*, i.e. not (of) age]

None. Last of the Little Hours of the divine office, recited at the ninth hour, 3 pm. – *Cf.* HORARIUM; SEXT; TERCE

Noon. Today we know noon as midday. Before the 14c however, the word was *none and referred to the ninth hour, which was around 3 pm.

Norbertines. Alternate name of Premonstratensians, after their founder St Norbert (1080–1134).

Norman Conquest. The successful invasion and conquest of England in 1066 by William, then duke of Normandy, after the famous battle fought at Hastings between King Harold II and the Normans on 14 October 1066.

Normangli [Normanangli]. Term used for the Normans who lived in England.

Norroy and Ulster. The third (English) King of *Arms, whose jurisdiction lies north of the river Trent and, latterly, Northern Ireland. [< OFr. *nord* = north + *roi* = king]

Northampton, Assize of. 1176. Ten years after the Assize of Clarendon, this assize repeated many of the earlier ordinances and criminal measures, while increasing some penalties. For example, if someone accused of robbery failed the ordeal of water, the punishment was increased from the loss of the right foot, to the loss of right foot and right hand. The robber was also required to leave the kingdom within 40 days. This was deemed in the interests of 'stern justice'. Other measures offered protection to various groups of people and property rights, e.g. of widows, and claims for inherited land in another's possession.

Novel disseisin. A possessory *assize which sought to find the rightful claimant of a property, a case which could easily be initiated by a writ from *chancery. The question to be answered by a jury brought together by the *sheriff and in the presence of a *justice-in-eyre was whether or not the claimant had the right to the property from which he had been evicted, i.e. disseised. It was a part of the much increased business of the royal justice system during the reign of Henry II. This procedure might have been used when a pilgrim returned home to find his land occupied by someone without title. – *Cf.* DISSEISIN; MORT D'ANCESTOR

Nowed. *Her.* A knot or something knotted, looking rather like a figure 8; most often of a snake and known as 'an adder nowed'.

Nudus nudum Christum sequi. Lit. 'to follow naked Christ naked'. The phrase was used of the many enthusiasts during the religious revival in the 12c who, wishing to emulate Christ, abjured wealth and its comforts.

Nulle terre sans seigneur. Lit. 'there is no land without a lord'. In England, after the Conquest, the king was the lord of all the land. – *Cf.* ALLODIUM; DOMINION DIRECTUM

Numbles [umbles]. Venison offal; also the surrounding meat; considered a delicacy by those who hunted.

Nuncio. The pope's ambassador, known properly as the Papal Nuncio. [< L *nuncio* = to announce] – *Cf. next*

Nuncius regis. King's messenger. The king had a body of messengers whose task was to carry writs, letters and any kind of document throughout the kingdom. (On one occasion a messenger was sent to deliver part of the quartered body of a man executed for treason.) They always travelled on horse. Messengers functioned in the same way in Europe, and were also employed by bishops, sheriffs, abbots and knights. There were places across the nation where horses could be changed, though a system of staging posts throughout England did not emerge until Tudor times. An attack on a messenger was deemed an attack on the king, which may have kept them safe to some extent. [< L *nuntius* = messenger] – *Cf.* CARECTARIUS; COKINI

Nutritus. Term used of a child *oblate raised to adulthood within a monastery. Many children were placed in monasteries by their families for various reasons. Bede, for example, was placed in the monastery at Jarrow at the age of seven. [< L *nutrio* = to raise or foster] – *Cf.* CONVERSUS

O

Oak Book. List of rules and regulations governing the use of the port of Southampton by shipping in the early 14c. It also contained a schedule of customs charges for the immense variety of goods being brought into England. Spices and dyes are notable: *brasil, cumin, rice, saffron, cloves and ginger are a few of the items specified. Sugar is one of these luxuries, referred to as *zucre* or *soucre*. The book is a useful record of just where shipping came from in the 14c: apart from places nearby such as Flanders and France, boats came from Genoa and nearby Savona, from Ancona, Venice, Catalonia and Portugal. Southampton shared this eastern trade via Italy with London: the Genoese traders tended to prefer Southampton, while the Venetians preferred London. Another part of the Oak Book set out local laws and regulations of the town of Southampton itself. These rules are all written in French.

Obedientiary. One who owes obedience. The word referred to that member of a monastery responsible for a particular aspect of the community's functioning, e.g. *cellarer, *fraterer, *precentor, *sacrist. He was also required to render appropriate annual accounts, usually at *Michaelmas, 29 September. The Latin form was *obedientiarius*

Obit. Mass said in commemoration of a person on the anniversary of their death. A sum of money, or endowment, was given to a monastery to ensure this was done each year. Frequently, such endowments included provision for a *pittance for each monk in the monastery. – *Cf.* BEDE-ROLL; LIBRI MEMORIALES; TRENTAL

Oblate. A child given by his parents to a monastery to be raised there; less commonly, a lay person connected with a monastery but without having taken vows. The practice of child oblation created difficulties if, as an adult, the oblate did not wish to join the community, for example in what to do with any property donated with him or her. By the 13c the giving of boys had virtually ceased, although girls continued to be given for some time. [< L *oblatus* = offered] – *Cf. next*; DONATUS; NUTRITUS; OBLEY

Oblation. Something given to God or a sacrifice so made; a gift or bequest to a church. – *Cf. previous*; ALTARAGE

Obley. An offering; later the wafer of the *eucharist. – *Cf.* OBLATE; OBLATION

Obolus [obole]. Orig. a Greek coin; a weight used by apothecaries; later, any coin of little value. [< Gr. *obolos* = coin, a sixth of a drachma]

Occitan. *See* LANGUE D'OC

Octave. The seventh day after a Church festival (which, by including the festival itself, is the eighth day). 'Octave' could also mean the span of these days, i.e. a week. [< L *octavus* = eighth] – *Cf.* QUINDENE

Ocularium. The horizontal slit in the *visor of a knight's helmet for seeing through. [< L *oculus* = eye] – *Cf.* ARMET; HEAUME

Oculus. An archdeacon; through him a bishop kept an eye on his diocese and exercised discipline. [< L *oculus* = eye]

Offertory. The placing of the bread and wine on the altar in the *eucharist; the *antiphon sung at this moment; time when the collection is made.

Oillagium. *Ullage. – *Cf.* -AGIUM

Oléron, laws of. Set of codes relating to maritime law thought to have been instituted in England by Richard I. They regulated all relationships between captains and their men, and their employers; they also had to do with the laws of wrecks. Some of the laws deal with violence onboard ship, e.g. if murder was committed at sea, the murderer should be tied to the body of the victim and thrown overboard. Another states that for punching someone a man should be ducked three times. They were first printed in 1494. (An equivalent collection of laws, though of earlier date, pertaining to France and Spain, was known as the *Consolat del Mar*.) The laws are to be found in the Black Book of the *Admiralty. Oléron is a small island in the bay of Biscay. – *Cf.* LEX MERCATORIA

Operatio castelli. Lit. 'castle work'. One of the services often mentioned in charters, from which a tenant might on occasion be exempted. The work was unspecified – the assumption being all knew what it involved – but most likely repair of walls and embankments was meant or building a specified length of wall. – *Cf.* TRIMODA NECESSITAS

Opinicus. *Her.* The opinicus was a fantastical vivid creature somewhat like a griffin with a lion's legs and body, an eagle's head, wings and a *curt tail. – *Cf.* DRAGON; GRIFFIN

Opus Anglicanum. Lit. 'English work'. In the 10c and 11c decorated textiles were often referred to as being distinctly English, notably gold embroidery. However, the reputation of this work lasted well into the 15c. By the 12c the very finest textiles were always assumed to be the work of English hands. (The English reputation for metal-work was equally high.) Most of this work was embroidery. St Dunstan is said to have designed stuffs to be embroidered, while the daughters of Edward the Elder were known for their skill. When William the Conqueror returned to Normandy the Normans were astonished by the richness of his English robes. The *Bayeux Tapestry, along with material (added in 934 by King Æthelstan) from St Cuthbert's sarcophagus form some important early examples of *opus Anglicanum*; later medieval examples have survived more extensively.

Opus Dei. Lit. 'the work of God'. Term used of the daily round of prayer and praise in a *cathedral, the organisation of which fell to the *precentor.

Or. *Her.* Orig. gold; also, the heraldic term for the *tincture gold. [< L *aurum* = gold]

Ora. *See* MARK 1

Oratores. *See* THREE ORDERS

Oratory. A small place for prayer, esp. private prayer; a small *shrine.

Orb. A globe of gold with a cross atop, part of the essential *regalia of a monarch, symbolising both the world and the power of the Church seen as blessing him who held it. – *Cf.* DALMATIC; SCEPTRE 1

Ordainers. The committee of barons and prelates who, opposing Edward II, imposed a series of ordinances (hence the name, Ordainers) upon the king for reform of government. The Ordainers were 21 in number. Among the demands of the barons were the following: the banishment of Piers Gaveston and other royal favourites who were seen to hold too great an influence over the king; the establishment of a baronial oligarchy to be the king's natural advisers; the barons to have the power to control all appointments of chief officials in the government and royal household; the king should not go to war or leave the country without baronial consent. – *Cf.* ORDINANCES OF 1311

Ordeal, trial by. In trial by ordeal, proof of guilt or innocence was determined by God, the accused being tested by an ordeal which proved innocence if no mark was caused by the trial itself. In the laws of Athelstan anyone undergoing this trial had to be blessed by a priest and live on bread, water and vegetables for three days. One trial involved the accused walking blindfold over red-hot ploughshares. God, it was believed, would guide the steps of the innocent; the guilty would burn their feet. Something equally unpleasant was done with boiling water. After this, the wounds were bandaged. If after three days the wounds appeared to be healing, innocence was proved; otherwise guilt was evident. Dunking displayed a paradox: water being the medium of baptism, it was considered sensitive both to guilt and to innocence. Thus if the water 'accepted' the accused, whose hands and feet were bound, they were innocent; the guilty were 'rejected' by water and floated. The length of rope or depth of sinking was set at 1½ ells, or some 5½ feet. During the *Angevin period, eight out of ten ordeals were of 'cold water', which were taken by the unfree, i.e. serfs, villeins etc. (Hot iron was taken by free men and women.) Pipe Roll records show that of the cold water ordeals, two out of three passed and were shown to be innocent. A priest was required to be present on these occasions; but the Lateran Council of 1215 condemned the practice and instructed priests to take no part. – *Cf.* BATTLE, TRIAL BY

Ordinances of 1311. Ordinances imposed on Edward II by the barons through parliament in the midst of his military incompetence and over-dependence on favourites. While there is no doubt the barons sought control of the king, this episode was an important part of the growth of parliament itself. It saw parliament's confidence in assenting to measures relating both to crown and to country. One of the provisions was the banishment of Edward's favourite and presumed lover, Piers Gaveston. Beyond Gaveston, there was nothing politically radical in the proposals: rather they sought to bring Edward back to a king's traditional advisers. They claimed the right to oversee senior appointments of the crown and household and also the right of assent to going to war. The group responsible for these ordinances was known as the *Ordainers.

Ordinary 1. An ordinance or regulation; a formula for doing something.

Ordinary 2. *Her.* A dictionary of heraldic bearings; one of the nine simple shapes or charges in *heraldry, sometimes called 'honourable ordinaries'. – *Cf.* BEND; CHEVRON 2; CHIEF; CROSS CRAMPONÉE; PALE; PILE 2; QUARTER 2; SALTIRE

Ordo equestris. Latin term for the Order of Knights.

Oriflamme. The silk banner of St Denis (patron saint of France), coloured sacred red or orange-red, which was given by the abbot of St Denis to the Capetian kings of France when they set out to war. The banner was known as *Monjoie*, the French battle-cry, and is often mentioned in the *Song of Roland*.

Original writ. Legal instrument bought by a plaintiff commanding the court of common pleas to deal with a particular case. This purchase only initiated the procedure, it did not buy a result.

Originalia Rolls. Rolls issued by the *chancery to the *exchequer with notification of payments, such as fines which were to be collected.

Orillion. A projection built onto a *bastion, reaching beyond the rampart.

Orphrey. Item of rich embroidery, made with gold; sometimes used for an elaborate *amice. [< L *aurifrisium*, a corruption of *aurum* = gold + *Phrygium*, thus Phrygian gold]

Orpiment. A yellow pigment, composed largely of arsenic trisulphide. [< L *aurum* = gold + *pigmentum* = colour] – *Cf.* REALGAR

Ostiarius [hostiarius]. Usher or doorkeeper, usually of *minor orders. By the late 13c, the *ostiarius* had become a member of the hanaper – responsible for rendering accounts – where he was next below the controller, himself next below the *chancellor. – *Cf.* HANAPER 2

Ostium ecclesiae. Lit. 'church door'. A distinctive feature of 15c ecclesiastical architecture was the spacious church door. They were places where business was done, contracts exchanged and wedding ceremonies began. Sometimes they were built with a room above, where the priest and *sacrist would sleep; this was convenient for their early start of the day with mass. This room was also useful for teaching choirboys.

Ostmen. Lit. 'eastmen'. *Viking settlers who created colonies in Ireland at Dublin, Waterford, Wexford and Limerick. The Irish Ostmen were driven out by Richard de Clare soon after he landed in Ireland in August 1170.

Outlaw. A person deemed unworthy of the protection afforded by the law. He was placed beyond justice and its benefits, much as *excommunication placed a person outside the Church and beyond salvation. It was relatively easy to become an outlaw. [< OE *utlaga, utlah* = an outlaw] – *Cf.* FRANK-PLEDGE

Outremer. Lit. 'overseas'. The title given to the lands held by crusaders in the Holy Land. – *Cf.* CRUSADES

Overslop. A cassock or gown; a loose, baggy garment; those worn by butchers identified their trade; abbr. as 'slop', whence our 'sloppy'.

Overt. *Her.* Describes a bird with wings spread about the fly. [< ME *overt* = open]

Ox. The main plough-beast until well after the 14c. In the 14c, an ox cost 13s 1¼d. In comparison, a sheep fetched just 1s 6d, a cow 9s 5d.

Oxford, Provincial Synod of. Held in 1409, this *synod determined to prohibit the translation of the Bible into English. It was thought that an English Bible would become a weapon in the hands of those without proper respect for authority, who would also begin to use it without being instructed in its proper use. Were they able to read for themselves, such readers might then ignore the glosses that explained the text in terms of received Church doctrine.

Oxford, Provisions of. These were set down at the parliament held at Oxford, June 1258. There was agreement between Henry III and the barons to reform royal powers in 1258 and to cut through bureaucracy – esp. regarding writs in common law which were stifled by *chancery and its standardised procedures. A council was established responsible to the barons in parliament. It was also felt that centralised bureaucracy gave the king undue power to interfere in the process of justice (e.g. forbidding writs to be issued against family or friends), which clearly breached both spirit and letter of clause 40 of *Magna Carta. It was a technical matter, but with profound implications for justice and access to it. – *Cf.* BARONS' WAR; MARLBOROUGH, STATUTE OF; QUERELA; WESTMINSTER, PROVISIONS OF

Oxford, University of. Though well established by 1167, it was not until 1571 that the university received from parliament an act of permanent incorporation. Until that act, the work of Robert Dudley, earl of Leicester, the university had been required to get a fresh charter with every change of monarch.

Oxgang. One eighth of a ploughland (*carucate); equiv. of a *bovata*.

Oyer and determiner. Lit. 'hear and decide'. *Oyer* is the legal term for the hearing of a case in court. However, the complete phrase is a 'commission of *oyer* and *determiner*' for a judge in *eyre to hear cases. *Oyer* shares its roots with *Oyez* = Hear me! uttered by the town crier, summoning people to hear his message.

P

Page. A young boy in the service of a knight. He might aspire to knighthood, and would serve his lord as did the *esquire. During battle the page would tend the *destriers* not in use.

Paint. Term used in the making of stained glass for the mixture of ground glass, metal oxide and flux which is applied to glass and then fired. – *Cf.* POT METAL

Palatinate. Territory ruled by a *palatine. In England, usually a *county in which a *tenant-in-chief had powers normally reserved to the king, e.g. the right to appoint a *justiciar, hold courts of exchequer and chancery and to coin money. The king's writ did not run in a county palatine.

Palatine. Lord of a territory or *county whose powers were similar to those usually only accorded a king. In a county palatine, the king's powers of justice and moneying were held by the lord, not the king. [< L *palatinus* = chamberlain or officer of a palace] – *Cf. previous*

Pale. *Her.* An *ordinary: a vertical stripe taking up a third of the area of the *shield.

Palet. A helmet, cap or other head-covering made of *cuir-bouilli.*

Palfrey. French term for a small horse such as was often used by women; definitely not a war horse. [< L *palfredus*] – *Cf.* DESTRIER; ROUNCY

Palimpsest. A *parchment MS partially or wholly reused, old matter being scraped off; also a brass plate which has been turned over and reused. The word is a 17c coinage. [< Gr. *palin* = again + *psestos* = rubbed]

Palisade. Wooden fence enclosing an area built defensively as a temporary shelter, or temporarily awaiting something more substantial made of stone. [< L *palus* = a pole or stake]

Pall. *Her.* A *charge of three bands in the form of a Y, charged with crosses.

Pallagium. Toll paid to a lord when using his port or dock for loading and unloading goods.

Pallium [pall]. Vestment of an archbishop's office; a band or belt worn round the shoulders with a flap or lappet front and back; by transference, the office of archbishop. The pallium was taken from the shrine of St Peter, which signified that the new archbishop's authority had been delegated by the apostle's successors. [< L *pallium* = a cloak (worn by philosophers)] – *Cf.* AD LIMINA; PETER'S PENCE

Palmer. A pilgrim, esp. one who returned from the Holy Land with a palm-leaf badge as a souvenir. The term was also used of *mendicant monks on a perpetual *pilgrimage from shrine to shrine. These latter often wore badges or small tokens as proof of having visited pilgrimage sites. Such tokens were sold at all sites. – *Cf.* SCALLOP

Paly. *Her.* Describes a shield divided into equal parts or stripes which are coloured or tintured alternately. [< OFr. *pale* < L *palus* = a stake or stick]

Panarius. Latin word for that part of a church near the door from which bread was handed out to the poor. [< L *panis* = bread]

Pannage. The right to feed pigs in a wood on beech-mast and acorns in autumn; also the fodder itself. In Latin, *pannagium*. – *Cf.* AVAGIUM; FORAGIUM

Pannus stragulatus. Lit. 'striped clothes'. The striped cloth given as part of their *livery to the servants of a lord or bishop.

Parage. Lineage or descent, particularly noble birth. 'Parage' was the English form. – *Cf.* IN PARAGIO

Parapet. Bank built on top of a wall for extra protection, or one built in front of a trench. [< Ital. *parapetto* = a breast-high wall]

Parcener. A partner; a person having a share in land with another. The Latin form is *parcenarius*. [< L *partitio* = divide, share] – *Cf.* IN PARAGIO

Parchment. The skin of a sheep or goat (and by extension often used more generally to include vellum), prepared for writing on; also used for the bindings of books. Preparation was a lengthy process: once the wool had been removed, the skin was soaked in lime to remove the flesh, then stretched on a frame, scraped with a *lunellum*, and treated with chalk to whiten the surface. [< L *pergamina* = writing material from Pergamum; also *Parthica pellis* = Parthian skin] – *Cf. next;* PERCAMINARIUS; VELLUM

Parchmenter. The maker of *parchment. Before the beginning of the 13c, most parchment was made in the monasteries by those who needed it. With the growth of the MS trade, and the opening of the universities, the parchment trade expanded beyond the monasteries.

Pardoner. A secular clerk or friar who travelled the country with *relics, issuing pardons in exchange for payment; one who sold *indulgences. They were also known as *questores*, i.e. askers, since they asked what sins needed expiation. Their official title was *quaestorii*. The office was abolished by the pope in 1562.

Park. An enclosed piece of land, held by royal grant, specifically for hunting. [< OE *pearruc* = an enclosure]

Parliament. Before the Conquest, Norman dukes had a *curia ducis*, through which they did business. In England, the equivalent was the **curia regis*, and a great council which met two or three times each year. Tenants-in-chief attended and advised the king; as did the Church's prelates. Petitions for justice and other pleas were dealt with by the *curia regis* and other courts, as were political matters. The Commons were at first knights summoned by the monarch in 1254. In time, those magnates who attended arrived by personal summons, which gave rise to the House of Lords, while sheriffs issued a general summons for representatives of the shires. By 1295 shires and the boroughs were represented, as were magnates. The **Hundred Years' War was the occasion for parliament to grant the king subsidies and taxes. All monarchs needed money and it was here that the Commons found its real power. In exchange for financial aid the crown made concessions and answered grievances. In the early 14c the Commons were meeting separately from the Lords, dealing with petitions and creating legislation to deal with grievances. By the end of the 14c, taxation was agreed by the Commons with the 'advice and assent of the Lords'. [< Fr. *parler* = talk]

Parliament, Houses of. There is said to have been a royal palace at Westminster during the reign of Cnut where the present Houses of Parliament are to be found. In any event, a palace was created by Edward the Confessor and extended by William the Conqueror, remaining in use until destroyed by fire in 1512. The Commons met in St Stephen's Chapel from the late 1540s. In 1834 fire destroyed the whole palace, after which the buildings we are familiar with were designed and built by Sir Charles Barry and Augustus Pugin. – *Cf.* Tally stick

Parmentarius. Latin word used of a tailor. The Norman-French was *parmentier*; *tailleur* was also used.

Parole. A prisoner's word of honour. Knights and magnates were expected to abide by their parole when captured and not try to escape. Under these terms a prisoner was allowed great freedom. It would not be chivalrous to break parole for that was breaking one's word – a great fault of honour. There was also a kind of bond here between equals, even if opponents in war. Indeed, the kinship appeared in their capturing each other, not killing each other. A captured knight, *baron or king, indeed, could be ransomed; a dead knight, baron or king was worthless. [< OFr. *parole* = something said.]

Parvis [parvyse]. The space within an enclosure in front of buildings such as cathedrals or large churches. *Parvis* is a French word, a corruption of the Latin *paradisus* = paradise or an enclosed garden. There was a *parvis* at *St Paul's Cathedral in London and it was there in the 14c that lawyers met for talk, disputation and consultation. – *Cf.* Serjeant-at-law

Parvus bussellus. Lit. 'a small bushel'. This term was used in some manorial accounts for what was actually a half bushel. It was the same measure as a *skep. [< L *parvus* = small + *bussellus* = a bushel]

Pas d'armes. Lit. 'passage of arms'. A variation of the *mêlée or joust in which a team or individual announced they would set themselves up to defend a particular place against any who chose to accept the challenge. These could well be lengthy affairs, with many contests using lance, sword, axe. One such contest in Burgundy, which involved 13 knights and squires, was spread out over six weeks – though without fighting every day. The challenge, in the form of shields fixed to a tree, or symbol thereof, would have been put up for any knight to accept. – *Cf.* PERRON 2; TREE OF HONOUR

Passant. *Her.* Term used of an animal which is moving to *dexter, i.e. to the right, with paws raised; in use the word follows the name of the animal it describes, e.g. lion passant. – *Cf.* GUARDANT; TRIPPING

Pastourelle. Song in which the heroine was a wise or foolish shepherdess; a form first found among *troubadours. – *Cf.* AUBADE; COURTLY LOVE; REVERDIE

Pasture, rights of. The right to graze animals on common land. The kinds of livestock permitted were always specified. – *Cf.* RIGHTS OF COMMON

Patent Rolls. *Cf.* LETTERS PATENT ROLLS

Paternoster. Lit. 'our father'. The first two Latin words of the Lord's Prayer; also special beads on a rosary, or a whole rosary.

Patonce. *Her.* A cross whose arms expand towards their ends, with floriate decorations. [ME < *potent* = a crutch with a cross-piece]

Patristic. Relating to the writings of the Church Fathers. [< L *pater* = father]

Patron. Someone who had the gift of a *benefice; someone who sponsored or supported another, e.g. an artist, writer, or building project. Attaching oneself to a lord or royal court was often the only path of employment for skilled artisans or writers, e.g. makers of illuminated MSS.

Patron saint. Saint associated with a trade or *guild; a particular saint to whom a person prays for protection through some specific association. Thus St Cecilia is patron saint of musicians, while St Jerome is patron saint of translators, and St Laurence of tanners.

Paul's window. A strange phrase found in Chaucer's *Miller's Tale* used of a pair of shoes worn by a dandyish clerk. The upper parts of these fancy shoes were cut away, somewhat like tracery, allowing the red hose to show through. The reference is to a *rosace in the old St Paul's Cathedral. The Latin phrase for these shoes was *calcei fenestrati*, i.e. window shoes.

Pavage. The right to take a toll towards the cost of paving the roads. – *Cf.* TRIMODA NECESSITAS

Pavilion. *Her.* A *charge representing a tent; any ornamented tent.

Pavis. Shield designed specifically as a protection against arrows, being larger than most and attached to the forearm, yet hardly hindering movement. The pavis was convex and large enough to protect the whole body, being used by infantry to protect themselves from whatever the enemy was firing at them. They were of particular use to crossbowmen, who took longer to reload than did longbowmen. A number could be set together to create a wall, something which was done at sieges. Such an arrangement was called a 'pavisade'. They are named after the town of Pavia, in Italy, where they were originally made. – *Cf.* ARCHERY

Paynim. A pagan or non-Christian, e.g. a *Saracen or Muslim; the pagan world generally. [< L *paganus* = pagan]

Pean. *Her.* The *fur with gold points or spots on a black background – the reverse of *ermine.

Peasants' Revolt. In 1381 a rebellion in response to government efforts to collect a much-disliked *poll tax, set at one shilling per man, confined largely to Kent and Essex, whose inhabitants marched on London, led by Wat Tyler. Jack Straw was named as one of the leaders, but that was most likely a pseudonym of Tyler's. They attacked the *Savoy, John of Gaunt's palace, and decapitated the archbishop of Canterbury. In June they were met by the young King Richard II, at Smithfield, where Tyler was killed. The Peasants' Revolt was part of the general disturbance of the 14c, which had begun with bad harvests, followed by the *Black Death in 1348.

Pecia. Tanner's term for a piece, used to refer to an animal skin treated and stretched, then trimmed, and ready for use as *vellum by scribe or illuminator. A section or pecia of a text was handed to several scribes, thus producing a MS quickly. [< medieval L *pecia* = piece] – *Cf.* QUIRE

Peck. Unit of measure for grain equal to one quarter of a *bushel.

Peculiar. Parish church owned by a monastery outside the diocese within which the church was, thus outwith the jurisdiction of its local bishop.

Pede pulverosus. *See* PIEPOUDRE

Pedesecus [sequipedus]. Lit. 'beside, by the feet'. Title of a person of apparently lowly position, sitting at someone's feet, but borne by a *thegn*, close to his king. A grant of land made by King Æthelbert in 858 was witnessed amongst others by Eastmund, described as *pedesecus*. In the list of subscribers, Eastmund was third, following only the king himself, and Æthelmod, *ealdorman*. In common with titles of apparently low status, the *pedesecus*, being a *thegn*, was likely very close to his lord. [< L *pes* = foot + *secus* = by, alongside] – *Cf.* ÆRENDRACA; STALLER

Pedites. Latin term for foot soldiers. [< L *pes* = foot]

Pele tower. Kind of fortification characteristic of the English–Scottish border. It was usually a small tower, perhaps a fortified house, designed as a refuge from raiding parties; sometimes surrounded by stakes and a ditch. Its size and strength were not intended to withstand a siege. – *Cf.* DUN

Pelican. A bird said to feed its young with its own blood by pecking its breast when needful; thus a symbol of self-sacrifice. The pelican was used in medieval art as a symbol of the Redeemer, i.e. Christ, the archetype of self-sacrifice. – *Cf.* VULN

Pelisse. Fur-lined overcoat, sometimes with sleeves, sometimes without. [< L *pellis* = pelt, hide, skin] – *Cf.* ERMINE 1; PELLETARIUS; PILCH

Pell. Two *rolls of *parchment, one of which records receipts and the other payments made by the *exchequer. The Pells was the office in which these documents were stored. [< AN *pell* < L *pellis* = skin]

Pellet 1. *Her.* A black spot, representing a cannon ball; a roundel. [< L *pila* = a ball] – *Cf.* ROUNDEL 2

Pellet 2. Small stone fired in large numbers from a mortar. [< L *pila* = a ball < pill]

Pellet bell. The bell on a tambourine whose striker is a small pellet; the bell on a clown or fool's clothing and/or shoes. – *Cf.* BALDRIC

Pelletarius [pelleciarius]. A skinner; sometimes also known as a 'fell-monger'. The Norman-French term was *pelletier*. – *Cf.* CORIARIUS

Pencel [pensil]. Small *pennon or streamer; also, in the late 14c, a token or favour, such as a handkerchief or scarf, given by a lady to a *knight at a *joust. The word is a form of *pennoncel.

Penitential pilgrimage. Sending a sinner on a long *pilgrimage was a good way of getting them out of the way. Thus a fornicating priest bringing disrespect on the Church might be sent to Compostella or Rome; or he might have to make such a journey year on year to different places. – *Cf.* INDULGENCES; JACOBIPETA; ROMIPETA; SCANDAL

Pennon. Long, narrow flag; an elongated triangle carried by a knight below the rank of *banneret. – *Cf. next;* PENCEL

Pennoncel. A small pennon worn on helmet or lance. – *Cf. previous*

Penny. The silver penny was the basic currency in England from the time of Offa (757–95) until Henry III. It was the only coin in circulation, though pennies were often cut in half or in quarters to provide halfpennies and farthings. Minting was confined to boroughs, most of which had a least one *moneyer. From the time of Edgar (959–75), coins regularly carried the names of both moneyer and minting-place, as well as that of the king who issued them. In 1279, there was an extensive recoinage when the halfpenny and *farthing were issued, as well as the *groat. For luxury items the gold *bezant was used and accepted from Byzantium to Carlisle or Dublin. A gold penny was issued by Henry III in 1257 worth 20 silver pennies, but it was not a success. – *Cf.* Sceatta; Sterling

Pentecost. The seventh Sunday after *Easter. The occasion celebrated was the descent of the Holy Spirit on the disciples. The event is recorded in Acts 2. – *Cf.* Whitsun

Pentecostals. Monies paid at *Whitsun by each household in a diocese to the mother church, as a token of obedience. These payments were sometimes known as 'smoke-farthings' as they were equivalent to a hearth tax. – *Cf. previous*

Penteulu. The captain or commander of a Welsh ruler's *teulu* or household troops. He was known in Latin as *princeps militiae* – *Cf.* Domus regis

Penthouse. Structure appended to the main part of a building; sometimes such an addition would have a sloping roof. By the 16c the word was also applied to the sloping roofs of a *real tennis court. [< L *appendo* = append] – *Cf. next*

Pentice. A first-floor extension, or projection, on the houses of the better-off, creating an extra room. Usually, they were supported by wooden columns or pillars. – *Cf. previous*

Penucella. *See* Pennoncel

Pepper. An imported commodity, pepper was an expensive item for any household. In the early 15c, black pepper cost 16d per pound, white pepper 24d per pound. It was brought to England by Genoese and Venetian merchants. [< OE *pipor* < L *piper* = pepper] – *Cf. next*; Piper

Pepperer. One of the many highly specific trades of the time. Pepperers dealt in pepper and spices; later they came to be known as 'grocers'. [< OE *pipor* < L *piper* = pepper] – *Cf. previous*

Per colos. Lit. 'by the spindle, *distaff'. When there was no male heir to an estate, who would have inherited entire, it went to daughters, who received equal shares. A version of the phrase might be 'on the distaff side'.

Percaminarius. Latin term for the maker and seller of *parchment, a *parchmenter.

Perch. Measure of length = 5½ yards; a *pole was the same measure. [< L *pertica* = a measuring rod]

Peregre iter arripuit. Lit. 'he set off on a pilgrimage'. Latin phrase used throughout the period, being found in Church documents, e.g. of someone sent on a *penitential *pilgrimage. The note of such a date might also be used to confirm a year in an *inquisition *post mortem*.

Peregrinus. Latin term used of both pilgrims and crusaders. – *Cf.* PILGRIM-AGE

Perron 1. Block of stone used as the base of e.g. a market cross or similar. [< Fr. *pierre* = a stone] – *Cf.* ELEANOR CROSSES

Perron 2. Not unlike the previous entry, this was sometimes a mound, sometimes a pillar, which featured in the more elaborate writings and practices of knightly contests. Its use at real tournaments may have been taken from Chrétien de Troyes's *Ywain* (*c.*1170–80) in which it served as the place where challenges were made; or if a pillar, where shields were hung waiting to be touched, which action served as the challenge. Sometimes there was a horn to be sounded to mark the challenge. – *Cf.* CLOUGES; CROSSES; PAS D'ARMES; TREE OF HONOUR

Pescary. *See* PISCARY

Peter's pence [Rom-feoh]. *Denarius Sancti Petri*. A penny tax each year on every house in England, collected at midsummer, and paid to the Holy See. Just when it began is not clear. A letter from Canute in 1031 mentions the penny owed to Rome. Claims were made by Matthew Paris and William of Malmesbury for, respectively, Offa and Æthelwulf as the initiators. Matthew said that Offa, in beginning the payment, intended it to support the English school and hostel for pilgrims in Rome. What prompted its remission may have been Alfred's payment *c.*882–4 of substantial arrears, sufficient for the pope, Marinus, to free the English in Rome of any tolls or taxes. After Alfred's reign, there are intermittent records of the 'pence' being paid until the reign of Henry VIII. It was payable on St Peter's Day, 1 August. – *Cf.* BENEFIT OF CLERGY; CHURCH COURTS; SCHOLA SAXONUM

Peytral [poitrel]. That piece of armour, heavily padded, which was designed to protect a horse's breast during battle or jousting. [< L *pectorale* = breast-plate]

Phala. One of the small buildings in the courtyard of a castle or fortified *manor house where weapons were kept.

Pheon. *Her.* A *charge displayed as the head or point of a javelin or arrow, with barbs on its inner side. These barbs are said to be *engrailed since they are indicated by round indentations.

Phlegm. One of the four bodily *humours of medieval physiology; being characterised as cold and moist, it was believed to induce apathy.

Pica. *See next*

Pie. Collection of rules used in the pre-Reformation Church of England showing how the coincidence of more than one office on the same day should be dealt with; an almanac and ordinal for reciting divine service. The Latin term *pica* is derisive, as it is associated with 'pie' = a magpie. It was criticised in the Book of Common Prayer.

Pied Friars. Colloquial term for the Friars of Blessed Mary, i.e. Friars *De Domina*; they were disbanded and obliged to join one of the major orders in the 14c. They were called 'pied' because of their brown and white *habit.

Piepoudre [pie-powder court]. Court presiding over a market, and all commercial dealings therein. It possessed the power to fine or expel any who transgressed, e.g. for short weights or low quality. The term comes from the French *pieds* = feet + *poudre* = powder. This was a reference to the dusty or powdery feet of pedlar or *chapman and other wandering sellers. The word was anglicised as 'Pie-powder court'. The Latin form was *pes pulverosus*.

Pike. Long, pointed weapon carried by foot soldiers, usually some 18–20 feet (5½–6m) in length. Used properly the formation of a compact group of pikes could hold off an attack by cavalry. Pikemen were of course vulnerable to the *longbowmen and their arrows. The Scots were notably successful when using the *schiltron of pikemen. [< OE *pic* = a pointed tool]

Pikes. Long, pointed extensions to shoes worn by men of fashion in the mid-15c (something like the winkle-pickers of the 1950s). Pikes were worn throughout Europe, but were considered outrageous enough for the pope, in 1468, to forbid pikes longer than two inches. Pikes almost a foot long were not unknown. Like much fashion, part of their purpose was to demonstrate and flaunt impracticality: such shoes would have been useless, even dangerous, in battle or at a joust. Men of the court were displaying their distance from men of action or soldiers. At that time, a firepike was what we call a poker. [< OE *pic* = a pointed tool] – *Cf.* POULAINE

Pilch. Fur-lined garment; also a woollen or leather garment. [< late OE *pylce* = cloak < L *pellis* = skin] – *Cf.* PELISSE

Pile 1. A javelin or an arrow; also the sharp, pointed end of a lance.

Pile 2. *Her.* A triangular shape, like the head of an arrow, formed by two lines pointing downwards.

Pilgrimage. Adam was the first pilgrim: after the expulsion from Eden life became exile; within life there is the journey towards salvation. The great time of pilgrimage was the 12–15c, esp. for ordinary people. But even in the 9c monks and kings made pilgrimage to Rome. Indeed, Alfred the Great went twice, in 853 and 855. Then the journey took up to two months. One pilgrim in the early 10c noted 79 stopping-places or pilgrim hostels for overnight stops. Only after the First *Crusade was preached in 1095 did the idea of going further than Rome become widespread. It is important to note that around Jerusalem, in Palestine, and in Egypt, the Saracens and others were very tolerant of early European Christians. So long as fair money was paid for what was required there was little tension. Indeed even when war was waged against them by virtue of their not being Christian, they at first simply laughed at the idea, thinking it absurd to fight for no reason, as they saw it. The Latin used of both pilgrim and crusader was *peregrinus*. – *Cf.* AD LIMINA; CRUSADES; PEREGRE ITER ARRIPUIT; PLACES OF PILGRIMAGE

Pillard. Lit. 'plunderer'. Term used in the phrase *chevalier pillard* = a plundering knight. Not all knights in Arthurian romance were noble and well behaved; rather there were killers and robbers in literature and the real world who could be called 'knights'. The 14c Latin form is *pilardus*. The German equiv. was *Raubritter*. [< Fr. *piller* = rob, plunder; from which our pillage]

Pillory. A device which held an offender by head and hands or by hands and feet for public punishment, where public humiliation was intense. Offenders were to be amerced the first two or three times, so long as the offence were not too grievous. However, the pillory's use was qualified: it was to be used without bodily peril to either man or woman. In the 12c Chester brewers of bad ale were put into the *cathedra stercoris*, i.e. the shit-seat or dung-seat. However, the pillory was not used as often as popular imagination has it. For instance, in London between 1347 and 1375 the pillory was only resorted to 23 times. – *Cf.* CUCK-STOOL; TOW

Pillory, judgement of the. In the mid-14c, this judgement provided articles of inquest into violations of assizes regarding bread and beer and their various measures; the price of wine was also included. A jury of 12 men gathered the various measures to be examined and everything was done publicly: nothing was concealed from public justice. A link was made between the price of wheat and that of ale, e.g. when a quarter of barley was sold for 2s, then four quarts of beer should be sold for 1d. Bakers were warned three times before sentencing to the *pillory if prices or weight of loaves were out of accord with the assize; butchers were punished if they sold contaminated, unwholesome or unfit meat or if the animal had died of *murrain. – *Cf. previous*

Pincerna. A *pincerna* was a butler in the household; from the 11c an important member of the royal household. – *Cf. next;* DAPIFER

Pincernarius. An officer of the buttery, i.e. a butler. – *Cf. previous*

Pinder [punder]. Officer of a *manor responsible for stray animals. In the *Boldon Book,* the existence of pinderland was mentioned. It indicated that whoever held pinderland should be the pinder, i.e. the officer responsible for strays. [< OE *pyndan* = to enclose or impound] – *Cf. next;* LEVANT; REEVE

Pinfold. A pen for holding stray cattle or sheep. [< OE *pundfald* = *pund* = a pound or enclosure + *fald* = a fold] – *Cf. previous*

Pipe Rolls. Records of the *exchequer, the financial section of the *curia regis;* yearly accounts of the royal income from *county sheriffs and other financial officials. The account of each shire (or other district) was entered on both sides of a single membrane made of two sheets of parchment sewn end to end; the membranes were then sewn together at the top, like a modern calendar, and rolled up, so that, as the *Dialogus de Scaccario* says, 'they look like a pipe'. The earliest Pipe Roll dates from 1130; the continuous sequence begins in 1155–6. – *Cf.* TALLY STICK

Piper. Latin word for *pepper. Thus black pepper was *piper niger;* white pepper *piper albus. Piperarius* was the Latin title of a *pepperer.

Piscary. The ancient right to take fish from ponds and pools and streams; the Latin word used in records was *piscaria.* [< L *piscis* = fish] – *Cf. next;* RIGHTS OF COMMON

Piscina. A fish-pond, often attached to monasteries (for eating fish on Fridays); a swimming pool; the large wash-basins found in monasteries. [< L *piscis* = fish] – *Cf. previous*

Pittance. A gift to a religious house for the provision of food and wine on special occasions, e.g. on the donor's anniversary, when prayers were said for his or her soul or on other specific festivals. Such gifts were most commonly for the provision of extra food and wine. [< L *pietas* = pity] – *Cf. next;* OBIT

Pittancer. That member of a monastery charged with the distribution of pittances. – *Cf. previous;* OBEDIENTIARY

Placebo. Lit. 'I shall please'. The *vespers of the dead, *placebo* being the first word of the *antiphon sung during the office of the dead.

Places of pilgrimage. There were four major sites of pilgrimage for the English: SS Peter and Paul in Rome, which included visiting the shrines in the city for 40 days, a quarantine; St James of Compostella in Spain; St Thomas at Canterbury; and the Three Kings at Cologne. – *Cf.* PILGRIMAGE; THOMIPETA

Placitum. Latin word for a law suit or plea; a case heard before a court. [< L *placeo* = to please]

Plague. Colloquial term for the disastrous outbreak of disease, esp. in 1348, and known in the words of Henry Knighton (d. 1396) as 'the general mortality of the world'. [< L *plaga* = a wound; later, a pestilence] – *Cf.* BLACK DEATH

Plainsong. Generic term for the unaccompanied music of monks singing in unison, e.g. *Gregorian chant. The rhythm of the song was and still is determined by the natural accents of the text being sung. The word 'plain' refers to the single line of melody, its monophony, and to the lack of a set rhythm.

Plantagenet. The dynastic kings of England from Henry II to Richard III, 1154–1485. 'Plantagenet' arose as the nickname of Count Geoffrey of Anjou (d. 1151), father of Henry II, apparently from his practice of sporting a sprig of broom (*planta genista*); another suggestion is that he favoured broom as cover in his hunting grounds. The plant was adopted as the family *crest. However, the use of the name dates from the 15c.

Plea Rolls. Rolls recording the proceedings of the court of common pleas, which was known as *De banco* = of the bench (of justices). The rolls date from 1190 and show the court met at Westminster. Most of the work involved civil disputes between private persons and such problems as land transactions.

Pleading, Statute of. Enacted in 1362, the statute stated that 'all pleas [in the king's courts] . . . shall be pleaded, shewed, defended, answered, debated, and judged in the English tongue'. – *Cf.* ENGLISH

Pleas of the Crown. The crown reserved certain grave crimes to its own jurisdiction, e.g. the harbouring of outlaws, ambush, forcible entry into a house. This ensured that local pressure or influence would not play a part in judgement.

Pleas of the Hall. One of the functions of the court of the *verge, to hear cases arising within the royal household and also within the verge itself, i.e. the surrounding area.

Plena arma. Lit. 'fully armed'. A knight or lord was required to possess *hauberk, shield and sword when answering the call to military service.

Plenary indulgence. Phrase used when a complete remission of punishment was granted. These were at first granted only on special occasions; in time more frequently. Pope Urban II (d. 1099) allowed such *indulgences to all crusaders when he remitted all their penances for full confession.

Plenus villanus. Lit. 'full villein'. A term sometimes found in reference to a *villein able to supply two oxen for the *plough-team. A villein able to supply one ox was known as a *dimidus villanus*.

Plough Day/Monday. First Monday after Epiphany (6 January), which marked the beginning of the ploughing season, when the ground had to be newly broken. – *Cf.* MIRACLE PLAY

Ploughland. *See* CARUCATE

Plough-scot. The *AS levy or tax of one penny paid each year on a plough, intended to fund local churches. – *Cf.* CIRICSCEAT; MORTUARY; SCOT; SOUL-SCOT

Plough-team. Two men worked the eight-ox plough-team: one guided the plough itself, and was known as the *conductor*; the other, the *fugator*, drove the oxen and also tended them during the year. There is a particularly good illustration of such a team and its two men in the *Luttrell Psalter* (fol. 170r). [*fugator* < L *fugo* = to drive; *conductor* = a guide, leader]

Plumbaria. A lead mine. Lead mines and mines for other mineral deposits on royal lands were rarely given away. A lead mine would make renders of lead slabs, of perhaps 250 slabs a year. [< L *plumbum* = lead] – *Cf.* PLUMBUM ALBUM

Plumber. Orig. a person who worked with lead, after the Latin *plumbum* = lead. Indeed English plumbers were in great demand on the continent: English lead roofed both Clairvaux and Rouen cathedrals in the 12c. However, lead was also used for rain-pipes and guttering, and the Romans had used it for carrying fresh water. The abbey at Bury St Edmunds had a two-mile-long system of lead pipes for its water supply. In 1091, the bishop of Coutances requested an English plumber be sent to mend the roof of his *cathedral which had been damaged by lightning. One Brismet, the plumber, was sent to help. – *Cf. previous and next*

Plumbum album. Lit. 'white lead', i.e. tin. – *Cf. previous*; PLUMBARIA

Plummet. A piece of lead, shaped like the modern pencil, used for drawing and marking lines on MSS. [< L *plumbum* = lead]

Pluralist. A cleric who held more than one Church office, e.g. *prebend or *benefice. It was common practice in this period. Many pluralists were foreigners appointed by the pope; such men were doubly resented. However, some senior members of the Church, e.g. Bishop Grosseteste (d. 1253), forswore the practice, encouraging others to do the same, esp. foreigners unable to speak English.

Po. A peacock or peahen.

Poitrel. *See* PEYTRAL

Poitrine pour justes. Armour breast-plate designed only for use in a *joust and not as sturdy or heavy as one built for real battle. [< Fr. *poitrine* = breast + *pour justes* = for jousts]

Pole. Unit of measure equal to 5½ yards; also known as a 'perch'. – *Cf.* ACRE; FURLONG

Poleaxe. A formidable weapon used in combat on foot by dismounted knights. It carried an axe, as its name suggests, but two other weapons were integrated: a hammer and a long spike. Poleaxes were usually long-handled, giving extra force to the blow delivered by a long swing, most effectively against the head. [< OE *pollax* = poll (i.e. head) + axe] – *Cf.* HALBERD

Policraticus. A work finished in 1159, written by John of Salisbury (*c.*1115–80), erstwhile secretary to Thomas Becket and later bishop of Chartres. Referred to sometimes as the Statesman's Book, it was intended as a philosophy of the contemporary state. The *Policraticus* is of real importance for being a truly medieval statement, appearing as it did before the work of Aristotle was available, which profoundly influenced later thinking.

Polinctor. Latin word for an undertaker. In a parish, the undertaker might also act as bellman and lamplighter.

Poll tax. Poll = head, as in head count. This tax was imposed on three occasions in the last quarter of the 14c. The first was that of 1377; this was followed in 1379 by a graduated tax. The latter's failure resulted in the removal of the *chancellor, Richard Scrope. In 1380, parliament permitted a further tax through the new chancellor, Simon Sudbury, archbishop of Canterbury. The tax was assessed as three groats on every man and woman over the age of 15. Its consequence at both times – 1379 and 1380 – was civil unrest, though the *Peasants' Revolt of 1381 was more serious, esp. in the loss of life.

Pollard. One of the false silver coins which entered England after Edward I's recoinage of 1279–80. They were so called because of the head they depicted. [< ME *poll* = a head] – *Cf.* CROCKARD

Pomace. The mash left after apples had been crushed in the making of cider. [< Fr. *pomme* = an apple] – *Cf. next*

Pomeis. *Her.* Round green shapes or roundels representing apples. [< Fr. *pomme* = an apple] – *Cf. previous*

Pommel. Spherical ornament at the top of tent or flag pole; the part at the front of a saddle. The term was also used of the knob or boss on the handle of a sword. These could be plain or ornamental but there were a great many styles. [< OFr. *pommel* = apple, fruit < L *pomus* = fruit]

Pone. A writ by which a suit was transferred from a *county court to a higher court. *Bracton said of it: 'When a plea begun by writ of right has, at the petition of the demandant, been transferred to the great court by *pone*, the tenant must be summoned to be present there to answer the demandant with respect thereto.' [< L *pono* = to place]

Pontage. The right to charge tolls to cross a bridge. The OE form was *brudtholl*, i.e. the right of toll; the Latin term was *pontagium*. In return the toller was required to maintain the bridge – a requirement frequently ignored. Often a small chapel was attached to a bridge. Hermits were known to take residence in such chapels and were givens alms by travellers, though often the *hermit was an unlicensed impostor. [< L *pons* = a bridge] – *Cf.* BARRAGIUM; RECLUSE; TRIMODA NECESSITAS

Pontarius. Latin term for a bridge-maker.

Pontifical. Book of office with the forms for the various rites performed by a bishop and the pope as bishop of Rome, e.g. ordination, consecration of a church, confirmation. [< L *pontifex* = a bishop]

Popinjay. Target for archers made from feathers or plumage attached to a pole; they resembled birds and were hung free to move.

Porcaria. Latin term for a pig-sty; the word was also used of that part of a *manor which was devoted to breeding pigs. Such farms would need access to *pannagium*. [< L *porcus* = a pig] – *Cf. next*

Porcarius. A pig-keeper, swineherd. – *Cf. previous*

Port. A walled town, esp. a market town; also gate or gateway set into the wall of such a town. [< L *portus* = a haven] – *Cf.* PORTMAN; PORTREEVE

Portcullis 1. Heavy grating of wood and metal which slid up and down, securing the entrance of a fortress or castle. [< OFr. *port* = door + *coulice* = sliding] – *Cf.* HERSE

Portcullis 2. *Her.* Vertical and horizontal lines crossing each other over a *field. – *Cf.* HERSE

Portcullis 3. *Her.* One of the four *pursuivants of the (English) College of Arms. The other three are *Blue Mantle, *Rouge Croix, and *Rouge Dragon. He is so named for the portcullis depicted on his badge. – *Cf.* ARMS, COLLEGE OF

Porteous. A portable *breviary. [< OFr. *portehors* < *porte* = carry + *hors* = outside]

Portman. Term for a town *burgess used before the 14c. *Port was the term used for a walled town, esp. one with a market. A portman was one of a group chosen to be responsible for a town's administration. – *Cf. next;* JURAT; PORTREEVE

Portman-moot. The gathering, i.e. *moot, of the men of a *port; sometimes also referred to as a *portmote*. As a court, it was distinct from any seigniorial/ lord's court, as was the *burh-moot*. – *Cf.* MOOT

Portmote. *See previous*

Portreeve. Chief officer of a town; someone with a rôle similar to mayor; also, the officer responsible for looking after the king's interests in London. [< OE *portgerefan*] – *Cf.* PORT and REEVE

Posse comitatus. Lit. 'force of the county'. The early English institution consisting of a shire's able-bodied citizens, who would be summoned to help a *sheriff or other officer of the law in maintaining public order, or chasing felons and such like. – *Cf.* COUNTY

Possessory assizes. Assizes established during the reign of Henry II dealing with questions of possession, as the name suggests. They were particularly important after the *Anarchy of Stephen's reign. – *Cf.* MORT D'ANCESTOR; NOVEL DISSEISIN

Posset. A drink, considered a delicacy, made from hot milk curdled with wine and sweetened with sugar, to which spices might be added.

Postern. Small side door to a castle, useful for getting in or out discreetly.

Pot metal. Technique for making stained glass by adding one or more metallic oxides to molten glass. – *Cf.* PAINT; YELLOW

Potell. A liquid measure equivalent to four pints. [< *pot* + *-ell* as dim.]

Potent [potencé]. *Her.* A T-shape or crutch. The term refers to one of the heraldic furs shown alternately as *argent or azure patches arranged so as to resemble a crutch. – *Cf.* COUNTER-POTENT

Potentiores. Lit. 'the powerful'. Term used of the senior men of the great London *guilds, those who controlled their guild and with others sought to influence and control London. The word was also used of men outside London, those who were wealthy and influential, being involved in local politics and sitting on town councils. The word was sometimes used to refer to the council on which the men sat. [< L *potens* = powerful] – *Cf.* BUZONE; POOR; PROBI HOMINES

Potestas. Lit. 'power'. In this period, in which all men up to the king had a lord, such men were said to be under the *potestas* of their lord. This power required service from the tenant and reciprocal protection for the tenant from the lord. Sons were also under the *potestas* of their father. This might be ended with the father's death, but also by the permanent banishment of the father, which was known as a 'civil death'.

Pottum fimare. The dung-cart, a necessity in every town and **burh*. [< L *pottum* = pot + *fimare* = dung, clay]

Poulaine. Long-pointed and very fashionable shoes; known in the AN as *souliers à la poulaine* as the shoes' style came from Poland. They were also known as 'crakows'. – *Cf.* PIKES

Poulter 1. That member of a noble or royal household whose duty was the provision of poultry and other foods; also the member of a monastery similarly charged. [< OFr. *poulet* = a chicken] – *Cf.* OBEDIENTIARY

Poulter 2. Metrical form of a poem written in lines alternating between 12 and 14 syllables.

Pound. English unit of weight derived from the Roman *libra ponda*; in currency 20 silver shilling coins or 240 pennies weighed 1 lb. Hence abbr. of monetary pound *libra* = L, stylised as £.

Praedial. Service or due owed a lord by a **serf or tenant which was attached to the **fief or tenure. These are distinguished from other services known as **'aids', which were deemed personal.

Praefectus. Latin term with varying uses. It was sometimes translated as **reeve (*gerefa*); but was also used of a town's head man and of the man in charge of a royal estate.

Praemunire, Statutes of. The statutes of 1353, 1365, 1393 were attempts to prevent the referral of English court judgements to a foreign state – which in effect meant appeals to the papacy, thus invoking papal authority. Later Henry VIII would use them in his conflict with Cardinal Wolsey in 1529. [L *praemunio* = safeguard, fortify, defend in advance]

Praepositus. The **reeve was so named in Latin records. [< L *praepositus* = placed in command; the person in front, representing the lord] – *Cf.* HIGH REEVE

Prebend. Stipend/income granted to a **canon or **prebendary; the money was provided via an endowment. [< L *praebeo* = to supply, to provide]

Prebendary. One who holds a **prebend; a **canon whose stipend was derived from a prebend.

Precarium 1 [precatio]. Additional services or **boon work required by a lord over and above those which formed a part of tenure. These were *ad precem* = at the request (of the lord). [< L *prex* = a request, a prayer]

Precarium 2. A loan received as a benefit by a tenant from a landowner. No set term or charge was specified. Often, too, the landowner was the patron of the tenant, his protector and lord. The land was held in *usufruct. The closest English word is 'loan'. Like any loan it could be called in; from this that we have 'precarious'.

Precentor. The director of singing in a *cathedral who was also responsible for choral services. His other responsibilities included being librarian and archivist. Further duties were maintaining the *mortuary roll and ensuring prayers for the dead were said when required, and choosing texts to be copied in the *scriptorium. [< L *praecentor* = leader in singing] – *Cf.* OBIT

Precursores. *See* PURVEYOR

Preequitator. Title used in royal account books for one of the attendants of the king's baggage train. He was a kind of outrider, working in conjunction with *sumpter men and the carters. [< L *prae* = before + *equitator* = rider on horseback] – *Cf.* BAGGAGE TRAIN

Premonstratensians. The monastic order was founded by St Norbert in 1120, at Prémontré in France. Its members wore a long white cloak and hood over a white cassock and were known as White Canons. They also wore a white cap or biretta. Like the Cistercian order, they preferred remote, unpopulated places, and were unafraid of hard manual labour. Again like the Cistercians, all their churches were dedicated to Our Lady. They arrived in England in 1143, founding their first house at Newham, eventually growing to 31 abbeys.

Prest. A financial device which enabled payments to be made in advance to members of the royal household and also departments of the household. It was often used outside England, when clerks and knights for example were away from their sources of income. Magnates had their own bankers, but most people relied upon prests, authorised by the treasurer of the *king's wardrobe. The accounts were maintained in a book known as *prestita privata*, i.e. private prests. [< OFr. *prester* = to lend]

Pretium corii. Lit. 'skin price'. This was the price required from a slave on his manumission: 30d had to be paid to the lord before witnesses. The *LHP adds that the skin price was 'a token that [the slave] may be worthy of it for ever'. – *Cf.* HYDGELD

Prime. The first of the hours of canonical prayer. – *Cf.* HORARIUM

Primer seisin. The claim of a lord to hold an estate after the death of its tenant until the heir had paid an appropriate *relief. Primer seisin was one of the *feudal incidents. If there was no heir, the land would *escheat to the lord. – *Cf.* SEISIN

Primum mobile. The tenth and outermost of the spheres which were thought to make up the universe in the system devised by Ptolemy, astronomer of Alexandria (d. *c.*165). This tenth sphere caused all other inner spheres to move in its revolution of 24 hours. [L *primum* = first + *mobile* = moving, i.e. first mover or first moving thing]

Prior provincial. The head of a province in the *Dominican order.

Prior. Superior of a religious house of canons or friars but deputy to an *abbot.

Priory. A house of canons regular; a monastery ruled by a *prior or a *convent by a prioress. – *Cf.* ALIEN PRIORY

Prisage. Toll levied by royal officials on provisions, esp. on wines. *Prisa* was the Latin term from the 11c. [< AN *prise* = to take]

Privy Council. The body of advisers appointed to advise the monarch. It was an offshoot of the *curia regis* composed of the king's tenants-in-chief, household officials, and indeed anyone else the king chose. From it grew larger councils, which in turn emerged as *parliament. It was named 'privy' as it was for the private advice of the monarch, although it lacks executive power.

Privy purse. A part of the *king's wardrobe. Purchases of such things as household stores, and the disbursement of small sums or payment to *mercenaries, were made through the purse; it was also used for receipt of payments made while the king was on his *itinerary.

Privy seal. A privy seal was in use during the reign of King John. From *c.*1230 – during Henry III's reign – it became a permanent feature of royal administration, being used to authenticate letters less formal than those issued by the *chancery. It was usually kept by the controller of the *king's wardrobe until 1313, when the post of keeper of the privy seal was created. By this time the keeper was an important officer of state and the office went out of court. Acquiring further importance, the privy seal was replaced for more secret purposes by that of the *signet. The privy seal ranked between the *great seal and the signet; it was known sometimes as a *secretum*, i.e. something separate, kept apart and thus secret. The office was abolished in 1884. – *Cf.* SECRETARIUS REGIS; SIGNET SEAL, OFFICE OF THE

Pro amore. Lit. 'for love'. Phrase used of certain grants made by the king. Part of a magnate's power resided in his ability to protect and advance those who owed him allegiance. Thus, a man favoured by the king was able to elicit pardons from the king – for a suitable sum of money. With such a grant, the magnate's own status was further enhanced. However, by the reign of

Henry II such grants had disappeared from the records.

Probi homines. Lit. 'honest, discreet men'. A rather vague term used to describe men deemed suitable to be councillors or men of local influence. They were necessarily free and successful, i.e. well off, having a business and possessing property. Today we might call them upright and middle-class. They were also known as *potentiores*, or in French *bons hommes*. – *Cf. next;* BUZONE; UCHELWR

Procer. Generic term used in Latin records for one of the men of power, or a leader, i.e. barons, lords, nobles, tribal chiefs etc. A more direct translation = magnate. – *Cf. previous*

Proctor. Someone employed to manage another's business affairs; a steward; also, a lawyer who worked in courts of *canon law. The term was used in the 13c and later of the official today called 'churchwarden'. He was responsible for managing the funds for a parish church's fabric maintenance. In the north of England, the proctor was also known as 'kirkmaster' or 'church *grieve'.

Proffer roll. A list compiled at feudal military musters by the *marshal or a deputy. Under the heading for each *tenant-in-chief they would list the names of all the *men-at-arms who were to serve; also included was the number of horses at the muster. – *Cf.* RESTAURATIO EQUORUM

Proper 1. Parts of the mass which change with the liturgical calendar or for a particular occasion; section of *breviary or *missal which contains the proper of the mass and offices proper to holy days.

Proper 2. *Her.* Describes an object as represented in its natural colours as opposed to (heraldically) conventional tinctures.

Protonotary. The chief clerk in the court of *chancery. [< Gk. *protos* = first + L *notarius* = notary, clerk]

Proux [preux]. Proud. A word 11c Norman aristocrats applied to themselves as they sought to become recognised as natives of Normandy – assimilated into the wider world of Franks – and not as new incomers or descendants of Vikings. – *Cf.* CHEVALIER; PROWESS

Provisor hospitii. Lit. 'provider of hospitality'. A *dapifer*, as overseer of a large establishment, was assisted by a *provisor hospitii*, who was his deputy and responsible for the daily work of supply.

Provisors, Statute of. Statute of February 1351 intended to prevent the pope from exercising authority within the Church of England and from giving his often non-English candidates lucrative benefices in England. The statute ordained that election to bishoprics was to be free; that patrons should be free to present their choice to a benefice; that should this not happen, the king would have the right to present; that anyone who sought recourse to papal authority would be under penalty. – *Cf.* PRAEMUNIRE, STATUTES OF; PROUX

Prowess. This was an essential quality of a knight, being a combination of skill with both daring and valour. Such a skill was both developed and demonstrated at tournaments, whether in the *mêlée or in single combat on foot with a sword or jousting. Before the Battle of Najera in 1367, the Black Prince said in a prayer that he was there 'for the maintenance of right, and for prowess and nobility . . . to gain a life of honour'. Prowess shares its etymology with *proux*. [< OFr. *prou* = worthy, valiant, brave] – *Cf.* COURAGE

Prydein. The Welsh name for Britain and Britannia; the Irish form is *Cruithin*. The English 'Britain' is derived from *Prydein*, the initial letter having changed over time. – *Cf.* BRUTUS

Psalters, illuminated. Psalters were illuminated as early as the 8c and 9c and until the beginning of the 14c they are easily the most numerous of illuminated MSS. Around 1220, portable MS volumes supplanted the huge tomes favoured in the preceding century. The change in size resulted in a more angular and necessarily more compact script. For example, the initial letters were smaller, and the text was written in double columns. – *Cf.* BREVIARY; ILLUMINATION

Psaltery. Plucked stringed musical instrument. – *Cf.* DULCIMER

Puer. Lit. 'a boy'. While usually meaning a boy, *puer* was also used to refer to a *vassal. This use is found in the *Bayeux Tapestry, when the text refers to the bishop of Bayeux's followers. The word is also found in the Lincolnshire placename Ashby Puerorum = Ashby of the boys, so named for its being a *prebend for the support of Lincoln Cathedral's choir boys.

Pui. An association formed in London in the 14c on the model of earlier *puis* established in France, for the encouragement of the art of *chanson* writing and singing. Ballads were particularly popular in the royal court at the time. The members of the Pui were all merchants of London, both English and French. The association had a 'prince' at its head, with the apostolic number of 12 companions, who were elected annually from all brothers of the association. Each year, after the election of the new prince who had written the best *chanson* of the year, all members processed through the streets of London.

Pulpitum. Double screen with a central doorway, separating monks in the choir from lay worshippers in the nave. During the service, both Epistle and *Gospel were read from it. It was also where the organ was housed. [< L *pulpitum* = a stage, a platform or scaffold]

Punder. *See* PINDER

Purfle. To decorate with embroidery or fur; also that decoration. – *Cf.* GRIS

Purpresture. Illegal enclosure of another's land; this included encroaching upon another's land and using it illegally. The word was used of raising fences to keep animals from cropland, such animals being of the *forest and the king's sport. Bracton also says, 'he who occupies [land], by exceeding the limits and boundaries of his land, is said to have committed a purpresture upon the king'. [< OFr. *porprendre* = to usurp, occupy < L *praehendo* = to take possession, to occupy] – *Cf.* DISSEISIN

Purpure. *Her.* The *tincture purple. It was indicated in black and white illustrations, by showing lines drawn from the shield's *sinister chief to *dexter base, i.e. from top left to bottom right. [< L *purpura* = purple-dyed cloth]

Pursuivant. One of the officers of the College of *Arms; junior to a *herald.

Purveyance. Provision or providence. During war in the 13c and 14c there was compulsory purchase of food for the king's army. However, it functioned like a levy as the buyer set the prices – which were lower than the current market. Additionally the food was frequently taken but not paid for. In 1352, Edward III accepted parliamentary legislation demanding his purveyors abide by regulations for fair prices and payment. This had little effect. – *Cf. next*

Purveyor. A royal official who arranged the king's accommodation during his itineraries. Traders were required to allow the king's purveyors first choice of all the goods on sale. Although payments were prescribed, a fair rate was rarely paid for supplies. Indeed there were frequent complaints that suppliers were not paid at all. Also, there were many impostors requisitioning for themselves. The name was changed from purveyor to *achatour* = buyer, in an attempt to eliminate corruption – a hopeful but futile exercise. The Latin term was *praecursor*. – *Cf. previous;* CLERK OF THE MARKET; ITINERARY

Put-log. As large buildings such as cathedrals were being constructed, put-logs were used as scaffolding to build up on what had been built before. Today rectangular holes in the walls of cathedrals can still be seen where these substantial pieces of wood were inserted. 'Put-log' is a 17c term.

Q

Qt. Abbr. of the Latin *quietus* = quit. The annotation was written in the margin of a roll, indicating payment had been made.

Quadra. A square loaf; also one quarter of such a loaf. – *Cf.* SIMNEL BREAD

Quadrellum. A quarrel; Latin synonym of *quarellus*. – *Cf.* QUARREL 1

Quadrivium. The four sciences, i.e. arithmetic, geometry, astronomy and music, which made up the higher division of study in the Middle Ages. [L *quadrivium* = the place where four paths meet] – *Cf.* TRIVIUM

Quaestorius. *See* PARDONER

Quare impedit. Lit. 'why does he impede?' A type of legal writ issued when presentation to a *benefice was being disputed. It required an answer from whoever was imposing the impediment.

Quarrel 1. Short 13c arrow with a four-sided head for a *crossbow. The Latin form was *quarellus* or **quadrellum*.

Quarrel 2. The 19c term for the square- or diamond-shaped pieces of glass found in the stained-glass windows of 15c cathedrals and churches.

Quarry. Those parts of a deer's body put on the animal's hide as reward for the dogs. [< OFr. *cuir* = leather, *curer* = disembowel]

Quartan ague. A fever which reoccurred every fourth day; one of the indeterminate febrile ailments of the period, *sweating sickness, probably influenza, which could be fatal. [< L *quartanus* = of the fourth] – *Cf.* AGUE

Quarter 1. Dismemberment of the body into four parts during execution, the victim having been previously hanged. When traitors were executed in this manner, a quarter would often enough be placed on Tower Bridge and left there; other parts might be distributed elsewhere. Heads of those treated with the mercy of the axe alone were also placed on the bridge for all to see. – *Cf.* NUNCIUS REGIS

Quarter 2. *Her.* A *charge which occupies a quarter of the *shield; an *honourable ordinary. As a verb 'quarter' indicated the placing of arms in the four parts of a shield, or adding another's arms, such as a husband's or wife's.

Quarter 3. Unit of weight, used of grain. One quarter = eight bushels; one *bushel = eight gallons. It was also known as a 'core'. – *Cf.* CHALDRON

Quarter Day. The four days of the year on which it was customary to pay rents or settle debts. They were Lady Day, 25 March; Midsummer Day, 24 June; Michaelmas, 29 September; Christmas, 25 December.

Quarter-staff. Wooden pole some six feet long used as a weapon by English peasants, usually tipped with iron.

Quaternion. Any group of four things or persons; also used of four sheets (of paper) folded once.

Quatrefoil. *Her.* A *charge in the form of four leaves attached to a central point, somewhat like a four-leafed clover.

Quean. A woman. The word's use was uncomplimentary, being later used of prostitutes. It shares its root with 'queen' but is a discrete word. [< OE *cwene* = a woman]

Querela. Lit. 'a plaint, a plea'. Latin term for one of the procedures imposed on Henry III in the provisions of *Oxford in May 1258. The *querela* was a simple oral complaint by which a legal action could be initiated. The barons sought to cut through excessive legal bureaucracy: the *querela* in its simplicity was the answer. *Bracton said: 'No one may sue without a writ [i.e. *querela*] since without a writ the other is not bound to answer.' The *querela*, being oral, bypassed the formal and lengthy procedures involved in getting written documents from *chancery. Although available to all, the barons had wanted the *querela* as a means of investigating royal officials without hindrance by other royal officers. All that was required was for a complaint to be made in a *county court in front of four knights – after that the king's justice was invoked. [< L *querelo* = to bring an action]

Quia Emptores, Statute of. 1290. Also called the Third Statute of Westminster, its purpose was similar to the Statute of *Mortmain. *Quia Emptores* restricted the letting out of land under terms which restricted a lord's dues. – *Cf.* JUDICIUM

Quindecima. Term used for a tax which required a fifteenth part. [< L *quindecim* = 15] – *Cf.* TITHING

Quindene [quinzaine]. Ecclesiastical usage indicating the fifteenth day (counting inclusively) after a particular holy day or Church festival, or the span of these 15 days; equivalent to our 'fortnight (from now)'. [< L *quindecim* = 15] – *Cf.* OCTAVE; QUINDECIMA

Quinsy [squinsy]. A severe inflammation of the throat; tonsillitis. [< L *quinancia*] – *Cf.* AGUE

Quintain. An object attached to a pole and used as a target by jousters with a lance, to train in accuracy. The target was attached to an arm which revolved when struck; the arm would spin and if struck inaccurately might hit the tyro *en passant*. [< L *quintana* = a place for military exercise]

Quintal. A weight of approx. 100 lb; also a hundredweight. [< L *centenarius* = numbering 100]

Quintessence. In medieval philosophy, the fifth essence or *element (after air, fire, water, earth) of which the celestial elements and regions were thought to be composed; sometimes thought to be an *elixir which cured all ills; latterly the most essential or purest part or quality of a person or thing. [< L *quinta* = fifth + *essentia* = essence]

Quinzaine. *See* QUINDENE

Quire. Four sheets of *parchment folded to make eight leaves – 16 pages – for a small book or pamphlet; later a gathering of sheets folded with others to make up a book. Such gatherings, identified by a sequence of letters or numbers to assist in putting together a complete book, are known as 'signatures'. – *Cf.* PECIA

Quit claim. A lord's release of all claims he may have had over a *villein in return for which he received a sum of money or *quit rent as compensation for this loss of services.

Quit rent. A rent paid in lieu of services otherwise owed. – *Cf. previous*

Quodlibet. Lit. 'what pleases or what you will'. As part of scholastic training, a question was proposed as an exercise in the abstract skills of argumentation and rhetoric. 'How many angels dance on the head of a pin?' might be one such question.

R

Rache. [ratch] A hunting dog, one which tracked by scent; a setter. [< OE *ræcc* = dog, a setter < OE *geræccan* = to reach, obtain] – *Cf.* GREYHOUND

Radman. A tenant who owed his lord the duty of armed escort. [< OE *rad* = riding, expedition] – *Cf.* GENEAT; RODKNIGHT

Ragemannus. Document from which were suspended tags with seals. – *Cf.* RAGMAN ROLL

Ragler. The chief officer of a *commote. The Latin documents used *raglottus*. [< W *rhaglaw*]

Ragman Roll. English term for the record of instruments of *homage made by the Scottish king and nobles to King Edward I in 1296. Later the Latin phrase *indenture ragmannice* was used. In *Piers Plowman*, ragman roll refers to a papal list with the names and seals of bishops attached. – *Cf.* RAGEMANNUS

Ramé. *Her.* Describes the antlers of a stag as of a different *tincture from its body. – *Cf.* ANIMÉ; BEQUE; CRINED; MEMBERED; UNGULED

Rampant. *Her.* Describes an animal, e.g. a lion, rearing up and standing on its hind legs, its fore legs raised. [< OFr. *ramper* = to climb]

Rampart. Mound of earth built defensively with a surrounding wall upon which there was space for defenders to walk around on patrol.

Ransom. A useful way of raising money during war; it was in each side's interest not to spill too much blood, as noble opponents were worth much more alive and ransomed than dead. The conditions of the captive were very different from those of a hostage and drew upon the chivalric tradition. Between England and France there was a great deal of ransoming in this period. The conditions of restraint were the captive's *parole. Thus, a French lord in England was treated as his rank demanded, being free and trusted to move about as he wished – anywhere but home. Froissart lamented the killing of captives. Chaucer was ransomed for £16 – paid by Edward III – after being captured at Rheims in 1360. [< OFr. *ransoun* < L *redemptio* = redemption] – *Cf.* RESTAURATIO EQUORUM; HOSTAGES

Rape 1. An administrative division of Sussex – Arundel, Bramber, Chichester, Hastings, Lewes, Pevensey – each of which comprised several hundreds. [< OE *rap* = rope; land was defined by being roped off] – *Cf.* LATHE; THACK AND RAPE; YOKE 1

Rape 2. Orig. the taking of a person or thing by force; if a woman was taken, the word did not necessarily imply sexual assault (which was a capital offence). The word was also used of elopement. [< AN *raper* < L *rapio* = to take by force]

Raven. Legends of the raven banners carried before *Viking armies proliferated both in England and Scandinavia from the 12c onwards. At least one such did exist: the levies of Devon captured it from a Viking force invading the *county in 878.

Ravissant. *Her.* About to pounce on prey.

Real. Royal, regal. Still found in use in 'real tennis', where real = royal. Thus realty is found on occasion = royalty. [< OFr. *real* = royal] – *Cf.* RYAL

Realgar. Red pigment composed largely of arsenic disulphide; also known as 'red arsenic' or 'red *orpiment'. [< Ar. *reh al-gha* = cave powder]

Reap-silver. Money paid in commutation of harvest work once owed to a lord, particularly by townsmen. [< OE *ripan* = to reap] – *Cf.* SOR-PENNY

Rearing. Term used for setting up timber-framed houses. They were almost prefabricated in sections, with plaster and flooring to be added later. Whereas peasants' houses might last only two or three years and were then replaced close by, these timber-framed houses could be dismantled and moved to a new site.

Reaver. A thief or robber. [< OE *reaf* = plunder, booty; *reafian* = to plunder]

Rebate 1. To remove the sharpness of a sword for safer use in a *tournament; also, to bring a falcon back to its handler's hand. – *Cf.* ARMS, STATUTE OF

Rebate 2. *Her.* To remove a part of a *charge; having points cut off.

Rebec [ribible]. Three-stringed musical instrument played with a bow. [< Ar. *rabab* = a stringed instrument resembling a fiddle] – *Cf.* Lute; Ribibour

Rebus. *Her.* An image which hints at or indicates the name of the bearer. Thus Shakespeare's rebus would show a man shaking a spear. – *Cf.* Canting arms

Receiver. Modern term for the chief administrators of the estates of the 13c and 14c magnates and later. A receiver would be based at the *caput honoris* from which all other manors were administered; he might have a *steward as his immediate junior, below whom there would be reeves and bailiffs on the various estates, tending to daily matters. Each year there would be an accounting of all monies, overseen by auditors. On some estates there would be a *view should the need be felt. – *Cf. Rectitudines Singularum Personarum*

Recet. That part of the field, at both ends of the lists or tilting lanes, where the knights waited before riding to make their pass against each other. [?< L *receptaculum* = a place to keep something L] – *Cf.* Berfrois; Tilt

Reclinatoria. *See* Leaning staffs

Recluse. Unlike a *hermit, a recluse never left his cave or hovel. Caves were used by a succession of recluses, each modifying the accommodation as he felt best.

Recreantia [recreantisa]. The state of being defeated in a *duellum,* and the acknowledgement of that defeat, for which a fine of 60s was payable, according to *Glanville. The AN word was *recreuz;* 'recreant' or 'recreancy' are English forms of the word, still carrying the sense of bad faith or apostasy. Glanville added that if a *duellum* could be avoided the prospect of death was obviated, as well as 'the opprobrium of a lasting infamy, of that dreadful and ignominious word that so disgracefully resounds from the mouth of the conquered champion'. That dreadful word was *craven. At this time the attempt to avoid a *duellum* was provided for in law, and was even considered desirable; however, the older chivalric sense of failure persisted in Glanville's words. *Bracton also mentions 'the hateful word' which was to be uttered at the end of a duel prompted by an accusation of theft. In this case the defeated had to admit theft as well as say 'Craven!' [< L *recreantia* = acknowledgement of defeat; OFr. *recroire* = surrender]

Recreation. Orig. a meal or nourishment, but after the 13c it signified a substantial meal taken outside the monastery's *frater and implied lax or nil observation of the monastic rule. – *Cf.* Conventualis

Rectitudines Singularum Personarum. *The Rights of Individual People.* An essay on estate management written *c*.1025, probably in Mercia. It treats of the various obligations and duties owed on an estate in late AS England. There are two versions: the earlier is in OE; the later is a Latin translation made in the 12c, which is taken to be accurate. The text is useful for the evidence it offers of agrarian conditions in England shortly before the time of Edward the Confessor; it shows also some of the features of the organisation of a *manor. – *Cf.* RECEIVER

Recursant. *Her.* Describes any figure – but most often an eagle – shown with its back towards the viewer. – *Cf.* REGARDANT

Reek-silver. Lit. 'smoke silver'. A hearth tax. – *Cf.* FUMAGIUM

Reeve. Generic term for an official, esp. a royal official. The king's estates were administered by reeves. It was a reeve who in **ASC* 787 rode out to meet the *Viking ships which turned up near Portland, Dorset, and was killed by them – the first recorded English victim of the Vikings. After 1066, the term is used of a village headman, the peasants' spokesman at the *manorial court. He cited the manor's customs, refuting demands by the lord's *bailiff or *steward. However, so reluctant were some men to accept the post that in some custom rolls it was noted that every holder of a *virgate could be compelled to accept. The reward was exemption from some or all labour services. The Latin term in the documents for the reeve was **praepositus*, i.e. the one 'in command' or 'in front'; also **praefectus*. The title of 'reeve' is to be found in the placename Reaveley in Northumbria. [< OE *gerefa, refa* = a high official, steward, reeve] – *Cf.* SHERIFF and FABLIAU

Regal. A reed-organ, small enough to be carried about by a minstrel band.

Regalia. Crown, orb, sceptre and other ornaments used at the coronation of English monarchs. In October 1216, King John lost his baggage train in crossing the Wash; amidst much royal treasure, the ancient regalia were lost, including the crown of Edward the Confessor. At Henry III's coronation at Gloucester Abbey, in lieu of a real crown, i.e. the one lost by John, the papal legate is said to have placed a chaplet or coronal of flowers on the child-king's head. An early representation of the regalia in use can be found in the *Bayeux Tapestry showing King Harold's coronation at Westminster in 1066. After Charles I's execution (1649) all royal regalia were melted down or sold off. [< L *regalis* = royal] – *Cf.* CHARING CROSS; ROYALTY; SUMPTER

Regalian right. Lit. 'royal right'. The right claimed by a monarch to the estates, income and other dues of a vacant bishopric. This claim often led to considerable delays in the election and appointing of a new bishop. [< L *regalis* = royal] – *Cf. previous*

Regard. Extra money paid by the king to one of his captains for each three-month period the captain kept a 30-man troop in service in France during the

*Hundred Years' War. It was introduced in 1345. This could amount to some 100 marks a quarter or £300 a year. – *Cf.* CONTRACT CAPTAIN; VADIA GUERRE

Regardant. *Her.* Describes a lion looking back over its shoulder. – *Cf.* RECURSANT

Regarder. The regarder was a knight responsible for checking local woods and forest areas every three years, reporting back to the forest court. There were 12 such knights. This inspection was known as the 'regard', which also referred to the area under his charge. He was required to check the metes and bounds of the forest and all things to do with the king's rights. These duties were set out in the Charter of the *Forest, 1217. The Latin was *regardator*. [< AN *regardour*]

Regent master. *See* SCOLAS REGERE

Regrate. The action of buying up goods in order to sell and make a middle-man's profit. – *Cf. next;* FORESTALLERS, STATUTE OF

Regrator [regrater]. The middleman in the scheme of medieval trade where artisans and bakers or brewers etc. sold their own produce. The regrator bought bread or fish or other goods to sell on his own behalf, perhaps as a street-hawker. He or she was bound by the terms of the relevant *assize which dealt with what was sold, e.g. he was not allowed to sell dearer than the price specified by assize. In Oxford, a certain number of regrators were licensed; in York, 14c city ordinances bound regrators tightly to the assize. Frequently, women were the petty traders in towns, finding their way into the courts for forestalling or as a regrator. [< OFr. *regrattier / regratteur* = a huckster] – *Cf. previous and next;* FORESTALLERS, STATUTE OF; HUCKSTER

Regratorie. The retail trade, that carried on by a *regrator. The word carried distinctly negative connotations: 'sharp practice' or 'hucksterism' are apt synonyms.

Regular clergy. Monks and nuns whose lives were subject to a rule, e.g. the Benedictines, Carthusians, Cistercians, Premonstratensians. The Latin *regula* = a rule.

Relics. Parts of the body or clothing of a saint or martyr or other person considered holy. They were an important part of religious life in this period. Small parts were particularly favoured, such as a finger, leg bone or part of a skull. Pieces of the Cross were esp. valued. Pilgrims would return to England having bought a relic as a memento of their journey and a sign of their faith. – *Cf.* RELIQUARY

Relief. Payment made to a lord on the taking up of an office or on inheriting an estate. In the case of bishoprics, it is not to be confused with *simony. Relief was one of the *feudal incidents and was a different kind of payment from the *heriot, which was a death payment. However, there were times when the two payments were used interchangeably, since both were the concomitants of a death. Attempts were made to curb the claiming of extortionate sums of money: *Magna Carta specified that a barony should have a relief of £100. This was intended to prevent excessive exactions on inheritance. The Latin word was *relevatio*. – *Cf.* CONTENEMENT

Reliquary. Small box or chest in which a saint's *relics were kept. As a saint's renown grew, so the reliquary played its part as the focus of pilgrimages. The *Bayeux Tapestry shows (the later King) Harold taking an oath to accept William, duke of Normandy, as king on Edward the Confessor's death. Harold's hand is seen to be resting on an object covered by decorated cloth; only afterwards did Harold learn that beneath the cloth was a reliquary, greatly enhancing the sanctity and power of his oath.

Remembrancer. Member of the *exchequer, whose function it was to enrol all matters that required 'remembering'. The king's remembrancer was responsible for collecting debts owed the king; the lord treasurer's remembrancer noted down matters of interest to his master.

Replevin. Conditional return of goods and *chattels distrained improperly. The condition was that the case should be heard in court; also that the court's decision be accepted. – *Cf.* DISTRAIN

Reprisal, right of. This right concerned unpaid bills. Town A was entitled to hold a man from Town B if a man of Town B owed money in Town A and was found there. It applied when town burgesses had done nothing about the complaint. The system was ended in 1287. – *Cf. next*

Reprise. Annual charge or payment made from a *manor's income.

Reproach. Medieval knights, those members of one of the chivalric orders or confraternities, were intended always to be without reproach, i.e. to remain a *chevalier sans reproche*. Breaking faith or defaulting on a promise involved, for example, being set free on condition of raising a ransom and not doing so. The means of making known such bad conduct could be to display the wrongdoer's coat of *arms upside-down. In one case, the aggrieved knight displayed the defaulter's arms reversed and attached to his horse's tail. Cowardice was a gross offence, as serious as treason. In these cases expulsion from the order followed. As a symbol of this the sword was broken and the spurs were cut from his heels – the dressing with spurs being an important part of the knighting ceremony. – *Cf.* CHIVALRY, ORDERS OF; CRAVEN; PAROLE

Requiem. Mass said for the repose of the souls of the dead, the first words of the *introit being *Requiem eternam dona eis* = Give them eternal rest.

Rere-brace. That piece of armour which covered the upper arm; later it was lengthened to cover the elbow.

Rere-dorter. Lit. 'rear of the dormitory'. A latrine accessible from the *dorter. It was sometimes referred to also as the *necessarium,* lit. 'the necessary'. All monasteries were founded close by running water. The rere-dorter was built where it would be constantly flushed by that water. – *Cf.* LONGAIGNE

Rere-mouse. *Her.* A bat; they were depicted 'spread-eagled'.

Ressort. In the 13c, the right of appeal available to any French *vassal to his lord's lord. It applied equally to the vassals of English kings in e.g. Gascony. Thus a French vassal could appeal over the English king's head. This was potentially a source of mischief to the English king, who was a vassal of the French king for his lands in France. The English kings sought to avoid the inherent complications, while the French king wished to perpetuate the situation as a means of controlling, in some small measure, the English.

Restauratio equorum. Lit. 'restoration of horses'. A 13–14c benefit scheme under which a man-at-arms' horse would be valued, so that compensation could be made if the animal died or was lost on active service. In 1360, at Rheims, the owner of a horse received £6 13s in recompense, a substantial sum of money. This system, however, was confined to the period of the three Edwards; by about 1370 the practice had been largely replaced by greater division of the spoils of war for the man-at-arms. – *Cf.* PROFFER ROLL; RANSOM

Retinentia. Term used of someone in the retinue of a lord or magnate. It did not distinguish between a follower, who owed his lord a life-time's service, and those who accompanied him on a particular campaign, in temporary employment. All members of the lord's *meinie could be counted within his *retinentia* but not the other way round. [< AN *retein* < L *retineo* = retain] – *Cf.* CONTRACT CAPTAIN

Retorna. *See* WRITS, RETURN OF

Retorted. *Her.* Twisted; used of serpents or snakes entwined around each other.

Revelins. Heavy shoes of undressed leather worn by English peasants.

Reverdie. Type of song brought to England by the court of the Angevins. They were spring songs, sung to celebrate the season of new growth and love. [< OFr. *reverie* = rejoicing < *rever* = to revel] – *Cf.* AUBADE; PASTOURELLE

Rex Anglorum. Lit. 'king of the English'. Latin phrase used from the 10c until late in the 12c, when it began to be replaced by *rex Angliae.* The first *rex Anglorum* was Æthelstan. Titles used by English and Norman kings were various but all were kings of people not of places. King John was the first *rex Angliae*.

Rhetor. A teacher of *rhetoric. [< Gk. *rhetor* = teacher of public speaking]

Rhetoric. The art of using language so as to persuade or influence others; a crucial part of the *trivium*. A set of rules was observed by either speaker or writer to achieve effective and persuasive expression. – *Cf. previous*

Rial. *See* RYAL

Ribald. A retainer who performed the meanest functions in a royal or noble household; also used of such men when recruited as an irregular soldiery. – *Cf. next*; RUTA; SCULLION

Ribaudaille [ribauz]. The men and women who followed an army and did much of the dirty work; a violent, unpleasant crowd. [< OFr. *ribauld* < OFr. *riber* = to pursue pleasure, to be licentious] – *Cf. previous*

Ribible. *See* REBEC

Ribibour [ribiber]. A lute-player. [< Ar. *rabab* = stringed instrument] – *Cf.* REBEC

Rider. According to *ASC, in 1085 William I dubbed his son Henry (later Henry I) a *ridere* at Westminster. The word *ridere* is used here synonymously with 'knight'.

Riding. One of three districts into which Yorkshire was divided, i.e. East, West and North [< ON *þriðjungr* = third part]

Rights of common. There were five rights of common: of pasture; of *estovers; of *turbary; in the soil; and of *piscary. – *Cf.* RIPARIES

Rinceau. Term for the foliate patterns used as a background in stained glass, or in moulding. The acanthus leaf was much favoured. [Fr. *rinceau*= foliage]

Riparies. The rights to the fish in river, stream or pond was jealously guarded by those entitled to them. Freshwater fish were a valuable source of protein, and were eaten every Friday (a fast day). When water-mills are mentioned in deeds, notice was always taken of fishing rights. Meadows also had their fishing rights added into their value. [< L *ripa* = a river bank] – *Cf.* RIGHTS OF COMMON

Riveling. A shoe made of untreated, i.e. raw skin.

Rockingham, Council of. Held in 1095, it was a part of the investiture controversy, concerned with whether a king or pope had the right to invest bishops. Lay investiture was seen by the Church as an encroachment. It was centred around Anselm's appointment as archbishop of Canterbury by William II Rufus in 1093. The controversy lasted for some two years. The council decided it could find no fault with Anselm, whose appointment was confirmed by the pope. The matter of lay investiture was resolved with a compromise by Henry I in 1107.

Rod. *See* PERCH

Rodknight. Holder of a form of *serjeanty or tenure of a fief, the service for which was riding with his lord or lady as specified by *Bracton. He was also known as a *'radman'.

Rogation. Prayers and litanies said on the Monday, Tuesday and Wednesday before Ascension Day form part of the 'Minor Rogation'. The 'Major Rogation' took place on 25 April, when prayers were said for the growing harvest.

Rolls. A class of documents used throughout medieval government. They were literally rolls of *parchment, going under a variety of names indicating their kind or which department of government generated them. Always in Latin, they were known collectively as *rotuli* (rolls). – *Cf. next;* FINE ROLLS; LETTERS PATENT ROLLS; PIPE ROLLS

Rolls Series. The collection of original source materials for the history of Britain during the medieval period. The Rolls Series is the short name for this series of texts published 'under the direction of the Master of the Rolls' and called *The Chronicles and Memorials of Great Britain and Ireland during the Middle Ages*. Publication began in 1858; some 250 volumes have been published since then. There are many associated volumes, such as *Foedera* and the Calendars of State Papers.

Romance 1. One of the many tales in verse popular at this time. Many dealt with legends and fables; others told chivalric stories or those involving heroic adventures. [< OFr. *romanz*]

Romance 2. The French language as used in this period, being distinct from Latin. More recently, the term includes all languages descended from Latin as a distinct language group. [< OFr. *romanz*]

Rome-scot. *See* PETER'S PENCE

Romfeoh [Rompenig]. *See* PETER'S PENCE

Romipeta. Term used in medieval documents for a pilgrim going to Rome. [< Rome + L *peto* = to make for] – *Cf.* JACOBIPETA; THOMIPETA

Rood 1. Measure of land = one quarter of an acre. The word was also used for a *perch.

Rood 2. The holy Cross. Many legends and lessons grew up around the symbol. One has the Cross itself being made of three kinds of tree: cypress, cedar and pine. This was seen as a symbol of the Trinity. These trees had grown from seeds given to Seth by an angel, which had been placed under the tongue of Adam on his death. One of the earliest English poems is the *Dream of the Rood*, parts of which were carved on the stone cross still to be seen at Ruthwell in Scotland.

Rosace. Modern term for a rose window, with plentiful stained glass, of the kind found in cathedrals, esp. of the 14c. – *Cf.* PAUL'S WINDOW

Roses, Wars of the. Dynastic conflict between the houses of York and Lancaster, taking place from roughly 1455 and ending at the Battle of Bosworth Field, 22 August 1485. At Bosworth, Henry Tudor defeated Richard III (the last king of England to die in battle); he later married into the house of York. In 1487 an impostor named Lambert Simnel claimed to be Edward, duke of Warwick, and the nephew of Edward IV. He succeeded in having himself crowned in Dublin as Edward VI. In England he was supported by the earl of Lincoln. At Stoke Simnel's followers met the king, Henry VII, whose forces won the day. With surprising leniency, Simnel was not executed but given a job in the royal kitchens.

Rota. The pope's signature set within a circle which was put on certain solemn documents issued by the papal chancery at Rome.

Rotulus. Latin word for a parchment roll of the kind used in medieval – and later – government administration. – *Cf.* ROLLS

Rouge Croix. One of the four *pursuivants of the (English) College of Arms. The other three are: *Blue Mantle, *Portcullis and *Rouge Dragon. – *Cf.* ARMS, COLLEGE OF

Rouge Dragon. One of the four *pursuivants of the (English) College of Arms. The other three are *Blue Mantle, *Portcullis and *Rouge Croix. – *Cf.* ARMS, COLLEGE OF

Rouncy. French term for a cob-like horse; an ordinary saddle-horse, particularly not a *destrier* yet suitable for carrying a soldier or for use as a packhorse. – *Cf.* PALFREY

Round house. A small round building, usually in a conspicuous place in a town, where local miscreants and runaways were imprisoned for a short time.

Roundel 1. Piece of circular metal attached to the handle of a sword to prevent the hand slipping.

Roundel 2. *Her.* Solid-coloured circular *charge whose meaning is defined by that colour. – *Cf.* POMEIS

Rousant. *Her.* Describes a bird in the act of taking flight.

Routier. Term for those we call *mercenaries. The Low Countries were a principal recruiting area for these very cosmopolitan bands of soldiers. They were made up from outlaws, spoiled priests, and any unsuited to civilian life and wanting adventure. During the 12c these men pillaged and ravaged their way through the lands of their foes and nominal friends fairly indiscriminately. Often uncontrollable, typically when their paymaster was short of funds and unable to pay, they would plunder promiscuously. The Latin form is *ruptarius. – Cf. BRABANTERS; RUTA; MERCENARIES; TRAILBASTON

Royalty. The right of a monarch to jurisdiction, a prerogative from which accrued payment in kind or coin. [< OFr. *roialte*] – *Cf.* REAL

Rubric. Heading of a chapter or document; these were intended to be distinctive and were therefore written in red ink. [< L *ruber*= red] – *Cf. next*; ILLUMINATION; MINIUM

Ruddle. Red ochre used by shepherds to mark their sheep. [< OE *rudu* = red] – *Cf. previous*

Runcinus. *See* ROUNCY

Ruptarius [rutharius]. Latin form of *routier. [< L *rumpo* = break, destroy] – *Cf.* RUTA

Rushes. Basic floor covering of rooms in a medieval castle, *manor or hovel. In a manor or castle hall tables were removed after eating and bedding set down on the rushes. – *Cf.* TABLE DORMANT

Ruta. Collective noun for a band or company of *routiers and their *sequela.

Ryal. English coin of Edward IV's reign, 1465; it was also known as a 'rose noble'. – *Cf.* REAL [< OFr. *real* = royal]

S

Sabaton. That piece of the suit of armour protecting the upper part of the foot, its scales overlapping to allow ease of movement. They were notably broad. Before the 15c, this piece was sometimes known as a *'solleret'.

Sabbatizare. Latin verb for observing the Sabbath, to sabbatise. Neither work nor play were permitted on a Sunday. However, such restrictions was widely ignored, there being ploughing and also the pleasures of markets and their crowds.

Sable. *Her.* Black; indicated in colourless illustrations by vertical and lateral cross-hatching.

Saca et soca. *See* SAKE AND SOKE

Sack of wool. Standard weight of a sack of wool for export was 364 lb; the standard calculation was that *c.*240 sheep were required to produce one sack. Wool was the most important English export of the 13c and 14c. There were some 50 grades of wool at the time; the finest in the 13c came from Tintern Abbey and Abbey Dore in the West Country and from Stanfield in Lincolnshire. A sack of such wool fetched 28 marks (£18) on the Flemish market, while lesser-rated wool would fetch 7–12 marks. In 1335–6 some 34,000 sacks of wool were sent to Flanders and Brabant. [OE *sæcc* = sackcloth] – *Cf.* SARPLER

Sack, friars of the. Colloquial name for the Friars of the Penance of Jesus Christ, the largest of the lesser groups of English friars. Their houses were all abandoned by 1314, the members being obliged to join one of the *mendicant orders.

Sackbut. Early form of the trombone, so named because of its resemblance to a *saqueboute.

Sacrabar. The public prosecutor in the *Danelaw. [< ON *sakaraberi*]

Sacramentary. Book which sets down the various prayers and rites to be performed at each of the sacraments.

Sacred Page, master of the. Synonym for a 'doctor of theology'.

Sacrist [sacristan]. The officer or *obedientiary of a monastery whose duties included ensuring the church and its contents were safe and secure, e.g. the silver and gold ornaments and vestments. 'Sacristan' is a later form. [< L *sacer* = sacred]

Safflower. Dried flowers of the safflower (*Carthamus tinctorius*) were used in the making of rouge and textile dyes.

Saffron. Dried stigmas of the crocus were used as a colouring and flavour in wines and cakes. It was used particularly in celebration after Lent. The name Saffron Walden in Essex commemorates a place renowned for growing the flowers for this use since the 14c.

Sagita. A bolt with a four-sided head fired by a *crossbow. [< L *sagittarius* = archer] – *Cf.* QUARREL 1

Sagmatarius. *See* SUMPTER

Sagum. A woollen cloak. The word was used first of the Roman military cloak; later, a similar civilian garment. There was a substantial trade of such garments with the Carolingian Empire in the late 8c. [L *sagum* = cloak] – *Cf.* SAY

Saint Anthony's fire. A disease known today as ergotism, caused by a fungus which contaminated bread made from damp flour.

Saint Paul's Cathedral. The first St Paul's Cathedral church in London was that of Mellitus, consecrated by Augustine and appointed bishop of London, which was dedicated to St Paul in *c.*603 and built by Æthelbert, king of Kent (d. 616). Another old St Paul's was completed in 1283. At that time it was the largest church in Europe and looked something like today's Notre Dame in Paris. Damaged beyond repair in the Great Fire of London in 1666, this St Paul's was replaced by Sir Christopher Wren's church.

Saint Paul's Cross. A stone cross in open space on the north-east side of *St Paul's Cathedral, first recorded in the 12c. It was by the cross that sermons were delivered, making it the pulpit of the cathedral and London. Around it, the London *folkmoot would meet to hear proclamations, papal bulls etc. read out. In one corner there was a belfry whose bell was used to summon Londoners. This was also the place where the men of London met before going out to battle, led in hereditary right by the lord of Castle Baynard. – *Cf.* BANNER

Saints, military. The popularity of military saints increased with the preaching of the First Crusade in 1095; St Michael, leader of the heavenly host, St James the Moor-slayer and St George, whose appearance with St Demetrius at the siege of Antioch, fighting on the side of the Christians, perhaps assisted his eventual acceptance as patron not only of England, but also Portugal, Catalonia, Venice and Genoa.

Sake and soke. Grants of sake and soke allowed the granter to intercept the fines and other profits of justice relating to his own estate which would otherwise have gone to the king; the rights of sake and soke are particularly associated with *bocland. [< OE *sacu* = dispute, esp. legal dispute; *socn* = enquiry, jurisdiction]

Saker. Female falcon (*Falco cherrug*), similar to the lanner, somewhat larger than the peregrine. The male was known as a 'sakeret' (with the dim. -et), it being smaller than the female.

Saladin tithe. *Tithe imposed after the fall of Jerusalem in 1187. It was a tax on movables – the first such personal tax in English history. The purpose was to raise funds for a crusade with the purpose of recapturing Jerusalem and other places in the Holy Land. It was named after Saladin, the one name known throughout Christendom as belonging to a Muslim leader and thus universally demonised. Dante placed him with virtuous non-Christians, 'solitary, set apart'.

Salamander. Pliny the Elder (AD 23–79) described the salamander as being so cold it could put out a fire, if dropped into one. Salamanders were also thought to be so poisonous that if one wrapped itself around a tree the fruit would be poisoned.

Salient. *Her.* Term used of a predatory animal shown as if leaping upwards onto its prey. A lion or wolf might be shown this way. [< L *salio* = to leap] – *Cf.* COUNTER-SALIENT; SPRINGING

Salle. In the 14c the walls of the rooms of wealthy magnates were covered by hangings. A suite of such hangings, or tapestries, was known as a *salle*. The finest such works came from Flanders – using English wool.

Salle du roy. French phrase used in the 14c for what would be known today as the king's flagship; however, it referred to the ship the king happened to be in, rather than to a purpose-built vessel. For example, Edward III was in a humble *cog during the Battle of Sluys in June 1340.

Sallet. A suit of armour's metal helmet with a section projecting backwards, so as to protect the back of the neck.

Sally port. Small fortified doorway from which defenders of a castle might 'make a sally', i.e. a brief sortie or attack with limited troops. [< OFr. *saillir* = to leap]

Saltire. *Her.* An *honourable ordinary, being a diagonal cross, i.e. *bend and bend *sinister, i.e. corner to corner, a St Andrew's cross (unlike St George's cross, which is vertical and lateral). [< OFr. *saultoir* = stile with crosspiece]

Salt-pan. Particularly common in eastern England, around the Wash; there are still remains of such pans. They collected salt-water; being heated from below, salt remained as water evaporated. The render or payment to a lord was often made up of combinations or fractions of the *ora, which was valued at 16d, as well as the salt itself. The Latin form is *salsa*. – *Cf.* MILL; SLITCH

Sambue. A woman's side-saddle. How much they were used is not clear.

Sanctorale. Annual cycle of services in the *breviary based around celebration of the feasts of the saints. [< L *sanctus* = holy]

Sanctuary. Immunity from prosecution, secured by placing oneself in a sacred place. Those churches which offered sanctuary had a knocker on the main door and the sanctuary seeker had only to touch it to be safe. Some of these knockers were rather elaborate, e.g. Durham Cathedral, while others were plain rings. At Durham, the seeker of sanctuary struck the great knocker, the door was opened and the Galilee Tower bell was rung. The malefactor then made full confession in front of witnesses of probity. At Westminster, there is today a portion of the abbey precincts still known as the Sanctuary.

The idea of sanctuary is found for the first time in 600 in the laws of Æthelberht. For all its apparent sanctity, there are many records of sanctuary being broken. In the register of the bishop of Lincoln, Oliver Sutton (1280–99), one can find penalties imposed upon a man for seriously injuring another he dragged forcibly from sanctuary. The penalties were for the injury – the use of force in a sacred place – and he was obliged both to pay doctor's fees and visit the injured man in prison and try to help him. However, the penalty for breaking sanctuary violently could be death. Taking a person from sanctuary was something for which there could be no compensation in the old English way of things. In certain circumstances a person could be removed on condition the death penalty would not be imposed. In English law, the sanctuary or asylum seeker was required either to submit to a trial or to take an oath to leave the kingdom; to return required the king's permission. The person in sanctuary was given 40 days to decide on a course to take, after which time he or she could be starved into submission. However, there were some 20 places in England where the king's law had no power and the refugee could stay for life. Kings Henry VIII and James I limited sanctuary; it finally disappeared in the 18c. [< L *sanctus* = holy] – *Cf.* ABJURE THE REALM; ASYLUM

Sanglier. A full-grown wild boar. The term was also used of the heraldic boar. – *Cf.* CLEYED

Sanguinati. The 12c Latin term used at Westminster and other cathedrals of those monks who had recently undergone blood-letting. These monks or canons were not expected to go to the stalls for service, instead they were allowed to use a side chapel, where seats were provided. – *Cf.* BLOOD-LETTING

Sapientes. *See* WITAN

Saqueboute. Lance with iron hook on one end used for pulling horsemen off their mounts in battle. – *Cf.* SACKBUT

Saracen. Person belonging to one of the nomadic peoples of the Syrian and Arabian deserts. They were fine guerrilla fighters who, as Muslims, fought against the Christian crusaders. Later, the word became a generic term for any non-Christian. It is remembered today in the names of many inns and pubs such as the Saracen's Head. [< Gr. *Sarakenos*] – *Cf.* CRUSADES; SARSENET

Sarhad. Injury money paid should a stallion injure someone outside the covering season. If this happened, the animal could be claimed as recompense. However, there was no claim to be made if the injury occurred during the season. [< OE *sar* = a sore or hurt] – *Cf.* WERGELD

Sarpler. Unit of weight for wool, being a little more than 2,240 lb. – *Cf.* SACK OF WOOL

Sarsenet [sarcenet]. Very fine, soft silk cloth; part of the trade in imported luxuries brought to England in the 12c and after from the East, often via Venice. It was named after the OFr. *drap sarrasinois* = *Saracen cloth; the French being garbled by the English. – *Cf.* TABARD

Sartis. *Cistercian house in Bedfordshire which took its name from *de assartis* = the clearing. The Cistercian order made a practice of searching out wilderness places to establish their monasteries. – *Cf.* ASSART

Sarum. The ecclesiastical name of Salisbury. Abbreviations were very common in Latin documents and the Latin name *Sarisburia* was abbreviated to *Sarz*. This may later have been misread and transcribed as Sarum.

Sarum Use. The order of service used in the Sarum, i.e. Salisbury, diocese, and indeed widely throughout England. A revision or new Sarum use emerged in the 14c and was used until the Reformation.

Sassenach. Scots' word for the English but a relic of the *Adventus Saxonum* when, to the inhabitants of Britain, all the newcomers were *Saxons. The Welsh equiv. is *saesneg*.

Savoy. Precinct of the Strand in London, which once possessed the right of *sanctuary. John of Gaunt had a palace there named Savoy, which was sacked and burned during the *Peasants' Revolt of 1381. However, they declined to take anything away, asserting they were lovers of truth and justice, not robbers or thieves.

Sax. *See* SEAX

Saxons. One of the Germanic peoples who settled Britain in the 5c and 6c. Their name is preserved in the kingdoms known as Sussex (South Saxons), Wessex (West Saxons), Middlesex and Essex (East Saxons). – *Cf.* ANGLES; SASSENACH

Say. Fine cloth somewhat like serge, blended with silk; later, it was wholly wool. [< L *sagae*] – *Cf.* SAGUM

Scaccarium Aaronis. Lit. 'Aaron's exchequer'. After the death of Aaron (the Jew) of Lincoln in 1185, a special department of the crown's *exchequer was created, his fortune and debts owed having escheated to the crown. Previously all his business had been done under royal protection. Apart from what the English king owed, among other debtors were the king of Scotland, the archbishop of Canterbury, several bishops, abbots and earls. Aaron had also provided the capital for the building of nine *Cistercian houses, and the abbeys of Peterborough and St Albans.

Scale armour. Armour made of overlapping scales or leaves, like those of the armadillo, allowing flexibility and movement.

Scallop. A shell worn by pilgrims on pilgrimage as a sign they had been to St James at Compostella. – *Cf.* PALMER

Scandal. Misbehaviour by a religious person resulting in discredit to religion or the Church; also, a troubled conscience occasioned by a respected person's misbehaviour. [< AN *scandle* < L *scandalum* = offence] – *Cf.* MISPRISION

Scantillon. A measuring device. – *Cf. next*

Scantling. A set of standardised dimensions used by carpenters and builders. – *Cf. previous*

Scapular. Garment worn by Benedictine monks in place of their cowl while working outside the house; it was worn shawl-like over the shoulders. [< L *scapula* = shoulder]

Scarlet. Type of fine, rich-quality English cloth, much valued on the continent; famously made in Stamford in Lincolnshire from the 12c. This cloth was not necessarily scarlet in colour: the term indicated its type and richness. Only later, by transference, did scarlet come to signify the colour. The dye was derived from dried insects (*Kermes ilicis*) found in the galls that form on the kermes oak (*Quercus coccifera*), which grew in Spain and Portugal. It was used in the English wool industry between the 12c and the 15c. *Scarletum* was one 12c Latin form, *exscarletum* and *ascarletum* others. [< OFr. *escarlate* < Persian *saqirlat* = scarlet cloth, a rich cloth < Ar. *siqillat* = fine cloth] – *Cf.* BRASIL; CRAMOISY; STAMFORT

Scat. A tribute payment or tax. [< OE *sceatt* = money, tribute] – *Cf.* SCEATTA

Scavage. A toll levied on merchant strangers and their goods in London and other towns. The Latin form was *scavagium*. – *Cf. next*

Scavager. London officer deputed to collect *scavage. Later, in the 16c, he kept the streets clean. [< scavenger]

Sceatta [sceat]. AS silver coin, the first English penny. Initially issued with good silver content; by the early 8c quality was deteriorating. Very debased coins, *sceattas* or *stycas*, were still being issued in Northumbria in the early 9c; by the end of that century all such coins were made of copper or brass. Some were issued by the archbishop of York. This coinage continued until 867. [< OE *sceatt* = money, tribute] – *Cf.* PENNY

Scedula. The loose leaf inserted into the register of a monastery on which were recorded notes of daily happenings and events. At the end of the year some of its contents were included in the chronicle being compiled at the monastery. Obviously the *scedula* was replaced each year. Often enough these notes were made not using a pen but *cum plumbo* = with lead, which when shaped conveniently could be used as a pencil. From *scedula* derives schedule.

Scegth. A warship; a light and fast craft, similar to those used by the Vikings. One bequeathed to Æthelred the Unready had 64 oars. In 1008 he ordered *scegths* to be built 'all over England'. [< ON *skeið* = a warship] – *Cf. next*

Scegthman. Generally a sailor or mariner; also used of pirates and Vikings. – *Cf. previous*

Sceptre 1. A decorated rod being a part of the royal *regalia, essential to the symbolism of a monarch's claim to power and authority. – *Cf. next*; DALMATIC; ORB

Sceptre 2. *Her.* A *charge representing the rod held by a monarch. – *Cf. previous*

Schiltron. A large but compact division of spearmen; a defensive formation of foot-soldiers forming a rectangle or oval, holding pikes or spears outwards so as to present a sharp fence to attackers. It was called a 'pike hedgehog'. This is not very different from the phalanx used by the Greeks and esp. the Spartans. It was a formation very difficult to break up directly with the spears holding off the knights on their *destriers*, for instance. However, they were vulnerable to archers and their blizzards of arrows. Once the formation was broken the knights could then charge in. William Wallace used this formation at the Battle of Stirling Bridge (1297) with success; also at Bannockburn in 1314. After that, the English knew better and used the bow and clouds of arrows to kill all in the formation. Then the knights and their horses could break through. Later, it evolved into the infantry 'square' as used by Wellington at Waterloo.

Schola Saxonum. Lit. 'Saxon school'. This was the permanent English community of pilgrims to be found in Rome, which had existed for some time by the mid-9c. It was sufficiently large to have been noted as contributing men for the defence of Rome in 846. However, it was destroyed by fire several times. One occasion, in 847, was much later the subject of a painting by Raphael, *Incendio del Borgo* (*Fire in the Borgo*), c.1511. After that fire, the pope issued in 854, a *bull organising the *Schola Saxonum* into a pilgrim community with property to support itself. The English themselves referred to this district of Rome as a *burh*; the Italian is *borgo*. – *Cf.* PETER'S PENCE

Scholium. An annotation or comment made by a scholar on an old MS.

Schoolman. A teacher at one of the medieval universities; a medieval scholastic, between the 9c and 14c, trained in philosophy and theology.

Schynbald. Metal plate which protected the shins of a knight in armour.

Scipbryce. The right to claim the wreckage of ships. [< OE *scip* = ship + *bryce* = break, fragment] – *Cf.* LAGAN

Scipflota. A sailor; also a pirate. – *Cf.* BUTESCARL; LITHESMAN

Scir. *See* SHIRE

Scirman. An official in the laws of Ine (688–94) in which he was considered one from whom justice could be demanded. He was precursor of the *sheriff. – *Cf. previous;* SHIRE

Scir-reeve. Shire-reeve, more familiarly, a sheriff. – *Cf.* HIGH REEVE

Scolas regere. Lit. 'to govern/direct school'. Phrase used in the institution of a *cathedral grammar school for the chancellor's duties.

Scop. An AS poet or minstrel.

Scot. Customary tax or contribution paid by tenants to their lord, also to the sheriff. [< OE *sceatta* = tribute, payment] – *Cf. next;* SCOT AND LOT

Scot and lot. A tax, i.e. *scot, levied on members of a borough in varying proportions or shares, i.e. lot. Behind it was the idea that those who shared in the obligations and responsibilities by paying tax would also share in the privileges. It was a mark of status.

Scot-ale. Combination of *scot = contribution + ale = festival or holiday at which ale was drunk. It was paid for by drinkers' contributions or share of the cost, usually exacted at the church by the vicar, sometimes by the lord of the *manor. – *Cf. previous;* BRIDALE

Scoti [Scotti]. Tribe or group of people speaking Gaelic living in the northeast of what is now Ireland. They began raiding in the 3c and then migrated to Scotland during the 5c. In early texts, references to Scotia or the Scoti are to these people. After migration the kingdom they founded was known as Dalriada, in what are now Argyll and Bute. Later, in the 9c the Scoti and Picts merged, and the former gave their name to the country. After about the 10c Scotia came to refer to Scotland.

Scottish Sea. Colloquial term for the great tract of mossy land which lay between the Clyde and the Forth. It served for some time as a natural border between Scotland and England.

Scriptorarius. Superintendent or principal scribe in a *scriptorium. He not only delegated tasks within the writing room, but also gave out the books to be read by his fellow monks. – *Cf. next*

Scriptorium. Lit. 'writing room' (in a monastery). The only means of reproducing any text or of making books was by hand until the advent of the printing press, *c*.1458. The scribe was a crucial part of society, writing letters for the illiterate, copying literary and legal texts or the Bible, or producing great works such as the *Lindisfarne Gospels*, the *Book of Cerne*, or the *Book of Kells*. A goose quill was used for text with ink made from gum and galls. Although many texts were illustrated in monasteries, by the 14c there were lay professionals who might be commissioned by an individual to produce something like the *Luttrell Psalter* or by a monastery which lacked the skills. A Bible might take three or four years. There had been scriptoria in monasteries since the 7c. – *Cf. previous;* SCRIVENER

Scriptory. An anglicised form of **scriptorium*.

Scrivener [scriveyn]. A scribe or copyist; someone who wrote professionally. There was always the problem inherent in copying of the transmission of errors, either through lack of attention to the text or through bad writing being mis-read. Authors themselves were always conscious of this potential problem. Chaucer mentions his copyist by name as Adam *scriveyn* and wishes him a bad case of scurf should he make mistakes. [< OFr. *escrivein* = writing]

Scullion. The lowliest domestic servant: the dish-washer/bottle-washer, night-soil disposer.

Scuta. *See* SHUTAGIUM

Scutage. A **fine or money paid in lieu of military service i.e. shield money; tax on an estate. The Latin form was *scutagium*. Land held of the king by tenants-in-chief owed military service, i.e. the supply of a specified number of knights when called upon. Henry II imposed such a tax every four years or so, at two marks (£1 6s 8d). It was basically a military tax; one which *Magna Carta affirmed could not be levied without the 'common counsel of the kingdom'. The purpose of levying a scutage in the late 12c and the 13c was to raise money to pay the wages of hired soldiers, who were beginning to predominate in armies of the time. In the late 12c, a knight was paid a daily wage of 1s, a foot soldier 1d or 2d. By the time of Edward III, *mercenaries were an essential part of the armies he mustered for use in the *Hundred Years' War. At this time knights' wages had gone up to 2s a day. Indeed, the *Dialogus de Scaccario* had this to say of scutage: 'The king decrees that a certain sum be paid from each knight's fief, namely, a mark or a pound, whence come the pay and gratuities for the soldiers. For the prince prefers to thrust into the vortex of war mercenary troops rather than domestic forces. And so this sum is paid in the name of shields and is therefore called scutage.' [< L *scutum* = shield] – *Cf. next;* ESCUAGE; KNIGHT'S FEE

Scutage Rolls. Exemptions from the payment of *scutage were enrolled under this head; also permission given to tenants-in-chief to collect scutage and summonses for military service. – *Cf. previous*

Scutifer. Shield-holder, i.e. *esquire. The term was also used of the 14c *hobelar or light cavalryman, whose horse was not barded or *coopertus. [< L scutum = shield] – Cf. BARD 1; SCUTAGE

Scyldburh. A shield-defence, a wall of shields held defensively by a row of soldiers. Such a defensive formation of man and shield was used by the English against Norman cavalry at the Battle of Hastings in 1066. This particular attack is shown in the *Bayeux Tapestry, when the Normans were stopped and beaten back. Shields locked together above soldiers' heads gave protection when approaching the walls of a castle under siege. [< OE scyld = shield + burh = a walled defence]

Sea-coal. So named to distinguish it from charcoal. The English did not use much sea-coal until c.1200. The sea-coal that was used came from the beaches of Northumberland and Durham having been washed ashore from seams exposed by the action of the sea. However, coals from Newcastle were arriving in London by c.1225; exports to Flanders expanded throughout the 13c.

Seam [seme]. The load carried by a pack-horse or sumpter-horse; also the harness of a pack-horse. [< OE seam = load, burden]

Seax. A short sword, sometimes a dagger, used by the *Saxons; from which their name. The OE handseax refers specifically to a dagger.

Secretarius regis. Lit. 'king's secretary'. During the first seven decades of the 14c, this term was often used of the keeper of the *privy seal.

Secrete et singillatim. Lit. 'secretly and one by one'. These were the terms under which a bishop or his agent, e.g. archdeacon, conducted interviews during the *visitation of a monastery. The purpose was to ensure there was no exertion of pressure or collusion in the giving of evidence of any wrongdoing. – Cf. COMPERTA; DETECTA

Secular clergy. The members of the *clergy who worked in the world and were not bound by the rules of a monastic order. They were clerics who had been admitted to one of the orders, but who did not live under a monastic rule, e.g. parish priests.

Sede vacante. Lit. 'the seat being vacant'. The phrase was used of a vacant bishopric.

Sedilia. Term used for the stalls of a church in the 11c. A seat or a group of seats for priests, canopied and decorated, near the altar.

Seely [sele]. Blessed, touched or favoured by God; fortunate, also innocent, or harmless or helpless; hence our word 'silly'. The word was applied to the mentally disturbed; cf. our use of 'touched' when describing someone's odd behaviour. The word was also applied to lepers. [< OE *sælig* = happy, fortunate] – *Cf.* HOLIDAY

Segno. A fencer's training aid comprising a plan marked out on the floor showing the correct positions of the feet for various cuts and thrusts.

Segreant. *Her.* Describes a griffin *rampant. Segreant was only ever used of the griffin.

Seisin. Freehold possession of land or goods and *chattels; also the taking of possession of land or goods. – *Cf.* DISSEISIN

Sejant. *Her.* Describes a beast sitting upright. [< OFr. *seant* < L *sedeo* = to sit]

Selion. A strip of arable land formed in the dividing of adjacent plots. [< AN *seillon* = a measure of land]

Selvage. Piece of woven edging used to finish a piece of cloth to prevent it unravelling. [< Du. *selfegge* = self-edge]

Sempstre. A seamstress.

Seneschal. *Steward or major-domo of a great estate; the official responsible for the estate's daily functioning, including sometimes responsibility for justice within the household. An AS seneschal was known as a *disc-thegn*, i.e. a dish-*thegn*. [< Germanic *seniskalkoz* < *seni* = old + *skalkoz* = a servant] – *Cf.* PINCERNA

Seneschaucie. A treatise setting out the rôles of officers and servants of a *manor, the most senior being the *seneschal or *reeve. It was written anonymously *c.*1270–80. It does not deal with any agricultural matters. Because custom and practice varied from region to region, its expression presents a somewhat idealised view of a manor. It begins: 'The seneschal of lands ought to be prudent, faithful and profitable; he ought to know the law of the realm'.

Septuagesima. The 70 days from the third Sunday before Lent, ending with the Saturday of Easter week. [< L *septuagesima* = seventieth]

Sepurture. *See* ENDORSED

Sequela. In feudal law the children of an unfree serf were not called *familia* or family but *sequela*, i.e. literally followers, with the sense of a brood or litter. In this sense of followers the word was also used for groups of *mercenaries. – *Cf.* RUTA

Sequipedus. *See* PEDESECUS

Seraphim. An order of six-winged angels, mentioned for example in Isaiah. – *Cf.* CHERUBIM

Serf. A labourer only slightly above a slave; one bound to work his lord's land, from whom he had land to feed himself and family; unlike a *sokeman he could not leave without permission. When the land's lord changed, the serf, and his family, was counted as part of the estate's *chattels. According to the *Rectitudines Singularum Personarum* a serf was to have a midwinter feast and another at Easter, some land and a *harvest handful, besides their needful dues. This system broke down after the *plague years of 1348, when such dues became money transactions, labour being in short supply. [< L *servus* = servant] – *Cf.* BLACK DEATH; CEORL; SEQUELA

Sergeant. A serving-man, one who attended his lord; also one who attended a knight on the field of battle and carried the lord's banner. [< L *servio* = to serve] – *Cf. next*; SERJEANT-AT-LAW

Sergeant-at-arms. At this period an officer of the crown, with authority to act in the king's name. – *Cf. previous and next*

Serjeant-at-law. At one time the highest rank of English barrister at the bar; it was abolished in the late 19c. Working in the court of common pleas, the serjeants-at-law had a monopoly on pleading cases. They were appointed by the king after 16 years of study and practice. Justices of the court of common pleas were chosen from their ranks. The title is a corrupt version of *serviens ad legem*, i.e. a law servant. They were serjeant-counters, i.e. pleaders who would frame the counts or charges involved in a case. Though similar in origin to 'sergeant', the spelling today of the word when referring to a law officer always uses a 'j'; however, use of a 'j' does not necessarily signify a law officer. In Chaucer's lifetime there were rarely more than 20 such officers. – *Cf.* PARVIS; SERGEANT

Serjeanty. Term (analogous with *thegnage) used for the tenure held by a *sergeant in return for which he served his lord by carrying his banner, making bows and arrows, and other such tasks. Other services could be as various as growing herbs, tending hounds when hurt, providing arrows, nursing sick falcons, providing fuel. A crucial aspect of a serjeanty was that neither knight service, nor *scutage were owed. *Magna Carta in 1215 stated that a serjeanty was both inalienable and impartible. *Bracton said the offices of serjeanties were 'infinite'. However, he did specify several: 'holding the pleas of their lords, or carrying letters within a certain precinct, or feeding greyhounds or harriers, or mewing hawks, or finding bows and arrows, or carrying them'. A serjeanty was also granted, for example, for taking royal money to the treasury at Winchester, before the 12c, after which time the treasury had moved to Westminster. The term was broad enough to cover also the tenure given by a great lord to various domestic servants. Cooks and porters, for instance, might be given some land, as might servants who helped during the hunting season. Such a tenure was exempt from such feudal dues as *wardship and *relief. These services were known as being *intrinsec. One of the grandest of serjeanties was that of the Dymokes of Scrivelsby, who were royal champions. [< L *serviens* = a servant] – *Cf.* RADMAN

Servantz corores. AN term for runaway servants or villeins. [< AN *servant* + *courir* = to run (away)]

Servitium debitum. Customary military service owed by a *vassal to his lord. This usually involved serving in the army for 40 days a year. The king's most important vassals would be required to supply a specified number of knights for duty in service of the king. The greater the lord, the greater the number of knights he would have to supply, that number being set in units of five or ten knights. The last summons for a levy of knights owing the *debitum* was by Richard II in June 1385. However, the rank and file soldier was still summoned and supplied by the boroughs and shires. [L *servitium* = service + *debitum* = of debts] – *Cf.* ARRAY, COMMISSION OF; SCUTAGE

Servus. Latin word used in *DB* and elsewhere for a *slave. In documents which recorded numbers of slaves, *servus* was used of the male slave, while *ancilla* was used of the female. – *Cf. next*

Servus casatus. Lit. 'a housed slave'. A slave with a cottage might even have a piece of land. Though not a free man, this slave was bound to his lord as any other tenant or *villein was. His status as slave was the added burden, one which the church sought to eliminate. Within a short time after the Conquest (1066) slavery had effectively disappeared from England with the blurring of distinction between *serf, *villein and slave dissolving. – *Cf. previous*

Sester [sextar]. A liquid measure, used esp. of honey. The actual capacity was variable – 24 and 23 ounces are recorded. As a dry measure, it was used of grain; 12 bushels in later Middle Ages. [< L *sextarius* = one sixth; in Roman measures, one sixth of a bucket (*congius*)]. – *Cf.* SEXTARY

-setla. The second element of words such as *cotsetla* and *ansetla*, meaning someone who sits or dwells. Thus *cotsetla* = a person who dwells in a cottage; *ansetla* = someone who dwells alone, i.e. a *hermit. There is also *fotsetla* which suggests someone sitting at another's feet; their function, though, is hard to guess. – *Cf.* PEDESECUS

Sevum. Suet, i.e. the fat found around an animal's liver. This was used by doctors as a treatment for liver problems in human beings. The suet was placed on the patient's body, close by the liver.

Sewer. A servant in the king's household; a *steward. He was responsible for seating guests at the table; he might also taste the food. [< OFr. *asseoir* = arrange a seat for another] – *Cf.* DAPIFER

Sext. The sixth canonical hour of the day; midday; second of three of the Little Hours. [< L *sextus* = sixth] – *Cf.* HORARIUM; NONE; TERCE

Sextary [sextar]. A measure equivalent to six pints. Some of those who lived in the king's household were entitled to a daily measure of wine, usually a sextary or proportions thereof. The chancellor, for example, was permitted one sextary of clear wine a day, while a sextary of wine was drawn every night for Henry I should he want it. [< L *sextarius* < *sext* = six] – *Cf.* CONGIUS; CONSTITUTIO DOMUS REGIS

Shalm. *See* SHAWM

Shambles. Orig. a footstool; then a table displaying wares for sale, most often meat; later, a street or passage of such tables, a meat market, e.g. the Shambles in York, whence our use of the word to indicate disorder. Shambles was known in 12c Latin as *carnificium*, a word used also of butchery. [< OE *sceamul, scamol* = footstool] – *Cf.* CHEPE

Shanks. The term for the fur from the legs of kids, goat or sheep, which was used to trim outer clothing. Less expensive than *marten or sable, it could be worn outside the house with no anxiety about its being damaged or dirtied. – *Cf.* MINIVER

Shaw. A small wood or copse. A line of trees used as the border of territory or a field. [< OE *sceaga* = edge of cultivated land] – *Cf.* WHITEBEAM

Shawm. A wind instrument similar to an oboe, with a double reed. [< ME *shallemalle* < OFr. *chalemel* < L *calamus* = reed]

Sheaf 1. A quiverful of two dozen arrows. [< OE *sceaf* = a bundle]

Sheaf 2. *Her.* A*charge which shows a sheaf of arrows. [< OE *sceaf* = a bundle]

Sheep. The presence of sheep throughout England in the medieval period is remembered in many placenames such as Shipton and Shipston. Approximately three-quarters of the livestock (excluding draught oxen) recorded in *DB* were sheep. In the 12c, they were mean creatures in comparison with today's. Their fleeces weighed 2 lb at best; today a fleece would be two or three times that weight. In the 14c there were as many as eight million sheep in England. The *wool industry was absolutely crucial to the English economy, with much being exported to Flanders. [< OE *sceap* = sheep]

Sheriff. Chief officer in a shire, i.e. the 'shire *reeve', representing the crown as its executive before the *Norman Conquest. The English office was amalgamated with that of the Norman *vicomte* (L = *vicecomes*) after 1066. William I separated secular and ecclesiastical courts, thus leaving the sheriff as the king's power in the *county. He summoned and led his shire's array of soldiery; he also executed all writs, and, for the first century after 1066, judged both criminal and civil cases. But from the time of Henry II, and the emergence of the *curia regis*, his powers were considerably restricted, jurisdiction over civil cases disappearing. His responsibilities thereafter were to investigate allegations of crime from within his shire, to try minor offences, but to hold those accused of serious crimes for the arrival of the justices-in-eyre. Today, the position remains as a ceremonial office. [< OE *scirgerefa* < *scir* = shire + *gerefa* = reeve] – *Cf.* INQUEST OF SHERIFFS; VISCOUNT

Sheriff's aid. Land tax received by sheriffs as payment for holding courts of shire and *hundred. Henry II intended to have the tax paid into the treasury. It was over whether or not the Church should pay this tax that Henry II and Thomas Becket as archbishop of Canterbury clashed so fiercely and publicly at a council held at Woodstock in 1163. Becket asserted the Church would not pay because the king was not entitled to it. There was an open debate which the king lost, the assembly siding with Becket.

Shield 1. A defensive implement, of wood or metal, sometimes circular, sometimes heart-shaped, secured to an arm by loops or a strap.

Shield 2. *Her.* The stylised heart shape used as the field for an *escutcheon. By the time of Edward, the Black Prince (d. 1376), the arms shown on a shield would depend on the occasion of use. There were shields for arms of war and shields of peace, with different arms for use at a *tournament. In Edward's case, the arms of war were the arms of England, whereas his arms of peace showed three ostrich feathers *argent on a field of *sable. – *Cf.* PAS D'ARMES

Shilling. Unit of weight equal to one twentieth of a pound; later the silver coin worth 12d, 20 of which made £1. – *Cf.* SOLIDUS

Shire. Orig. a sphere of jurisdiction or command; thus the area over which such authority was exercised. The earliest shires (in Wessex) were commanded by *ealdormen*; by the late 10c, when the *ealdorman*'s powers were more extensive, they were administered by sheriffs. By the same period, the shires were divided into hundreds (in the north, wapentakes). From the 12c, they were also called 'counties'. Latin form is *scira*. [< OE *scir* = division, sphere of control, shire]

Short-cross penny. New coin of 1180 replacing the issue of coins known today as *Tealby coins. A new coin was a necessity, the existing coinage being crude, and of poor quality. These new coins were of high quality, being 95 per cent silver; they continued in use until the reign of Henry III. The 'short cross' of their name refers to the cross on the reverse, which is noticeably smaller than that found on earlier issues. The coins of Henry III's reign were known as 'long cross', as the cross on the reverse extended to the edge of the coin. There were 11 mints in use: London, Carlisle, Exeter, Lincoln, Northampton, Norwich, Oxford, Wilton, Winchester, Worcester and York. When minted in London, some 20 moneyers were employed; there were eight in York, Lincoln and Winchester. – *Cf.* MONEYER; MONEYERS, ASSIZE OF

Shrievalty. The office of a sheriff, his jurisdiction. [< *shrive, shrieve* = an old form of sheriff] – *Cf.* SHERIFF

Shrine. Orig. a box or chest; also a *reliquary with a tomb or special box-like container. Harold Godwineson is to be seen on the *Bayeux tapestry swearing an oath to William, duke of Normandy, with his hand on just such a reliquary. Later a shrine became an elaborate tomb and place of worship if that of a saint, e.g. St Thomas Becket.

Shutagium. The fare for using a 'shout' or barge, a 'shout' being a small river taxi, also known as *scuta, shuta* and *schoutum*; the bargeman was a *shutarius*. [< Du. *schute* = a flat-bottomed boat]

Siege 1. The chair for a person of high rank, thus Siege Perilous, the one unoccupied seat at King Arthur's Round Table, to be occupied only by the one who would achieve the *Grail.

Siege 2. A military siege involved surrounding a town with the intention of starving the inhabitants into surrender; later, a privy. Orig. a siege was the place where herons waited for prey to approach.

Signet seal, office of the. After the office of the *privy seal went 'out of court' in the 14c, the signet-seal evolved, allowing the king to continue sending instructions. In this period the seal's keeper was always a *clerk, never a bishop, with up to 10 clerks under him. (By the 16c, its keeper came to be called the 'secretary of state'.) The king's more personal letters were written in this office, as were his instructions to the privy seal to issue letters or warrants, including warrants to *chancery.

Signifer. Term used by Bede of a king's standard-bearer. In the 14c the word was used of an armorial bearing. [< L *signum* = a sign]

Signum. Lit. 'a sign'. When a document, such as a charter, was witnessed, several people would add their mark, usually a cross, i.e. their *signa*. These documents are one way historians can trace the movements of members of the royal courts of this period. Over time, some of the crosses became distinctive through use; some are quickly recognisable to the practised eye.

Silvaticus. Term used in the Latin records for an outlaw living in the woods and forests. Many men so described were among those dispossessed after the Conquest. [< L *silva* = a wood.]

Simnel bread. Bread made with finest flour. There were two kinds of simnel, a superior or royal simnel and a salt simnel. Such breads were also quite large. A superior simnel would feed four men; a salt only two men. A loaf was intended for one man, as part of his *livery. The Latin form is *simenellus*. [< OFr. *simenel* < L *simila* = a fine flour] – *Cf.* WASTEL

Simony. The buying and selling of ecclesiastical pardons and offices or benefices. In the literature of the 13c and 14c, there was much poetry written against both simony and avarice, particularly greed amongst the *clergy and friars. An anonymous poem *The Simonie*, also titled *On the Evil Times of Edward II*, was written *c*.1320. It is a satire aimed at the entire Church hierarchy from pope to local priest. [< Simon Magus, who in the 1c wanted to buy the power of transmitting the Holy Spirit.]

Sindon. A fine linen; muslin or *cambric. [< L *sindon* = muslin] – *Cf.* SARSENET; TABARD

Sine prole. Lit. 'without issue'. The Latin law term used to state that a man died without a 'male heir of his body'.

Singular. 15c hunter's term for a group of wild boar; that for dislodging a boar from its lair was 'rearing' it.

Sinister. *Her.* The left-hand side. In *heraldry, left and right are determined from the holder of a shield's point of view, not from the onlooker's. [< L *sinister* = left, left hand] – *Cf.* DEXTER

Sins, seven deadly. The sins were: pride or vainglory; covetousness; lust (expressed in *incontinence); envy; gluttony, which included drunkenness; anger; and sloth, of which *accidie was an expression.

Siserary. Corrupt form of *certiorari*.

Sixhynde. Man with a *wergeld* of 600s; found in early West Saxon law codes, but apparently obsolete by the 10c, though the 600s *wergeld* is mentioned in the *Leges Henrici Primi*. A man worth 200s was *twyhynde*; one worth 1,200s *twelfhynde*. – *Cf.* WERGELD

Skald. A Scandinavian court poet or bard; like many such singer-poets he was itinerant; also like a poet laureate, he would compose poems for occasions, such as a battle. After the *Norman Conquest of 1066, a skald named Thorkill, once under the patronage of Earl Waltheof, wrote a lament in Old Norse for the lost *AS world after Waltheof's execution in 1076. Another skald named Sighvatr wrote a poem, *Tøgdrápa*, about King Cnut. Its refrain runs 'Cnut is the foremost sovereign under heaven'. – *Cf.* STALLER

Skep. Dry measure in the 13c equivalent to a half-*bushel. There were eight skeps in a *quarter, though the bushel was the unit most frequently used. The skep itself was orig. a basket which came to hold half a bushel. The Latin form of skep is *eskippa*. [< OE *sceppe* = a dry measure] – *Cf.* PARVUS BUSSELLUS

Skivinus. An official of the London commune; also, a steward of a *guild. The English form is 'skivin'.

Slave. Some 25,000 slaves are mentioned in *DB*. However, after the Conquest, slaves as a class disappeared or rather were absorbed into the villeins or serfs. In the AS world slaves were a large group, particularly in the southwest peninsula and Wessex. For example, Cornwall had 1,160 slaves, Devon 3,290 and Somerset 2,110, whereas only one is mentioned in Huntingdonshire and none in Lincolnshire. The Normans were less concerned with legal status; what concerned them was the work a person could do. [< *Sclavus* = Slav] – *Cf. next*

Slavery. Slavery was often the fate of soldiers captured on a battlefield, as well as those captured at sea by pirates. The *AS enslaved many *Britons, most of whom worked on the land. Those who worked for the AS aristocracy within the house might well have had an easier life but their status remained the lowest. Vikings also had slaves; indeed they traded in slaves. In England in the 11c perhaps 5–10 per cent of the population was enslaved. Archbishops Lanfranc and Anselm did much to eliminate the practice in England. – *Cf.* BARBARIAN

Slitch [sleech]. The sandy silt above the usual tide-line left after the high spring tides, as a result of which it had a high salt content. This silt was gathered into a trench known as a 'kinch', over which fresh water was passed. The resulting salt as brine was then drained in a wooden receptacle; this brine was taken to the boiling pan. The word 'slitch' was used in Lancashire and the Solway; in the Lincolnshire salt industry the equivalent word used was 'muldefang' or 'mould'. – *Cf.* SALT-PAN

Slop 1. A bag with magic powers, used to steal milk from cows.

Slop 2. A loose baggy garment. – *Cf.* OVERSLOP

Smaragd. An emerald. [< L *smaragdus* = green precious stone, e.g. emerald; also beryl, jasper]

Smoke-farthing. A small payment made at *Whitsun by all households of a diocese, as a sign of obedience to the Church. – *Cf.* PENTECOSTALS

Snecca [Esnecca]. A warship, perhaps somewhat smaller than a *scegth*. Henry II possessed such a ship in the late 12c, which was berthed at Southampton; its master was paid 12d a day. [< ON *snekkja*, OE *snacc* = warship]

Soca. *See* SOKE

Soca faldae. *See* FOLD SOKE

Socage. Tenure of land for which a rent of money or kind – such as labour at sowing time and harvest or ploughing – was given but which did not include military service. [< 12c L *socagium* = form of free tenure]

Socherie. The manufacture of ploughshares; a maker of ploughshares = *sochier* [< Fr. *soc* = ploughshare]

Soil, in the. Ancient right to take gravel and stones and sand. – *Cf.* RIGHTS OF COMMON

Soke. A lord's jurisdictional right over the district attached to a *manor, with the right to receive fines and other dues; later, this included the exclusive right within a district to mill corn – the mill being built and held by the lord as a means of extra income, esp. after the *plague of 1348. [< OE *socn* = right of jurisdiction] – *Cf.* SAKE AND SOKE; SOKEN

Sokeland. Hamlets or small villages occupied by men and women owing service to their lord. – *Cf. next;* SOKE

Sokeman. A free man holding land in *socage; a man under jurisdiction (i.e. *soke) of his *lord.

Soken. Obligation of tenants to use the local mill; the mill's right to tenants' custom. [< OE *socn* = right of jurisdiction, of taking fines] – *Cf.* SOKE

Sol. *Her.* The tincture *or as used in a *blazon.

Solar [solar]. A sunny room; an upper room designed to catch the sun; a garret; a private chamber. [< L *sol* = the sun, *solarium* = a terrace, a room at the top of a house]

Solatium. Lit. 'solace'. Term used sometimes in older histories for what might well be called 'sweeteners' or 'hush money'. The gift was usually a pension or a small estate, being given to a nuisance.

Solidatae. Wages. *Cf. next;* LIBERATIONES

Solidus. After the English adoption of the *denarius*, 12 *denarii* made one *solidus* (hence s and d in predecimal £sd), while 20 *solidi* made £1. [< L *solidus* = solid, not hollow, thus genuine] – *Cf.* POUND; SHILLING

Solleret. A metal shoe, made with overlapping plates, which were part of a complete suit of armour. [< OFr. *soller* = a shoe] – *Cf.* SABATON

Somier. A pack-horse. – *Cf.* DESTRIER

Sore. Term used of a hawk in its first year before it has moulted, still bearing its red plumage.

Sor-penny. The fee paid to a lord by townsmen for free pasture. – *Cf.* REAP-SILVER

Soul-scot [corpse-present]. The last payment of the dead made by the living.

Since AS times, the soul-scot levy (also known as the *'mortuary') was made upon the deceased's goods: the bed he or she died in, the best beast or horse, or whatever, would be given to the Church, while something else was given to the lord. If the best horse was not good enough or worthy of the lord, then a sum of money would be agreed. Of course, the higher the rank of the dead person, the more valuable the 'present' would have to be. – *Cf.* SCOT; WAX-SCOT

Sow. A wheeled structure allowing besiegers to approach a castle or fortified *manor, with a roof for protection against rocks or hot oil dropped by defenders: in essence, a siege engine. – *Cf.* BEREFREDUM

Spangen helmet. A helmet made up from metal plates bound together in bands and secured with rivets, secured beneath the chin by a buckle. [< German *Spang* = a buckle]

Spaulder. Armour to protect the shoulder comprising lames or thin metal plates stretching downwards. [< OFr. *espalde* < L *spatula* = shoulder-blade]

Speaker. The member of parliament elected by his peers in the Commons to act as their representative and moderator of their debates. The first speaker, Peter de la Mare, was appointed during the Good Parliament of 1376. During the reign of Henry V, Thomas Chaucer, the son of Geoffrey Chaucer, was speaker. In the 14c, once the Commons had reached a decision, it was the speaker who would deliver it to the Lords. In the French of the time it was the speaker *qui avoit les paroles pur les Communes d'Engleterre en cest Parlement* = who has the words of the Commons of this parliament.

Spence. A colloquial contraction of 'dispense', applying to a small room in the buttery of a large establishment; perhaps also a larder. [< OFr. *dispenser* = to hand out, distribute]

Spicery. In the royal household, the spicery took in a great many items. Wax, napery, cloth, canvas and spices were all acquired through the great wardrobe. These goods were then distributed to the appropriate officers.

Spigurnel. Title of the sealer of writs in *chancery in the 13–14c. It was he who actually used the seal on documents, assisted by the *chauffer, or chafe wax. The title is found as a surname in the 14c. The Latin form is *spigurnellus*.

Spinster. Orig. used simply of a woman who spun wool or linen for a living; only in the 18c did the word come to denote an unmarried woman.

Spiritualities. Income of the Church derived from sources such as *tithes and offerings, these sources being exclusive to the Church. – *Cf.* TEMPORALI-TIES

Splendour. *Her.* Describes the sun shown with a face surrounded by rays.

Springald. Military machine used for throwing rocks, using the same principle as a catapult. [< OFr. *espringalle* < *espringeur* = a spring] – *Cf.* Mangonel; Trebuchet

Springing. *Her.* Describes animals of the chase, e.g. deer, when shown leaping. – *Cf.* Salient

Spurrier. A maker of spurs. – *Cf.* Lorimer

Squint. *See* Hagioscope

Squire. A young man, usually noble, or the unknighted son of a knight, who, in preparation for his knighthood, attended a knight. Squires also served in bishops' households. Their pay was a *mark (13s 4d) a year or perhaps as much as £1. 'Squire' and 'esquire' are synonymous. – *Cf.* Commensalis; Destrier; Esquire

Staggard. A male red deer in its fourth year. – *Cf.* Brocket

Staller. Lit. 'a place man'. An important officer of the royal household, perhaps equiv. to the 10c *pedesecus*. The title's origin is disputed; since the earliest known stallers were Danes, it was perhaps introduced in the time of Cnut. Since it is not recorded in contemporary sources until Edward the Confessor's reign, it has been seen as an English equivalent of the continental *constable. [OE *steallere* < ON *stallari* = marshal; or < L *constabularius* = man in charge of the stables]

Stamfort [stanforte]. Generic term for an English cloth or worsted yarn, or worsted-woollen. The term's derivation is either from the cloth-making town of Stamford, Lincolnshire, or *stamen forte* = strong, warp yarn or worsted. – *Cf.* Scarlet; Staple 1

Stance. Enclosure on the side of one of the old drove-roads in which animals were confined for safety overnight.

Standard. Flag held high in battle displaying each side's or its leader's *arms; showing an armed force where to rally. The loss of a standard signified a battle lost and humiliation. In the *Bayeux Tapestry there appears to be a *wyvern standard being carried before the figure of King Harold, who is shown with an arrow in his eye, i.e. at the moment of his death.

Stank. A pond or pool often enough with fish; also a moat, again with fish.

Stannary. Those areas of Devon and Cornwall having tin mines. The stannaries had their own courts, customs and privileges. – *Cf. next*

Stannum. Orig. an alloy of silver and lead. – *Cf. previous*

Staple 1. A town in England or on the continent to which English trade in *wool and other goods was confined. From the reign of Edward I, the first was Dordrecht, followed by Antwerp, Bruges and Middelburg (in Zeeland). In the Statute of Staples (1354) the staple towns under the crown were set as Bristol, Canterbury, Carmarthen, Chichester, Cork, Drogheda, Dublin, Exeter, Lincoln, London, Newcastle, Norwich, Waterford, Winchester and York; from 1392, the continental staple town was fixed at Calais (until Calais was retaken by France in 1558). – *Cf. next*; WOOL

Staple 2. The word was used of a particular fineness and length of wool fibre. – *Cf.* STAMFORT

Statant. *Her.* This term is used to describe an animal shown standing still.

Stationarius. Lit. 'stationer'. A dealer in MSS; particularly one in a university who kept texts, which were hired out for copying. Such MS texts were required to be authenticated by those nominated by a university; were the text found to be inaccurate the stock might well be destroyed. A price list was set and established. Such a dealer was not permitted to sell to anyone who would make a profit by selling on what he had bought. The association of these MS dealers became a *guild in 1403 and was known as The Stationers' Company. [< L *stationarius* = someone stationary, in a fixed place; later = a shopkeeper with a fixed place of business.]

Steelyard. *See* HANSEATIC LEAGUE

Sterling. Term used for the fineness of coins. Once thought to be so called because some coins had a star; another suggested derivation was from *Easterlings, who were coiners brought to England by Henry II to improve the currency. Foreign copies of the English *penny known as 'esterling' were esp. common in the late 13c. In 1213, when King John swore fealty to the pope, he also swore to pay for ever *mille marcas sterlingorum* = 1,000 marks of sterling. Now, however, it is suggested sterling is derived from OE *steor* = firm.

Steward. Official in charge of the daily running of a castle/house; a domestic rather than a military officer, though such duties were taken on in an abbot's household, for instance. The word was also used in combination with 'high', of a person able to advance and protect the interests of a monastery or abbey at court; consequently the holder was a person of noble birth or a lay magnate with influence at court. They were in effect lobbyists. Fees were payable. These were not great sums (perhaps 40s) but held multiply they could be well worthwhile; also being such a steward came with the perk of ample hospitality when visiting his charge. During the reign of Henry I (1100–35) there were perhaps four stewards with the title; at other times there may have been as many as five. They seem to have been verbal, *ad hoc* appointments of the people who actually did the work. The post may also have been at times hereditary; in these cases the person bore the title but probably as an honorary position. Such appointments were begun by the Norman kings; subsequent monarchs did the same. The Scottish surname Stewart relates to the royal steward. – *Cf.* DAPIFER; GREEN CLOTH; SENESCHAL

Stew-pond. A pond or tank in which fish were kept for eating.

Sticha [stica, stick]. A quantity of eels, usually 25.

Stint. Limitation imposed on the rights to pasture and other matters on a *manor; also, as a verb, the simple matter of stopping someone or something. Latterly, it is a measure of quantity or rather a lack of what is considered sufficient. [< OE *styntan* = to dull]

Stipendarius. Latin word used by AN chroniclers for a *mercenary. [< L *stipendium* = wages] – *Cf.* LITHESMAN

Stirk. A young heifer or bullock under two years of age; the word is still in use in the north of England.

Stoc. In placenames, *stoc* = a religious place, a secondary settlement or *cell of a monastery. It occurs in Stoke, for example. [< OE *stoc* = a dwelling]

Stock. Container or box in which cloth was put, where it was beaten in the fulling process. – *Cf.* FULL; SWINGLE

Stole. Ecclesiastical vestment, being a strip of cloth or silk worn around the neck and falling to the knees. [< L *stola* = a cloak-like outer garment]

Stool, groom of the. One of the gentlemen of the privy chamber who served the king in the more private rooms of the palace. It was the groom's duty to empty the royal chamber-pot; this intimacy put him among the most senior of the gentlemen, ranking him below the vice-chamberlain. 'Stole' is found sometimes as a variant spelling. – *Cf. next*

Stool-room. The king's lavatory within the confines of the privy chamber. [< OE *stol* = stool, chair] – *Cf. previous*; EASEMENT ROOM; LONGAIGNE

Stow. A place or locality; also a place with religious or holy associations. – *Cf.* STOC; WÆLSTOW

Stræt. A street, a highway; the surface was often paved, being a relic of Roman construction. When 'street' forms part of a placename, it usually commemorates a Roman road. [< L *strata* = a paved way] – *Cf.* GATE 2

Strætbreche. The offence of digging up a road, or blocking or obstructing in some fashion. The fine payable as compensation was 100s. [< OE *stræt* = road, street + *brece* = break]

Streapeles. Leggings, worn from knee to ankle; breeches. [< OE *strapulas* = leggings] – *Cf.* HODDEN GREY

Stubble-goose. *See* MICHAELMAS GOOSE

Studium generale. Lit. 'general study'. The phrase was used of a university before the word 'university' was coined.

Styca. Northumbrian word for the **sceatta*; the 9c Northumbrian coin was made of silver, zinc and copper. [< OE *stycce* = a piece (of money)]

Subinfeudation. Modern term for the practice of a **vassal having vassals of his own. – *Cf.* ENFEOFF; FEUDALISM; JUDICIUM; MESNE

Subtlety. This word was used of usually sweet cakes and confections, often in the form of table decoration. These were sometimes served between courses. [< L *subtilitas* = fineness of detail]

Succentor. Subcantor. Orig. the person who led the singing of choir and congregation; the deputy of the **precentor; usually a **minor canon.

Succurrendum. *See* AD SUCCURRENDUM

Suit. The obligatory attendance at his lord's court by a tenant. This was known as 'suit of court'.

Sulong. A Kentish measurement equivalent to two hides. – *Cf.* JUGUM

Summagium. Latin word for the obligation to supply pack-horses for carrying loads. Were a **fine paid in lieu of such service, the term *pro summagio* was used. – *Cf.* –AGIUM; SUMPTER

Summoner. Official attached to an ecclesiastical court, whose duty was to bring to court those summoned by the archdeacon for offences against **canon law. By the time Chaucer wrote *The Friar's Tale*, they were regarded as snoops and blackmailers. The Latin for summoner is *summonitor*. – *Cf.* PARDONER

Sumpter. A packhorse; also the driver of a sumpter horse. This was the kind of horse used in great numbers in a **baggage train. Sumpter bears no relation to sumptuary. [< AN *sumer* < L *sagmarius, sagmatarius* = a saddle] – *Cf.* REGALIA

Sumptuary regulations. In Edward III's reign regulations sought to establish rules of dress so as to ensure people did not dress 'above their station'. The law of 1363 condemned 'outrageous and excessive apparel of diverse people, contrary to their estate and degree'. Indeed, these regulations also sought to prescribe the kinds of food appropriate to each **degree. For example, it stated that servants should have only one meal of flesh or fish in the day, and that their other food should consist of milk, butter and cheese. [< L *sumptuarius* = relating to expenditure; *sumptus* = expense] – *Cf. previous*; GARÇONS; MINIVER

Sunneniht. Lit. 'the night before Sunday', i.e. Saturday night.

Supporter. *Her.* Figure used to support an *escutcheon. Usually they were identical, one on each side of the escutcheon.

Surcoat. Outer coat of rich material, also worn over a suit of armour, decorated sometimes with heraldic coats of *arms; later, such a coat worn shortened was one of the signs of knighthood. [< Fr. *sur* = over]

Surtout. *Her.* Describes an *escutcheon placed at the centre of a coat of *arms.

Suspendatur. Lit. 'let him be hanged'. The word indicated a criminal's sentence.

Swan. Swans have been royal birds since the 12c and were served at great feasts. A keeper of the king's swans appeared in the 14c, while a law of 1482 restricted the ownership of swans to men worth more than 5 marks a year. Swans appear as supporters on the Vintners' Company's coat of *arms. The Vintners, as also the Dyers, still mark Thames swans each year by clipping their bills. – *Cf.* SUPPORTER

Swanimote [swainmote]. A court held three times each year before the forest verderers. This court had nothing to do with the birds, the swans; rather, the jurymen were swains employed in the forest, i.e. herdsmen. It was established under the *Forest Charter of 1217, whose purpose was to oversee the pasturing of pigs and cattle in the king's forests; also ensuring animals were cleared at times when they might interfere with the forest's life, e.g. during fawning and the hunting season.

Swans, Feast of the. The occasion at Westminster, on Whit Sunday, 1306, when Edward I knighted his son, the prince of Wales, later Edward II. Almost 300 other young man came to be knighted at the same time. It was a great event, with the old king inspired by chivalric ideals. The feast takes its name from the two swans which were laid on the table, and over which Edward I swore to fight the Scots and infidels in the Holy Land.

Sweating sickness. An often fatal illness, named from one of its symptoms; probably a true influenza. Between 1315 and 1322 there was a series of epidemics accompanied by bad harvests and starvation. At the same time there were outbreaks of *murrain. The result was that a great many people died, perhaps one in five of the population: all that before the next generation was visited by the *Black Death. – *Cf.* AGUE; QUARTAN AGUE

Swingle. Piece of wood, somewhat sword-like in shape, used for beating and scraping flax. The process was similar to the winnowing of grain, removing unwanted particles. A swingle functioned much like a flail. [< OE *swingel* = a whip or rod] – *Cf.* STOCK

Swingletree. A kind of shock absorber of reins and tracers, which equalised the strains when horse and cart changed directions. It was also known later as a whippletree. [< OE *swingle* = piece of wood]

Sylfdema. Lit. 'self-appointed'. One of the four kinds of monk, as described in an AS version of the rule of St Benedict. According to that rule the *sylfdema* had never adhered to any rule nor been taught by a master: they were 'soft as lead'. They went about in twos or threes or even singly 'without a shepherd, not enclosed in the Lord's sheepfold'. They just followed 'the enjoyment of their will instead of a rule; whatever they think fit or choose to do they call holy'. – *Cf.* MYNSTERMON; WESTENSETLA; WIDSCRITHUL

Synod. An assembly of *clergy from a church or diocese. [< Gr. *sunodos* = a meeting]

Synodsman. Layman expected to attend a bishop's *visitation or a *synod.

T

T/O map. A conceptual diagram of the world, with a T-shape within an O creating three parts which represent the three continents, i.e. Europe, Asia and Africa. The O represented the ocean surrounding the world. The perpendicular bar of the T represented the Mediterranean, while the lateral bar represented the river Nile, separating Asia and Africa and the River Dnieper separating Europe and Asia. – *Cf.* MAPPA MUNDI

Tabard. Outer garment made of coarse material worn coat-like by peasants and ordinary town dwellers; later, *c.*1420–50, worn as an open garment by a knight over his armour and displaying his armorial bearings. – *Cf.* SARSENET

Table dormant. Table of fixed position in the hall or main room of a house. Most tables were trestle tables, to be dismantled after use, so creating more space in the main public room. A table dormant implied its owner had ample space and money enough for such a solid piece of work.

Tabor. Small drum used by minstrels as an accompaniment to other musicians. It was an instrument which required little skill but keeping time. It could also be used in conjunction with a fife, played by the same person. [?< *tabira* = Persian drum]

Taeog. An unfree Welsh tenant; equivalent of the English *serf.

Tail. Subsidy or tax levied by the king; an irregular, even, arbitrary impost. The Latin form is *tallium*. – *Cf.* TALLAGE

Taillé. *Her.* Term used to describe a shield divided in half by a line from *sinister *chief to *dexter base.

Taint. Damage or blemish in a hawk's plumage due to poor diet. – *Cf.* ATTAINT 2

Tainus regis. Lit. 'king's *thegn*'. Although *DB* occasionally applies the term to great pre-Conquest landholders subject only to the king, it is primarily used of lesser royal officials, whose expertise was necessary to the incoming Norman administration and who therefore continued to hold land in 1086. These *taini regis* held their lands by *thegnage, a tenure analogous to *serjeanty and soon amalgamated with it. Many 13c serjeanties can be traced back to lands held by *taini regis* in 1086. – *Cf.* THEGN

Tale. Payment by tale was the literal counting out of the coins, rather than by weight. – *Cf.* AD PONDUM

Tallage. Tax imposed by both the Norman and the early *Plantagenet kings upon towns and *demesne lands of the crown. Royal tallages were sometimes imposed before parliament claimed its right of review of money matters. A *villein would also have to pay his lord tallage among other dues. Tallage became the word for any impost demanded by a superior. The Latin is *tallagium*. [< OFr. *taillet* = a subsidy or tax] – *Cf. next;* TAIL

Tally stick. A stick marked with cuts or notches, which indicated payment made, it was then cut in half lengthwise by the talliator so each party to the transaction had a copy of the exchange, in effect a receipt. These sticks were also used as money within departments of the *exchequer for instance. Tally sticks continued in use until 1826. [< L *talea* = a stick] – *Cf. previous*

Talu. An accusation; also a claim, i.e. to a piece of land. [< OE *talu* = statement, claim, action at law] – *Cf.* AGNUNG

Tang. That unseen part of a sword securing it within the handle.

Tanner. A man who tanned skins and hides using tannin (made from bark). He was not permitted to make shoes from his finished work. The Latin is *tannerus*. – *Cf.* CORIARIUS; TAWYER, WHITE

Tappestere. A woman who served drink in an *ale-house; a female tapster. [< OE *tæppian* = to open a cask or barrel] – *Cf.* -ESTERE

Targe. Small round shield, also known as a *'buckler', used by troops on foot.

Tasse [tasset]. That part of a suit of armour making a skirt of scales or over-lapping plates designed to protect hips and thighs.

Tau cross. A (walking) stick with a T-shaped handle carried by a bishop as a sign of his office. [Gr. *tau* = a letter resembling the letter T]

Taw. Verb used for the preparation of leather, esp. without tannin. Such a craftsman was known as a *'tawyer'. From the OE noun *taw* = an implement, the modern 'tool' is derived. Then as now, *taw* and tool, share the same slang reference to the male genitalia. [< OE *tawian* = to prepare, make ready]

Tawdry lace. Cheap goods sold at the annual St Audrey's fair, whose name time garbled into our 'tawdry'. St Audrey (d. 679) was Æthelthryth (Etheldreda), foundress of a double monastery at Ely. – *Cf.* VERNICLE

Tawyer, white [whittawer]. A craftsman who prepared and dressed leather without recourse to tannin – hence the use of 'white'. Instead of tannin, he would use a mixture of alum and salt. The result was a pale or white, soft leather. – *Cf.* TAW

Tealby coins. Hoard of 12c coins found in the Lincolnshire village of Tealby. They were 90 per cent silver pennies, all bearing the name Henry II, and dating between 1158 and 1180. Such coins are named Tealby as those found in the village serve as exemplars. – *Cf.* SHORT-CROSS PENNY

Team. Right of a lord to supervise the vouching for the quality of goods and the presenting of evidence of the right to sell presented goods. [OE *getieman* = to vouch to warranty] – *Cf.* TOLL AND TEAM; VOUCHING TO WARRANTY

Tegnus. *See* THEGN

Teithi. A breeding stallion. It was deemed to be a *teithi* if it could cover two mares in quick succession. At this time, the quality of offspring was thought to be the 'gift' of the stallion, not the mare.

Templars. *See* KNIGHTS TEMPLAR

Temple. The church of the *Knights Templar. The first to be built in England was in Holborn, not far from today's Chancery Lane, then known as New Lane, after they acquired the land in 1130. The church was built with a round nave, after the Holy Sepulchre in Jerusalem. This became known as the Old Temple when a new site was found on the banks of the Thames. The New Temple was consecrated in 1185.

Tempora minutionis. Lit. 'times of lessening'. – *Cf.* BLOOD-LETTING

Temporalities. Used of the lay or secular possessions of the Church, but par-ticularly of those which provided income and revenue for religious establishments and senior clerics such as bishops. [< L *temporalitas* = the temporal world] – *Cf.* DE INTENDENDO; GLEBE; SPIRITUALITIES

Tenant. In this period, the king was the great landlord; from him downwards land was held by tenure with various dues and obligations. A tenant could be duke or peasant. [< L *teneo* = to hold] – *Cf. next;* FEE SIMPLE

Tenant-in-chief [tenant-in-capite]. – In the great chain of feudal allegiance from monarch down to peasant, the tenant-in-chief held his land directly of the king; the Church and earls were all tenants-in-chief. In *DB* the tenants-in-chief were listed at the beginning of each county, each being given a separate section. The term *honour is used of all the fiefs held by a tenant, even if in more than one *county. – *Cf.* ALIENATION; IN CHIEF

Tenement. The holding of land of a lord by freehold or other kinds of tenure; later, any building used as a living accommodation. [< L *teneo* = to hold]

Tenné. *Her.* Tawny or orange-brown *tincture.

Tenser. Someone who lived in a town but who was not a free man, having to pay for the privilege of remaining there. – *Cf. next*

Tenseries. Protection money. During the *Anarchy of Stephen's reign, rebel lords imposed tenseries on towns: arbitrary impositions to raise money. Failure to pay made the towns' people liable to torture or a speedy death. These are mentioned in the *ASC for the year 1137. *Tenseria* was the 12c form. [< L *tenso* = to protect] – *Cf. previous*

Tenter. Frame on which material was secured by hooks so as to dry without shrinkage or loss of shape. From this we have 'on tenter-hooks'. [< L *tendo* = to stretch]

Terce. Third canonical hour of the day for prayer, i.e. 9 am; one of the Little Hours of the divine office. [< L *tertius* = third] – *Cf.* HORARIUM; NONE; SEXT

Termagant. Imaginary god supposed by ill-informed Christians to be worshipped by Muslims.

Termor. A person who held land for a set term, i.e. a number of years or until he died. [< AN *terme* = set period of time]

Terra regis. Lit. 'the king's land'. Phrase used in *DB for all the land still in the king's possession, i.e. that which had not been given to one of his barons or other person in return for services. The term continued in use well into the 12c, when there was still much land held by the king himself. Such land was known as the 'royal *demesne'. However, this was not a static portfolio.

Terrae carucae. Lit. 'plough-lands'. The long, narrow field of the long acre was necessitated by the plough-team of eight oxen. Such rigs were cumbersome and could not turn so neatly as the small team of two animals – or even people – pulling the light plough known as the *aratra*, a plough known to the Romans. The oxen needed more space to turn in, making the 'long acre' a practical solution. – *Cf.* ACRE; ARATURA; CARUCA

Terrae datae. Lit. 'land given'. Broad term used of land which had been granted by the king. The term was used in the *exchequer for accounting for diminished income from the counties via the *sheriff. Land which had been granted to a tenant no longer contributed to the *county *farm.

Terram depopulare. *See* CHEVAUCHÉES

Terrier. List of tenants with details of their various holdings, rents and duties; it later became a detailed record of boundaries and acreages. [< L *terra* = land] – *Cf.* CADASTRAL MAP

Tester 1. Although originally used of the canopy over a bed, it was also used of the canopy or the sounding-board of a pulpit. [< OFr. *teste* = a head]

Tester 2. Head-piece of a suit of armour. [< OFr. *teste* = a head]

Teston. Shilling coin issued by Henry VII.

Teulu. Welsh ruler's household troops, or the royal body-guard, maintained by him, and who fought closely with him and were expected to die with him if need be. – *Cf.* COMITATUS 1

Textura. Modern term for a form of *black letter script used from the mid-14c. Letters were formed by vertical strokes – known as 'minims' – often close together and joined top and bottom, making it difficult to read today. It is most often found in the opening words of charters and inscriptions on monuments. – *Cf.* INSULAR; MINUSCULE

Thack and rape. The thatch cover of a hayrick and the supporting rope ties. [< OE *þæc* = roof]

Thane. *See next*

Thegn [thane]. Originally meaning a servant, the term was applied from the late 9c to members of the AS aristocracy, whose *wergeld* was 1,200s. In Latin texts they were called *ministri*, which carries the same connotations. The standing of a *thegn* depended on that of his lord: one who served the king was a king's *thegn*; one who served a lord other than the king (i.e. bishop, abbot, earl or greater *thegn*) was a median (i.e. middling) *thegn*. All were noble and outranked the *ceorl*; distinctions between them were marked by the amount due as *heriot*. Duties of the median *thegn* were set out in *Rectitudines Singularum Personarum*: 'The law of the *thegn* is that he be entitled to his book-right, and that he shall contribute three things in respect of his land: armed service, and the repairing of fortresses and work on bridges [the *trimoda necessitas]. Also in respect of many estates, further service arises on the king's order such as service connected with the deer fence [*deorhege] at the king's residence, and equipping a guardship, and guarding the coast, and guarding the lord, and military watch, almsgiving and church dues, and many other things.' Such duties were owed by the king's *thegn* to the king himself. The latinised forms are *tainus, teignus*. [< OE *ðegen* = servant, follower] – *Cf.* TAINUS REGIS

Thegnage. The holding of land in return for service; a holder could be a royal officer (*tainus regis*) or a lesser *thegn*. It was analogous to *serjeanty, with which it was amalgamated after 1066.

Thesaurarius. Latin word for a treasurer.

Theta. The Greek letter *theta* was a symbol of death in this period (the Greek for death is *thanatos*). It was also used in the various account books to indicate a cancelled entry. Arab mathematicians recognised its value and incorporated it in the mid-10c as zero, a concept of Indian origin.

Thing. Norse word for a meeting or assembly. The word can be found in placenames such as Thingoe in Suffolk, which comes from the ON *Þinghaugr* = assembly mound, or Tynwald, the still-existing Manx parliament; in Scandinavia and subsequently in England the burial mound of a chieftain was often used as a meeting place.

Third penny. The earl's share of the revenues accruing from his *shire; the other two pennies went to the king.

Thomipeta. Term used of a person going on a *pilgrimage to St Thomas Becket's shrine in Canterbury. [< Thomas + L *peta* = seeker] – *Cf.* JACOBIPETA; ROMIPETA

Thrall. A slave.

Three Orders. A concept common both in England and the continent. It first appears as a developed idea in King Alfred's writing where he says: 'a king must have his land fully manned: he must have praying men (*gebedemen*), fighting men (*fyrdmen*) and working men (*weorcmen*)'. In Latin texts they were *oratores*, *bellatores* and *laboratores* – broadly, monks and priests, warriors and the peasants upon whose labour all depended. This idea was not intended as a literal description of society, rather it was a vision of the ideal community in which all worked together and contributed to the common good.

Thrimsetel. A throne. [< OE *þrim* = glory + *setel* = seat; thus the throne is the 'glory seat'] – *Cf.* SIEGE 1

Thrymsa [trymes]. AS gold or silver coin minted from *c.*630, at first copying Roman style, then after *c.*660 adopting distinctive AS decoration. Though initially issued in gold, by *c.*650 the *thrymsa* was being alloyed with silver; by 675 it was a wholly silver coin. In *c.*1000 the *thrymsa* was equal in value to 3d. [< L *tremis* = a Roman coin]

Thwaite. Naturalised Norwegian word = a clearing in a wood or land reclaimed for arable. It is commonly found for example on the NW coast of England, indicating settlements of Norwegian sailors who came from Ireland. [< ON *þveit*]

Tierce. *Her.* A *charge divided into three equal parts, each differently tinctured.

Tilt. Barrier separating knightly jousters designed to prevent converging horses from colliding with each other. The word came by transference to apply to the sport of jousting; also the place became the tilt-yard. The use of a barrier emerged when jousting was becoming more a sport and display of skill, rather than just practice in an art of war. While still dangerous, the intent was not to cause injury so much as simply to unseat one's opponent and thereby gain praise; indeed points were scored by various hits. It was at this time that *chivalry was becoming self-conscious and tournaments expensive shows. There is a tilt-yard at Kenilworth Castle which may date to Richard I's reign. – *Cf.* RECET

Timber. Term used for a collection or bundle of 40 furs or skins. The Latin word was *timbria*; *tymbris* was also used.

Timbre. *Crest worn on a knight's helmet; also, the crest placed over the heraldic shield.

Timbrel. A popular instrument in this period, very like the modern tambourine.

Tincture. *Her.* Term for a colour, *metal or *fur used in coats of *arms and blazons. [< L *tinctura* = a dye]

Tippet. A long piece of material, like a scarf, or streamer, worn at the neck or arm, sometimes attached to a hood. It was also like a small cape and was worn like a shawl. These latter were worn both by men and women, plain and fancy. In the 19c a 'Tyburn tippet' was the colloquial phrase for the hangman's noose. – *Cf.* TYBURN

Tir gwelyog. *See* GWELY

Tire. Clothing in general; it is a form of 'attire'. Later, in the 15c, 'tire' was used of a fashionable woman's headdress; it was *atour* anglicised.

Tirones. Young men, young soldiers. The Latin word on the *Bayeux Tapestry = *pueri*. At one point Odo, bishop of Bayeux, is shown encouraging them. The word was also used, somewhat later, for the young fighters who hired themselves out as champions in civil duels. As their name suggests, they were young, beginners, tiros; certainly they were unknighted. When hired they would have had servants with them, adding to the costs of their employer. [< L *tiro* = a young soldier, a beginner, a young recruit] – *Cf.* DUELLUM; PUER

Tithe. A tenth part. It referred to the tenth part of the harvest, or general agricultural produce, for the support of Church and clergyman. Tithes were also referred to as 'greater' and 'lesser' tithes: the greater were those of wood, corn, hay; the lesser comprised milling and fishing, salt-making and young animals. – *Cf. next*

Tithing. Orig. one tenth of a *hundred; later, the 10 householders of a *frankpledge. A later Latin word is *decania*. – *Cf. previous*

Tithingman. The leader of a tithing and parish peace officer. – *Cf. previous*

Tod. A measure of weight equal to 28 lb, used in weighing wool. However, such measures were liable to much local variation.

Toft. Site of a homestead and its various outbuildings; a field larger than the space occupied by a house; a small hill in an area of flat land. The word is found in placenames in the East Midlands, e.g. Huttoft (Lincs) = a homestead on a hill-spur, Sandtoft (Lincs) = a homestead on sandy soil.

Toft and croft. A holding comprising both homestead and its associated arable land.

Toison. *Her.* French word used sometimes for a fleece (of a lamb) when used as a *charge.

Toll and team. Term describing wide-ranging rights of a lord. In AS law, 'toll' indicated the lord's right to take payment, i.e. commission on the sale of cattle or goods within his estate. 'Team' indicated the lord's right to take the fines from those accused of stealing cattle; also it indicated the power to oversee the presentation of evidence of the right to sell presented goods. When new town charters were granted, 'toll and team' was usually included from the beginning. It was one of the rights granted in the Charter of the *Cinque Ports of 1155. [< 11c L *teloneum* = toll, tax < Gr. *telos* = tax] – *Cf. next*

Tollere. A tax gatherer. The job is remembered in the name of Tollerton (tollere + *-ton), in north Yorkshire. [< 11c L *teloneum* = toll, tax < Gr. *telos* = tax] – *Cf. previous*

-ton. Placename suffix = homestead. In early examples, the probable meaning = estate, as in numerous instances of Kingston = king's estate. Increasing use of -ton after *c*.900 has been taken to indicate the rise of compact estates in the hands of *thegns*, e.g. Wigston in Sussex = Wigstan's homestead, also Alston, Derbyshire, = Alwine's. From *tun* we have 'town'. [< OE *tun* = fence, hence enclosure round a house, hence homestead, village, town] – *Cf.* -BY

Tonsure. The shaving of the head on acceptance into a religious community, in imitation of Christ's crown of thorns; its style however was a source of contention between branches of the early Christian Church. The Irish tonsure up to the 8c was different – the front of the scalp was shaved. The adoption of the Roman style was a sign of the final dominance of Roman over the Irish or Celtic Church. [< L *tondeo* = to cut or shear]

Torche-cul. Straw for use in a latrine. The phrase can be read in two ways, offering a nice colloquial play on words. *Torche* can mean either a 'torch' for the giving of light for which straw could be used, or as a noun meaning 'wipe'. Thus *torche-cul* means either an 'arse-torch' or an 'arse-wipe'. – *Cf.* LONGAIGNE

Tornatio. Term used for the collision of two knights charging each other, whether in real war or during a *tournament. [< L *tornus* = a turn] – *Cf.* TILT

Torse. *Her.* Wreath-like band of material worn around a helmet. It was useful for identification and could be highly decorative at a *tournament. – *Cf.* COG-NISANCE

Torteau. *Her.* A *roundel *gules, representing a round loaf of bread. [< OFr. *tortel* = cake]

Totus comitatus. Phrase used in charters of earldoms granted by William I to his followers in the great distribution of land following the Conquest = the total or complete rights of an earl. As a *tenant-in-chief, such a lord would not worry about others' powers within his shire, only the king's. Such a *fief would have the power of appointing the *sheriff, the collection of the *third penny, and other matters. The earl might or might not have the right of acting as *justiciar in his shire. Although the phrase suggests a clear-cut set of rights and privileges, in fact each was resolved on its own merits.

Touch. Term used for an assay mark. In a statute of 1423 provincial assay towns were required to have 'divers touches' so that each town could be identified by its touch. All smiths had to add the touch before any item was 'set to sell'. – *Cf.* HALLMARK

Tourn. Circuit of his *county or jurisdiction made by a *sheriff twice each year; the visit of the court to each *hundred. [< OFr. *tourner* = turn, rotate]

Tournaments. Introduced to England as *Conflictus Gallicus*, a tournament was a somewhat chaotic affair, known as a *'mêlée' – from which our use of the word. At first, the mêlée took place in open countryside, with a large number of knights and their attendants. The purpose was to take as many prisoners as possible, in conditions very similar to real conflict, so that they could be ransomed, for substantial sums of money, as well as to capture horse and weapons, expensive items. It was a dangerous business. In time, rules changed, as did the climate of ideas. With the emergence of *chivalry as an ideal, the conduct of tournaments was constrained somewhat. Single combat emerged, in which knights broke lances and scored points, in a joust, before fighting on foot with sword and mace. The Church banned them, seeing them as a waste of energy and lives which could be better used in defence of the Church. In England they were banned by Henry II. However, in Richard I's reign they were permitted under licence. The tournament became fashionable, with lords competing against each other in organising the most elaborate and extravagant shows, both in England and in France. *Prowess in a tournament was good for a man's reputation at court, while also being excellent practice for war. Henry IV was a great hero in England before he took the crown because of his prowess as a jouster. Much of the conduct of tournaments owed a great deal to literature, in particular to Froissart and the Arthurian Cycle. *Turneamentum* was the Latin form; 'tourney' was also used. [< OFr. *tournei* < L *tornus* = turn] – *Cf.* JOUST OF PEACE; JOUST OF WAR

Tourney. *See previous.*

Tow. Cheap coarse hemp or flax for low-quality spinning. Tow was bound on a *distaff which was carried by a woman on her way to the *pillory for punishment. To have 'tow on the distaff' meant one had ample work. – *Cf.* DISTAFF

Tractatus de Legibus et Consuetudinibus Regni Angliae. *Treatise on the Laws and Customs of the Kingdom of England*, c.1188. Attributed to Ranulph de Glanville (d. 1190), this is a text on English common law. Crucially, Glanville concentrated on decisions of justices as a basis for that law, i.e. on *jus*, or on what had been done and decided in the past.

Trailbaston. Violent thugs and bandits – *mercenaries – who hired out their services during the reign of Edward I; later, the ordinances issued to control them. The first commissions of trailbaston were instituted by Edward I in 1304, a time of public disorder. They were intended to deal not only with outlaws but also those who supported them and benefited from their crimes. There is an outlaw's song dating to c.1305 in which the need to bribe sheriffs is lamented. [< trail + baston = a club, thus a person who trails a club; as we say someone's 'knuckles scrape the ground'.] – *Cf.* BASTON; ROUTIER

Traiz. The game of draughts, played in a manner very similar to the modern game. [< OFr. *trait* = a move, in chess or draughts]

Transfluent. *Her.* Term used of water shown flowing through the arches of a bridge.

Transfretation. Modern term for the crossing of the Channel by English monarchs in this period; based on the 12c Latin *transfretatio* = crossing the sea. [< L *trans* = across + *fretum* = a strait or narrow sea]

Translation. The transfer of a bishop between sees; also, the removal of the remains of a saint from one place to another. In this latter case the move was usually to a specially prepared and dedicated shrine, done with solemn ceremony.

Transumpt. Word sometimes used for a copy or transcript of a record or legal document. [< L *transsumo* = to transcribe] – *Cf.* ENGROSS 2

Trapper. *See next*

Trappings [trapper]. The decorated or ornamental cover of a horse's saddle or harness, sometimes with mail beneath; the more elaborate trappings covered the animal completely but for eye-holes and an opening for the muzzle. [< Fr. *drap* = a cover]

TRE. Acronym used in *DB*, being the scribe's shorthand for *tempore regis Edwardi* = in the time of King Edward (the Confessor). *DB* was ordered in 1085 to ascertain contemporary values of land and to compare them with those of King Edward's reign, i.e. in 1065.

Treason. The breaking of allegiance to the crown and state; it often entailed plotting against the reigning monarch, i.e. high treason. 'Petty treason' was the killing of someone owed allegiance. Treason was the favoured charge of convenience used by one court faction to do down another. [< L *trado* = to betray]

Trebuchet. Machine for throwing or catapulting rocks during a siege. The device got its power from a counterweight which, when freed, released an arm which slung a missile. It was more accurate than its cousin, the *mangonel. The trebuchet was used to create further alarm and despondency among those it attacked when human and animal corpses were thrown into the castle or town under siege. [< OFr. *trebucher* = to overturn, to stumble, to overthrow] – *Cf.* CUCK-STOOL

Tree. In many poems and prose texts of this period, the 'tree' had become a symbol of the Cross. By the time of John Wyclif (d. 1384), it had become almost a commonplace. Central to Wyclif's thought was the excessive worldliness of the Church; one of his Twelve Conclusions was set firmly against the use of images 'of tre and ston' – *tre* also signified the Cross, here and in other medieval writing.

Tree of honour. Such a tree served as the place where knights' shields were fixed by way of challenge. Any knight wishing to take up the challenge would tap one or all the shields; terms and time and place would then be agreed for the jousting and fighting on foot. – *Cf.* Clouges; Gauntlet; Pas d'armes

Treflé. *See* Botony

Trefoil. *Her.* Decoration in three parts, as a clover leaf; the word is also used architecturally. [< L *trifolium* = with three leaves]

Trencher. Piece of wood on which meat was carved. The word had orig. been used of the knife which carved. It was also a thick piece of bread which served as a plate and was given to the poor or the dogs when the meal was finished. A mid-15c rhyme describes how to 'cut [venison] in the pasty and lay it on trencher'. [< OFr. *trenchier* = a cut, a cut through] – *Cf.* Manchet 1

Trental. Church term for 30 masses said for the dead. An *obit might specify a number of trentals to be said for a named person; money being bequeathed for trentals. [< L *trentalis* = 30] – *Cf.* Libri memoriales

Trespass. Transgression or offence other than *treason or felony; a civil wrong for which payment might be a redress; particularly an offence against another's property. [< OFr. *trespasser* = to go or pass beyond]

Treuga Dei. *See* Truce of God

Trial by combat [trial by battle]. An aspect of Norman law brought to England by the Conquest of 1066. It was believed that right would always triumph, even in physical contests. The practice had largely died out by the late 13c, though examples can be found as late as the 15c. – *Cf.* Duellum

Trian. *Her.* 'In trian aspect' refers to a figure showing only three-quarters, turned partially forwards.

Tribal Hidage. A document whose purpose and origin are not entirely clear. It comprises a list of assessments, using the *hide as the base unit. These assessments are thought to be for payments of *tribute to an unknown overlord. It is believed to date to the 7c; but the only extant MS is 11c. The 'tribes' enumerated included Mercians, South, West and East Saxons, men of Kent and Lindsey, and many others. However, Northumbrian peoples are not included. This suggests two possibilities: that the *Tribal Hidage* was produced for a Mercian king with no power over Northumbria, or for a Northumbrian king who required no list of his own territory and attendant tributes.

Tribute. Payment by a *vassal to his lord; money (usually) paid to ensure protection, e.g. money paid to Vikings at various times to stop raiding or to ensure peace.

Triduum. The three principal days of Easter, i.e. Maundy Thursday, Good Friday and Holy Saturday.

Trimoda necessitas. Three obligations, i.e. *necessitas*, owed by AS tenants and landholders: armed service in the **fyrd*, the repair of forts and bridge building. These obligations were the only ones ever exempted from any grants of immunities. Sometimes one finds *trinoda* rather than *trimoda*; the English phrase 'common burdens' is also used. [< L *trimoda* = three modes or ways + *necessitas* = obligation] – *Cf.* THEGN

Trinovantum [Troynovant]. Name given to an ancient London by Geoffrey of Monmouth. He claimed that Trinovantum actually meant *Troia nova*, or New Troy. This ties in with the legend of Britain being founded by **Brutus, the great-grandson of Aeneas, after the fall of Troy. – *Cf.* BRUTUS

Trippant. *See next*

Tripping [trippant]. *Her.* Term used of a stag or deer depicted walking and looking to the **dexter side with one front foot poised off the ground. When animals other than deer were shown the term used was **passant.

Triton. *Her.* Triton was one of the minor gods of classical mythology. Heraldically, the word indicated the shell of a sea snail.

Trivet 1. Iron tripod arrangement for holding a kettle or cooking pot over a fire. – *Cf. next*

Trivet 2. *Her.* A charge showing a tripod or a stand with three feet. – *Cf. previous*

Trivium. The three disciplines of grammar, rhetoric and logic, which made up part of scholastic study; the trivium was viewed as preparatory to the more advanced **quadrivium*.

Tron. Weighing machine used in public places, e.g. a market; later, the word came to be used to name a place in a town. The official who weighed goods was known as the *tronator*. [< OFr. *trone* < L *trutina* = a pair of scales, a balance] – *Cf. next*

Tronage. Charge for weighing goods on a **tron; also the right to levy such a charge. The Latin equivalent was *tronagium*.

Trope. A trope was a word or phrase added and sung as embellishment during divine office or the mass. After the 12c, the word was used of a book containing sequences of tropes.

Troubadour. A 11–13c writer of songs about **courtly love and **chivalry in Provençal. [< Fr. *trouer* = to find, invent, compose] – *Cf. next;* FABLEOR; SKALD

Trouvère. The northern equivalent of the **troubadour; from the 11c to 14c *trouvères* were composers of **chansons de geste* and *fabliaux*. The difference in temperament between the two is striking, the Provençal courts being smaller, less powerful, yet wealthier than those of the north. – *Cf.* SKALD

Truce of God. Latin *Treuga Dei,* or *Treva Dei.* In the 10c Wido, bishop of Puy, persuaded knights and peasants to swear to protect Church property and not to plunder. At a more formal level, it can be traced back to the *Synod of Elne in 1027, which suspended all warfare from Saturday night until prime on Monday. This oath-taking spread widely, with the pacific intent deepening until, in theory, there were left only 80 days in any year in which waging war was permissible. To begin with, war was not permitted between sunset on Wednesday and sunrise on Monday of each week; saints' days also were included, as were festivals. The truce lasted during the seasons of Lent and Advent, the three great vigils and feasts of the Blessed Virgin, and those of the 12 apostles and a few other saints. The Synod of Thérouanne decreed a Truce of God in 1063, while the Council of Clermont in 1095 pronounced a truce for all Christendom. Such a truce was impractical, but it grew from a noble impulse. It was precursor to the king's peace in England, where the kind of private warring which occurred on the continent, at which the truce was aimed, was not possible. The avowed purpose of the 'truce' was to prevent Christian from fighting and killing Christian, esp. when there were so many infidels in the world and the Holy Land needed liberation. – *Cf.* FIGHTING SEASON

Truncagium. Latin term for the obligation of some tenures which required the supply and carting of timber. The English form is 'truncage'. [< L *truncum* = a trunk (of a tree)]

Truncheon. Something broken or cut off, a fragment, usually of a spear or *lance; also, the shaft of a spear; the stump of a tree; then a thick stick or cudgel; a staff of office. When, in the 14c the king witnessed a duel at Smithfield or Cheapside, and he threw his truncheon onto the field, it was a sign the duel was to end, usually to prevent a death. – *Cf.* BATON 2

Tucker. A finisher of cloth; someone who fulled and dressed cloth. [< tuck = to fold or flatten] – *Cf.* FULLER

Tufter. Dog trained to drive deer out of cover.

Tumbrel. From the 16c a contraption for the ducking in water of minor criminals, named from the tipping cart which carried and tipped night soil; the sense of earlier usages is not clear. – *Cf.* CUCK-STOOL

Tun. Container of wine holding *c.*200–250 gallons. In 1201, an audit of King John's wine-holdings showed that he had 700 tuns in various palaces, castles and hunting-lodges. – *Cf.* BUTT 1; HOGSHEAD

-tun. *See* -TON

Tunicle. Part of the vestment worn by a bishop next to the *dalmatic during celebration of the *eucharist.

Tunnage [tonnage]. Duty levied on imported wine arriving in tuns or casks, after the 13c.

Turbary, rights of. The right to dig and take turf and peat for fuel. [< OFr. *turberie* < L *turba* = a turf] – *Cf.* RIGHTS OF COMMON

Turret 1. Small tower projecting outwards from the main structure of a castle; later a movable construct to be moved against an enemy gate or wall with troops within, protected from hot oil etc.

Turret 2. *Her.* One small tower on top of another larger.

Twelve Conclusions. Twelve articles, demanding Church reform, which were posted on the doors of Westminster Hall and *St Paul's Cathedral in February 1395 by Lollards. (Cf. Martin Luther's similar action with his theses at Wittenberg in October 1517.)

Tyburn. Stream in London (no longer visible), which gave its name to the place of public execution used from *c.*1300 till the late 18c, from which the gallows are known as a 'Tyburn tree'. Tyburn was near to the modern Marble Arch. [OE *ty* < *tynan* = to enclose + *burn* = a stream]

Tynell. Word used occasionally for the king's household. [?< OE *tynan* = to enclose]

Tywysog. Welsh title, the Latin for which was *princeps*, adopted by Owain Gwynedd (d. 1170). Although he had done homage to Henry II, Owain chose the title *princeps* rather than *arglwydd*, which other Welsh rulers were using in place of *brenin*.

U

Uchelwr. Term for Welshmen who were free landholders. In time the term came to apply to families from whom local leaders were selected; those who considered themselves born to lead. They were similar as a class to the English *probi homines*.

Ullage. Measure of deficiency or deficit, i.e. the amount required to fill a cask or barrel; the quantity of wine needed to make good losses by leakage. The Latin term used in account books was *oillagium*.

Ultima voluntas. Lit. 'last wish'. A person's last spoken words and wishes became their will as certainly as those committed to paper. This was enforceable both in lay courts and Church courts. Church courts had cognisance of many matters we would consider the province of secular courts alone. – *Cf.* ECCLESIASTICAL COURTS

Ultra mare. Lit. 'across the sea', i.e. the continent or most particularly the Holy Land. – *Cf.* TRANSFRETATION

Umbrel [umbril]. The visor of a knight's metal helmet. [< OFr. *ombrel* = shade]

Umbri-wiken. Lit. 'ember-weeks'. – *Cf.* EMBER DAYS

Uncial. Name of a script, which indicated it was 'inch high'; in use from the 4c in Greek and Latin MSS until well after the 16c. The earliest known example of the work of a European monk/scribe was written in uncial *c.*517. The word uncial itself was not known to those who used the script, being coined in the 17c. [< L *uncia* = twelfth part] – *Cf.* INSULAR; MINUSCULE

Undee [undy]. *Her.* Wavy; a wavy, undulating line.

Undersettle. Lit. 'settle under (someone else)'. Term used of the servants and occasional labourers who settled on small plots of land established by enterprising peasants. These plots of land were small and unlikely to have been sufficient for an adequate living.

Unguled. *Her.* Term describing an animal whose hoofs are shown in a *tincture different from that of the body. [< L *ungula* = a hoof] – *Cf.* ANIMÉ; BEQUE; CRINED; MEMBERED; RAMÉ

Unknown Charter of Liberties. Document from *c.*1214/15 which formed some part in the drafting of what became *Magna Carta. Its occasion was possibly the gathering of northern barons at Stamford. It begins with the re-affirmation of the coronation charter of Henry I. It then describes various concessions which King John offered as remedies to the grievances complained of: no arbitrary judgement, amendments to marriage and wardship law, various abuses of relief, restriction on liability for service abroad. These and other matters emerge in the final document known as Magna Carta. The original document is in the Archive Royaume in Paris.

Unnithing. An honest man, someone not dishonest, not a rogue, not a *nithing. It is used in *ASC* for 1087, when William Rufus was calling for soldiers before besieging Rochester during the rebellion of his half-brother, Odo, bishop of Bayeux.

Unræd. Lit. 'unwise, unguided, ill-advised'. The word was used of Æthelred II because of his apparent inadequacies as ruler in the face of the Viking threat.

Urdee [urdy]. *Her.* A cross pointed at the ends.

Ursinarius. *See* BEARWARD

Usher. There were several ushers in the royal household, attached to various departments. For example, the usher of the (king's) chamber was responsible for making the king's bed.

Usucapion. Title to property through long possession, *per usucapionem.* *Bracton said 'dominion of corporeal things' could be achieved 'by long, continuous and peaceful possession: by time and without livery, but how long that time must be is not specified by law but left to rightly exercised discretion'. He also specified two other paths to possession of corporeal things as being by *livery and title.

Usufruct. Modern term for the use and enjoyment of the income from a piece land with the proviso that it should not be damaged or diminished. Thus land given as a loan conveyed the usufruct, not the land itself. [< L *usus* = use + *fructus* = fruit; thus, use of the fruits.] – *Cf.* PRECARIUM 2

Usury. OE law stated that any compensation for lending money, i.e. interest or making a profit from lending, was usury; later the word was applied to excessive interest rates. The Greek word for 'interest' was *tokos* = offspring. From this, usury was thought of as the breeding of money from money and therefore against nature and forbidden to Christians. Some members of the Jewish community became immensely wealthy by lending money. They also enjoyed special protection of the crown, as on their death the crown took possession of unpaid notes and therefore of monies yet to be paid. Christian lenders from Lombardy got round the proscriptions against interest by making 'charges' for services rendered. Frequently, interest charges of whichever kind of up to 60 per cent and more were imposed. One way of by-passing the problem of usury was by this means: a knight borrows money, which will be repaid on three successive Easter days. The note specifies £30 but the knight promises to pay 10 marks three times. Thus, if he fails to repay the actual loan of 30 marks, he is bound to pay £30, which gives the lenders interest of 33.3 per cent. A more concrete example is that of Henry IV. Over the course of his reign, Henry borrowed as much as £150,000, or rather, he signed notes to that value. What he actually received was only £130,000: thus 'charges'. A 14c quotation sums up a deep anxiety about borrowing money and payment of interest: 'He who taketh usury goeth to hell; he who taketh none liveth on the verge of beggary.' It is no surprise that the papacy and English monarchs were always in debt. – *Cf.* SCACCARIUM AARONIS

Utrum. An *assize of *utrum* was called by a writ to determine the status of the holding of a property of land, as to whether it had lay status or not. [< L *utrum* = whether]

V

Vaccary. Farm with dairy cows or cattle. In the 13–14c, many of these were to be found in Yorkshire and Lancashire, on land not suitable for arable crops. [< L *vacca* = a cow]

Vadia guerre. Lit. 'war wages'. These were essentially accounts itemising the payroll of the army, listing all who had received money and how much. They were organised by retinue within the army, containing summaries of all personnel with information such as each man's length of service. *Pono ad vadia* = to put on the payroll. These account *rolls can now be found in the Public Record Office and the British Library. [< *vador* = to accept sureties + *guerre* = war] – *Cf.* REGARD

Vadimonia. Broadly, a pledge or guarantee. When charters were given to towns by the king, they confirmed all previous grants, privileges and lands, freedom from taxes and other benefits. *Vadimonia* was included in such a charter, confirming all lands mortgaged to the town. [< L *vadio* = to give surety or security]

Vair 1. The fur of a squirrel; its grey and white was used as distinctive decoration. – *Cf.* MINIVER

Vair 2. *Her.* One of the chief *furs, with alternating azure and *argent bell shapes. – *Cf.* COUNTER-VAIR; ERMINE 1

Valance. Piece of material attached to an altar cloth and which hung downwards; also used around the bottom of a bed, to conceal the space beneath.

Valettus. A post of close attendance on the king, given to those young and well-born. It could include duties such as making the king's bed, though this would not have been deemed demeaning. It was a post Geoffrey Chaucer filled for King Edward III. – *Cf.* COMMENSALIS

Vallate. Being encircled by a *rampart or wall. – *Cf.* BIVALLATE

Valor. Lit. 'value'. In the 14c, particularly after the *Black Death, the lords of large honours began to have estimates drawn up of just how much ought to be produced yearly by a *manor. It was an annual means of checking that there was no theft or incompetence at work, diminishing the land's productiveness and value, particularly if the manor was not the *caput honoris*. – *Cf.* VIEW

Vambrace 1 [avawmbrace, vantbrace]. Piece of armour for the fore-arm, in tubular or part-tubular form, made either of metal or of *cuir-bouilli*. [< OFr. *avant* = before + *bras* = arm] – *Cf.* BRACER

Vambrace 2. *Her.* An arm sheathed in armour.

Vamplate. The circular plate – of leather or metal – attached to a *lance intended to protect the hand or deflect an opponent's weapon.

Varlet. A lowly servant, a menial; a young boy acting as a groom; an attendant on a knight. Only in the 16c did the word acquire negative connotations. – *Cf. next*

Varlet des chiens. Hound or dog handler. This was the first position in which a boy interested in hunting might make a career for himself. He would handle the hounds for a senior aide. – *Cf. previous;* AIDE DE LA VENERIE; LYMER

Varvel. Metal ring attached to a hawk's *jess, so connecting it to the leash.

Vasconicus. Latin form of Gascon; found in *Rotuli Vasconie*, the *rolls recording royal correspondence with Gascony.

Vassal. Person holding land of a lord to whom he owed loyalty and homage; the most onerous duty was military service, with various payments due to the lord on specified occasions such as the lord's daughter's marriage. [< L *vassallus* = a servant or retainer]

Vasta. Lit. 'waste (land)'. References in *DB* to *vasta* have been taken to refer to land laid waste by William I's armies, e.g. in Sussex before the Battle of Hastings, and Yorkshire after the *harrying of the North. 'Waste', however, can also indicate land which did not produce an income (for example, because it was exempt) or for which no information was forthcoming.

Vauntmure [vaumure]. An outer wall, one set well in front of a main fortified wall. [< OFr. *vaunt* = forward + *mure* = wall] – *Cf.* VALLATE

Vavasour. A freeman holding land of a *baron, thus ranking below him. In a list in *LHP* of the kinds of people who should attend a *county court – the shire moot, held twice a year – the vavasour is included alongside such men as the *reeve (*praepositus*) and *steward (*praefectus*), implying a distinct place for him in the medieval order – a middle ranker. [?< L *vassus vassorum* = vassal of vassals]

Vellum. Skin of a calf, treated so as to be suitable for writing on. Something like 120 animals were killed to provide sufficient skins to be turned into vellum for an illuminated *codex of the Bible. Skins of the 12c are often yellower than those of later dates as a weaker lime-water solution was used in the bleaching process. [< OFr. *vel* = a calf]

Venalis locus. Lit. 'a place where things are for sale'. The Latin term used in some charters to indicate a market.

Venerable. Title conferred on archdeacons and clerics worthy of great respect, e.g. Bede; also conferred in the Roman Catholic Church on those who are past the first step towards canonisation. [< L *venerari* = to venerate]

Venire facias. Lit. 'may you cause to come'. A writ issued to a *sheriff instructing him to summon a jury; writs issued to summon knights and burgesses to *parliament in 1275 were *venire facias.*

Ventail. *See* AVENTAIL

Venture. Adventure. 'Venture' was used in the 14c as a sophistical synonym for *'tournament', when these were banned by royal decree. The Latin word *fortunium* was used of ventures, as well as of good fortune.

Verderer [verder]. Officer of the crown who imposed *forest laws. – *Cf.* SWANIMOTE; VERT AND VENISON

Verdoy. *Her.* A border with flowers and leaves and fruit. [< OFr. *verd, vert* = green] – *Cf.* VERT

Verge. The verge was that area which stretched for 12 miles around wherever it was the itinerant royal household happened to be; because the household was always on the move, the boundaries of the verge were constantly moving. The marshal of the household was in charge of discipline of the royal staff; further, he had the right to try all crimes which occurred within this area. – *Cf. next;* CLERK OF THE MARKET; MARSHALSEA

Verge, court of the. The legal arm of the royal household, its jurisdiction defined by the *verge. Throughout the 14c there were serious problems created by the *steward exercising his authority in ways felt to be beyond his writ. He would, for instance, impose fines on towns when a single trader had breached the *assize. Another anomalous circumstance occurred when the royal household was in London. The city of London complained that criminals were crossing the river to Southwark, thus placing themselves beyond the city's reach because the court and *marshalsea claimed jurisdiction there. – *Cf. previous;* CLERK OF THE MARKET

Vermeil. Vermillion. – *Cf. next*

Vermillion. The colour derived from *cinnabar.

Vernicle. A portrait of Christ's head as it was said to have been imprinted on St Veronica's handkerchief, which she used to wipe his face on his way to crucifixion. [vernicle = corruption of Veronica + -le acting as a dim.] – *Cf.* TAWDRY LACE

Vert [Her.; orig. verd]. The *tincture green. Use of the word is one sign of the persistence of spoken French in England. [< OFr. *verd* = green] – *Cf.* VERDOY

Vert and venison. The greenery and deer of the king's forest. Special courts were established to protect the greenery on which the deer fed, thus, for example, excluding pigs even in the autumn from feeding on beech mast. From the time of the Norman kings, forests in England were fiercely protected to ensure the king's hunting was unimpaired, and the forests stocked with plenty of venison on the hoof. – *Cf.* KING'S VERT; VERDERER

Vertant. *Her.* Adjective for a *charge which is curving or bent. [< L *verto* = to turn]

Vespers [evensong]. One of the day's canonical hours of prayer, vespers is for the early evening. – *Cf.* HORARIUM

Vestiarius. Latin term for the keeper of the *king's wardrobe. – *Cf. next;* HRÆGLTHEGN

Vestiary. A wardrobe for storing clothes, e.g. of the king or in a monastery. [< L *vestiarium* = a clothes' chest or cupboard] – *Cf. previous*

Vexillatores. Latin word for the banner-bearers in *miracle plays. When such plays were put on in the streets, these banner-bearers would go ahead and banns were read announcing the subject of the scenes to follow. [< L *vexillum* = a standard]

Via Francigena. Lit. 'the French way or road'. From the 10c the routes – of which there were many – taken by pilgrims from north-west Europe to Rome. – *Cf.* ROMIPETA

Viander. The man or officer who provided victuals or viands in a household.

Viator. *See* CURSORES

Vicar. A person who represents another, i.e. the rector in a parish being God's representative; these duties were carried out for the *benefice or part thereof. [< L *vicarius* = substitute]

Vice [vis]. A spiral staircase. This word was also used of the screw mechanism of the early printing press. [< Fr. *vis* = a vine, thus like the twisting tendrils of the vine.]

Victum vel stipendum. Lit. 'victuals and/or stipend', i.e. wages. Latin term for payments made to soldiers of the *fyrd. It seems likely the *victum* element was paid in cash before the soldier went away, while the stipend, as wages, was paid on his return. These payments were made under the obligation of localities to support a set number of soldiers called to serve in the *fyrd. – *Cf.* VADIA GUERRE

Vidimus. An authenticated, witnessed, copy of a document. [< L *vidimus* = we have seen]

Vielle. Stringed instrument played with a bow; but also a hurdy-gurdy, which required different skills.

View. Term used for the intermediate audit of a *manor or estate of a lord for one of many reasons. It might have been felt that money was not being properly accounted for, that there were problems with leases. Such a visit would have been at the instigation of a *receiver, delegated to his *steward and perhaps accompanied by an auditor. – *Cf.* VALOR

Vigilium. Latin term for a small group of the king's bodyguards.

Vignette. Decorative design on the page of a book based upon vine leaves; any curvilinear design frequently found in illuminated MSS; later a small scene with one or two figures at the bottom of a page but without a border. [< OFr. *vigne* = vine] – *Cf.* CROCKET

Viking. Scandinavians who raided Britain and the continent from the 8c to the 11c. At much the same time, traders and raiders set out from Sweden and moved into modern Russia. In Russian chronicles, these 9c Swedish Vikings were referred to as Varangians. The first recorded Viking attack in England was on Lindisfarne in 793; their first on mainland England was in Lindsey in 841. 'Viking' always implies raiding, but many Norsemen were (also) traders and farmers. Countless settlements were made in the East Midlands of England by Danes, while Norwegians, navigating from so much further north, favoured the western isles of Scotland and Ireland. Vikings began settling in eastern England in 877, though armies had over-wintered many times, e.g. at Repton in 873–4. From this time the *Danelaw really emerges into English history. [OE *wicing* = pirate]

Vill. The smallest unit of administration; equivalent to today's parish. There are some 13,000 vills named in *DB*.

Villata. The body of villeins of a particular *manor. It was the *villata* which elected the *reeve. – *Cf.* HOMAGE 2

Villein. Peasant occupying land subject to a lord. He was effectively tied to the land and the *manor, and not permitted to leave without permission. [< L *villa* = a farm] – *Cf. next;* BONDUS

Villeinage. Tenure by which a villein held his land; it was known as 'tenure by villeinage' or 'in villeinage'. The Latin form used was *villanagium*. – *Cf. previous;* BONDUS

Vintinary [vintiner]. A commander of 20 soldiers. [< L *vintinarius*] – *Cf.* CENTENER; DECURIA

Vintry. A district in the city of London where the vintners lived and stored their wine imports. [< AN *vintner* < L *vinum* = wine]

Virgate. Measure of land of approx. 20 to 30 acres; one quarter of a *hide; an English yardland. [< L *virga* = a (measuring) rod] – *Cf.* FARTHINGLAND; YARDLAND

Virole. *Her.* A ring which encircles a hunting horn or bugle.

Virtue. Medieval theology asserted there were three theological virtues: faith, hope and charity (I Corinthians); there were also four cardinal (Christian) virtues: justice, prudence, temperance, fortitude.

Viscount. Orig. an official (*vicomte, vicecomes*) representing a count or duke, esp. in 11c Normandy. In 12c England, *vicecomes* was used in Latin sources as the equivalent of *sheriff. In the later medieval hierarchy, a viscount was of noble birth ranking below an earl but above a *baron. [< L *vice* = in place of + count]

Visitation. A bishop's visit to one of the religious houses within his jurisdiction. It was intended as an examination of how the order's rules were or were not being observed and how well the monastery was functioning. Such tours of inspection were made every three years or so. Evidence and disclosures (*dicta* and *detectiones*) were taken: anything from ill-prepared food to ill-managed finances to the name of the abbot's mistress – all were known as *detecta. [< AN *visitacioun* < L *visitatio* = a visit of inspection, a visitation] – *Cf.* COMPERTA

Visor 1. The front of a helmet of a suit of armour with openings to see through, later able to be raised. [< OFr. *vis* = a face] – *Cf.* AVENTAIL; MISERICORD 1; UMBREL

Visor 2. *Her.* A *charge whose placing indicated rank.

Vitri historiales. Lit. 'storytelling windows'. Term used for the stained-glass windows depicting biblical figures or stories. They were very important in a world of illiterates in the telling of biblical stories but could be expensive, costing up to 2s each.

Vivum gagum. Lit. 'living gage or pledge'. A form of loan which was repaid by e.g. handing over the proceeds of the crop from an estate. It differed from a mortgage, where both interest and principal must be repaid, because the *vivum gagum* required only the principal to be paid – interest being illegal – while property was held as surety only until the debt was repaid. This ensured that the land pledged would eventually be returned. The *vivum* could also discreetly conceal interest payments. A mortgage is a dead (Fr. *mort* = dead) pledge. [< L *vivum* = living + *gagum* = gage i.e. pledge] – *Cf.* GAGE; USURY

Voider. A piece of armour to protect parts of the body unprotected by the main pieces, e.g. knee and elbow. So named because a voider kept things away.

Voire. Lit. 'in truth, indeed'. Answer made e.g. when doing homage to the French king. Thus in June 1329, Edward III said *Voire* = Truly, when doing homage for Aquitaine to King Philip of France.

Volant 1. An additional piece of armour used to protect the face.

Volant 2. *Her.* Flying, e.g. birds in flight with wings spread.

Vorant. *Her.* Term used when the *charge is a fish or dolphin swallowing a fish. *Engoulant* is a synonym. [< L *voro* = to devour] – *Cf.* ENGOULED

Vouching to warranty. Term for the process under which sellers of goods were required to provide assurances that their wares had been acquired honestly, thus protecting buyers against criminal charges should the goods prove to have been stolen. – *Cf.* TEAM

Voussoir. The wedge-shaped stones which form an arch. [Fr. *voussure* = a curve]

Vow. A promise made to God voluntarily; a solemn commitment to do or not do something, e.g. a vow of chastity taken after the death of wife or husband was not uncommon in the 13c and after. Monks took three vows: the vow to poverty was against the deceits of the world; that to chastity was against the lusts and disturbances of the flesh; that to obedience was against the tricks and snares of the devil. – *Cf.* INCONTINENCE

Vowess. A woman who took a vow of chastity. Usually, such women were widows; however sometimes such a vow was taken within a marriage. One part of the vow was thereafter to wear plain, modest clothes, long and black to conceal her shape, as well as hands and feet. (These resembled nuns' habits.)

Vulgate. Lit. 'in common use'. A 17c term used of the *Bible as translated into Latin by St Jerome and completed in 405; its 'commonness' comes from its widespread use, not its language. The text was that found in almost all Latin quotations from the Bible during this period. Its translation into English was at the heart of Lollardy and the Reformation in England: the Church resisted what it saw as a weakening of its authority were everyone able to read the Bible and think for themselves. The Douai Bible is a translation of the Vulgate text. [cf. L *vulgaris* = commonplace, of the people]

Vulgus. Latin word used in documents for the 'Commons' of parliament. Later the word came to be applied to the general public. [< L *vulgus* = the common people]

Vuln. *Her.* A wound. [< L *vulnus* = a wound]

W

Wælreaf. The offence of stripping a dead man of his clothing or arms, whether or not he was buried. [< OE *wæl* = dead body + *reaf* = plunder]

Wælstow. The field or place of slaughter. The phrase is used in **ASC* after a battle. [OE *wæl* = slaughter, the dead + *stow* = place] – *Cf.* STOW

Wafery. That part of a large household where wafers and sweet biscuits etc. were made.

Waif and stray. A piece of live property – cow or sheep – found without an apparent owner, which became the lord of the *manor's if it was not claimed within a customary period of time.

Wainage. Implements required by a *villein to carry out his work; also the wagons and team of an estate. When a man was amerced, the amount was judged according to his station but his wainage was exempt from confiscation. *Bracton compared the villein's wainage with a merchant's merchandise, which was also exempt from amercement. This was intended to ensure that a man could still earn a living after punishment. [< AL *wainagium*]

Wait. A minstrel or musician of a band in the service of a city, such as London, rather than the king or magnate. They were provided with a *livery and badge to wear, and played at local festivals and fairs.

Waita. A castle watchman's fee; not a high-ranking post; perhaps akin to the porter in the opening scene of *Macbeth*. – *Cf.* WARDA CASTRI

Wake. Lit. 'vigil, watch'; also, a celebration. Annual festival in a parish; orig. on the feast of the local church's patron, and occasion for having a holiday, for village sports, dancing, etc. Still used in northern England of annual holidays.

Wakefield plays. Collection of 32 plays dating from *c*.1425. A MS still extant is dated to 1485 by evidence of the handwriting. It would seem that these plays were part of a cycle put on by crafts of the town; this is deduced from the headings given to several of the plays. For example, one is headed 'lyster play', a lyster being a dyer; another is called 'barkers', another 'glover', a fourth 'fysher'. Several of the plays were taken from the York cycle; but the treatment is somewhat different. There is, however, distinct textual evidence for one particular writer, known today as the Wakefield Master. He wrote five plays using a distinctive long stanza, and more alliteration than elsewhere in the collection. The master's contributions included *Noah* and *Magnus Herodes* (Great Herod) or the Innocents; also two *Pastores* plays, i.e. concerning the shepherds. In Bethlehem, one of the shepherds addresses the Christ child: 'Hail, little, tiny mop [child]/ Of our creed thou art crop [complete, come to fruition]'. – *Cf.* CHESTER PLAYS; MIRACLE PLAY; MYSTERY PLAY; YORK PLAYS

Wales. *See* WELSH

Walker. Surname derived from the work of the *fuller, who 'walked' on his cloth.

Wallia. Latinate form of Wales, used for example by Matthew Paris on his map of Britain *c*.1250.

Walton Ordinances. 1338. These were a set of instructions drawn up for the administration of the kingdom while Edward III was away, fighting in France.

Wand. A Sussex measure of land = 10 yokes = *c*.500 acres. The Latin form is *wendus*. – *Cf.* RAPE 1

Wands. *Her.* The gathered branches of an osier.

Wanlace. *See* WINDAS

Wapentake. Term used in the *Danelaw for a division or subdivision of a *county; also the court of such a division; equivalent to a southern English *hundred. 'Wapentake' = literally a 'weapon take', i.e. a place to which arms were not taken, only being taken up after the meeting.

War rides. *See* CHEVAUCHÉES

Warble. Falconer's term for the bird's crossing its wings across its back when settling on its perch.

Ward. Section or division of a town or city which had its own *alderman and court. In London there were 24 wards, each of which had its own court. A *wardmoot was similar in function to the court of a rural *hundred. The duty of a watchman/sentinel was 'to hold ward'. [< OE *weard* = watch] – *Cf.* WATCH

Warda castri. Lit. 'castle guard'; abbr. sometimes as *warda*. One of the duties owed by a tenant by way of his knight service, another of which, for example, was *equitatio*. The knights of an *honour would have shared duties of castle guard; they might well have had the duty of guard at a king's castle such as Windsor. This latter would have arisen through their lord's *servitium debitum*. However, as with *scutage, such duty could have been commuted to a money payment. – *Cf.* WAITA

Wardmoot. The *moot or court which served a *ward; its function was similar to rural courts. In the city of London, the wardmoot was a meeting of the liverymen of a ward. – *Cf.* WARD

Ward-penny [guard-penny]. A payment made in lieu of performing guard duty. The Latin form was *warpenna*.

Wardship. A lord's right to and lucrative control of the *fief of a dead lord whose heir is a minor; in such an event the revenues of the estate were the guardian's to use as he wished. The fief was supposed to be handed over to the ward in good condition. In many cases, the wardship was bought, often from the king. [< OE *weard* = watch]

Warranty. A pledge or guarantee. Legal obligation taken on by a lord when *homage had been made by a man on becoming seised of land or an estate. Homage incurred the obligation of protection, and should the lord fail in this, the warranty obliged the lord to grant an *escambium* by way of replacement. By the end of the 12c, such a warranty was transferable by inheritance from lord to inheriting son. The word is a variation of guaranty. – *Cf.* SEISIN

Warren. Land reserved for the rearing of game; also, land set aside for rearing rabbits. Free warren = the right to have game, also to hunt game.

Warrener. A man or servant in charge of a *warren, esp. a rabbit warren.

Wastel. Bread made from the finest flour. There were three degrees or qualities of wheat, best, second, and third. Wastel has nothing to do with waste. [< OFr. *guastel*] – *Cf.* ASSIZE; PILLORY; SIMNEL BREAD; TORTEAU

Watch. The keeping guard and maintenance of order in a town or borough during the night. – *Cf.* WARD

Wattle. Stakes interwoven with twigs/branches to make a fence or wall; also wattle and daub = the use of mud and clay 'daubed' on a wattle wall.

Wax-scot. One of the compulsory payments required of parishioners since AS times. As its name suggests, it was to pay for candles, the lights of the church or chapel. The Latin form is *ceragium* – *Cf.* SOUL-SCOT

Way-going crop. The crop allowed to a tenant upon leaving land he has rented.

Weald. *See* WOLD

Wealh. OE for a Welshman; the plural *wealas* gives modern English 'Wales'. – *Cf.* WELSH

Wealhgerefa. Lit. 'Welsh *reeve', i.e. the administrator required perhaps to collect taxes from the Welsh. He was also probably required to patrol and maintain the Welsh border. The word is found in *ASC* for 897.

Webbe. A weaver; the female form is webster.

Wedd. A pledge or security. The word was used also in *wedd-brother* meaning a pledged brother, akin to blood brotherhood but without the blood pledge. A *wedd-loga* was someone who broke their troth or pledge. – Cf. GAGE

Weld. A plant of the mignonette family, *Reseda luteola*, used as a source of yellow for dyeing purposes.

Welsh. Modern form of the name used by the AS for the people of Wales (which like Walach and Vlach is derived ultimately from the Germanic word meaning 'foreign' or 'foreigner'). *Waleis*, the AN form, is still found in the Scottish name Wallace. Wales was one of the places the ancient or native Britons migrated to or were driven to (Cornwall and Brittany were other refuges). [< OE *Wealh/Walh*] – Cf. BRITONS; WEALH

Wendus. *See* WAND

Wergeld [weregild]. Lit. 'man payment'. AS custom and law valued people in pecuniary terms according to their rank. For example in Mercia a *ceorl*'s life was worth 200s; a *thegn* was worth 1,200s; an *earl, next below the king, was worth 6,000s. In the years immediately following the Conquest of 1066, *wergeld* was applied to Normans killed by the English. If a Norman was killed but no killer found, then the *hundred had to come up with the appropriate sum. This applied also if the identity of the murder victim was unknown – the assumption by the Normans being the victim might be one of their own, while an extra penalty could not do much harm and it might discourage violence. During William I's reign when *wergeld* was being paid, the value of a horse if part of the payment was set at 20s. In the charter given to London by Henry I a citizen of the city was worth 100s. The Latin form was *weregeldum*. – Cf. BLOODWITE; FEUDALISM; MURDRUM; SARHAD; SIXHYNDE

Westensetla. Lit. 'settler in the wilds'. One of the four kinds of monk, as described in an AS version of the rule of St Benedict. According to that rule, these hermits or anchorites were experienced in religious life and were not full of a beginner's fervour. Through probation in a monastery they learned with the help of others to fight the devil, and were well prepared for 'the single-handed combat of the wilderness . . . against the vices of the flesh and their evil thoughts'. [< OE *westen* = waste, wilds + *setla* = settler] – Cf. MYNSTERMON; SYLFDEMA; WIDSCRITHUL

Westminster, Council of. 1138. At this council, summoned by the austere Cluniac cardinal, Alberic, *sumptuary regulations for nuns were tightened. They were forbidden to wear any furs – *vair, *gris, *sable, *ermine – except pelisses, or pilches, which were plain unadorned lamb or goat skin or cloth so lined.

Westminster, Provisions of. 1259. Under these terms Henry III surrendered control of government to a baronial council with an agenda of institutional reform. The provisions were both revised and reissued by the king in 1263, while a further revision in 1267 produced the Statute of *Marlborough.

Wethersilver. Customary rent, orig. payment of a wether (a castrated ram) to the landlord's flock; later commuted to a payment of silver coin. – *Cf.* ALBA FIRMA

Wheel. *Her.* This *charge was a Catherine wheel, after that on which St Catherine was martyred in the 4c. The heraldic wheel, like the original, was shown with curved spikes.

Whiffler. An attendant who carried a battle axe or spear; one who used a spear or staff to clear a way through a crowd. [< OE *wifel* = a javelin]

Whippletree. *See* SWINGLETREE

Whitby, Synod of. 664. The calculation of the date for *Easter was a fractious issue in the early Western Church, there being two 'schools' of calculation, the Irish and the Roman. At Whitby the issue was finally resolved in favour of the Roman mode after Bishop Colman lost the debate and withdrew to Iona. This permitted a reorganisation of the English Church by Theodore, archbishop of Canterbury.

White City. London was known as the White City *c.*1420. The name came from the almost universal use of lime-wash (a preservative) on the outside of buildings. The White Tower was aptly named. Indeed care for its exterior was such that gutters collecting rainwater were designed to ensure rain did not splash out of them, spoiling the whiteness of its great walls.

White Ship. This ship sank with great consequences for the English throne on 25 November 1120 while leaving port to cross the Channel to England. The crew were mostly drunk, as was the captain. Many members of the royal household were on board and perished, chief among them being William the Ætheling, son of Henry I and heir to the throne. The death of young William left the kingdom without an heir apparent; Henry's attempt to make his daughter Matilda his heir resulted in civil war.

Whitebeam. Two varieties are of interest here: the common whitebeam (*Sorbus aria*), and Swedish whitebeam (*S. intermedia* = *S. suecica*). They bear distinctive white flowers and their leaves are generally lighter than other deciduous trees such as beech, birch, oak. The underside of the whitebeam is particularly light in colour and distinctive. They are thought to have been used as markers or borders of territory, their leaves' light colouring being clear at a distance. – *Cf.* HAW

Whitsun. The holiday and festival days celebrating Whit Sunday or *Pentecost. Parishes celebrated with games and much *scot-ale. The word is OE *Hwita Sunnandæg*, i.e. White Sunday. The first component 'Whit' (white) comes from the custom of the newly baptised wearing white robes; '-sun' is an abbr. of 'Sunday'. – *Cf.* DOMINICA IN ALBIS

Whittawer. A white tawyer; known in Latin as *tannator albus*. – *Cf.* TANNER; TAWYER, WHITE

Wic. *See* WYCH

Wicgerefa. A town *reeve; also the chief officer of London in the 7c and later. – *Cf.* HIGH REEVE

Wich. *See* WYCH

Wick. A house or place to live; later, a village or hamlet. This word is also found in placenames as the place where certain food was grown, e.g. Berwick = a barley farm, Chiswick = a cheese farm. [< OE *wic* = dwelling, house < L *vicus* = village, a street of houses, a living place] – *Cf.* BERE; WYCH

-wick. Suffix indicating possession of a post or office, e.g. *bailiwick. [< OE *wice* = office, function] – *Cf.* WICKNER

Wickham. A settlement in some way connected with an old Roman *vicus*, e.g. Wickham in Essex. [< OE combination of *wic*(k) + *ham*] – *Cf. previous*

Wickner. *Bailiff, steward; the collector of a lord of the *manor's dues, i.e. rents and fines. The Latin form is *wikenarius*. [< OE *wicnere* = bailiff, steward]

Widscrithul. A wandering monk. One of the four kinds of monk, as described in an AS version of the rule of St Benedict. The *widscrithul* was the monk who spent his life wandering about, staying in different *cells for a few days at a time, always wandering, 'given up to pleasure and the evils of gluttony, and worse in all ways than the self-appointed ones', i.e. the *sylfdema*. – *Cf.* MYNSTERMON; WESTENSETLA

Wifle. A battle axe, javelin or spear. – *Cf.* WHIFFLER

Wimple. Headdress worn by women from the 12c to 14c. How much of the forehead was visible or not was for a while a measure of modesty – or immodesty: hair was removed so as to move the hair-line back. The wimple was also used by nuns until recently. Apart from its first use as a lay woman's headwear, wimple was also used as a verb meaning 'to veil'. [< G *wimple* = *pennon] – *Cf.* ATOUR

Winchester, Council of. Held at Easter 1070, at which Stigand, archbishop of Canterbury, was deposed. It decreed that a canon may not be married, but priests in villages need not send away their wives.

Winchester, Treaty of. November 1153. Drawn up between King Stephen and Henry, duke of Normandy and Aquitaine, before becoming king as Henry II. It resolved the issues of Stephen's hold on the English throne and the succession. Conflict during Stephen's reign had begun with Henry's mother. Matilda, who had challenged the king in support of her son's claim to the throne. By 1153, England had been through the *Anarchy. Various other matters were included in the treaty, which attempted to undo the many ills and seizures of property during that time. What it did do was to settle the succession on Stephen's death and ensure there would be no conflict over that succession. – *Cf.* WHITE SHIP

Windas. A small winch-link mechanism for setting a crossbow to fire.

Windle. A measure of grain equal to three bushels.

Windmill. Windmills first appeared in England in the 1180s. They were a source of power for grinding corn and also for fulling mills. Windmills were found in places where there were few or no fast-flowing streams and rivers which could be used for water power, i.e. mostly in the eastern counties. There is some evidence that the first appeared in Yorkshire in the mid-1180s, and one is known to have been built in 1191 at Bury St Edmunds. They were favoured by lords, who could earn extra money from them by making it obligatory for tenants to use their mills. – *Cf.* BANALITY

Windsor herald. Title of the *herald of the Order of the *Garter.

Wista. Word used of a *virgate or a *yardland in some parts of the south of England. [< OE *wist* = provision, nourishment]

Wita. A wise man. – *Cf. next;* WITENAGEMOT

Witan. Wise men; *sapientes* in Latin. – *Cf.* WITENAGEMOT

Witch. The belief in witches and their ability to cast spells was widespread, but with none of the hysteria that characterised the witch trials of the post-medieval period. By the 14c, the Church had come to reverse its earlier position, that witchcraft was an unreal delusion (and hence witches were to be pitied rather than persecuted), to one in which witches were equated with *heretics. [< OE *wicce* = bad, wicked] – *Cf.* CHICHIVACHE

Wite. A penalty paid to the crown for injury caused to a third party. From this grew the 'king's peace', for the breaking of which penalties were duly codified. – *Cf.* BLOODWITE; BOT 1

Witenagemot. Assembly of the king's *witan, i.e. wise men; analogous to the post-1066 great council. [< OE *witan* = wise men + *gemot* = a meeting] – *Cf.* BUREWARMOT

Witenmoot. *See previous*

Within the verge. Term used of the knights and bannerets, also the esquires, who were summoned to join the king when he went to war. They formed part of the king's household or *familia regis* throughout the campaign. – *Cf.* DOMUS REGIS; VERGE

Withy. A flexible branch of the willow used for tying and binding. – *Cf.* LAQUEUS

Woad. Woad was used as a source of blue until the 19c, when chemists produced synthetic colours. Woad came from a member of the mustard family, *Isatis tinctoria*, whose leaves were fermented, that process expressing the dye. [< OE = *wad*]

Wold. Forest land, wooded uplands; now, open country with small rolling hills, or moorland; used to refer to parts of north Yorkshire and parts of central Lincolnshire, i.e. the Wolds; cognate with Weald, used of land in Sussex and Kent. – *Cf.* ANDRED

Wolf. There were enough wolves in England during the reign of King John (1199–1216) for a bounty of 5s to be offered for their catching and killing. There are many AS placenames which indicate the presence of wolves, e.g. Woolley in Yorkshire, [< wolves' + OE *leah* = wood] and Woolmer in Hampshire, [< wolves' + OE *mere* = lake]. In 1209 two colts were killed and eaten by wolves in Hampshire. There are also sufficient records of wolves being caught in the king's forests to make it unsurprising that during the 1130s there were full-time royal wolf hunters, with a pack of two dozen hounds and also greyhounds. A wolf-catcher in Worcestershire in the early 13c was paid 3s a year. No records survive to show how many, if any, he caught, or whether indeed there were any wolves left in that part of England. Certainly, wolves were killing deer in the Forest of Dean in 1290s. Wolves appear to have survived in England until the 17c, and longer in Scotland.

Wonderful Parliament. The parliament summoned to meet on 1 October 1386 to discuss the threat of invasion by the French. An extraordinary subsidy of four fifteenths was being requested by the king, Richard II. Instead of debate on that the king found himself under attack because of favourites much disliked by the Commons. Ill-feeling predominated and, in a moment of bizarre folly, Richard threatened to appeal to the king of France for assistance. However, parliament prevailed and secured the impeachment of Suffolk, the treasurer. Relations between king and parliament continued to be bad.

Wong [wang]. A field, piece of common land; a garden.

Woodland trees. Medieval England was thickly wooded, even close to settlements. The most common woodland trees were the oak and the ash, particularly if the land was clay. (The sycamore was only introduced to England in the 16c.) However, on the chalky downs beech woods were vast. Lime, maple and elm preferred lowlands. The birch was found where it is today, in thinning woods, and also on neglected ground. – *Cf.* AFFORESTATION; FOREST ASSIZES

Woodstock, Assize of. 1184. Also known as the Assize of the *Forest. – *Cf.* FOREST ASSIZES

Woodward. The keeper or officer in charge of a wood. – *Cf.* WARD

Wool. In the late 13c, there were some eight million sheep in England; the wool trade was the single most important export and the basis of crucial taxation. Monasteries had great flocks on their granges, particularly the Cistercian order in their out of the way places. However, the trade began to lose its dominance in the late 14c. – *Cf.* DORDRECHT BONDS; SACK OF WOOL; STAPLE 2

Woolsack. The large red cushion, stuffed with wool, on which the lord *chancellor sits as speaker of the House of Lords. It signified just how vital the wool trade was to the national economy. At first it was simply a sack filled with wool for the judges' comfort when they attended the House of Lords. – *Cf. previous*; SACK OF WOOL

Worth. An enclosed or self-contained place like a homestead or farm; curtilage. [< OE *worð* = soil, homestead] – *Cf. next*

Worthig. The enclosure of a *ceorl's piece of land which he was required to keep fenced; the requirement had purpose since he was not entitled to compensation if a wandering animal got onto his land through a gap in the fence. – *Cf. previous*

Writ of summons. Writs were issued by the king to summon tenants-in-chief and others of the baronage to attend parliament on a specified day. Some received regular summonses to each parliament; others received only one. In time the summonses were issued to some of barons for every session of parliament and this would become a right inherited by the son. From this a set body within the baronage was distinguished from the rest. It was this which created the Lords and the House of Lords.

Writs, return of. Writs usually were executed by a *sheriff. However, in a *franchise or *manor having 'return of writs', the sheriff could not act. Rather a precept was sent to the *bailiff, who would execute the writ and then inform the sheriff. The sheriff, in turn, would then endorse the original writ, and return it to the first, issuing court. The Latin word used was *retorna*.

Wych [wich]. A salt works or salt pit; also one of the towns in Cheshire and remembered in names such as Droitwich. Similar to *wick but used here only in relation to places with salt. [< OE *wic* = a living place or village]

Wylisc. *Welsh; those living in Wales. – *Cf.* WEALH

Wytword. A small bequest made to a parish church, to pay for lights perhaps, or as a contribution to the maintenance of the church's fabric.

Wyvern. *Her.* Winged dragon with feet like an eagle's, and barbed tail; very similar to the Wessex dragon. It was thought to symbolise pestilence and plague. – *Cf.* COCKATRICE

X

Xenodochium. A place set up on pilgrim routes for their and other travellers' use as an overnight hostel.

Y

Yale. *Her.* Mythical beast used as a badge, but of rare occurrence. The yale was a creature about the size of a horse, somewhat like an antelope, with horns and tusks. The horns were able to move and turn independently; the tail was like that of a lion. The yale was used as a *supporter of the *escutcheon of John, duke of Bedford (d. 1435), and third son of Henry IV. It was first described by Pliny.

Yard 1. Enclosed piece of land attached to a building. It also came to indicate a space where animals were kept.

Yard 2. The measure we know as being three feet was originally a 'cloth measure'. The Latin *tres pedes faciunt ulnam* = three feet make a yard (*ulna* = a yard). However, *ulna* originally meant the length of an outstretched arm (*ulna* also being the anatomical term for the fore-arm). There is a story which has Henry I making the length of his own outstretched arm the standard. – *Cf.* CUBIT

Yardland [yard of land]. Orig. a 7c *tenement which was created by taking one *rood (one quarter of an *acre) from every acre in a *hide. Later, it determined the relationship between lord and tenant in which the tenant is a freeman working a quarter hide or *virgate at an agreed rent; the lord was obliged to provide a house if he wished both work and rent. – *Cf. next;* FURLONG

Yardling. A *villein holding a *yardland.

Year books. These works were an important, if little known, part of early printing in England. However, the texts themselves are the work of unknown hands. It is thought that they were produced by law students, who took notes in the courts and organised them for teaching and, of course, for printing. William de Mechlinia was their earliest printer, but it was Richard Pynson who produced the largest sequence of these books when William ceased printing in 1490. They were closely studied both by students and practising lawyers. Manuscript copies date from the last quarter of the 13c. It is certain that they would have been widely available at the *Inns of Court. As a series, the year books continued until the 1530s. That they were well used can be seen in the marks and underlinings in copies, both MS and printed, to be found in law libraries today. – *Cf.* BRACTON; *Tractatus de Legibus*

Yellow. Experimentation in the 14c resulted in a yellow for use in stained glass being made with silver nitrate. – *Cf.* MADDER; ORPIMENT; POT METAL

Yelm. Basic bundle of straw used by a thatcher when thatching a roof. [< OE *gilm* = a handful, a sheaf]

Yeoman. Holder of a small estate, of perhaps 60 acres or more. He was a freeholder, whose land was worth 40s but he was not one of the gentry. Also, one of the attendants in a royal or other household, more than a groom but less than a *squire. Sometimes a yeoman would have a specific rôle, e.g. yeoman of the *king's wardrobe in the royal household.

Yett. A metal grating, sometimes with a wood backing, with locking bars and hinges used to secure and barricade narrow passages against attack. They are still to be found in many churches on the English–Scottish border; these churches have extra protection, e.g. stone-vaulted ceilings which would not burn. The villagers would hide themselves in stone towers during murderous cross-border raids, using a yett in a specially narrowed passage which could be defended easily and was fire-proof. 'Yett' is a northern form of 'gate'.

Yoke 1. Kentish area of land = *c*.50–60 acres. – *Cf.* RAPE 1; WAND

Yoke 2. Wooden frame which linked oxen together and to the plough; also, three spears joined together beneath which defeated soldiers were made to march as a sign of that defeat.

York plays. A cycle of *mystery plays performed at York. They are first mentioned in 1387, although by that time they had a history behind them – just how long is uncertain. Certainly, by 1397 they were famous enough to prompt a visit by Richard II. – *Cf.* CHESTER PLAYS; MIRACLE PLAY; MYSTERY PLAY; WAKEFIELD PLAYS

Yrthling. Lit. 'earthling'. A husbandman or farmer.

Z

Zelator. A zealot; a zealous defender or supporter (of a person or idea). [< Gk. *zelo* = to be zealous]

REGNAL DATES

OF THE KINGS OF WESSEX AND OF ENGLAND

Kings of Wessex

Ecgberht	802–839 – effectively first king of England
Æthelwulf	839–856/858 – son of Ecgberht
Æthelbald	855/856–860 – son of Æthelwulf
Æthelberht	860–865/866 – son of Æthelwulf
Æthelred I	865/866–871 – son of Æthelwulf
Alfred the Great	871–899 – brother of Æthelred I
Edward the Elder	899–924 – son of Alfred the Great

Kings of England

Æthelstan	925–939 – son of Edward the Elder
Edmund I	939–946 – son of Edward the Elder
Eadred	946–955 – son of Edward the Elder
Eadwig	955–959 – son of Edmund I
Edgar	959–975 – son of Edmund I
Edward the Martyr	975–978 – son of Edgar
Æthelred II the Unready	978–1013 – son of Edgar
Sweyn Forkbeard	1013–1014 – Danish, took throne from exiled Æthelred II
Æthelred II the Unready	1014–1016 (restored)
Edmund II Ironside	1016 – son of Æthelred II
Cnut	1016–1035 – Danish, son of Sweyn, elected by English *witenagemot*
Harold I Harefoot	1035–1040 – Anglo-Danish, son of Cnut
Harthacnut	1040–1042 – Danish, son of Cnut
Edward the Confessor	1042–1066 – son of Æthelred II
Harold II	1066 – last Anglo-Saxon king
William I the Conqueror	1066–1087 – Norman, overthrew Harold II at Hastings
William II	1087–1100 – son of William I
Henry I	1100–1135 – son of William I
Stephen	1135–1154 – nephew of Henry I
Henry II	1154–1189 – grandson of Henry I
Richard I	1189–1199 – son of Henry II
John	1199–1216 – son of Henry II
Henry III	1216–1272 – son of John
Edward I	1272–1307 – son of Henry III

Edward II	1307–1327 – son of Edward I
Edward III	1327–1377 – son of Edward II
Richard II	1377–1399 – grandson of Edward III
Henry IV	1399–1413 – seized throne from Richard II
Henry V	1413–1422 – son of Henry IV
Henry VI	1422–1461 – son of Henry V
Edward IV	1461–1470 – seized throne from Henry VI
Henry VI	1470–1471 (restored)
Edward IV	1471–1483 (restored)
Edward V	1483 – son of Edward IV
Richard III	1483–1485 – seized throne from Edward V
Henry VII	1485–1509 – took throne after killing Richard III on Bosworth Field

SELECT BIBLIOGRAPHY

The purpose of this bibliography is to provide pointers to some major histories and a few more precisely focused titles, as well as translations of important texts. More detailed bibliographies are to be found in the works listed here.

The first group of titles provides translations of texts and documents of the period. It should be noted that the Phillimore edition of *Domesday Book*, edited by John Morris, is published county by county, and includes a copy of the original text with *en face* translation. The first and second volumes of *English Historical Documents* include a translation of the *Anglo-Saxon Chronicle*; the second also offers a translation of the *Dialogue of the Exchequer*.

Amt, E., *Medieval England, 1000–1500, A Reader* (Ontario, 2001)

Douglas, D. C., and G. W. Greenaway, *English Historical Documents 1042–1189*, vol. 2 (London, 1968)

Downer, L. J., ed and trans., *Leges Henrici Primi* (Oxford, 1996)

Geoffrey of Monmouth, *The History of the Kings of Britain* (London, 1966)

Malory, Thomas, *Le Morte D'Arthur* (London, 2000)

Morris, J., *Domesday Book*, 36 vols. (Chichester, 1986)

Swanton, M., ed. and trans., *The Anglo-Saxon Chronicles* (London, 1996)

Whitelock, D., *English Historical Documents c.500–1042*, vol. 1 (London, 1968)

Williams, A., and G. H. Martin, *Domesday Book: A Complete Translation* (London, 2002)

The following titles provide a broad narrative account of the history and culture of the period covered by this dictionary.

Barlow, F., *The Feudal Kingdom of England 1042–1216*, 2nd edn (London, 1963)

Bartlett, R., *England under the Norman and Angevin Kings 1075–1225* (Oxford, 2000)

Blair, P. H., *An Introduction to Anglo-Saxon England*, 2nd edn (Cambridge, 1997)

Brown, R. A., *The Normans and the Norman Conquest*, 2nd edn (Woodbridge, 1987)

Carpenter, D., *The Struggle for Mastery, Britain, 1066-1284* (London, 2003)

Chibnall, M., *Anglo-Norman England, 1066–1166* (Oxford, 1986)

Chibnall, M., *The World of Orderic Vitalis* (Woodbridge, 2001)

Huizinga, J., *The Waning of the Middle Ages* (London, 1990)

Lapidge, M., *et al.*, *The Blackwell Encyclopedia of Anglo-Saxon England* (Oxford, 2001)

Maitland, F. M., *Domesday Book and Beyond* (New York, 1966)

Myres, J. N. L., *The English Settlements* (Oxford, 1986)

Pevsner, N., *The Buildings of England* (London)

Poole, A. L., *Domesday Book to* Magna Carta, *1087–1216*, 2nd edn (Oxford, 1958)

Southern, R. W., *The Making of the Middle Ages* (London, 1953)

Stenton, F. M., *Anglo-Saxon England*, 3rd edn (Oxford, 1997)

The monographs below offer more sharply focused work.

Ayton, A., *Knights and Warhorses: Military Service and the English Aristocracy under Edward III* (Woodbridge, 1999)

Barber, R., *The Knight and Chivalry*, revised edn (Woodbridge, 1995)

Barber, R., *The Arthurian Legends, An Illustrated Anthology* (Woodbridge, 1991)

Barker, J., *The Tournament in England, 1100–1400* (Woodbridge, 1986)

Crouch, D., *The Normans – The History of a Dynasty* (Hambledon and London, 2002)

Davies, R. R., *The First English Empire, Power and Identities in the British Isles, 1093–1343* (Oxford, 2000)

Dyer, C., *Making a Living in the Middle Ages, The People of Britain 850–1520* (New Haven and London, 2002)

Hollister, C. W., *Anglo-Saxon Military Institutions on the Eve of the Norman Conquest* (Oxford, 1998)

Hyland, A., *The Horse in the Middle Ages* (Stroud, 1999)

McFarlane, K. B., *The Nobility of Later Medieval England* (Oxford, 1973)

Stenton, D. M., *English Society in the Early Middle Ages*, 4th edn (London, 1991)

Stenton, F. M., *et al.*, *The Bayeux Tapestry* (London, 1957)

Walker, I. W., *Mercia and the Making of England* (Stroud, 2000)

Williams, A., *The English and the Norman Conquest* (Woodbridge, 1997)

Williams, A., *Kingship and Government in Pre-Conquest England c.500–1066* (London, 1999)